THE MANY ROOMS OF THIS HOUSE

Diversity and Toronto's Places
of Worship since 1840

Places of worship are the true building blocks of communities where people of various genders, age, and class interact with each other on a regular basis. These places are also rallying points for immigrants, helping them make the transition to a new, and often hostile environment.

The Many Rooms of This House is a story about the rise and decline of religion in Toronto over the past 160 years. Unlike other studies that concentrate on specific denominations, or ecclesiastical politics, Roberto Perin's ecumenical approach focuses on the physical places of worship and the local clergy and congregants that gather there. Perin's timely and nuanced analysis reveals how the growing wealth of the city stimulated congregations to compete with one another over the size, style, materials, and decoration of their places of worship. However, the rise of individualism and declining church attendance has led to church closings, the breakdown of church communities, and in some cases, redevelopment and cooperation among congregations of varied faiths. Perin's fascinating work is a lens to understanding how this once overwhelmingly Protestant city became a symbol of diversity.

ROBERTO PERIN is a professor in the Department of History at Glendon College, York University.

The Many Rooms
of This House

*Diversity and Toronto's Places
of Worship since 1840*

ROBERTO PERIN

UNIVERSITY OF TORONTO PRESS
Toronto Buffalo London

© University of Toronto Press 2017
Toronto Buffalo London
www.utppublishing.com
Printed in Canada

ISBN 978-1-4875-0027-6 (cloth)
ISBN 978-1-4875-2017-5 (paper)

Printed on acid-free, 100% post-consumer recycled paper
with vegetable-based inks.

___

Library and Archives Canada Cataloguing in Publication

Perin, Roberto, author
The many rooms of this house : diversity and Toronto's places of
worship since 1840 / Roberto Perin.

Includes bibliographical references and index.
ISBN 978-1-4875-0027-6 (cloth)   ISBN 978-1-4875-2017-5 (paper)

1. Religious pluralism – Ontario – Toronto – History. 2. Toronto
(Ont.) – Religion. I. Title.

BL2530.C3P47 2017   200.9713′541   C2016-908189-3

___

This book has been published with the help of a grant from the Federation
for the Humanities and Social Sciences, through the Awards to Scholarly
Publications Program, using funds provided by the Social Sciences and
Humanities Research Council of Canada.

University of Toronto Press acknowledges the financial assistance to its
publishing program of the Canada Council for the Arts and the Ontario Arts
Council, an agency of the Government of Ontario.

Funded by the   Financé par le
Government   gouvernement
of Canada   du Canada

Canadä

Contents

Tables

Illustrations

THE MANY ROOMS OF THIS HOUSE

Diversity and Toronto's Places
of Worship since 1840

Introduction

A city of churches: if we were to guess which nineteenth-century Canadian locality those words described, we would most likely say Montreal, which during that century was the North American capital of a resurgent and assertive Catholicism, and one whose built religious heritage dating back to the founding of New France two centuries earlier by then included Jewish and many varieties of Protestant places of worship. The correct answer, however, is Toronto. That city does not immediately come to mind in part because we tend to think of nineteenth-century Toronto chiefly in economic terms – as a city grown wealthy from commerce, a financial powerhouse eager to overtake Montreal as Canada's great metropolis, a rapidly industrializing centre where capitalists and skilled workers alike found their interests served, albeit in far different measure.

But this is precisely why religion mattered. As William Westfall argued so convincingly in *Two Worlds: The Protestant Culture of Nineteenth-Century Ontario*, Ontarians and English-speaking Canadians slowly came to see religion as a vital counterweight to the materialistic impulse of capitalism: without it, society would simply go awry. Religion provided both a moral sanction for the emergent economic order and a transcendent vision of what the proper accumulation of riches could bring: the Lord's Dominion. A social consensus was constructed around this vision that was articulated by a broad range of the social and intellectual elite, whether they were businessmen, politicians, clerics, or other shapers of opinion. Religion thus occupied an important public space in Toronto. But it also mattered to the common people. In his late-nineteenth-century survey of the city's places of worship, published as *Robertson's Landmarks of Toronto*, journalist John Ross Robertson showed that religious services were very well attended. In fact, many Torontonians went to church twice on Sunday, morning and evening. Religion maintained this pre-eminence until after the Second World War, when, as we will see, consumer capitalism, by then a truly mass phenomenon, finally supplanted it.

The following chapters track the rise, success, and decline of religion in Toronto over the past century and a half. This is not a study of church hierarchies, structures, or major institutions; nor of ecclesiastical politics, church–state relations, or disputes over dogma and belief. The focus here is not on individuals' faith and motives, but on religion as a social phenomenon: how it shaped society and how in turn it was shaped by broader historical forces. The focus is also resolutely local, on parishes and congregations within a defined space. Scholars of architectural history have been partial to such an approach, but their attention has long been oriented towards the buildings themselves: their style, their symbolism, the materials used to construct them, how they were built, and, at times, the relationship between the architect or builder and his patrons. The actors remain eerily absent from that stage. So our attention will be mainly on the actors, although themes of architectural interest will not be ignored.

In Canada, the history of parishes and congregations has largely been left to amateurs, many of them commissioned by specific places of worship to mark an anniversary. These works are not uninteresting and often contain valuable facts and details, but they are for the most part celebratory, detached from the broader historical context, and therefore devoid of interpretation. Fortunately, there are exceptions to this rather lacklustre pattern. A few professional historians have produced solid and useful studies, which the present book uses and cites. Still, the best work in this genre undoubtedly belongs to Quebec historian Lucia Ferretti, whose book *Entre voisins* examines the working-class parish of St-Pierre-Apôtre in the east end of Montreal, which was under the care of the Oblates of Mary Immaculate, a French-based community that dominated the Catholic Church in the Canadian West until the First World War. Her monograph highlights the crucial role the parish played in helping migrants from the Quebec countryside adjust to urban life at a time when they were pouring into the metropolis in search of work. Through the multitude of parish-based organizations they joined, these migrants developed a strong sense of community that gave them the confidence to move forward in an alien environment. Here, finally, is a study that gives real meaning to the collective experience of parish life.

Recently, a Religious Studies professor at Queen's University, William Closson James, has broken new ground. Instead of focusing on a parish or congregation, his *God's Plenty: Religious Diversity in Kingston* looks at all places of worship within the city's perimeter. In many ways, his book and the present one are strikingly similar, even though their authors were blissfully unaware of the each other's research. Both works have a firm geographic foundation – that is, they study all places of worship within a clearly defined space. They are inclusive in terms of the worshippers and expressions of worship examined: the faithful comprise "old stock" as well as new and less recent immigrants; eschewing artificial and often partisan categories of "church" and "sect," the two books incorporate manifestations of religion that are both mainstream and unconventional, traditional and syncretic, Western and Eastern, monotheistic and polytheistic. Thus, the distinctive features of those religious expressions are given less weight than what they have in common. The physical structures within which people worship include edifices commonly associated with the divine, but also unusual spaces such as storefronts or garages. Finally, both studies rely on an extensive body of oral interviews.

That said, there are significant differences between this book and James's. *God's Plenty* draws on a diversity of disciplines and sources that enrich the field of Religious Studies. Among its many scholarly and literary references are historical ones, but the book's focus is essentially contemporary – its purpose is to take stock of Kingston's current religious culture. Consequently, chapters are organized according to broad religious categories: mainline, evangelical, proselytizing, liberal, ethnic, and so on. By contrast, *The Many Rooms of This House* is historical in approach, organization, and perspective, encompassing existing places of worship as well as those that have vanished. It explores current manifestations of diversity as well as past ones. It seeks to measure the effects of time on space and culture, examining how neighbourhoods change and are reinvented by economic and social forces that shape the urban landscape and how worship and the sociability it generates are influenced by broader cultural, intellectual, and social currents.

No one can dispute that places of worship were chiefly houses of prayer. But it would be a mistake to see them only in that light. They were also building blocks of community, in that within their walls people differentiated by gender, age, and often social class regularly came together and interacted. And for immigrants, they were a rallying point, bringing the group together and helping it make the transition to a new and alien environment. Places of worship were not, of course, the only such spaces. The workplace was another; in fact, men, women, and children spent more time at work than at prayer. Given the volatile character of labour relations in Canada, especially before the Second World War, it could even be argued that bonds of solidarity were stronger among workers than among parishioners or congregants. Other sites of socialization and community building were mutual aid and fraternal associations (Elks, Foresters, Kiwanis) or ethnically based ones (Orange Lodge, St Andrew's Society, St George's Society).

What made places of worship unique, however, was that, unlike workplaces, they were largely voluntary, even though individuals might feel a moral obligation to participate regularly. Unlike fraternal or mutual aid associations and most workplaces, they catered to entire families, thus providing sites for cross-generational encounter and communication. Rebellious teenage sons might pose particular problems of integration and involvement, but fairly successful strategies were devised to overcome that obstacle. Parishioners and congregants joined together, contributing money and at times their labour to build sacred structures, Sunday schools, and adjoining halls. In prosperous times, significant sums of money were expended to equip these buildings and embellish sanctuaries with carved furniture, stained glass windows, murals, mosaics, and organs. Financial support was also extended to clergy, Sunday school teachers, and missionaries at home and abroad. Finally, parishes and congregations offered members a range of spiritual *and* temporal activities. As religion increasingly asserted itself within the public sphere, it nourished ever greater ambitions regarding the services it could provide the local community.

Parishioners and congregants were certainly active participants, but they were also acted *upon* by external forces. They were confronted by issues of class, gender, nation, ethnicity, and race generated by industrialization, imperialism (including the world wars), and, as mentioned earlier, the rise of consumer culture. How people responded to these issues within their places of worship are topics of interest to this study. As well, this book will explore the extent to which their religious denomination shaped their behaviour and their attitudes.

It is tempting to give this story a Whig interpretation, with Toronto evolving from a uniformly dour, narrow-minded, Protestant nineteenth-century backwater into the pluralistic, cosmopolitan, and accepting metropolis it is today. Although undoubtedly dear to contemporary civic boosters, that caricature has no basis in fact. Toronto has always been an immigrant town. It is true that in the nineteenth century, most newcomers were from the British Isles; however, that geographic point of origin encompassed a diversity of peoples difficult to discern today. To cite the most obvious example, Irish Catholics – especially those of peasant stock – were widely regarded in English-speaking countries in the nineteenth century as racially inferior. What's more, ethnic distinctions were complicated by religious ones, and this generated endless permutations and combinations such as Scots Baptists, Irish Anglicans, English Catholics, and Welsh Presbyterians, to name but a few. Also, it is hard to appreciate today just how fractured Protestantism was in Canada until the last quarter of the nineteenth century. Mainstream denominations like the Methodists and the Presbyterians were splintered into three or four rival groupings, each with its own organization and hierarchy, often reflecting a distinct ethnic culture. Meanwhile, Anglicanism had become an uneasy amalgam of Low Church, which subscribed to a plain form of worship and a more evangelical Protestant church polity, and High Church, which cherished a more elaborate ritual inspired by Catholic notions of the Eucharist and the veneration of the saints, chief among whom was the Virgin Mary. Many Anglicans chose a middle way, borrowing elements from each faction but not identifying with either. Protestantism was therefore far from being monolithic in the second half of the nineteenth century.

At the beginning of the twentieth century, immigrants from eastern and southern Europe became a visible presence in the downtown core, where earlier waves of newcomers had once lived. Irish Catholics gave way to Jews from eastern European towns (*shtetls*), who became the new "other." By this time, Irish Catholics were joining the Canadian mainstream, and the new arrivals may well have accelerated that process, thereby prompting the receiving society to redefine itself so as to accommodate the descendants of a group once viewed as pariahs. This process repeated itself after the Second World War as Italian peasants replaced Jews, and again after 1967, when visible minority immigrants displaced those of European descent. Toronto has always been diverse, and each new wave of immigration has accelerated the previous wave's arduous journey to acceptance, besides causing the receiving society to again reformulate its own identity. Toronto has successively defined itself as Protestant, as British (including Irish Catholics), as Canadian (including Jews), as multicultural (including other Europeans), and as diverse (including racialized, gendered, as well as physically and mentally challenged groups).

This project began more than a decade ago when, with Professor Gabriele Scardellato, a friend and colleague in the Graduate History Program, I started documenting on paper and in photographs the places of worship in our neighbourhood. We were fascinated by the linguistic, ethnic, racial, and denominational mix we encountered. Each week our investigation took us farther afield both spatially and temporally. Eventually we delineated a sector of Toronto we loosely termed the West End, bounded on the east by University Avenue/Avenue Road, on the north by St Clair Avenue, on the west by the old City of Toronto limits (roughly the Humber River), and on the south by Lake Ontario. After identifying more than 250 places of worship within this perimeter, we wound up our investigation and posted the results on a website, http://www .glendon.yorku.ca/placesofworship/index.html. This resource contains a map of the area divided into nine subsections that, when called up, show the locations of places of worship, with corresponding photographs and brief descriptions. For each subregion and for the area as a whole, statistics are provided on the number of places of worship by denomination, as well as by race and ethnicity. Our survey encompasses buildings that were specifically erected as houses of prayer, whether or not they are still so today, as well as storefronts and other structures now serving such ends. To be considered, however, the current edifices had to display a sign or some other symbol indicating that it was open for pubic worship.

Research and writing require that choices be made. We were tempted to extend the boundaries of this inquiry to include other areas of Toronto, such as the historic centre, the East End, or the northern fringes. Given the already broad scope of this study, however, such an undertaking would have been foolhardy. As a historian specializing in immigration, I found the West End to be of particular interest because of its marked ethnic and racial diversity – a trait that coincided with the arrival of non-British immigrants to the city and is still very much in evidence today. Ethnicity and race add complexity and depth to a study of urban space. The East End, by contrast, was historically more ethnically homogeneous, anchored in its British origins and English Canadian identity. The area featured one lone synagogue to the West End's sixty, and only in 1972 did Italians there receive religious services that their West End cousins had already enjoyed for more than half a century. Ethnic and racial diversity came late to this part of Toronto, and when it did, it mirrored new immigration currents developing in the wake of the 1967 Immigration Act. As a result, around the time that the East End's Italians began worshipping in their language, Sikhs and Muslims were establishing their own places of worship there. Sooner or later, though, each part of Toronto experienced the same broad changes described in the pages that follow: industrialization, immigration, suburbanization, imperialism, and consumer capitalism. Diversity too was a given for all areas, expressed perhaps in religious more than ethnic and racial terms. In this context it is useful to point out that in North America, Toronto was an early outpost of Pentecostalism, and that it was in the East End that it first found expression. While it would be interesting and worthwhile to examine and compare different parts of the city, it would doubtless reveal variations in degree and timing rather than in substance.

We tend to think of places of worship as fixed, static, and silent landmarks, somewhat like the famous stone heads on Easter Island. But in reality they are both witnesses to and markers of change within the urban landscape. In this inquiry, I purposely chose an area large enough to allow for the observation of a number of phenomena related to urban change. One of these was the reinforcement of Protestantism. As Toronto's growing wealth depended less on trade in agricultural produce and more on the production of manufactured goods, especially industrial machinery, Protestantism became more self-confident and demonstrative. Churches competed with one another over size as well as materials, style of construction, music, and artistic decoration. Comparing church buildings of the 1860s with those erected just twenty years later makes this transition immediately obvious. Another phenomenon was the consolidation of commercial space in the downtown core. In the 1880s, an almost manic era of church construction, few imagined that Queen Street West would gradually lose its residential character and become solidly commercial. Thirty years later, parishioners and congregants were confronted with hard decisions. St Margaret's Anglican on Spadina south of Queen became a business space. Today, the building's origins can only be discerned from the rear, where the apse can still be seen. At the same time, commercialization offered opportunities for newer religious groups with fewer resources to gain a foothold in the city. This is vividly illustrated by a commercial building at 450 Spadina, south of College: at the turn of the twentieth century it served as a meeting place for a variety of small groups, including the Disciples of Christ, the Mennonite Brethren in Christ, the Swedenborgians, the Pentecostal League, the Christian Workers, and English-speaking Lutherans.

As older residential areas declined, newer ones emerged on the periphery. The churches along Avenue Road, and those on St Clair east of Bathurst, are eloquent examples of middle- and upper-class suburbanization. The churches on Christie Street testify to the same phenomenon, but in relation to the working class. Urban development entailed not only the city's appropriation of adjoining agricultural land, but also the annexation of the neighbouring towns of Brockton, Parkdale, the Junction, and Swansea. Village churches gave way to larger structures, such as those along Annette Street in the Junction, reflecting the increased wealth that came with industrial development linked to Toronto's proximity. Others, such as St Mark's Parkdale, preserved their small-town charm.

Immigration is another phenomenon that can be tracked through places of worship. For the better part of the twentieth century, the eastern part of the West End was a major immigrant reception area. Today it is not always easy to appreciate the dynamic movement of immigrant groups that took place there. At times, urban archaeology is called for, as in the above-mentioned case of St Margaret's Anglican. A glance at the cornerstone of Chinese Grace Baptist Church, for example, reveals that it was originally First Ukrainian Presbyterian. Similarly, research in city directories disclosed to us that Fung Loy Kok Taoist Temple was initially a Polish synagogue. The most outstanding examples of such changes are two small churches, originally known as College Street Baptist and Hope Congregational. In less than a century, they accommodated groups as diverse as Welsh Presbyterians, Slovak Lutherans, Greek Orthodox, and Italian members of the United Church, as well as German and Danish Lutherans.

Before the Second World War, the largest non-British immigrant group to settle in Toronto were Jews. They established a number of synagogues in the West End, many of which were *stiblach* set up in existing residential spaces such as apartments or houses. In the 1950s and 1960s, suburbanization enticed most Jews northward along the Bathurst corridor. Old *shuls* were closed, and congregations amalgamated and began life anew on Toronto's fringes. Half of the West End's synagogues were demolished; others were passed on to other religious communities, or they were converted to secular purposes. But many former *stiblach* still stand and await an urban archaeologist to bring them to public awareness. By 2000, only five synagogues were left to bear witness to the Jewish presence in the West End, four of these in what had been the city's Jewish heartland. The other is located in the Junction, a reminder of the important Jewish working-class presence in the town's burgeoning industries before the First World War.

While many other immigrant groups will be examined in subsequent chapters, Jews illustrate how useful places of worship can be for tracking population movements across the city. Today, however, it is clear that the West End has ceased to be Toronto's major immigrant reception area. Indeed, newcomers, admitted under the points system inaugurated by the 1967 Immigration Act, no longer come mainly from Europe, the country's traditional source of recruitment. Rather than initially settling in the downtown core as their predecessors had done, newer immigrants from Asia, Africa, the Caribbean, and Latin America go directly to Scarborough, Mississauga, Markham, and Brampton. Be that as it may, the West End continues to bear witness to changing population movements, albeit less intensely than before. Mirroring the importance of Asian immigration is the fact that today the West End boasts more Buddhist temples than either United or Presbyterian churches.

This detail hints at another significant socio-cultural phenomenon: secularization. Suburbanization affected Jews, but even more so the old stock population. The desertion of the downtown by this cohort doubtless contributed to the emptying of West End churches. A number of surveys have established that regular church attendance dropped steadily after the 1960s. Declining membership made it ever harder for churches to meet the costs of maintenance and repair, as well as rising heating bills. As a result, since the 1960s a staggering forty-one mainline Protestant churches or congregations have had to close in the West End. Almost half this total were demolished or destroyed by fire, some of them in suspicious circumstances. A number of others became secular spaces, such as condominiums, community centres, halls, or theatres.

Divided into four distinct, forty-year time periods, this study focuses on two major themes. The first relates to space and time. Here attention is given to the development of places of worship across the West End landscape, as well as specific parts of it, and the major events that affected that development, be they economic booms, depressions, or wars. The second is broadly conceived under the rubric of fellowship, that is, the many and varied activities generated by places of worship. What was it that brought people together under one roof, and how did this associational life change over time? The first chapter, dedicated to the early period in the development of places of worship, examines the two themes in tandem. In subsequent chapters, these themes are studied separately within the time periods indicated.

The periods chosen are significant in a number of ways. Between 1840 and 1880, Toronto evolved from a colonial outpost into an industrial city. The religiosity characterizing the former slowly gave way to one that reflected a maturing and established community. Associational life expressed itself during this period in terms of institution building: the church, the Sunday school, the choir, the women's associations, all of these elements were fundamental to the well-being and growth of parishes and congregations. The years 1880 to 1920 marked the consolidation of Toronto's economic power as well as the triumph of British imperialism and evangelical Protestantism. The city and its places of worship were self-assured in their British Protestant identity, which profoundly marked even the cultures of Catholic and Jewish minorities. Church buildings attained their accomplished forms, and associational life became multifaceted in an effort to fulfil the promise of a full-orbed Christianity. The years 1920 to 1960 were in one sense an extension of the previous one, but in another they represented a break with it. Although Toronto strengthened its claim to being Canada's economic capital, the exuberant era of church building had definitely come to an end. While associational life more or less maintained its steady pace, depression and war severely affected its development. Meanwhile, activities once considered part of the religious sphere, such as social work, were taken over by professionals or well-funded service clubs. The ambition of full-orbed religion was being challenged. Finally, the years 1960 to 2000 marked a decisive rupture. Toronto's economic primacy spurred postwar immigration that turned the city into an ethnically, racially, and religiously plural society. At the same time, however, the advent of consumer capitalism heralded a drastic drop in religious practice and self-identity, leading to church closings. The demise of the family as an economic unit and the concurrent rise of an assertive individualism had a profound impact on the sense of community. Places of worship that had once nurtured such feelings were no longer spaces where men and women of diverse ages and backgrounds gathered. The rich associational life of the past had withered, and what remained was often in the hands of an older cohort unsupported by younger ones. Thus, while it is necessary to celebrate and cherish diversity, is it yet possible for us to find an ethos that brings us together and gives us a common sense of purpose as places of worship once did?

A grant from the Multiculturalism Branch of the Department of Canadian Heritage made the research for this project possible. The monies allocated were mostly used to hire an army of graduate students whose motivation and interest provided me with invaluable material and insights. A number of these students have gone on to careers in academia. I would like to express my sincere thanks to Michael Akladios, Liliya Bogutska, Dr Denise Challenger, Ryan Cowling, Eileen Doucet, Jeet Heer, Tricia Hong, Lawrence Horowitz, Helen Kim, Kevin Ladouceur, Jérôme Laflamme, Dr Julia Lalande, Dr Kenneth Lan, Dr Susana Miranda, Ana Mitrovič, Dr Stuart Parker, Lori Pucar, Dr Audrey Pyée, Divya Segal, Dr Todd Stubbs, Krista Taves, Jeff Watson, and Dr Todd Webb. I am also grateful to Drs Janet McLellan, Elaine Gold, Judith Szapor, and Henriette Donner, who already had their doctorates when they assisted me with this research. I am also indebted to Professors Matteo Sanfilippo and Gabriele Scardellato, who read the manuscript in its entirety. I would like to express my gratitude to Leslie Scrivener of the *Toronto Star* and to reporters at CJBC, Toronto's French-language radio station, for their sustained support and interest in this project. A special word of thanks goes to Mariana Paralles for her superb work on the website, as well as to Glendon College's IT office. Finally, I am indebted to the anonymous readers of this manuscript whose suggestions for revision were extremely helpful and very much appreciated, and to the copy editor, Matthew Kudelka, who did superb work at once time-consuming and meticulous.

Chapter One

Consolidating Protestantism, 1840–1880

The Union of the Canadas in 1841 accelerated the growth of an ambitious provincial town just recently renamed Toronto. From 1851 to 1881 the city's population nearly trebled, from 31,000 to 86,000. This increase was due largely to immigration originating in part in the surrounding countryside, but more especially in the British Isles (the enormous Famine Irish migration, for instance, took place in the late 1840s). Toronto reaped the benefits of significant improvements in transportation, such as the imposing canal work done in the 1840s along the lower Great Lakes and the St Lawrence River and especially the massive railway construction of the 1850s that secured its status as a hub of continental trade and the metropolis of a large and prosperous hinterland. No mere satellite of Montreal, then the undisputed commercial and economic capital of the Canadas, Toronto could ship produce directly to Atlantic ports in the United States via the Erie Canal. The railway made possible the creation of a large internal market and therefore the local production of goods. This process was helped along by a number of factors, the most important being the Crimean War (1853–6) which had cut off Britain's regular supply of wheat from the Russian empire, compelling it to turn to North America; the American Civil War, which stimulated Canada's industrial production by reducing the importation of goods manufactured south of the border; commercial policies such as the Reciprocity Treaty in natural goods with the United States (1854–66); the Galt tariff of 1858–9, which served to protect nascent industries; and, finally, the National Policy of 1878 that placed Toronto at the core of Canada's industrial heartland of southwestern Ontario. At the end of this period, the city's wealth was no longer essentially dependent on agriculture. It had a diversified economy with a firm industrial base.

Attracted by opportunity, immigrants poured into the city. It may surprise today's observers amazed by the high proportion of foreigners living in Toronto that in 1851, fully two-thirds of the city's population had been born abroad; by 1871, half of them had been. After the Famine Migration, more than one-quarter of Torontonians were Catholics; by 1871, one-fifth were. That decline took place despite the city's overall prosperity because the economic cycle with its booms and busts created insecurity and unemployment for the most vulnerable social classes, prompting a number of newcomers to move on in search of a more stable future. It must be said too that Toronto was not welcoming to Irish Catholic immigrants, who were singled out in the press and in public speeches as prone to drink, crime, filth, stupidity, and depravity. Many held the Catholic Church responsible for this state of affairs, claiming that it instilled subservient and indolent attitudes in its members. In some quarters, there was panic at the thought that Catholics would continue to arrive in ever larger numbers and subvert Canada's character. As a result, membership skyrocketed in Orange Lodges, which were seen as defenders of society's core values, and Orange Day parades became salutary reminders of Canada's supposedly unalterable character.[1]

For all of Catholicism's perceived dangers, Toronto remained staunchly Protestant. The adherents of various branches of the mainstream denominations – Anglican, Presbyterian, and Methodist – constituted two-thirds of the population in 1851 and nearly three-quarters of the total in 1881. Contrary to popular conceptions of nineteenth-century Toronto as dourly Presbyterian or dryly Methodist, Anglicans were the largest Protestant contingent, claiming close to 40 per cent of the city's population. In 1851 they outstripped the other two groups, combined and by 1881 they equalled their joint total. Methodists, for their part, went from 13 per cent of inhabitants in 1851 to just under 20 per cent thirty years later, surpassing the Presbyterians, who remained steady at over 15 per cent. Those indicating they had no religion or declining to state their denominational affiliation were a mere fraction of 1 per cent of the population.[2] This is no indication of Torontonians' level or intensity of faith and religious practice, but it does underline the importance of religion in personal and collective identity in this period.

The Denominational Context

Immigrants had come to Toronto with religious affiliations based in part on different national traditions and in part on schisms that had taken place over time within them. Issues that had caused division involved dogma of course, but also church governance or polity, as well as churchs–state relations. Anglicanism was born when King Henry VIII (1509–47) broke with Rome in 1530, declaring himself head of the Church in England. But it was his daughter, Queen Elizabeth I (1558–1603), who devised the *via media*, a broad compromise, as she saw it, between Catholicism and Protestantism, both of which threatened to tear apart her kingdom. Basically, both tendencies were tolerated, but not their extreme expressions: the principle of Royal supremacy was sacred and could not be questioned. Anglicanism retained Catholicism's hierarchical structure, with a primate, archbishops, bishops, priests, and faithful organized territorially by parish and diocese. The Church became established in England, enjoying state support and patronage.[3]

Meanwhile in Scotland, the Reformation had become forthrightly Protestant by the mid-sixteenth century. Founded by John Knox (1514–1572), Presbyterianism aligned itself with the ideas of Swiss reformer Jean Calvin (1509–1564), who held pessimistic views about human nature, already expressed by St Augustine (354–430) in the fifth century: humankind was so sinful that it could do nothing to secure its own salvation. God alone could effect it. Calvin added that from the beginning of time, God had determined who were the elect and who were the damned; thus, every person's fate was predestined. This was the doctrine of predestination that in the popular mind made Presbyterians so dour. On the question of governance, Presbyterianism discarded the individual offices of bishop, primate, and supreme head of the Church, replacing these with hierarchical bodies that were elective and collective – namely sessions (local), presbyteries (district), synods (regional), and the General Assembly (denominational). Presbyterianism became the Established Church in Scotland, and it was precisely this privileged relationship with the state that caused conflict. In the eighteenth century a schism developed over the practice of lay patronage whereby wealthy laymen made appointments to church offices. In the following century, the very notion of Church Establishment led in 1843 to the Great Disruption and the creation of Free Church of Scotland. In both these rifts, the issue was the ability of the Church to govern itself without outside or state interference.[4]

Some Protestant groups, called dissenters, rejected the Elizabethan compromise and the very notion of Church Establishment. Two such groups of most interest to us are the Congregationalists and the Baptists. The first made church governance the central feature of their denomination, refusing to accept any form of overarching ecclesiastical authority, whether exercised individually as in Anglicanism or collectively as in Presbyterianism. Instead, power was vested exclusively in the local congregation, which was entirely autonomous, hence the name. By contrast, Baptists were distinguished not by questions of governance but doctrine: they emphatically rejected infant baptism, arguing that the sacrament should be reserved for adult believers, who alone were capable of committing themselves to the Christian ideal. Soon a schism occurred within this denomination over the doctrine of predestination: some embraced Calvin's ideas on this question, while others adopted a mainstream approach.

England was also the cradle of Methodism, even though its founder, John Wesley (1703–1791), remained an Anglican minister until his death. Reacting against the rigid formalism and arid rationalism of eighteenth-century Anglicanism, Wesley emphasized personal conversion understood as an intimate and emotional turning point (Wesley himself felt a "warming of the heart") whereby the individual surrendered to the Holy Spirit, experienced spiritual rebirth, and became wholly dedicated to personal sanctification. This last objective required that followers give up frivolous pursuits such as dancing, card playing, smoking, and especially drinking. Indeed, total abstinence from alcohol became Methodism's trademark in the popular mind. After the founder's demise, the movement became a proper denomination known as the Wesleyan Methodist Church, adopting a collective and elective model of government similar to Presbyterianism.[5] Almost immediately, however, dissension broke out. The New Connexion was fiercely committed to the issue of equal representation of the laity and clergy in ecclesiastical bodies. In the early nineteenth century, Primitive Methodism asserted itself as a more popular, more fervid, more decentralized, and more institutionally democratic movement than its Wesleyan counterpart, which strove instead for respectability in its membership, worship, and politics. Meanwhile, the doctrine of predestination was dividing the Methodists as it had done the Baptists before them, with the Church in Wales strongly supporting it. All of these varieties of Methodism were present in Toronto.

As for Catholicism, the Council of Trent (1545–1563) tackled some of the excesses that had led to the Reformation, while at the same time taking a firm stand *against* Protestantism. The Catholics who settled in Toronto were very much the products of this Counter-Reformation. The council reaffirmed the hierarchical nature of ecclesiastical authority, especially its right to teach and thereby direct the faithful, emphasizing the age-old distinction between clergy and laity. The latter had to submit to the Church's judgment not only in interpreting scripture but also in the conduct of their moral affairs. Institutional oversight of the laity became more systematic. Parish priests, who were to be trained as much as possible in diocesan seminaries and supervised by their bishops, were expected personally to know their flock. The laity in turn had to belong to specific territorial parishes, where they were required to take the sacraments and fulfil their other religious obligations. The veneration of Mary and the saints was strongly encouraged through a series of new devotional practices that were personal, demonstrative, and emotive, intended to bind the laity to these powerful celestial go-betweens. In the nineteenth century, the First Vatican Council (1870) took the notion of ecclesiastical authority one step further by declaring the pope personally infallible in matters of dogma and morals. At the same time, the control exerted by the Papal Curia over the Church worldwide increased, facilitated by new technologies of communication and transportation. Meanwhile, the devotions to Mary and the saints were given renewed vigour, and new ones were created.[6]

While the hostility between Catholicism and Protestantism remained strong in the nineteenth century, the distinctions within Protestant denominations, especially within Methodism and Presbyterianism, gradually lost their relevance. A move to unite the different wings of these churches gathered momentum, culminating in the creation of the Presbyterian Church in Canada in 1875 and the Methodist Church in 1884. But more importantly, there emerged what historian William Westfall has termed an evangelical consensus among mainstream Protestants, made possible by the separation in 1854 of church and state, the Anglican Church becoming formally disestablished. This consensus, from which only High Church Anglicans were excluded, was based on the belief in the inerrancy of the Bible, the need to evangelize those who ignored Christian truth, and the progress of humankind leading to the thousand-year reign of Christ on earth. It was also profoundly anti-Catholic, not necessarily in a violent way (although that element was certainly present) but rather in its representation of Catholicism as a system of values diametrically opposed to British ones. Canadian evangelicalism in the later nineteenth century was optimistic, positivist, activist, and dogmatic.

Worship in mid-Victorian Toronto followed two distinct models that determined the organization of space inside churches. Evangelical Protestants were focused on the word, that is, on the minister's sermon. Interiors were therefore centred on the pulpit, an elevated piece of furniture usually made of wood, sometimes of stone, from which the minister spoke, elaborating on a biblical text to make a point about doctrine, moral behaviour, personal spirituality, or even contemporary events. Services included the singing of psalms or hymns by a choir as well as the entire congregation. When it was incorporated in worship, the organ was normally placed either behind the pulpit or in the gallery above the main entrance. A wooden communion table, generally found in front of the pulpit, was employed on those occasions, sometimes weekly, monthly, or quarterly, when the congregation received the sacrament. In order not to detract from the centrality of the word, ornamentation was kept to a minimum, being limited to wood and iron work and possibly some stained glass windows.

Revivals were a much sought after objective in evangelical Protestant congregations. Charismatic preachers, whether home-grown or brought in from the outside, would attempt to arouse religious fervour in their listeners and bring about their spiritual or moral regeneration. Inevitably, speakers focused on humanity's utter depravity, the urgency of conversion, God's saving grace, and the horrors of eternal damnation. Sermons were highly charged affairs designed to produce the maximum emotional impact on listeners. Apart from worship, congregational life was structured around a number of organizations, the most important in this early period being the Sunday school, where children of different ages received religious instruction, and the women's association, which was responsible for fundraising either for the congregation or for Christian missions.

By contrast, the focus for Catholics and many Anglicans was on the altar or communion table that recalled the Last Supper, the meal before the crucifixion when Christ enjoined his followers to eat his flesh and drink his blood in order to perpetuate his memory after his death. In addition to the liturgy of the word, which was shared with evangelical Protestants, Catholic and Anglican clergy re-enacted the Last Supper through the liturgy of the Eucharist. In churches typically shaped like a cross, priests stood at the head of the congregation in the apse, while the laity sat in the nave and transepts, the body and arms of the building. In Catholic worship, congregants were not assigned an active role; they were merely expected to pray quietly. In order to inspire prayer, the church was elaborately decorated with paintings, statuary, and stained glass windows. The altar, usually a fixed and elevated structure, was embellished with embroidered cloths, candles, and flowers, all meant to excite reverence. Organ music and choral singing were intended to heighten this atmosphere of reverence and prayer.

To engage them in a deeper religious life, the Holy See under Pope Pius IX (1846–78) encouraged the laity to do devotions outside of Sunday mass focused on the veneration of the sacrament and to recite the rosary while meditating on the sufferings and triumphs of Jesus and his mother Mary. Historian Brian Clarke has described the "devotional revolution" that took place among Irish immigrants, many of whom had practised back home a peasant type of Catholicism that incorporated superstitions, fables, and folk customs. Through the efforts of Bishops Armand De Charbonnel (1850–60) and John Joseph Lynch (1860–88) of Toronto and with the active collaboration of female congregants, parish life revolved around pious lay associations, which included confraternities and temperance and charitable organizations (such as the St Vincent de Paul Society), as well as a variety of religious practices, the most common being the Forty Hours devotion, novenas in preparation for major feast days, and missions, a Catholic term designating practices roughly similar to revivals.[7] Ironically, all of these rituals regarded as orthodox by Catholic ecclesiastical authorities were judged to be obscurantist and idolatrous by Protestant evangelicals. Despite the obvious differences, congregational life was remarkably similar to that of parishes. The faithful were grouped together by gender and age in edifying, philanthropic, instructional, and proselytizing activities under the guidance of an ever-present clergy.

The Geography of Worship

Patrons and the Populace

As its population grew, Toronto expanded westward along the King and Queen Street axes from its historic core just west of the Don River. The geographic focus of this study is the West End. The area at first encompassed the City of Toronto west of College Park Avenue (now University Avenue), and a number of outlying villages not yet incorporated

BLOOR ST. W.
AVENUE RD. →
OSSINGTON AVE.
COLLEGE ST.
DUNDAS ST. W.
BATHURST ST.
SPADINA AVE.
UNIVERSITY AVE.
QUEEN ST. W.
KING ST. W.
FRONT ST.
Methodist/United
Presbyterian
Anglican
Catholic
Baptist
Other
0
500
1000 m
N
Boundary of the
City of Toronto,
1834-1998.
MAP
AREA

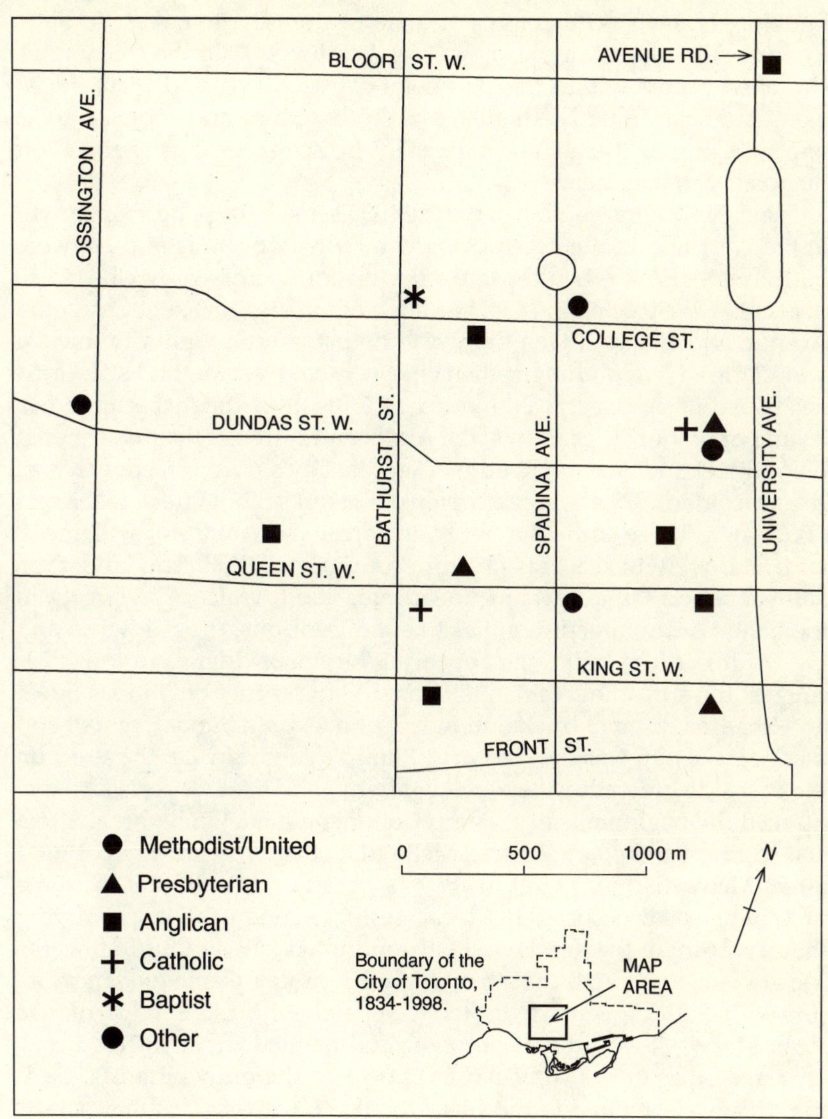

Map 1.1

into the city, such as Brockton, Parkdale, Seaton, Carlton, West Toronto, Runnymede, and Swansea, as well as Wychwood. Of the thirty-three churches erected within this perimeter between 1840 and 1880, eleven were Anglican, nine Methodist, six Presbyterian, and four Catholic. Baptist, Congregational, and Protestant Episcopal groups rounded off the total with one each.

The dates of construction of these edifices make the pattern of growth in the West End immediately apparent. Fully two-thirds of them were built in the 1870s, when the city's population increased by close to 50 per cent.[8] Constructed in 1874, Wesley Methodist, situated at Ossington Avenue and Dundas, was the westernmost church within municipal boundaries. It was founded when Queen Street West Methodist, located near Spadina Avenue, was divided as a result of the increasing Wesleyan population. Meanwhile, the Anglican Church of the Redeemer at Bloor Street and Avenue Road marked the city's northern edge. It was constructed in 1879 after the division of St Paul's Bloor Street, to the east of our area. These edifices roughly demarcated the limits of settlement, which, as we will see, was far from contiguous: the urban landscape still contained large tracts of unoccupied land, which was largely in the hands of prominent families like the Denisons, the Baldwins, and the Boultons. The buildings appearing on major arteries in the 1870s suggest the spread of residential areas. At the corner of Dundas Street and Spadina, a small brick building acting as both Sunday school and place of worship was the start of St Phillip's Anglican. Up the street on the east side of Spadina between Baldwin and D'Arcy streets a chapel marked the beginnings of Western Congregational. On Bathurst Street just south of Bloor, a Primitive Methodist chapel (the future Bathurst Street Methodist) was built in 1869 as a result of a split that for some unknown reason occurred in a local Wesleyan congregation, prompting the departure of the Sunday school superintendent and his followers.[9] Meanwhile, just across the street, Catholics built a plain wooden structure with Gothic accents dedicated to St Peter. Acting as a chapel of ease for St Mary's, it would only become a full-fledged parish in 1896.

Sacred structures also began to appear in the outlying areas. Carlton Village developed in the 1840s thanks to the railways that passed through it.[10] The date of construction of its first church, St Mark's Anglican, is uncertain, although the first baptism was performed in 1854. It was an unassuming country edifice that provided a plain service, so it is unlikely that any architect was involved in its design.[11] During that decade, a small Methodist church made of brick and stone appeared in the same area. The land around the Davenport ridge had seen scattered settlement by farmers, mostly of English origin, starting in the early nineteenth century. One of the pioneers was Bartholomew Bull, a native of Tipperary, Ireland, whose father had personally known John Wesley back in England. In 1818, prayer meetings began at Bull's house and subsequently in neighbouring barns and stables. A small frame structure was finally erected in the late 1840s, soon to be replaced by the brick structure. Egerton Ryerson, Superintendent of Education for Canada West, often preached to this zealous congregation.[12]

In the village of Brockton, to the southeast, St Anne's Anglican was the first sacred site to be erected. Situated at Dufferin Street north of Dundas where the current church is now located, the small red brick structure with a framed front porch was built in the English Country Gothic style by architect Kivas Tully,[13] an immigrant from County Laois, Ireland. Pew rents were apparently charged on Sunday morning, but not in the evening.[14] Farther to the west, two modest edifices were added to the religious landscape. St Helen's Catholic, initially located at Lansdowne Avenue and Dundas, became a full-fledged parish in 1875. Meanwhile, students at Knox College, the Presbyterian divinity school, who had been given preaching assignments in the town over the summer break, recommended that a church be built there. They also agreed to assume temporary responsibility for conducting services until more permanent arrangements could be made. Accordingly, a building seating five hundred went up on Dundas Street at St Clarens.

In the adjacent village of Parkdale to the southwest, three small churches materialized in quick succession. Wesleyan Methodists put up a small frame structure seating two hundred; and Anglicans erected an even smaller wooden building, the embryonic St Mark's (not to be confused with the homonymous church in Carlton Village); while local Presbyterians who had gone to Brockton to worship decided to build a brick edifice seating four hundred people on Dunn Avenue.[15] Wychwood, the area around St Clair Avenue and Christie, was described by contemporaries as follows: "Looking southward appears in the distance the scattered houses and the newly opened angular streets which mark the progress of the expanding city … To the north, the dotted homesteads, the patches of bush and the fields of waving grain appear."[16] There, Toronto's two Primitive Methodist congregations financially supported a mission, which opened in 1877. Richard Punnett, a pious local resident, donated land on St Clair Avenue. In one day the following year a raising bee constructed the frame of a roughcast structure

Table 1.1. The cost of sacred spaces, 1840–80

St George the Martyr Anglican	$24,000	1844
Queen Street Methodist	$46,000 (lot and building)	1857
St Stephen-in-the-Fields Anglican (first)	$10,000	1858
St Patrick Catholic (first)	$60,000 (lot and buildings)	1869
Wesley Methodist	$8,500	1874
Ascension Anglican	$36,500 (lot and buildings)	1875
St Andrew's Presbyterian	$85,000	1876
Erskine Presbyterian	$32,000 (lot and building)	1878
Broadway Tabernacle (first)	$16,000	1879

seating one hundred people. Thus Zion Methodist was born. The Bathurst Street congregation supplied discarded benches and a melodeon, apparently "the first musical instrument possessed by the new movement."[17] A Sunday school with forty students was immediately created; so was a choir.

As may already be apparent, almost two-thirds of the thirty-three churches constructed in this period were transitory. But it is interesting to note that of the thirteen permanent buildings erected in the area, six were Anglican and three Presbyterian – a measure of the wealth and importance of these two denominations. By contrast, only one was Catholic, indicating the relative poverty of a denomination largely comprised of recent immigrants. Clearly, not all churches were created equal (see table 1.1). The ones that made an early impact on the landscape by their size and style of architecture were often products of the patronage of wealthy and influential Torontonians. Among these were members of the old Tory elite, people with connections to the Family Compact that would rule the province until the Union of the Canadas in 1841. For example, a Conservative politician and Orangeman, D'Arcy Boulton Junior, donated the land for St George the Martyr Anglican. The descendant of three generations of men who stood at the very centre of power, he lived in the Grange, a stately Georgian manor built by his grandfather in 1817 and adjacent to the new church. Boulton's nephew, John D'Arcy Caley, son of a Tory cabinet minister, would later become St George's rector. Designed in the Gothic style by architect Henry Bower Lane, a relative of Boulton's by marriage, and built in 1844 of brick dressed with Ohio stone, St George the Martyr had a timbered ceiling and stained glass windows, and seated 750 people. It had an organ manufactured by Samuel R. Warren, who had come to Montreal from the United States in 1836 and remained active there for close to half a century. St George's steeple rose 160 feet from the ground. A condition of its consecration was that the building be free of debt. The church was therefore consecrated by Bishop John Strachan of Toronto (1839–1867) in 1853. No pew rents were charged, seats being entirely free. Revenues were generated from parishioners' Sunday offerings and other sources such as the Sunday school.

Similarly, the Anglican church of the Ascension, built in 1875 on Richmond Street west of Simcoe (demolished), had its entire debt cancelled and a large organ installed thanks to a bequest by Samuel Bois Smith Junior. The son of a British army officer who had been intimately associated with the colonial administration (he was even acting governor of the province for a short time), Smith occupied the politically key position of Clerk of the Executive Council during the Union of the Canadas. For its part, St Stephen-in-the-Fields, located on College Street just west of Spadina, was entirely paid for by Robert Brittain Denison, son of George Taylor Denison Sr, a prominent member of the Tory military establishment and the owner of extensive West End properties.[18] The church was designed by Thomas Fuller, a renowned architect responsible for the Centre Block of the Canadian Parliament and a future Chief Dominion Architect. Denison's patronage, however, proved to be a mixed blessing: for some unknown reason, he took offence one Sunday at what the rector said in his sermon and in protest walked out of the church, threatening to take his family to another place of worship. The diocesan authorities reacted by moving the clergyman to another parish. The next incumbent seemed to be more acceptable, given that he would remain at his post for the next half-century. The incident was probably what prompted the diocese to take full control of the church in 1863.[19] After a fire ravaged the building two years later, a new one was immediately constructed in the Early English Gothic style, seating six hundred faithful according to plans by architectural partners Thomas Gundry and Henry Langley.[20] The church underwent several enlargements in subsequent years to accommodate a congregation that had expanded from its modest working-class origins. Pew rents were no more charged here than at St George the Martyr. It is likely that Denison's half-brother, Richard Lippincott Denison, donated the land for St Anne's Brockton. Before the church's construction, worship had taken place in a private chapel seating fifty people in Dover Court on Denison's ample West End estate.

1.1 St Stephen-in-the-Fields (second church)
The Denison family, prominent landholders in the West End closely connected to the Tory establishment, donated the land and the money for the first church, which was built in 1858. Gutted by fire a short time later, it was quickly rebuilt. It is a fine example of a Gothic Revival country church, although the awkward rear addition of 1890 spoils the building's line somewhat. (Toronto Reference Library)

Patronage was not the sole preserve of rich and powerful Anglicans. Lawyer and businessman Angus Duncan MacDonell, whose Loyalist forebears had established close links to the Family Compact and who was co-founder with his brother of the Quebec and Lake Superior Mining Association in the 1840s, had given the land on which the first St Helen's Catholic stood.[21] New Connexion Methodists found their patrons in Robert Wilkes, a native of County Leitrim, Ireland, one-time Liberal Member of Parliament for Toronto Centre, and vice-president of the Canadian Bank of Commerce, and his wife Martha Cooke. Previously, worshippers had gathered in a small frame mission station, which had been transported on rollers northward to the new site on College Street east of Spadina, a fairly common practice at the time. Robertson described the surrounding area roughly between Queen Street and Bloor as "one unbroken common, where the troops drilled and the boys played cricket and baseball."[22] Once plans for a Gothic-style white brick church were approved, Wilkes apparently instructed the bank manager to advance whatever sum the trustees requested.[23] The cornerstone of the edifice was laid by Mrs Wilkes. Meanwhile, the original frame structure was moved to the back of the property to serve as a Sunday school.

Located at Portland Street below King, St John the Evangelist rose on a two-acre site donated not by a notable, but by the government itself so that the British military stationed at nearby Fort York until their withdrawal from Canada in 1870 would not have to march all the way to St James Cathedral for Sunday worship. The first building was a low, roughcast frame structure, but despite its modest appearance, founding members included prominent Toronto figures such as the eminent jurists and businessmen.[24] The local elite were doubtless drawn to the church by the presence of British officers, as well as to the adjacent historic cemetery dating back to 1793. Perhaps for this reason, St John the Evangelist boasted stained glass windows and a Warren organ. As with most other Anglican places of worship, this one had no pew rents.

Presbyterians connected to the Established Church erected the new St Andrew's at the corner of King Street and Simcoe on the southeastern fringe of our area. The old church, built years earlier in the historic centre, could no longer hold all of its congregants, who were divided over the location of the new place of worship. A majority favoured the current site because of its prestigious surroundings across the street from Government House, diagonally opposite Upper Canada College, and close to the provincial Parliament on Front Street. In the immediate area resided legislators, bank executives, jurists, and successful professionals.[25] Architect William George Storm designed the building using lavish materials: Georgetown stone dressed with Ohio sandstone, and with Bay of Fundy granite for the pillars. The architecturally eclectic structure, which far outstripped the cost of all other churches, appealed to Romantic sensibilities à la Robert Louis Stevenson. Clergyman and writer Charles Pelham Mulvany likened it to a medieval castle and regarded it as "one of the most beautiful buildings in this or any other city on the continent of America."[26] Designed in the Romanesque style,

1.2 Interior of St John the Evangelist Anglican (demolished)
More like a table, the unadorned altar was typical of Anglican church
chancels prior to the Oxford Movement. (Toronto Public Library)

the edifice had turrets on either side of the main entrance and a tower 116 feet high on the southwest corner. The cornerstone was laid in the presence of Senator John Macdonald, a Methodist, wealthy wholesale merchant, and philanthropist, as well as by Auditor General William Cayley, an Anglican well connected by birth and marriage to leading figures in the Family Compact.[27] The inside of the building was organized as a semi-circular amphitheatre on two levels, a style that would become standard for North American Protestant churches. Pew rents were charged so that social status determined seating. Doubtless the highest-paid cleric in the city, Daniel James Macdonnell, who served the congregation from 1870 to 1896, was reputed to be the best preacher in Toronto – according to some people, in the entire country. Irrespective of denominational affiliation, he was a very popular choice for the evening service because he often chose to speak on contemporary or controversial issues.

Like St Andrew's, Erskine Presbyterian had been established years earlier just to the east of our area, and the sale of the old building allowed the congregation to erect a more elaborate and expensive one in the West End. The church's name recalled Ebeneezer Erskine (1680–1754) and his brother Ralph (1685–1752), leaders of the eighteenth-century Secession movement within the Church of Scotland. The particular issues that provoked the schism had long lost their relevance, and this congregation was evidently now anxious to proclaim its social standing. In the event, the political elite turned out in full force for the laying of the cornerstone. In attendance were the Governor General, the Prime Minister, the Lieutenant-Governor, and the Premier of Ontario and the Mayor of Toronto. Perhaps more than Anglicans, Presbyterians were remarkably successful despite their relatively small numbers at mobilizing high-profile figures for such events. The new edifice was located on Simcoe Street just opposite Christ Church First Reformed Episcopal. Architects William Frederick McCaw and Edward Lennox devised a handsome structure in the English Gothic style made of white brick trimmed with Ohio stone. It had a bell tower measuring 135 feet at the side of the elaborate main entrance, as well as an unusual and attractive semicircular vestibule that followed the shape of the nave. Together with draw seats, the building accommodated more than 1,000 worshippers. With carpeted floor and cushioned pews, Robertson deemed it "one of the prettiest and cosiest churches" in the city.[28]

If perhaps not within the inner circles of power, local notables who formed a social stratum below the elite also acted as church patrons.

1.3 St Andrew's Presbyterian
Built in the Romanesque style with a Romantic twist to the exotic towers,
it was one of the city's elite churches situated in what was then an upscale
neighbourhood. Its long-serving minister, D.J. Macdonnell, voted the most
popular preacher in the city, was tried in ecclesiastical court for heresy in
the 1870s. (Toronto Public Library)

St Mark's (Carlton Village) stood on a property donated by Samuel Thompson, an immigrant from London who became a printer, newspaper editor, and staunch Tory advocate throughout the troubled 1830s and 1840s. By contrast, George Cooper was socially prominent in his community. A wealthy farmer and Bartholomew Bull's immediate neighbour in Davenport, he made possible the erection of a brick building for the local Methodist congregation. For his part, Yorkshire-born John Bugg represented a new breed of notable whose activities reflected the new economic and political order. A builder, alderman, and magistrate, he gave land for a Primitive Methodist chapel at Queen Street west of Bathurst (the future Euclid Avenue Methodist).[29] Most congregants were like him immigrants from Yorkshire (and their offspring), who had settled in Upper Canada as part of the huge wave of British immigration following the Napoleonic Wars.[30] John McMurrich, a Scottish immigrant turned businessman, chair of the Board of Education, and provincial politician, provided generous financial and other assistance for the Free Presbyterian congregation that was created at Denison Avenue north of Queen. Like their coreligionists in Scotland, these members had seceded from the Established Church following the Disruption of 1843. They created a mission in the West End in 1856 and five years later built their church, named West Presbyterian. The rather austere exterior was described by architect and academic Eric Arthur as very attractive.[31] Be that as it may, the unknown architect certainly offered a unique response to the standard Romanesque or Gothic-style facades of the period. In less than twenty years, however, the building would be entirely inadequate to the needs of the expanding congregation. A larger edifice in the Gothic style seating 1,000 faithful was built in 1879 just up the street according to plans by architect Henry Bauld Gordon.[32]

Methodists affiliated with the British Wesleyan Conference had been the first in the West End to choose a permanent site for their church. But the property was not donated; it had to be purchased from John Henry Dunn, popular Tory politician and a long-time Receiver General of Upper Canada.[33] After its early beginnings, Queen Street West Methodist assumed its final form in 1857. Seating 1,000 people, it was enlarged a few years later to accommodate five hundred more.[34] Designed by William George Storm, himself an evangelical Anglican but coming from a devoutly Methodist family, it combined Gothic and Romanesque features with entirely unprepossessing results.[35] At the time of its construction, it was the largest Methodist temple, surpassing the mother church

1.4 West Presbyterian (demolished)
Erected in 1860 thanks to a donation by the local and provincial politician
John McMurrich, it was a plain structure in line with the newly estab-
lished Free Church, which rejected the status of the Established Church of
Scotland. It became a Church of Christ in 1885 and a Christian Workers'
church in 1892. (Toronto Public Library)

on Richmond Street not only in seating capacity and membership but in
Sunday school enrolment as well. It would, however, soon be overtaken
by the more architecturally accomplished Metropolitan Methodist on
Queen Street East, with which it would engage in competition for social
prestige and influence, including in the musical realm.

Under the dynamic leadership of congregant John Baxter, alderman for St Patrick's Ward, a choir and orchestra were established and
a Warren organ purchased. Baxter, a countertenor, was at the heart of
the musical life of a structure blessed with excellent acoustics. He was

responsible for the first public performance there of George Frederick Handel's *Messiah*, which was sung by many members of his choir. The church also drew famous preachers from abroad such as the American Phoebe Palmer, originator of Holiness movement, who led a powerful revival here in 1857, and the British evangelist, Morley Punshon, who delivered his first Toronto lecture here a decade later. In keeping with its social standing, the church was fully carpeted, and the pews, for which a rental fee was charged, were cushioned. This was in marked contrast to the earlier church with its high-backed box pews with doors, reflecting a simpler and more financially modest era.[36] Wesleyans also put up a plain brick chapel on University Avenue and Elm that would later serve diverse groups, such as Jews and African Americans.[37]

As mentioned earlier, a new place of worship called Wesley Methodist seating five hundred people was erected farther to the west. It was made of wood with white brick facing according to a plain design by architect Almond E. Paull, an immigrant from Cornwall. The choirmaster and long-serving superintendent of the Sunday school was Robert Awde, an Englishman from Durham and butcher by trade who later received a government appointment as food inspector. An amateur poet, he acquired a modicum of fame for the songs he wrote to welcome the Governor General, the Marquis of Lorne, and his wife Princess Louise, daughter of Queen Victoria. These songs were "in wide circulation and were frequently sung by school children on public and patriotic occasions."[38]

Catholics, who like many Methodists in this period generally could not count on well-established benefactors to help them out, chose a site on Bathurst Street at Richmond for the first St Mary's church. One hesitates to call this a permanent edifice, plagued as it was by severe structural problems that led to its demolition a few years later. Nor did the building that replaced it fare any better. Only in the 1880s were these issues satisfactorily resolved with the construction of the church we see today. Nevertheless, the parish, the third in the city, boasted a school and a presbytery to house its priests, both built in 1860. Lay associations included a number of temperance or total abstinence societies. According to Brian Clarke, St Mary's had a diverse and fairly prosperous working-class population twenty years after its founding. At the eastern edge of the West End, on St Patrick Street just west of University Avenue and north of Dundas, stood St Patrick's, a yellow brick structure designed by Henry Langley in the Gothic style, seating eight hundred parishioners, and completed in 1869. Its lofty spire challenged St George the Martyr's on the West End skyline. In addition to the church proper, the property had a presbytery and a separate school taught by Christian Brothers. The heavy debt incurred to build these structures was apparently still unpaid some twenty years later. This is not surprising, given that most parishioners were recent immigrants from Ireland and of modest circumstances. In fact, Clarke describes the parish as solidly working class and the poorest in the city.[39]

Along College Street, fledgling congregations emerged in the 1870s, following the early lead of St Stephen-in-the-Fields Anglican. At the corner of Bathurst, Presbyterians erected a small roughcast mission station. A minister was inducted in 1875.[40] Baptists also made their formal appearance in the area after conducting a two-year missionary campaign that included outdoor preaching in the summer. Land was purchased by congregant Thomas Lailey, who became personally liable for its payment. Following the creation of the Sunday school, a chapel was built one block east of where the Presbyterians had theirs. The thirty-five founding members chose their pastor, elected their deacons, and adopted the New Hampshire Articles of Faith, a fairly tolerant doctrinal statement formulated in the United States in 1833. This poorer congregation had to content itself with the gift of a silver communion service presented by Ulster immigrant William McMaster and his American wife Susan. A wealthy dry goods merchant and first president of the Canadian Bank of Commerce, McMaster was at this very time financing the construction of the impressive Jarvis Street Baptist to the east of our area. A gallery was soon added to the College Street church in order to accommodate the growing congregation. which held its first picnic on the banks of the Humber River in order to strengthen fellowship. Five years after its founding, the congregation became self-sustaining. An organist was then hired, and the Women's Missionary Association formed.[41]

Ritual Wars

Scattered evidence in the previous pages indicates that Toronto's churches were also sites of conflict. Tensions were strong in the 1870s not only between Catholics and Protestants but also within particular denominations. St Mary was the scene in 1875 of one of the famous Jubilee Riots. These affrays fortunately did not involve loss of life, although many injuries were reported. Nor is there any certainty about the number of people involved because of the difficulty of distinguishing actual participants from curious onlookers. At issue, however, was the right of Catholics to hold religious processions on city streets. The faithful taking part in these sacred events were the object of jeers, insults, and worse still, stones thrown by Orangemen, who, it must be said, received in kind what they doled out. Random shots were also fired. The police and the army performed their duty, separating the hostile contenders, charging at rioters with batons and at one point with guns drawn, and finally confiscating weapons. A number of arrests were made. These incidents revealed how public officials such as the Orange mayor of Toronto, Francis Medcalf, paid lip service to civil liberties, while pressing the provincial legislature to ban processions. He also implied that Catholics, by their obstinacy, had provoked the disturbances. This was the line taken as well by the Conservative Party organ, *The Leader*, which blithely associated the processions with Fenianism, a North American Irish expatriate movement that advocated the violent overthrow of British rule in Ireland. Catholics, it appeared, had breached an unwritten rule established by the Protestant majority that religious events should take place in enclosed spaces, certainly not on city streets.[42]

As Presbyterians and Methodists gradually resolved their internal differences and moved in tandem towards an evangelical consensus, Anglicans felt the strains of division. As long as Catholicism had posed a threat to the legitimacy of the state in England, the *via media* or Elizabethan Settlement held firm. But by the middle of the nineteenth century, the menace had long receded, despite what a headstrong anti-papist lobby maintained. In this changing climate, the Oxford Movement was born. Inspired by what they saw as the unity of medieval Christendom, a group of clergymen affiliated with Oxford University sought to reconnect Anglicanism with its historical roots by emphasizing Christ's presence in the Eucharist. The movement was not uniform. It produced some spectacular defections, such as John Henry Newman (1801–1890) and Henry Manning (1808–1892), whose conversions earned them each a Cardinal's hat. The majority, however, remained faithful to their Anglican faith.

In Toronto, the first church to be influenced by the Oxford Movement was Holy Trinity, to the east of our area. However, a new parish named St Matthias was created in 1873 in the developing western edge of the city close to Trinity Bellwoods Park. Built of two-toned brick, it resembled a charming little country church because of its unassuming architecture. Its high-pitched timbered ceiling and stained-glass windows were the only structural adornments. Unlike many congregations striving for respectability, St Matthias was not carpeted. Its plain, unvarnished pine pews were available free of charge. Standing in a poor part

1.5 St Matthias Anglican
This modest church in a working-class neighbourhood became the first in
the West End to adopt a Eucharist-centred liturgy promoted by the Oxford
Movement. A bastion of Anglo-Catholicism, it provoked sometimes violent
responses from Protestant zealots. (Gabriele Scardellato)

of the city where modest-sized homes were the norm, the church was heavily involved in the distribution of fuel and clothing to local English immigrants caught in the depression of 1873.[43] This suggests that the parish was composed at least in part of recent arrivals.

St Matthias became the second parish after Holy Trinity whose choir wore surplices – a real flashpoint for evangelicals, who saw this innovation as the thin edge of the wedge of Popery. Extremists broke into the church and vandalized the altar, which had been carved by students at the Diocesan Theological Institute, an institution founded in Cobourg by Bishop Strachan. The altar, dressed in rich cloths, displayed words stressing the centrality of communion. Years later, journalist John Ross Robertson reported: "The marks of its defacement are yet distinctly visible in its beautiful carvings."[44] The parish was home to the Toronto chapter of the Confraternity of the Blessed Sacrament, founded in London, England, in 1862 to promote the veneration of Christ's presence in the Eucharist. Members were encouraged to fast before taking communion. The priest at St Matthias wore liturgical dress historically associated with the Catholic mass – that is, a chasuble, maniple, and stole – and like his Catholic counterpart, he had his back turned to the congregation. "So he does exactly like the mayor of a town," explained Robertson to his readers, "who goes up with the corporation and the citizens to present an address to the Queen."[45] Evangelicals remained unmoved by such rationalizations. For them, the priest's position created an air of secrecy and superstitious mystery, setting him apart from the people and contravening the cherished Reformation belief in the priesthood of all believers. Still, the parish enjoyed the full support of the professors at nearby Trinity College, then located in Trinity Bellwoods Park, who were identified with the High Church party.[46]

The second parish in the area to be influenced by the Oxford Movement was St Thomas, founded a year after St Matthias in 1874 and originally located in Seaton Village, northwest of Bloor and Bathurst Streets. Its benefactor was American-born William Russell Bartlett, a long-time civil servant who, as commissioner and visiting superintendent in the Indian Department, had sold Ontario settlers large tracts of land apparently ceded by First Nations peoples.[47] The small frame roughcast building was designed by architect Frank Darling, son of Charles Stewart, rector of Holy Trinity Church and leader of the High Church group in Toronto. Frank's brother Charles would serve for many years as rector of St Mary Magdalene, also associated with the High Church movement. St Thomas assisted English immigrants who had settled in

1.6 The choir at St Thomas's Anglican
This composite photograph, very popular in the nineteenth century, shows
the men and boys' choir wearing surplices, condemned as Popish by many
Protestants. (Toronto Reference Library)

Seaton in the 1860s and who, lacking any kind of religious organization,
recited Matins and Evensong in one others' homes. Seats at St Thomas
were free.[48]

The ritualist turn taken by High Church parishes was firmly resisted
by the evangelical Anglicans who founded the Church of the Ascension
mentioned above. Canon Edmund Baldwin, a cousin of Reform leader
Robert Baldwin, had considered St George's to be too High Church, and
he left it, taking a number of wealthy parishioners with him, when their
candidate for people's warden was defeated. That failed candidate had
been Kivas Tully, architect of St Anne's.[49] To ensure that the Church of

the Ascension remained "Protestant and Evangelical," the property was entrusted to trustees rather than, as was usually the case, the diocese. Edmund Baldwin's son, Hugh Grassett Baldwin, would later become its rector. The new church sat nine hundred faithful, making it at the time the largest and most expensive Anglican church to be built in the West End. No pew rents were charged.[50] Designed by Frank Darling, it was constructed in brick with stone dressing in the Gothic style and had a bell tower at the side of the main entrance. A plain, unadorned table (as opposed to an altar) stood at the centre of the chancel, a strikingly symbolic downgrading of the significance of the Eucharist.[51] The most prominent member of this church was Goldwin Smith, intellectual, polemicist, and occupant of the Grange after his marriage in 1875 to Harriet, daughter-in-law of D'Arcy Boulton Junior.

Another Low Church parish emerged with the creation of the Church of the Redeemer. It was designed by architects James Avon Smith and John Gemmell in the Early English Gothic style and accommodated eight hundred people. Expensive materials were used in its construction: the exterior was of stone, and the interior of brick, with two granite pillars supporting the junction of the transepts to the nave. Like St Andrew's Presbyterian, this was a rich man's church. Among its prominent parishioners were a Chief Justice of the Court of Queen's Bench and former mayor of Toronto, a renowned lawyer and arbitrator,[52] and William George Storm.[53] In fact, Storm designed the adjacent large rectory described by Robertson as "the finest in the city."[54] In contrast to other Anglican churches in the area, this one charged pew rents.

Some evangelicals severed their connection with Anglicanism altogether, affiliating instead with the Reformed Episcopals, a denomination founded in the United States in reaction to ritualism. In 1876, this breakaway group chose a site on Simcoe Street at the corner of Elm to erect a church in the Romanesque style with a truncated belfry, named Christ Church First Reformed Episcopal. Rejecting the idea of Christ's presence in the Eucharist, they did away entirely with the altar, placing the pulpit front and centre in the sanctuary. A prominent member of this congregation was E.F. (Ned) Clarke. A native of County Cavan, Ireland, and a committed Orangeman, he led the famous Printers' Strike of 1872 against George Brown's *Globe*. He went on to be mayor of Toronto (1888–91) and Conservative MP (1896–1905).

Presbyterians too showed signs of division. Prior to the move to St Andrew's new location, the minister, James Macdonnell, was accused of heresy for a sermon in which he expressed long-held doubts about the compatibility of the Calvinist doctrine of predestination with the New Testament's portrayal of God as infinitely loving and merciful. An ecclesiastical trial was held in 1875 that severely tested the new union of Presbyterians achieved just the previous year. Macdonnell was brought before the General Assembly, the Church's highest-ranking body in Canada. The controversy was resolved after nearly two years of wheeling and dealing. The ensuing compromise statement succeeded in defusing a potential time bomb.[55] Still, it exposed a doctrinaire current within Canadian Presbyterianism that accused the Established Church party of moral and doctrinal laxity. This dispute essentially concerned the clergy; another one engaged the laity, especially at St Andrew's but also elsewhere. The issue was the use of musical instruments in worship, specifically the organ, and it was as divisive in Presbyterianism as surplices were in Anglicanism, portending for some the slippery slope to Romanism. The anti-instruments faction regarded a cappella singing as the only acceptable form of music in Christian worship, so when a cabinet organ was introduced at St Andrew's in 1859, a parishioner objected. The matter was brought before the Synod, which ordered its removal. Only years later would individual congregations finally be allowed the option of using musical instruments in worship if they so chose. In 1885 a magnificent Warren organ, costing $13,000 (it seems nothing was done cheaply at St Andrew's), was finally installed.[56]

Beginning in the early 1840s, more churches were founded in the West End as the city expanded to the north and west. Meanwhile Wychwood, Carlton Village, Brockton, and Parkdale all had chapels that highlighted the recent development of these municipalities. Some places of worship were markers of a group's recent arrival and ethnicity. Catholic churches were frequented largely but not exclusively by Irish immigrants struggling to insert themselves and their families into the local economy. It is more difficult to categorize Protestant churches as ethnic because newcomers were often thrown together with congregants who had immigrated earlier or were born on the continent. As well, religion and ethnicity were not coterminous in Britain: Scots, Irish, and English could be Anglican, Methodist, Presbyterian, or Baptist, just to name the major denominations. Protestants also tended to intermarry, especially after the first generation in Toronto, thus blurring ethnic distinctions. Finally, a congregation's ethnic character could be altered by the addition of a new cohort to the original membership.

Places of worship seemed to reproduce class distinctions, often morally sanctioning such divisions. Individuals could flaunt their social standing by donating land or assuming the costs of a church's construction, as did D'Arcy Boulton Junior, Samuel B. Smith, and Robert Brittain Denison. The Anglican parishes of the Redeemer and St John the Evangelist and the Presbyterian ones of St Andrew's and Erskine clearly denoted wealth and prestige. Their churches, generally built by well-established architects who used costly construction materials, contrasted sharply with the frame or plain brick structures erected by Baptists, Methodists, and even Anglicans in outlying areas. Zion Methodist and Parkdale Methodist offer examples of the cooperative and popular building techniques used by people of modest means. Yet the congregations to which wealthy patrons made major contributions were not uniformly of the same social class. As well, timing is an important factor to consider. Comparing well-established churches such as St George the Martyr and Queen Street Methodist with pioneering ones such as Davenport Road Methodist and St Mark's Carlton Village may not be appropriate. And while Catholic churches suggested working-class status, St Patrick's was built by a reputable architect and St Mary's was a socially mixed parish. So on the whole, most sacred spaces were situated between the two extremes of wealth illustrated above and exhibited a degree of social heterogeneity.

This does not mean that they were sites of harmony. Churches could and did mirror ethnic, inter-denominational, and intra-denominational tensions, as is vividly illustrated by the dissension at St George the Martyr over ritualism and the subsequent founding of the Church of the Ascension. After the Protestant Episcopal Divinity School (later known as Wycliffe College) was founded in 1877, parishes recruited their clergy either from there or from Trinity College depending on whether they were High Church or Low Church. Surplices for choirs and the use of candles in worship became points of demarcation between these two currents. At St Andrew's Presbyterian, as we have seen, the introduction of musical instruments sparked vigorous protest, delaying the purchase of an organ for a generation. While explicitly doctrinal controversies were rare, they did exist, as demonstrated by D.J. Macdonell's heresy trial. Meanwhile, at St George the Martyr, John D'Arcy Cayley and John Langtry confronted each other over the issue of higher biblical criticism. All of these questions, however, were kept contained at the clerical or parish level. They did not disturb the relative calm that, with the notable exception of the Jubilee Riots, which coincided with the ritualist controversy in the Anglican Church, characterized Christian worship in the city.

In the end, the centrifugal forces of class and sectarianism proved to be weaker than the centripetal ones. Churches succeeded in bringing people together, and music played an important role – perhaps a key one – in this process. Robertson commented on the excellence of the music at Queen Street Methodist, St George the Martyr, and the Church of the Redeemer. He was also impressed by how the parishioners at the Church of the Ascension participated in congregational singing. Sunday schools were another critical component of church life, often serving as embryonic places of worship and consolidating ties between families and particular churches. In many parishes and congregations, among the first organizations to be founded were women's associations, in particular those that supported missionary activity, which underscores the significant role played by women in organized religious life. For Irish and English newcomers, churches were expressions of collective identity against the challenges posed by immigration and the homogenizing North American environment. Paradoxically, these institutions actually facilitated immigrant integration. For example, the Catholic clergy inhibited expressions of the peasant religiosity of the home country among Irish immigrants, inculcating in them instead a standard Ultramontane practice promoted by the Holy See throughout the world. While Catholicism continued to be reviled in Protestant North America, it nevertheless acquired greater respectability by rooting out all manifestations of peasant religion brought over by rural immigrants.

Chapter Two

An Era of Exuberance, 1880–1920

Like an earthquake, the formidable forces of industrialization reshaped the urban landscape. The effect was sudden, quick, extensive, and completely unexpected. Rich and poor alike moved house in response to the increasing concentration of commercial and industrial establishments in the downtown core and along its corridors. Even recent arrivals from Europe eventually had to abandon the crowded and insalubrious St John's Ward with its profusion of cheap housing as government, business, financial, and health care institutions vied with one another for a portion of downtown space. Religion was not spared from these dramatic changes. Churches built in the expansive 1880s and distinguished in the early years by a flourishing associational life were but empty shells twenty years later. Tough choices had to be made: follow the movement of people away from the downtown, or remain and adapt to change. The first option led at times to closings and demolitions. More often, however, it triggered a process whereby ethno-religious groups in some way connected to the new industrial reality took over existing structures. Since the technology and managerial culture underpinning the new industrial reality were as a rule of American origin, a number of religious groups associated with the Second or Third Great Awakening in the United States made their appearance in Toronto. Christian Science, Christian and Missionary Alliance, Mormons, Pentecostals, and Christadelphians settled within or near the downtown core. Meanwhile migrants from the Ontario countryside or continental Europe, who formed the backbone of the unskilled labour force, took over a number of churches vacated by older, well-established congregations.

A good illustration of the point being made here is Erskine Presbyterian. Initially located to the east of our area, the congregation decided to

2.1 Erskine Presbyterian (demolished)
Like its rival St Andrew's, this church served an elite congregation residing
in what was then a prosperous suburb close to where Queen's Park would
stand. Built in the Gothic style, it was located on Elm Street at Simcoe.
(Toronto Reference Library)

move to a more respectable neighbourhood close to the soon-to-be-built provincial Parliament at Queen's Park. The lot and the building cost the princely sum of $34,000, part of which was covered by the sale of the old church. After a disastrous fire in 1884, which left only the shell of the structure, the congregation spent another $20,000 to erect a new edifice accommodating more than 1,000 people. Membership stood at 600 in the early 1890s. The Sunday school had 350 scholars, and the library held 600 books. Its minister enjoyed a salary of $2,400 a year. A plethora of organizations had flourished, divided by gender and age groups. The congregation supported an East End mission on Duchess Street that ran, among other things, a savings bank and child care classes. It also provided financial aid to a missionary teacher in the New Hebrides.[1]

By the First World War, however, the situation had changed dramatically. As a *Toronto Star* reporter observed in rather shaky prose: "Today the building alone remains of the church life, standing a monument to early Presbyterian Toronto in a sea of gesticulating Yiddish [*sic*] and factory whistles. The giant commerce has come in and possessed the land."[2] The congregation responded by merging with St Paul's on Bathurst Street north of Bloor, in whose vicinity more than half of Erskine's members now lived. Erskine's wealthy congregants exemplified Torontonians' willingness to make significant capital outlays to build and support the activities of their places of worship. No matter how rich or powerful, however, they could not arrest or temper the forces of industrialism on the urban landscape.

Hogtown, as the industrial city came to be nicknamed because of its extensive meat-packing facilities, changed dramatically in the forty years after 1880. Its population increased sixfold, from 86,000 to more than 500,000. Overseas immigration continued to be a significant factor in this increase, but proportionally less so than in the previous period. The foreign-born still accounted for more than one-third of Toronto's inhabitants; between 1891 and 1921 their numbers climbed from 51,000 to almost 200,000. Internal migration also played a part in this growth. Plants first established in outlying areas, together with their workers, moved to the city as part of a process of industrial concentration. The farm machinery firm of Hart Massey, for example, came to Toronto from Newcastle in 1879, absorbing a number of smaller enterprises over the years and merging with a major rival, the Harris plant of Brantford. By the end of the century, with its unshakable control of the Canadian market, the Massey-Harris operations on King Street West comprised the single largest factory in the city.[3]

This example highlights two important and doubtless interrelated events. The first was Prime Minister John A. Macdonald's National Policy, all three elements of which were salient in Toronto's growth: the transcontinental railway transformed the city's market from a regional one into a national one in which it was able to enjoy commercial superiority, buying cheaply and selling dearly; the tariff protected home-based industries from foreign competition; and immigration expanded the national market while also attracting both highly skilled workers without the cost of training them and unskilled ones who performed work that native-born Canadians disdained. The second, as we have seen, was horizontal integration. Toronto was situated in the most populous and, more importantly, the richest part of the country. Economies of scale encouraged businessmen to locate their enterprises there. By 1880 the city already had a solid and varied industrial base that spanned the spectrum from light industries, such as clothing and shoe manufacturing, to heavy ones, such as the production of industrial machinery. Those enterprises that survived the cyclical downturns of the years from 1873 to 1896 often absorbed smaller ones in the same sector, as Massey did, thus reducing the costs of production and increasing their profit margins. When in 1896 the rise in commodity prices put an end to the world trade slump, Toronto's solid financial institutions, which had backed these mergers with their capital, invested heavily in the resource sector, but also in transportation as well as in urban utilities and real estate. This was the era of vertical integration, during which enterprises – now impersonal conglomerates whose boards of directors included entrepreneurs, lawyers, and politicians – sought to bring under their ownership every aspect of production in one economic sector, from the extraction of raw materials to the selling of finished products. Huge fortunes were made in this period. The most graphic demonstration of this wealth is Casa Loma, Sir Henry Pellatt's ninety-eight-room residence, a *folie de grandeur* costing $3.5 million. Meanwhile, unskilled workers often did not earn enough to provide for their families, and unions had managed to organize only a small fraction of the labour force.

The Demographics of Religion

Toronto continued to be overwhelmingly Protestant, with the four main denominations (Anglican, Presbyterian, Methodist, and Baptist) claiming more than three-quarters of its inhabitants. If to these we add members of smaller Protestant groups, that proportion was just over four-fifths. Indeed, a plethora of new denominations made their appearance in the West End. At first they worshipped separately at Broadway Hall on Spadina Avenue just south of College, but many of them would later find permanent facilities. While Protestants increased their share of the Toronto population, Catholics fell precipitously from 18 per cent to an all-time low of 12 per cent in 1921. Jews, the first non-Christian group, became statistically significant during this period, increasing from 1.5 per cent in 1901 to 6.5 per cent in 1920. People claiming no denominational attachment or simply no religion continued to be marginal.[4] Torontonians were also becoming somewhat ethnically diverse. The proportional increase in Jews reflected the large number of newcomers arriving from eastern Europe. Similarly, Toronto's Catholics, as a result of immigration, now included Italians, Poles, and Ukrainians. Unlike in the previous era, some Protestants were now not of British extraction or culture. They included Finns and Germans as well as Chinese. Immigration also accounted for the presence of the Orthodox faith in Toronto; Russians were the first of its adherents to appear in the West End.

Between 1880 and 1920 the West End could count 115 new permanent places of worship, a ninefold rise over the previous period and larger than the overall demographic increase. Parishioners and congregants spent significant sums on their sacred sites – on average, tens of thousands of dollars per unit. Structures costing less than $10,000 tended to be found in solidly working-class neighbourhoods, such the Junction and Christie Pits, or they belonged to smaller denominations, such as Congregationalists. In any event, there were notable exceptions in both these cases: Western Congregational, Royce Avenue Presbyterian, and Perth Avenue Methodist were both costlier and larger. As table 2.1 indicates, church construction made a noteworthy contribution to the urban economy and to the building trades in particular, including manufacturers of stained glass.

It comes as somewhat of a surprise that the largest number of churches, twenty-two in all, were built by Methodists even though numerically they continued to lag behind Anglicans. In fact, their percentage of the overall population actually dropped from 23 to 16 per cent in the first two decades of the new century. By contrast, the Presbyterians, whose portion of the population rose from 17 to 22 per cent between 1881 and 1921, built nineteen churches. Anglicans and

Table 2.1. The cost of sacred spaces, 1880–1920

	Cost ($)	Year
St Mark's Parkdale Anglican	6,500 (lot and building)	1880
St Thomas Anglican	20,000 (lot and building)	1882
Parkdale Congregational	3,000 (lot and building)	1883
St Phillip's Anglican	17,000	1884
College Street Presbyterian	29,000	1885
Beverley Street Baptist (second)	12,500	1886
Cowan Avenue Methodist	16,000	1886
St Paul's Methodist	40,000 (lot and building	1887
Bloor Street Presbyterian	16,000	1887
Clinton Street Methodist	14,000 (lot and building)	1887
Dovercourt Road Baptist	28,000	1887
St Clarens Avenue Methodist	4,000	1887
Trinity Methodist	130,000	1888
Western Congregational	20,000 (lot and building)	1888
Walmer Road Baptist (first)	45,000	1888
College Street Baptist (second)	57,000	1888
Clinton Street Methodist	30,000	1888
St Mark's Presbyterian	12,000	1888
Epworth Methodist	5,000	1888
St Paul's Presbyterian	36,000	1888
Parkdale Presbyterian	40,000	1888
Royce Avenue Baptist	5,000	1888
Annette Street Baptist (first)	5,000 (lot and building)	1888
Zion Methodist (first)	10,000	1889
Chalmers Presbyterian	40,000	1889
Lansdowne Avenue Baptist	6,000	1889
Parkdale Methodist	77,000 (lot and building)	1889
Perth Avenue Methodist (first)	7,000	1889
St Margaret Anglican	12,000	1890
Keele Street Church of Christ	6,500	1890
High Park Methodist (second)	7,500 (lot and building)	1890
Cecil Street Church of Christ	27,000 (lot and building)	1891
Messiah Anglican	35,000	1891
Walmer Road Baptist (second)	70,000	1891
Hope Congregational	6,000 (lot and building)	1891
Centennial Methodist (first)	13,000 (lot and building)	1891
St John the Evangelist Anglican (second)	16,000	1892
St Cyprian's Anglican (first)	4,500	1892
Crawford Street Methodist	13,000	1892
Bethany Chapel	9,000	1893

	Cost ($)	Year
Memorial Baptist	13,000	1897
Olivet Baptist	8,000 (lot and building)	1901
St Francis Catholic (first)	20,000	1902
Christie Street Baptist	3,000	1902
Bathurst Street Disciples of Christ	9,000 (lot and building)	1903
Victoria Presbyterian	40,000	1903
Goel Tzedec Synagogue	65,000	1905
Chevra Tefillah Synagogue	30,000	1905
Christian Workers Tabernacle	20,000	1906
St Cyprian's Anglican (second)	15,000	1906
First Baptist	15,000	1907
St Anne's Anglican	55,000	1907
High Park Methodist (third)	36,000	1907
St Helen's Catholic	97,000 (lot and building)	1908
Westmoreland Avenue Methodist	45,000	1908
Wychwood Presbyterian	30,000	1910
St Stanislaus Polish Catholic	30,000	1911
High Park Baptist	60,000	1912
St Josaphat Ukrainian Catholic	31,000	1913
St Francis Catholic (second)	115,000	1914
Dewi Sant Presbyterian	6,000	1917
Dufferin Street Baptist	17,000	1918

Baptists erected seventeen and fourteen churches respectively. Despite the Baptists' small numbers (they never surpassed 6 per cent of the population, a peak reached in 1891 and 1901), they were, to borrow a common expression at the time, active "church planters." Why were Anglicans, who still accounted for one-third of the population in 1921, apparently so sluggish? It could be argued that they had a head start in the earlier period and that their churches could, in any event, be found in all parts of the West End. By 1920 Anglicans had just slightly fewer permanent religious structures than Methodists and Presbyterians. It might also be that Anglicans were present in greater numbers in other parts of the city. Further research would have to be conducted to confirm this hypothesis. With eleven churches to their credit, Catholics were making up for their underrepresentation in the earlier era. As well, Jews made a substantial contribution to Toronto's religious architecture, given their numbers, by erecting two synagogues, thus diversifying the city's landscape.

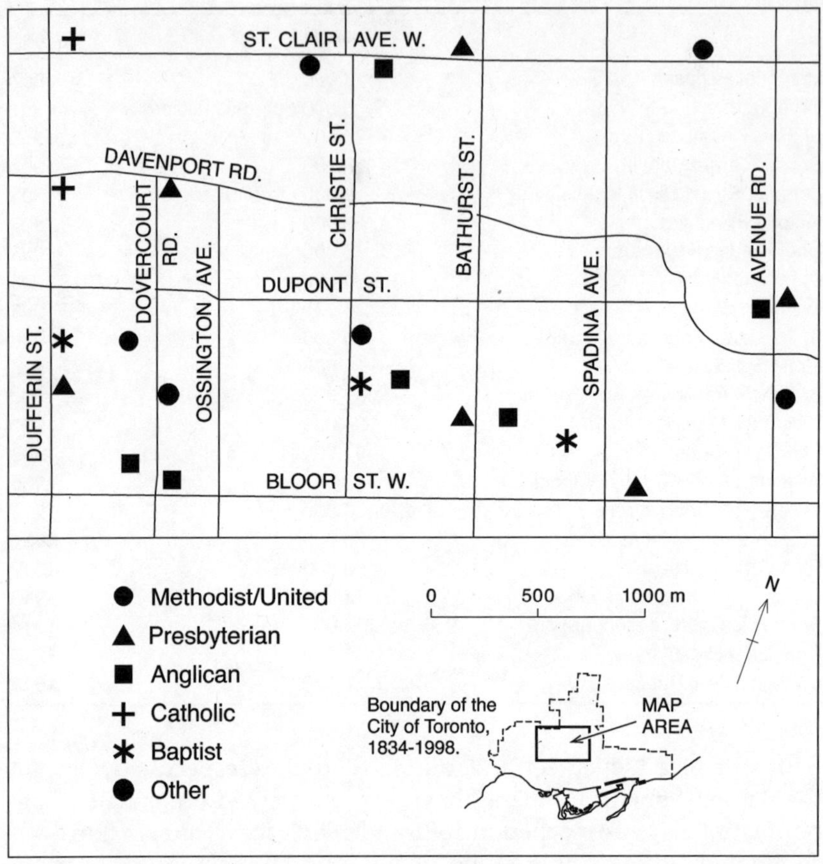

Map 2.1

Just under half the new West End sacred structures were substantial ones, seating between 700 and 2,000 people. Twenty-two of them were built between 1884 and 1892, an era marked by civic optimism, pride, and ambition. Twenty-eight more went up in the decade after 1906, which also coincided with a period of prosperity, expansion, and boosterism. Once again, it was the Methodists who put up the most and biggest buildings. Churches such as Bathurst Street, Trinity, Centennial, and Timothy Eaton Memorial were and still are veritable landmarks.[5] Presbyterians came second, although on the whole, their buildings were not as capacious

AVENUE RD.
DUFFERIN ST.
OSSINGTON AVE.
BLOOR ST. W.
COLLEGE ST.
BATHURST ST.
SPADINA AVE.
UNIVERSITY AVE.
DUNDAS ST. W.
QUEEN ST. W.
KING ST. W.
Methodist/United
Congregational
Presbyterian
Anglican
Catholic
Baptist
Jewish
Other
0
500
1000 m
N
Boundary of the City of Toronto, 1834-1998.
MAP AREA

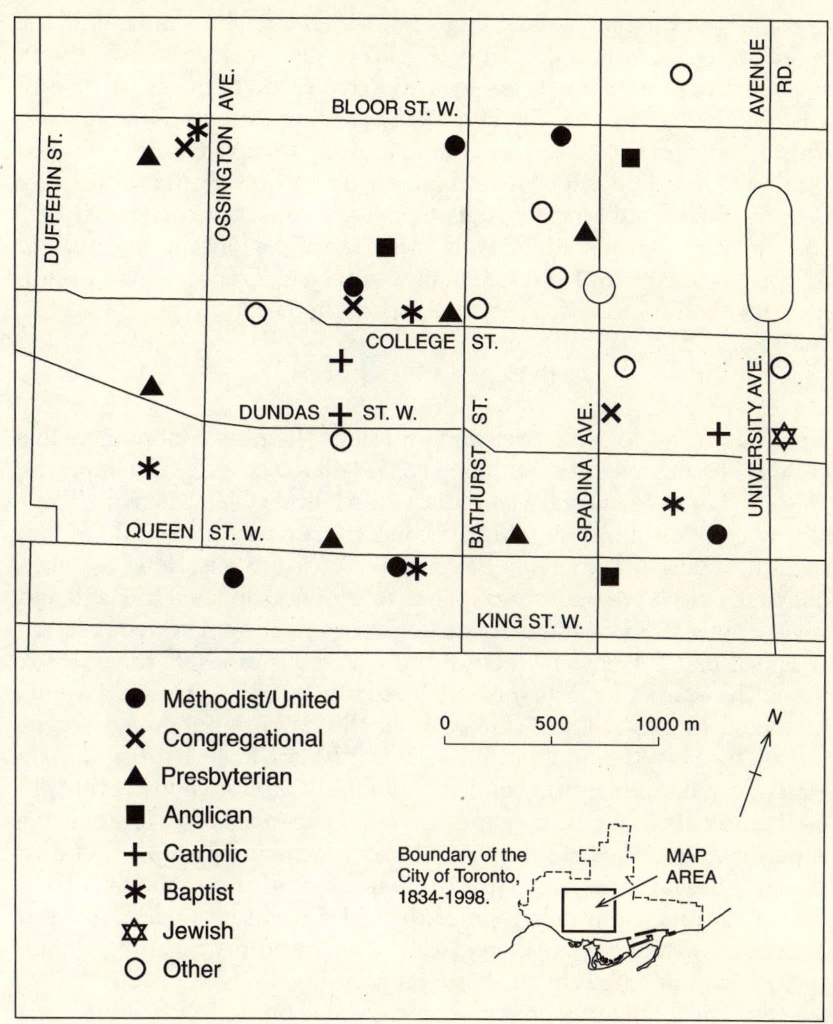

Map 2.2

as the largest Methodist ones; they also tended to be built later. With the exception of St Anne's Brockton, Anglicans also seemed satisfied with smaller structures. Baptists too seemed to have caught the mood of optimism and expansion of the late 1880s, erecting Walmer Road, Dovercourt Road, and College Street.[6] Catholics were relative latecomers when it came to building imposing structures. Apart from St Mary on lower Bathurst Street, built in 1885, the others were constructed between 1908 and the war. They include St Patrick, St Francis, St Vincent de Paul, and the very attractive St Helen's. Finally, with Goel Tzedec, Eastern European Jews announced that they had arrived in the city.

Patrons and Architects

Benefactions by Toronto's rich and prominent families continued in this period. The Eatons, for example, assumed all the costs for the imposing Timothy Eaton Memorial Methodist Church on St Clair Avenue at Warren, which the family would subsequently run as a personal fiefdom until the death of Lady Flora Eaton in 1970. Meanwhile, Robert Walker, one of the city's wealthiest dry goods merchants, donated the land and covered one-third of the construction cost for St Paul's Methodist on Avenue Road at Webster, where Timothy Eaton's imposing funeral took place. The Masseys, for their part, paid for the building of Euclid Avenue Methodist (third) on Queen Street, while the Harrises put up most of the money for both the first and the second Walmer Road Baptist. Elmore Harris, scion of this farm implements family and a leading evangelical, became its first minister, and his brother-in-law, J.N. Shenstone, the superintendent of its Sunday school and a member of its board of deacons.[7] William Davies, an Oxfordshire immigrant and millionaire meat packer, assumed the mortgage of the old Tecumseth Road Baptist at Richmond so that it could be replaced by a new edifice renamed Memorial. He also donated the property on Margueretta Street south of College on which Olivet Baptist rose, and the one on Roncesvalles Avenue at Hewitt where High Park Baptist now stands.[8] Thomas Lailey, a leading member of College Street Baptist, meanwhile deeded land located at Dovercourt Road and Argyle, where Dovercourt Road Baptist was built; and John Stark, a member of the board of trustees of Toronto Baptist College (forerunner of McMaster University), gave the property on Ossington Avenue at Bloor where the homonymous church was built. [9]

The Presbyterians found a generous donor in John Wanless, a jewellery manufacturer, school trustee, and alderman. He provided the land for the Wychwood and Davenport churches, as well as for Evangel Hall, the mission on Queen Street run by Knox Church, where he was an elder. He also paid for Davenport's furnishings and organ, as well as for the musical instruments for its noteworthy orchestra. William Mortimer Clark, bank director, chairman of the board of management of Knox College, vice-president of the militant Protestant Equal Rights Association, and future Lieutenant-Governor of Ontario, gave the land on which St Paul's Presbyterian stood on Barton Avenue at Bathurst. Robert Dale offered a property on Queen Street where in 1916 the congregants of St Mark's Presbyterian erected their church, renamed Dale in his honour. Finally, Edward Dawes gave the land on which the first St Mary the Virgin Anglican stood.

The names of many well-established architects are associated with about two-thirds of the West End's places of worship (see table 2.2).

These architects were often chosen on the basis of their denominational or evangelical allegiances. While Anglicans called on a wide variety of individuals or firms for their churches, High Churchmen had a penchant for Frank Darling and Birmingham-born Eden Smith, who built in the Arts and Crafts style. The evangelical Grant Helliwell, who served as Sunday school superintendent at the Church of the Messiah for thirty-three years, was a favourite of Low Churchmen. Together with Henry Bauld Gordon, a member of Knox Presbyterian, Helliwell designed five out of thirteen Presbyterian churches; William Rufus Gregg, the son of a professor at Knox College, and James Wilson Gray – like Gordon, an active Knox congregant – produced two church designs each. Finally, partners James Avon Smith and John Gemmell, both of whom were Scottish-born, created plans for three other Presbyterian places of worship. For its part, the Catholic archdiocese practically elevated Arthur Holmes, a London-born convert to Catholicism, to the status of official architect; he designed five of the nine professionally commissioned Catholic churches. Baptists were partial to one of their own, Edmund Burke, who was also a favourite of the McMasters. He and his various partners worked on five of the seven Baptist sanctuaries.[10] The two synagogues erected in the West End were the work of Gentiles, since there were no Jewish architects in Toronto at the time.

Large denominations were not alone in making use of professionals. Smaller ones, mostly of American origin, did so as well. One of these was the Reorganized Church of Latter-Day Saints. An outgrowth of the Second Great Awakening in the early nineteenth century, this denomination was established by Joseph Smith III, son of

Table 2.2. Architects of West End places of worship, 1880–1920

Architects	Year	Places of Worship
Solon Spencer Bemen	1915	First Church Christ Scientist
Francis Brown	1901	Olivet Baptist
	1903	Grace Evangelical
	1906	Ossington Baptist
	1910	St Jude Anglican
Charles Acton Bond	1908	Reorganized Mormons
Edmund Burke & John	1897	Memorial Baptist
Horwood	1907	High Park Methodist
William Burns	1910	Howard Park Methodist
James Coxhead	1883	Parkdale Congregational
Joseph Connolly	1885	St Mary's Catholic
James Michael Cowan	1915	St.Vincent de Paul Catholic
Frank Darling	1888	St Mary Magdalene Anglican
A.R. Denison	1884	St Philip's Anglican
James Ellis	1890	Church of Christ, Junction
James Ellis & W. Connery	1903	Victoria Presbyterian
	1910	Humberside Baptist
	1911	Knesseth Israel Synagogue
J. Falloon & R.C. Windeyer	1885	St Alban the Martyr Anglican
Henry Bauld Gordon	1889	Chalmers Presbyterian
H.B. Gordon & G. Helliwell	1888	Bathurst Street Methodist
	1888	Parkdale Presbyterian
	1888	Western Congregational
	1891	Messiah Anglican
	1906	Covenant Presbyterian
	1907	Bonar Presbyterian
	1910	Epiphany Anglican
	1912	West Presbyterian (3rd church)
	1914	Epworth Methodist
James Wilson Gray	1906	St Paul's Presbyterian
	1907	Knox Presbyterian
William Rufus Gregg	1887	Bloor Street Presbyterian
	1905	Dovercourt Presbyterian
Arthur Holmes	1902	Holy Family Catholic
	1908	St Patrick's Catholic (second)
	1908	St Helen's Catholic
	1913	St Clare Catholic
	1914	St Francis Catholic (second)
J.C.B. Horwood & M. White	1911	Western Baptist
William Ford Howland	1907	St Anne's Anglican

Architects	Year	Places of Worship
Wilm Knox & John Elliott	1891	Cecil Street Church of Christ
Henry Langley & E. Burke	1873	College Street Baptist
	1886	Beverley Street Baptist
	1887	Dovercourt Road Baptist
	1888	Trinity Methodist
	1888	Walmer Road Baptist
	1888	College Street Baptist (second)
	1889	Parkdale Methodist
	1889	St Mary the Virgin Anglican
Langley, E. Langley & Burke	1880	St Mark's Anglican, Parkdale
W.A. Langton	1890	St Margaret's Anglican
	1913	St Mary the Virgin Anglican (second)
Simon Larke	1892	Crawford Street Methodist
E. J. Lennox	1889	Broadway/Spadina Avenue Methodist
William G. Malcolmson	1903	Bathurst Street Disciples of Christ
George M. Miller	1904	Euclid Avenue Methodist
	1907	First Baptist
	1908	College Street Methodist
	1908	Westmoreland Methodist
	1908	North Parkdale Methodist
Herbert George Paull	1912	Dale Presbyterian
Albert Asa Post	1909	St Cecilia's Catholic
Charles J. Read	1902	St Francis Catholic (first)
Henry Simpson	1893	Bethany
Eden Smith	1892	St John Anglican (Garrison)
	1893	St Thomas Anglican
	1906	St Cyprian Anglican
James Avon Smith	1916	Morningside Avenue Presbyterian
J.A. Smith & John Gemmell	1885	College Street Presbyterian
	1886	Cowan Avenue Methodist
	1886	New Richmond Methodist
	1887	Clinton Street Methodist
	1887	St Paul's Methodist
	1910	New Jerusalem (Swedenborgian)
William L. Symonds	1907	Goel Tzedec Synagogue
Charles Frederick Wagner	1911	St Paul's English Lutheran
F. Wickson & A. Gregg	1913	T. Eaton Memorial Methodist

the founder of Mormonism, who broke with Brigham Young, the denomination's second president, advocating a more standard form of Protestantism.[11] Another was Christian Science, a group based on faith healing and the rejection of conventional medicine founded by Mary Baker Eddy. The prosperous Toronto congregation invited a celebrated Chicago architect to design its grandiose, Classical-style temple on St George Street at Lowther. A third denomination was the Church of Christ, also a product of the Second Great Awakening, which aimed to unite Christians around core dogmas with clear biblical foundations. Toronto members commissioned three churches. The smallest of these, on Keele Street at Annette, which accommodated one hundred faithful, was designed by a prolific Junction architect. Meanwhile, partners with numerous commissions in Toronto and Cleveland produced plans for the largest and most imposing building, on Cecil Street just off Spadina, which seated six hundred.[12] The middle one, on Bathurst Street just north of College, was the work of a Hamilton-born professional architect who arrived at perhaps the most original design of the three. Finally, there were the congregants of Bethany Chapel, who at first shunned denominational labels but later joined the Christian and Missionary Alliance (CMA), a fundamentalist group established by Canadian-born A.B. Simpson during the Third Great Awakening in the latter half of the nineteenth century. A highly original architectural design, Bethany became the CMA's mother church in Canada.

Other small denominations were of continental European origins. Lutherans had twin congregations in the West End. St Paul's, doubtless serving the English-speaking offspring of northern European immigrants, was designed by a professional who had trained with Helliwell and Gordon and who was himself the son of a very successful German building contractor.[13] St John's, meanwhile, was a German-language congregation whose chapel was conceived by a German-born, Ottawa-based architect.[14] The Church of the New Jerusalem followed the teachings of Emanuel Swedenborg, an eighteenth-century Swedish scientist, philosopher, and theologian, who began to have mystical visions in later life. This denomination was structured along congregational lines and followed Swedenborg's writings, which attempted to achieve a synthesis between matter and spirit through the person of Jesus. Their temple was erected on College Street at Euclid according to plans by a highly productive architectural duo.

2.2 Olivet Church of the New Jerusalem (demolished)
Situated on Elm Grove Avenue at Melbourne in the comfortable suburb
of Parkdale, the edifice's rationalist style recalls the eighteenth-century
origins of the movement founded in Sweden by Emanuel Swedenborg,
who influenced figures such as Balzac, Beaudelaire, Blake, Conan Doyle,
Emerson, and Jung. (Toronto Reference Library)

One might expect the West End's places of worship to be concentrated in the core area south of Bloor Street between University
and Lansdowne Avenues. Indeed, about half of them, including the
substantial ones, were. The rest were fairly evenly divided between
the areas situated to the west and those to the north. Parkdale alone

claimed 10 per cent of the West End's places of worship, most of which were built in the 1880s – an indication of the town's rapid development in that decade. Costly structures erected by Methodists, Presbyterians, Anglicans, and even Catholics denoted the suburbs' sustained wealth. And in neighbouring High Park, members of these same denominations expended significant sums of money on imposing places of worship. The area north of Bloor contained a higher proportion of substantial structures, most of them concentrated along Avenue Road, St Clair Avenue, and Bloor Street east of Bathurst, signalling the neighbourhood's elevated social status. In the segment west of Bathurst up to and including the Junction, very few permanent places of worship appeared before 1906. In general, these were modest structures found on or near secondary arteries in working-class neighbourhoods.

Structural Change

In the evolution of Toronto's places of worship, change occurred because of two related phenomena. The first was structural – in particular, the way in which the city's economy shaped the urban environment. The second was conjunctural, encompassing major events such as depressions, wars, and social upheavals, all of which had a direct impact on parishes and congregations.

The industrial economy required a rationalization of the city's space: it made economic sense for businesses and industries to locate close to one another in the downtown core and along major transportation corridors created by the railways. This process entailed the increasing segregation of social space. Wealthier inhabitants deserted the old neighbourhoods, which were becoming more commercial and industrial, and settled in the greener, healthier, and quieter suburbs. At the same time, wage workers sought cheaper housing close to their places of employment. This phenomenon repeated itself on the outskirts of Toronto. Parkdale and High Park, areas situated well away from factories, became desirable residential neighbourhoods, whereas Brockton and the Junction, bordered by railway tracks and businesses, were clearly meant to house workers.

In periods of growth, the industrial economy had an insatiable appetite for labour. This was the case, as we have seen, in the 1880s and in the decade before the First World War, when many unskilled workers were recruited from Asia and continental Europe to occupy specific niches in Toronto's labour market. For example, Jews tended to work in the clothing industry (which was that group's largest single employer), and Italians as builders of roads, sewers, and other urban infrastructure. Macedonians gravitated towards meat packing and tanning, Chinese towards laundries and restaurants.[15]

Closings

The changing social and ethnic environment had a profound impact on places of worship in the downtown core. (See table 2.4). Four of these did not survive the transition. St Margaret's Anglican, a rather grim and heavy structure, had been built to accommodate seven hundred people. Located on Spadina Avenue just south of Queen, it was closed less than twenty years after it was built, and turned into a factory – a telling commentary on the neighbourhood's evolution. Bethany Chapel had an even briefer existence. Standing on the northwest fringe of St John's Ward, it survived only seventeen years before having to make way for the Toronto Hospital, a fate linked to the increasingly specialized use of downtown space. The surrounding area would in fact be earmarked for large-scale institutions such as government buildings, insurance companies, hospitals, and educational establishments.[16] The dedication of a new CMA temple, Parkdale Tabernacle on Queen Street, took place in 1909 in the presence of A.B. Simpson, Elmore Harris, and Peter W. Philpott, about whom more will be said below.[17]

Two other churches succumbed to the wreckers. As we saw at the beginning of this chapter, Erskine Presbyterian, situated across the street from Bethany Chapel, was closed in 1915. The fourth place of worship to be demolished was the Church of the Ascension. Apparently the decision was made without the prior knowledge or consent of the rector, J.E. Gibson. A social activist, Gibson flouted the diocese's decision by buying a nearby YWCA building and turning it into a church, to be used as a base for work among the immigrant poor. Gibson set up a forty-bed hostel for single men in the building as well as a fresh-air camp on Lake Simcoe for people who could not afford recreational space in the countryside. On Sundays after the evening service, he led discussion groups on economics and religion to raise parishioners' awareness of broader social issues. But the diocesan authorities were diffident.

Gibson's project, they contended, was not financially accountable, nor did it conform to the norms of regular parish work. They wanted it closed. The rector carried on a protracted legal battle in the civil courts, which he finally lost in 1933.[18]

New Departures

Elite churches too were faced with difficult choices. Newspaper editor John Ross Robertson noted on a visit to St John the Evangelist that it had become working class in composition: "The transfer of the residential centre to the north-east sadly crippled the church, so that, in that respect, it has very largely lost its ancient prestige and influence."[19] The old, badly deteriorating frame structure was finally replaced in 1893 by a new building – a relatively cheap one, given the congregation's modest means. At St Andrew's, attendance and revenues dropped within a dozen or so years after its construction in the wake of the departure from the neighbourhood of the provincial Parliament and Upper Canada College. The option of starting afresh elsewhere was therefore given serious consideration. The new minister openly deplored the dreadful state of the church's finances. In a Sunday sermon he pointedly remarked that he had not cashed his paycheque for fear of putting St Andrew's bank account into deficit (see table 2.3 for some ministers' salaries). He stunned the congregation by announcing his resignation only eighteen months after his installation. The trustees immediately adopted a damage control strategy. In an effort both to salvage the congregation's tarnished reputation and in their search for a successor, they publicly refuted the minister's assertions with detailed facts and figures.[20]

While the congregants at St Andrew's decided to stay, those at New Richmond Methodist voted to go. Built in 1886 on McCaul Street just north of Queen by the prominent architectural team of Smith and Gemmell to replace the original church on Richmond Street, it was Methodism's flagship in the West End, with a seating capacity of 1,400. Because of declining membership, the congregation could not meet its financial obligations. The company holding the hefty $28,000 mortgage threatened legal action. The minister had to accept a salary half of what he might expect at a church of equivalent size elsewhere. The neighbourhood was changing visibly, with homes being turned into boarding houses to accommodate recently arrived Jewish and Italian immigrants. While two leading Methodist ministers were opposed to

2.3 New Richmond Methodist became Beth Hamidrash Hagodol
Chevra Tehillim (Russian) Synagogue (demolished)
Built in 1886 with a capacity of 1,400 congregants, this dour and heavy
Romanesque church lost congregants as eastern and southern European
immigrants settled in its vicinity. Unable to meet its debts, it was sold in
1905. This picture was taken shortly before the building was demolished
in 1956. (Toronto Reference Library)

the move, likening it to "surrendering a fort, and accepting defeat in
doing so,"[21] hard-nosed industrialist Chester Daniel Massey wanted
the property sold. And so it came to pass: New Richmond Methodist
became Beth Hamidrash Hagodol Chevra Tehillim, colloquially known
as the Russian Synagogue. The fort had indeed fallen.

2.4 Beverley Street Baptist
Changing downtown demographics turned this church, built in 1886 with
the financial assistance of the prominent McMaster family, into a Baptist
centre for proselytizing immigrants just before the First World War. It
became Toronto Chinese Baptist in 1975, serving congregants in Cantonese
and Mandarin. (Toronto Reference Library)

A block away, Beverley Street Baptist faced similar challenges. Erected
on land donated by William McMaster, the pleasing polychromatic
brick structure was designed by Henry Langley and Edmund Burke.
The congregation, which now included Goldwin Smith, who lived just
across the street, clearly looked to the future with confidence. Within a
quarter of a century, however, "weakened by the suburban exodus to
a state of dependency," the church considered merging with a larger
congregation. But the Board of Home Missions, determined "to battle ...
the wickedness and worldliness of downtown environs," came up with
an alternative plan: in return for a yearly rent paid by the board to the
church, a small Russian mission mostly comprised of sojourners would

Table 2.3. Salaries paid to some clergymen, 1870–1920

	Salary ($)	Year
St Andrew's Presbyterian	2,000	1871
College Street Baptist	600	1873
Wesley Methodist	2,000	1880s
Chalmers Presbyterian	900	1883
Parkdale Presbyterian	1,400	1886
College Street Presbyterian	2,000	1887
College Street Baptist (second)	1,000	1887
Erskine Presbyterian	2,400	1892
Knox Presbyterian	2,500	1901
New Richmond Methodist	1,000	1905
Centennial Methodist	1,400	1907
High Park Baptist	1,000	1908
Dufferin Street Presbyterian	700	1911
Keele Street Church of Christ	1,000	1913

share the premises and have a space for worship, a reading room, and a printing press.[22]

Farther west, another Baptist church faced similar challenges. Tecumseth Street Baptist's origins went back to 1873, when a Sunday school was created to reach out to the rougher elements of the local population. According to Robertson, the school was nicknamed "the Soudan, owing to the 'Arab' propensities of a number of boys attending. One of the [teachers] once attempted to put a boy out for disorderly conduct, a not infrequent occurrence, and was promptly stabbed in the thigh."[23] William Davies donated money for a church named Memorial following the death his daughter Ellen, an active collaborator in the Sunday school. It was Davies's intention that the building's simplicity should stand in stark contrast to the offensive lavishness of the McMasters' Jarvis Street church.[24] Designed by Edmund Burke and John Horwood, the brick and half-timbered building seated seven hundred. One of Davies's daughters, Mrs E.T. Fox, laid the cornerstone, while two other family members paid for the organ, pulpit, and carpets. In less than fifteen years, however, membership had dropped by half. Rechristened Memorial Institute in 1911, it was taken over by Walmer Road Baptist as an experiment in social outreach.[25] It was as though Memorial had come full circle.

Table 2.4. Changes to West End places of worship before 1920

Name	Change	Year
Wesleyan Methodist	Goel Tzedec Synagogue	1885
West Presbyterian	Church of Christ	1885
College Street Baptist (first)	Christ Church Reformed Episcopal	1889
Denison Ave. Church of Christ	Christian Workers	1890
Christ Church Reformed Episcopal	Christian Science	1891
Cowan Avenue Methodist	Cowan Avenue Presbyterian	1895
Hope Congregational/Bethel	Clinton Street Christian Workers	1904
Sheridan Avenue Baptist	demolished	1905
Church of Christ Scientist	Bethel Mennonite Brethren in Christ	1906
St Clarens Avenue Methodist	demolished	1907
New Richmond Methodist	Chevra Tehillim Synagogue	1907
Denison Ave. Christian Workers	demolished	1908
St Patrick Catholic	Our Lady of Mount Carmel Italian	1908
St Margaret Anglican	Closed	1909
Parkdale Congregational	demolished	1909
Bethany	demolished	1910
West Presbyterian (second)	Polish Catholics	1911
Fern Avenue Presbyterian	Church of Christ	1911
St Mark Presbyterian	demolished	1912
Memorial Baptist	Memorial Institute	1912
St Francis Catholic	St Agnes (Italian)	1913
Goel Tzedec	African Methodist Episcopal	1913
Clinton Street Christian Workers	Dewi Sant Welsh Presbyterian	1915
Erskine Presbyterian	demolished	1915
Royce Avenue Baptist	Resurrection Russian Orthodox	1915
Resurrection Russian Orthodox	Ukrainian Presbyterian	1919
Ascension Anglican	demolished	1919
St Mary the Virgin Anglican	Apostolic Faith	1919
Zion Congregational/Concord Avenue Pentecostal	demolished	1920
Brock Avenue People's mission	Salvation Army hall	1920

New Occupants

Other places of worship welcomed new tenants or changed religious affiliation. The building on Simcoe Street at Elm vacated by the cash-strapped congregants of Christ Church Reformed Episcopal was occupied by Christian Science. Established and led by an American couple recently settled in Toronto, the affluent congregation grew so rapidly that it acquired the building in the midst of the economic depression of the 1890s. Within the same decade, however, the structure could no longer hold the expanding congregation and was torn down. On the same site a new and larger brick structure seating seven hundred people was built.[26] Meanwhile, the first West Presbyterian church became Church of Christ. This denomination, which had taken root in the Ontario countryside, counted among its early Toronto members men successful in business and public life.[27] Active in the city since the 1840s, the Church of Christ appeared in the West End forty years later, using community halls for worship and Sunday school. Shortly after the move to West Presbyterian, the first regular pastor arrived from Ohio. The small congregation, numbering less than two hundred, grew in these years as a result of migration from the countryside. In 1889, however, a split occurred over two issues: the first was the use of the organ in worship – a question, as we have seen, that had divided Presbyterians (see table 2.5 for the cost of some organs);[28] the second was the role assigned to the pastor. A minority upheld a cappella singing, rejecting the use of any musical instrument in worship. They also strictly interpreted the doctrine of the priesthood of all believers to mean that no member was more qualified than any other to preach. According to this view, no special training was required to be a pastor. The minority

Table 2.5. The cost of some church organs

	Cost ($)	Year
Queen Street Methodist	4,000	1870s
St Thomas Anglican	3,000/19,000	1882/1917
St Andrew's Presbyterian	13,000	1885
Ossington Avenue Baptist	50	1886
St Paul's Methodist	3,000	1887
Parkdale Presbyerian	2,000	1888
Royce Avenue Baptist	500	1888
Westmoreland Avenue Methodist	3,200	1890s
First Church of Christ Scientist	2,000	1898
Chalmers Presbyterian	3,000	1898
St Clarens Methodist	140	1899
Cowan Avenue Presbyterian	2,000	1900
St Mary the Virgin (second)	2,000	1914
Cecil Street Church of Christ	1,600	1915

faction was temporarily forced to hold services in community halls once again. The majority moved to the Cecil Street location, where they purchased a pipe organ and supported a woman missionary in Japan. The Junction members of the majority, led by Daniel Webster Clendenan, an American-born lawyer and land speculator and first mayor of the municipality, faced serious financial difficulties. They resorted to tent meetings as a way to boost membership.[29]

Reflecting the growing proletarianization of the neighbourhood around Queen and Bathurst, a fundamentalist, working-class denomination with a congregational structure, established in 1892 and known as Christian Workers, took over the old West Presbyterian. The group's founder, Peter W. Philpott, had been a brigadier in the Salvation Army but had broken with that denomination because of its hierarchical structure and what he perceived as the immodest and privileged lifestyle of its officers.[30] Christian Workers spread quickly, taking over a chapel in Brockton[31] and absorbing two congregational churches.[32] They erected their flagship Missionary Tabernacle, a plain brick structure on Bathurst Street south of Dundas; a second, modest edifice went up on Robert Street just north of College.

Working-Class Religiosity

Philpott's discontent and restlessness were shared by evangelists of various Protestant persuasions such as John Salmon, George Fisher, and Joseph Wild, to name but a few. Tapping into a Protestant sensibility that felt orphaned in the push to unite the various currents of Methodism and Presbyterianism, they rejected the straightjacket of mainstream Protestantism with its cushioned pews, carpeted churches, and formalistic worship. They were stirred instead by Phoebe Palmer's Holiness Movement, which had unleashed a powerful North Atlantic revivalist current with its vision of individual Christian perfection through an intimate and emotional relationship with Jesus. They yearned to rekindle the flame of primitive Christianity expressed at Pentecost when the Holy Spirit appeared as a powerful wind and a shower of tongues of fire physically forcing Christ's disciples out of their timid seclusion and into the world as forthright evangelists.

In Toronto the movement had a disruptive effect on individuals and entire congregations, especially those subscribing to a congregational form of organization. Having rejected the idea of overarching governing structures, such congregations were especially vulnerable to new religious currents. Under the immensely popular pastorate of Joseph Wild, an ardent imperialist and anti-Catholic who had been voted the most popular preacher in Ontario by readers of the *Toronto Daily Mail*,[33] the church on Clinton Street dropped its Congregational affiliation and changed its name to Bethel, suggesting a more revivalist and fundamentalist turn.[34] Wild went on to become pastor of Zion Congregational, where in 1905 he preached a sermon titled "Prophetic Outcome of the Next Fifty Years of Some of the Present Agitation," an indication of things to come.[35] After a visit in 1907 by Charles Fox Parham, a founder of American Pentecostalism, Zion's entire congregation converted to that faith, the first in the West End to do so. Although the church was demolished around 1920, it is quite likely that the congregation continued under the name Apostolic Faith at the first St Mary the Virgin Anglican on Delaware Street just north of Bloor.

The death of the Pentecostal congregation's first pastor brought together an interesting group of clerics at his funeral. They were Ellen Hebden, founder of the East End mission and Pentecostalism's iconic figure in Toronto, George Fisher, ex-Salvationist and ex-Christian Worker, and John Salmon, ex-Methodist and ex-Congregationalist. The movements that had engaged them were both class- and religious-based. These figures rebelled against the bourgeoisification of Protestantism with its concerns over cosy church interiors and balanced accounts. They sought instead to instil passion in faith by emphasizing the disruptive and exhilarating power of the Holy Spirit. This brand of Protestantism, pessimistic about human nature, stressing emotion as the key to an immediate and urgent spiritual rebirth, anxiously awaiting Christ's Second Coming, and awed by the Holy Spirit's power of permanent regeneration, spawned a variety of groups in Toronto that were very much aware of their common outlook.

Della Lehman Lageer articulated this view from the pew. A young, single seamstress from the countryside, she had found work in Toronto with a Jewish employer. In the absence of family, she experienced fellowship at the Bethel Mennonite Chapel, one of the many denominations that over the years had occupied Forester's Hall on Brunswick Avenue above Harbord. This congregation belonged to the Mennonite Brethren in Christ, which rejected Mennonites' traditional communitarian focus in favour of the more personal and emotional religiosity of the Third Great Awakening. In a diary she kept in 1910–11 and again sporadically after the war, Lageer noted: "We girls certainly have lots of fun discussing the preachers. Oliver Panabaker [a friend] has agreed to get me one if he can but not much danger [*sic*]."[36] Even after marriage, the seamstress spent most of her free time at church and missionary conferences. Commenting on a sermon given by the Pentecostal George Fisher, she wrote:

> I enjoyed them so much. Text 2 Peter 16–19. The word of God once instilled in the heart, more sure than any feeling the only thing that lasts, not only to be sanctified but to keep at it, pray to be closer to Jesus daily. Until the day dawn [*sic*] – conversion. The day star arise [*sic*] in your hearts – meaning sanctification … I told [Carrie] it was more enjoyable than going to the show.

Lageer felt equally at home among Christian Workers, Baptists, Pentecostals, and fundamentalist Presbyterians,[37] a perspective shared by her pastor, C.H. Good, who noted that Christian Workers, Plymouth Brethren, and Free Methodists attended his services, one of which had been "out of the ordinary" with "an altar full of seekers."[38] Clearly these denominations viewed one another not as rivals or competitors, but as partakers in a common religious culture.

Places of Worship for Non-British Immigrants

Having few resources at their disposal, recent immigrants from continental Europe tended to reuse existing places of worship. Yiddish-speaking Jews settled in St John's Ward, where cheap housing, proximity to work, and the multi-functional character of the district encouraged enterprise among family members, who worked as a unit in order to accumulate savings. Newcomers identified themselves with their *landsleit* (i.e., people from the same hometown), socializing primarily with them, and with them forming *landsmanshaftn*, self-help organizations that provided a cushion against illness, sudden loss of income, and death. Feeling little affinity with the assimilated English-speaking Jews of Holy Blossom Temple, they soon established their own synagogues. The Litvaks, or Lithuanians, formed a congregation calling itself Goel Tzedec (Righteous Redeemer), which occupied the chapel that Wesleyan Methodists had built on University Avenue that had become the Elm Street Mission.

In the first dozen or so years of the twentieth century, Catholic immigrants of non-British origin were also settling in Toronto. The Italians came mostly from the *Mezzogiorno* (South), and the Ukrainians and

2.5 St Patrick's Catholic became Our Lady of Mount Carmel
Built of brick in 1869, this Gothic-style church served an Irish congregation, which was accommodated in a new, larger stone church a block
farther west in 1908. The original structure then became the city's first
Italian-language parish. Since 1975 it has served Cantonese and Mandarin
speakers. (Toronto Reference Library)

Poles from the Austro-Hungarian province of Galicia, as well as from the *guberniyas* of Kielce and Radom in the Russian Empire, provinces where incidentally many Jewish immigrants originated.[39] As with the Jews, these immigrants' primary identity was with their hometown, which formed the basis of informal networks to help them find lodging, labour, and assistance when needed.

Initially the archdiocese of Toronto did little for these newcomers. Archbishop Dennis O'Connor (1899–1908) argued that they were too few in number and not financially stable enough to warrant assistance. But the Holy See grew deeply worried about the activities of Protestant proselytizers, who had found intermediaries to speak to these immigrants directly in their own language, offering them all manner of material assistance, along with Bibles. Through the Apostolic Delegate, Rome's representative in Ottawa, pressure was brought to bear on Archbishop Fergus McEvay (1908–11), O'Connor's successor, to adopt a more proactive approach. In 1908, St Patrick's Church, renamed Our Lady of Mount Carmel, was set aside for Italians, many of whom lived close by in St John's Ward. That same year, a new and more commodious stone church named in honour of St Patrick was erected on McCaul Street just north of Dundas for English-speaking parishioners. The archdiocese followed the same strategy six years later in response to Italians moving out of St John's Ward to the area around College Street at Grace. The modest brick church on Dundas Street at Grace, dedicated in 1902 to St Francis, became an Italian-language parish called St Agnes. Up the street on Grace Street at Mansfield, a substantial stone edifice, the reborn St Francis, catered to English speakers. Finally, a mission was founded in 1915 on Dufferin Street just south of Davenport to serve the families of Italians working in the nearby industrial plants. This basement structure, initially dedicated to St Clement, would serve as their church for the next twenty years.[40]

After the Italians, it was the turn of the Poles. In 1911 a gift from brewer Eugene O'Keefe, a native of County Cork in Ireland, allowed the archdiocese to purchase the second West Presbyterian Church and turn it into the Polish-language parish of St Stanislaus. The benefactor's daughter, Helen French, paid for the interior renovations. Four years later a modest church honouring the Nativity of Our Lady of Częstochowa was erected on Davenport Road near Old Weston in the Junction. The name recalled the national Polish shrine in Częstochowa, then in the Russian Empire, with its miraculous image of the Jasna Góra (Black Madonna). This became the second parish serving Poles who

2.6 St Stanislaus Polish Catholic
In another example of early suburbanization, the second West Presbyterian, constructed in 1879, became St Stanislaus Polish Catholic in 1911 thanks to a donation by brewer Eugene O'Keefe. A schism occurred in the interwar period that led to the creation by dissidents of a Polish National Catholic parish. (Gabriele Scardellato)

worked in the nearby CPR workshops, the Heintzman piano factory, or the needle trades. From the start, it was beset by financial difficulties because of parishioners' inability to pay off the large loan that had been taken out to build it.[41]

In 1908, Ukrainians temporarily moved into the first St Helen's Church after a new, larger, and more beautiful building had been erected close by on Dundas Street for English-speaking parishioners. These immigrants were heavily concentrated in the Junction and, like their Polish counterparts, worked in its many factories. Finding clergy to serve them proved very difficult, for they belonged to the Uniate Church, which had entered into communion with Rome in the late sixteenth century on the condition that it be allowed to preserve its Orthodox liturgy and discipline. Because almost all Uniate priests were married, the Holy See had forbidden their transfer to the Americas. So Archbishop Neil McNeil (1912–34) decided to train celibate Uniate priests in his new diocesan seminary of St Augustine, another of Eugene O'Keefe's gifts to the archdiocese. Meanwhile, the first Ukrainian Church of St Josaphat, a harmonious square brick structure with a defining central bell tower topped by an onion-shaped dome, was constructed in the Junction on Franklin Street south of Dupont. The basilica-style interior, with its characteristic flat ceiling from which was suspended an elegant chandelier, had no iconostasis (a wooden screen separating the nave from the sanctuary in Orthodox places of worship), probably because of the cost involved in constructing one. Instead, four round columns divided the sanctuary from the nave.[42] The newly appointed bishop, Nikita Budka, whose authority extended over Ukrainians across Canada, consecrated the church in 1914. The altar was imported from Lwów, in Galicia, and the heating system was supplied free of charge by the neighbouring Gurney factory. Contrary to Orthodox practice where the faithful stood for the liturgy, oak benches were introduced in 1917, accommodating seven hundred people.[43]

Worship in Non-Institutional Spaces

Some people gathered together in buildings not specifically designed as places of worship. Most often, this phenomenon involved working-class families, including immigrant ones, whose means were limited. But there were exceptions. Spiritualism, for instance, could not be characterized as primarily working class. Its followers, the most famous among them being William Lyon Mackenzie King, believed it was possible to commune with the dead. Spiritualists gathered together in private homes and halls to hold seances and pray, as numerous newspaper advertisements of the day made abundantly clear.[44] Spiritualism reached its peak as a movement around the turn of the twentieth century. A church was actually built in 1917 on Dovercourt Road north of Bloor in memory of Emma Hardinge Britten (1823–1899), an English-born clairvoyant and early propagator of Spiritualism in the English-speaking world. By then, however, the movement was in decline.

Ten Jewish congregations established synagogues in private residences (called *stiblach* in Yiddish). Five of these were temporary pending a move to more permanent quarters.[45] Torah Emeth (Truth of the Torah) on D'Arcy Street shared its building with a Talmud Torah. Both institutions spoke to the divisions among Toronto's Jews – a feature of most immigrant communities in the early years of settlement. As latecomers to Toronto, Polish Jews resented the domination of Lithuanian Jews, whose sense of superiority sprang from the brilliant centres of Jewish learning back in the Vilnius General Governorate in the Russian Empire. Polish Jews wanted their distinctiveness and their status as the city's largest Jewish group to be recognized. Yehuda Leib Rosenberg, born near Radomsko, Piotrków *guberniya* in Poland, aspired to the title of chief rabbi. When non-Polish Jews refused him that honour, Mordecai Richler's learned maternal grandfather left for Montreal. In the meantime he had managed to establish Eitz Chaim, a Talmud Torah, which asserted its uniqueness over the existing one by having Yiddish, the popular tongue of eastern European Jews, as the medium of instruction rather than Hebrew, the language of learning. Despite this acknowledgment of popular culture, radical ideas were unwelcome in the school, and religion was stressed over secular subjects.[46]

Tzemach Tzedec Anshei Libavitch Nusach Ari (Righteous Scion of the Men of Libavitch) comprised, not natives from the Russian town of Lyubavichi as the name suggests, but followers of Rabbi Zalman Shneur, founder of the Chabad branch of Chassidism, now headquartered in Brooklyn.[47] In 1914, ten years after its founding, the synagogue moved to Denison Avenue south of Dundas. In 1917 it hosted the inauguration of the Mizrachi Talmud Torah, a school committed to a Zionist ideology in which religion was placed at the core of Jewish identity.[48] Yavneh Zion, a synagogue connected with the Zion Institute on Beverley Street and Cecil, was named after the town in Israel where rabbinic Judaism had taken root after the destruction of the temple in Jerusalem in the year 70. At its inauguration in 1917, the rabbi, Jacob Gordon, made an impassioned speech in support of Zionism weeks before the Balfour Declaration expressing the British government's approval of the establishment of a Jewish national home in Palestine.[49]

The Plymouth Brethren utterly rejected the notion of an ordained clergy and believed that worship could take place anywhere. This Christian denomination, established in post-Napoleonic Britain by John Nelson Darby (1800–1882), a disillusioned Anglican clergyman, strictly adhered to the idea of the priesthood of all believers, the imminence of Christ's Second Coming, and a literal interpretation of the Bible. Brethren began to do missionary work in Toronto's West End in the 1870s alongside Baptists and worshipped both in community halls and in private homes. They also attended, as we have seen, other like-minded fundamentalist congregations. Discrete Plymouth Brethren worship sites were eventually built, but these were unadorned one-storey roughcast structures and were called Gospel Halls, as distinct from churches, to distance them from the trappings of institutional Christianity. That these buildings were located in solid working-class neighbourhoods points to the class character of the denomination. The first such building went up in 1896 on Brock Avenue south of Dundas and was apparently linked to the arrival in Toronto of two Glaswegian Brethren, Donald Munro and Donald Ross.[50] Three other Gospel Halls were erected in quick succession, two in the Junction and one on Lansdowne Avenue at Wallace. Without a doubt, however, their most interesting structure was built in 1917 for the hearing-impaired on College Street at Shaw; it was called Maranatha Hall for the Deaf. Maranatha, an Aramaic expression meaning "Come O Lord," was a reference to the impending return of Christ.[51]

Mainstream Protestant denominations tended to use converted residences as sites for their work among immigrants. In 1909, Presbyterians took over the Finnish Hall, located in a private home on Mitchell Avenue west of Tecumseth, to nurture an embryonic congregation made up mostly of female domestics. Since the Finnish government strongly discouraged Lutheran ministers from immigrating to North America, the Toronto group had at first hired a US-trained Finnish Congregational minister; but they soon must have realized the material benefits of affiliating with a mainstream Canadian Church. In the event, the Presbyterians organized activities such as adult English classes and a youth club, while the Women's Auxiliary looked after domestics in need.[52]

In 1917, to promote their work among the Chinese, the Presbyterian Church spent $25,000 to purchase two adjacent houses on University Avenue north of Dundas Street. An additional $20,000 was laid out on renovations and furnishings. The newly inaugurated Chinese Christian Association comprised a place of worship on the ground floor, students' quarters on the upper levels, a reading room supplied with newspapers and books, a kindergarten, a classroom for language instruction that doubled as a Sunday school, and, finally, a gymnasium.[53] For their part, the Methodists established an Italian mission in the West End in 1907, taking over a building previously occupied by Presbyterians on Claremont Street below Dundas. Offering a variety of services, including free language classes, a kindergarten, and social assistance, the Methodist endeavour preceded by four years the creation of the nearby Italian-language Catholic parish of St Agnes.[54]

Conjunctural Pressures

The Depression of the 1890s

Besides the structural transformations outlined above, Toronto's places of worship were subject to conjunctural ones, among which was the depression of the early 1890s, which had a dramatic impact on existing congregations as well as on church building. Only fifteen years after being established, Christ Church Reformed Episcopal was sold in 1891 because the congregants were unable to maintain it. They moved into a smaller and less inspiring building on College Street that had been vacated by Baptists. But the most obvious casualty of the depression was the Anglican Church of St Alban the Martyr on Albany Avenue north of Bloor. Bishop Arthur Sweatman (1879–1909) had conceived a grandiose if somewhat impractical plan to build a cathedral in order to free himself of his dependence on the trustees of St James Cathedral. Construction began in 1885 in what was then a sparsely inhabited part of Toronto. By 1891 the chancel and choir had been finished in full-blown Gothic style. At that point, however, work stopped because of the depression; it would not resume for another twenty years. At that point, Ralph Cram, architect of Saint John the Divine Episcopal Cathedral in New York, produced revised plans. The cornerstone was laid by the Governor General, Prince Arthur, Duke of Connaught, a son of Queen Victoria, and the rest of the foundations were laid. With the outbreak of the First World

War, work again came to a halt; after the war, the diocesan synod voted against resuming construction.[55] Bishop Sweatman's dream was never realized.

The depression slowed the development of a number of churches. Covenant Presbyterian began on Davenport Road as a mission conducted by Knox College students, but the congregation did not acquire its first pastor until almost twenty years later. It was another six years before land for a new church was purchased, and seven more years before the imposing if somewhat austere stone edifice was erected on Avenue Road and Roxborough.[56] The beginnings of St Mark's Presbyterian were equally modest. Originally a mission school of St Andrew's, the building was moved on rollers twice before finally coming to rest on King Street and Tecumseth. In the late 1880s it underwent costly renovations related to its enlargement; then in 1912 the decision was made to tear it down. In spite of the war, a new large brick building was completed four years later, on Queen Street at Bellwoods.[57]

Like St Mark's, Dovercourt Presbyterian was a roughcast structure. It was moved on rollers from Dufferin Street to Dovercourt Road. When in 1894 many parishioners lost their jobs as a result of the depression, the minister raised funds and proceeded to hire them to enlarge the building.[58] It was replaced by a solid brick structure at the corner of Hepbourne Street in 1905. The depression forced several families of the embryonic congregation of Wychwood Presbyterian to move away. Unable to meet the mortgage payments on land purchased thanks in part to a donation by the Lieutenant-Governor of Ontario, Sir Alexander Campbell, the remaining members lost the property. Twenty years later, the current brick church trimmed with white sandstone was built.[59] Finally, Morningside Presbyterian's early growth had been spurred by the founding in the town of Swansea of two important enterprises, the Iron Works and the Bolt Works. The collapse of both enterprises during the depression left the congregation in the lurch. Twenty years after its founding in 1889, the first minister arrived. Almost another decade went by, before the stone church we see today was erected.[60]

The First World War and Its Aftermath

The First World War too had a negative impact on parishes and congregations, although it is remembered in histories and on commemorative plaques as a noble and selfless sacrifice rather than a calamity, which is the term used to describe the depression of the 1890s. Clergymen of various denominations felt moved to abandon their pastoral charges temporarily in order to contribute to the war effort. J.D. Morrow, minister at Dale Presbyterian, enlisted in the Sportsman's Battalion. By the time he returned to Toronto, his health was so severely impaired that he was unable to resume his duties. John McNeill, pastor of Walmer Road Baptist, served from 1916 to 1918 as YMCA chaplain; George Pidgeon left his position as associate minister at Bloor Street Presbyterian to preach to the Second Division in England and France in 1917–18. The rector of the Anglican Church of the Ascension and the pastor of College Street Baptist also went overseas, as did Nestore Cacciapuoti, minister at the Italian Methodist missions, who served in Italy when that country entered the war on the Allied side in 1915. Meanwhile, the German American minister at Western Baptist abandoned his charge to return to the neutral United States. The minister at Ossington Avenue Baptist, to express a spirit of sacrifice, voluntarily reduced his salary for the duration of the war.[61]

The absence, temporary or otherwise, of so many congregants, especially young men, had a profound long-term impact on congregational life. In general, the larger churches had the greatest number of men and women serving in the war. With six hundred recruits by 1917, the contribution of St Mary's Catholic was unusually large compared to those of St Peter's, St Patrick's, Holy Family, and St Vincent de Paul, which were well below the mean of 10 per cent of all parishioners enlisted.[62] Fragmentary evidence from the West End's Protestant churches shows the heavy toll exacted by war (see table 2.6).

Fatalities included Murray Winchester, the son of the minister at Knox Presbyterian, who died at Vimy Ridge, and the son of architect Grant Helliwell.

Many churches played an active part in the recruitment of troops. In December 1915, Broadway Tabernacle announced a "Grand Union Recruiting service" featuring three senior officers and patriotic music.[63] A similar service was held at Timothy Eaton Memorial Methodist, where the guest preacher was C.A. Williams, Quebec's chief recruitment officer and pastor of the premier Methodist church in Montreal, St James.[64] Protestant and Catholic clergymen, as well as rabbis, did not hesitate to express strong support for the Allied cause from the pulpit. Parkdale Methodist's Hiram Hull gave an evening address titled "Kaiser Saul," comparing the German Emperor to Saul, the benighted king of Israel who had failed to heed God's word and

Table 2.6. Responses to the First World War

Place of worship	Recruits	Deaths
College Street Presbyterian	301	47
Wesley Methodist	280	
Epiphany Anglican	265	41
St John's Anglican Humberside		39
Walmer Road Baptist	177	25
Spadina Avenue Methodist		23
College Street Baptist	127	22
T. Eaton Memorial Methodist	118	20
Knox Presbyterian	113 (by 1916)	
Italian Methodist missions	80	
Dewi Sant Welsh Presbyterian	56	
Messiah Anglican		17
Ossington Avenue Baptist	60	15
Dufferin Street Baptist		11

committed suicide.[65] Meanwhile, at nearby Western Baptist, the minister spoke on the topic "Scientific Evidence of the Kaiser's Insanity." F.D. Morrow, the idiosyncratic pastor at Dale Presbyterian, composed a special hymn titled "Our Brave Soldier Boys" which, newspapers announced, he would sing to his congregation on a Sunday designated as Soldiers' Day.[66]

On 1 January 1915 and 1916, Toronto's churches and synagogues observed special days of prayer for an Allied victory, which were held throughout the empire. In an ardently patriotic sermon delivered at *Chevra Tehillim*, Jacob Gordon, a Russian-born and -educated rabbi, maintained that England was the champion of liberty for the Jews – a fact secretly acknowledged by their German coreligionists.[67] At a mass meeting of Jews held at Massey Hall to express support for the Allies, Gordon's American-trained English-speaking assistant at Goel Tzedec, Julius Price, offered a brief prayer in English for Britain, which prompted a journalist to comment in amazement that it "might have been delivered by a Christian minister."[68] In the speech that followed, Price declared: "We Jewish ministers are proud to be citizens of an Empire that is willing to risk its prestige to fight a philosophy that God forbids." A few months earlier, commenting on the German navy's torpedoing of the passenger ship *Lusitania* with heavy loss of civilian life, the young

2.7 Goel Tzedec Synagogue (demolished)
This synagogue was founded by Lithuanian Jews who rejected Holy Blossom's deviation from Orthodox practices. A testimony to the enhanced social standing achieved by some Jewish immigrants at the turn of the twentieth century, it too began to stray from orthodoxy. (Author)

rabbi contended that Germany had thereby proved her *kultur* to be a fraud: she had signed her own death warrant, and civilization had a duty to obliterate this terrible curse.[69] The minister at the pacifist Bethel Mennonite Chapel urged his congregants to demonstrate their loyalty by participating in Red Cross relief work. By 1918 they were openly praying for the Allies' victory and for those congregants at war, who were described as "the self-sacrificing sons of our Empire."[70] For the parishioners of St Stanislaus and Nativity of Our Lady of Częstochowa, the war had special meaning because it offered the possibility of Polish national independence. Money was collected and recruits were sent to advance this cause, possibly draining the scarce resources of the latter parish and certainly straining relations with Ukrainian Catholics, whose compatriots back home would later find themselves a subjugated minority in an independent Poland.[71]

After the war, congregations memorialized the men and women who had served and those who had died in the conflict. In a solemn service held in 1919 at Epiphany Anglican in Parkdale, Sir Arthur Currie, commander of the Canadian Expeditionary Force, unveiled a tablet, a stained glass window, and the carved oak panelling in the chancel, all intended to remember the war dead. A tablet at the second St Mary the Virgin Anglican on Westmoreland Avenue above Bloor was unveiled by Lieutenant-Governor Henry Cockshutt and dedicated by Bishop James Sweeny (1909–40). At Redeemer Anglican a transept window in honour of the parish's servicemen and women was inaugurated at a service led by a congregant whose sons had died in action. Memorial windows were dedicated at Western Baptist and the following Anglican churches: St Michael and All Angels, St Anne's, St John's Humberside, and St Martin-in-the-Fields. In other parishes, the commemoration took different forms: an organ at Dufferin Street Presbyterian, a baptistery at St Thomas Anglican; a parish hall at Messiah Anglican; a new altar at St Cyprian's Anglican; a polychrome crucifix sculpted by Frances Loring and decorated by Group of Seven painter Franz Johnston at St Mary Magdalene Anglican.[72]

The Russian Revolution

In 1917, just as the war was reaching its climax, the October Revolution in Russia disrupted a number of Eastern European congregations in Toronto. Because of factionalism caused by the Bolshevik takeover, the parishioners of the Russian Orthodox Church of the Resurrection lost possession of a small church seating one hundred people that they had occupied in the Junction since 1915. Previously known as Royce Avenue Baptist, the building was then occupied by Ukrainian Presbyterians, whose minister was Pavlo Krat, a former leader of the Social Democratic Party who was now opposed to Bolshevism and who had recently converted to Presbyteriansim.[73] Meanwhile, the Russian Baptist mission operating out of the Beverley Street church barely survived the defection of its new minister and a majority of congregants "under the destructive influence of Bolshevism." The faithful remnant had to wait until 1923 for a replacement.[74]

At the nearby Ukrainian Church of St Josaphat, elements of the Russian–Ukrainian Social Revolutionary Group – who apparently were not even members of the parish – challenged the episcopal ownership of church property. They must have exerted considerable influence on parishioners, for the pastor angrily resigned his charge and locked up the building for three weeks.[75] Jews, for their part, became deeply disquieted by the pogroms that followed Ukraine's brief moment of independence from 1917 to 1920. They called a mass protest meeting at Massey Hall at which Rabbi Gordon spoke in Yiddish before an audience of 4,000. Christian clerics were also in attendance, including the Anglican assistant bishop W.D. Reeve, F.H. Cosgrove, professor at Trinity College, the Methodist Salem Bland, and the Catholic Lancelot Minehan.[76] That same year, St Stanislaus Polish Catholic was shaken by a conflict between the laity and their pastor, Leopold Blum, who was even accused of embezzling parish funds. Parishioners demanded exclusive control of the church's finances and the right to set the priest's salary. Even though clashes of this kind were not unusual in Canadian ecclesiastical history and both parties appealed to the archdiocese for support, there is little doubt that the October Revolution contributed to the parishioners' mood of defiance.[77]

In an era of tremendous industrial and urban growth throughout North America, places of worship mobilized the financial resources of communities. As Toronto's population increased exponentially, so did its number of churches, in fact more so. An impressive number of new ones were built, and older ones abandoned by their former owners were reoccupied, while a number of residential spaces were appropriated for religious purposes. Considerable sums of money were invested by the wealthy and not so wealthy in the construction or renovation of sacred spaces, as well as in furnishings for them, including organs. Such spaces often encompassed Sunday schools, church halls, and manses or presbyteries. At the same time, the faithful committed themselves to regular ongoing disbursements to pay for the upkeep of clergy and missionaries at home and abroad, as well as musicians, choirs, vestments, and other adornments. These expenditures did not include the ones incurred by organizations based in parishes or congregations, whose activities will be examined in the next chapter. In other words, when parishioners or congregants decided to build a church, they incurred not only a heavy debt linked to the mortgage (unless there happened to be a patron among them), but also recurring yearly financial obligations.

Industrialization fostered social segregation that saw the wealthier members of society deserting the downtown to live in desirable suburban areas, mainly north of Bloor Street and west of the CPR tracks. Their spiritual needs were cared for by such churches as Bloor Street Presbyterian, Knox Presbyterian, Trinity Methodist, Walmer Road Baptist, Redeemer Anglican, Messiah Anglican, St Paul's Methodist, Eaton Memorial Methodist, Parkdale Methodist, Parkdale Presbyterian, Victoria Presbyterian, and High Park Methodist. These costly and lavish edifices were monuments as much to social prominence and economic power as to faith. Wealthy eastern European Jews could not yet aspire to live in these new residential neighbourhoods beside their "social betters" of British origin. Their synagogue, Goel Tzedec, would remain firmly embedded in the downtown for many years to come.

These social divisions developed in such a way that a number of parishes and congregations suddenly found themselves in working-class neighbourhoods. A few, such as St John the Evangelist, apparently adapted to change. Others grudgingly acknowledged "defeat" – to borrow the term applied to New Richmond Methodist's closing. Lamenting the passing of the era of social integration when rich and poor lived side by side, Torontonians of British stock associated the social decline of old neighbourhoods with the newly arrived immigrants – the "gesticulating Yiddish," as a *Toronto Star* journalist so charmingly put it – holding them responsible for a phenomenon clearly beyond the latter's control. In addition to class, ethnicity provided yet another reason for disdaining the new residents of the downtown core. Missions were set up by Protestant denominations not only to convert the foreigners but also to impart proper British values: the future of *the* nation depended on it. But was there not an element of condescension in the fact that immigrants who attended these missions worshipped in reconverted houses instead of proper churches? Be that as it may, Jewish, Italian, Polish, and Ukrainian immigrants in this period took over a number of places of worship, which effectively became working-class congregations. A number of the Catholic churches they occupied were often right next to the newer, more imposing ones established by the archdiocese for the English-language faithful. Still, newcomers at least had churches in which to worship, and in the case of St Stanislaus, a most respectable one indeed.

A number of new denominations drew upon an essentially working-class following. The Salvation Army, Christian Workers, Plymouth

Brethren, and Pentecostals, among others, had a class appeal because of their disdain of formalism, their straightforwardness, their simplicity, and their emotional intensity. But this should not obscure the fact that, taken together, they comprised only a tiny minority of Toronto's Christians. While these were indeed working-class denominations, they were not denominations of the working class: more workers and their families were found in mainstream Christian churches. It is tempting when studying this era of social segregation to see a polarized religious environment in which only working-class or bourgeois congregations and parishes existed. The truth, however, is that there were a number of middling churches where social mixing did occur, not only at worship, but also in various church-related activities such as Sunday school. While Timothy Eaton may not have shared his pew with a day labourer, shopkeepers, professionals, businessmen, and skilled and unskilled workers alike did rub elbows with one another in a number of churches and synagogues.

Another instrument of social contact, if not cohesion, was the various outreach programs run by congregations and parishes in the West End. The major Presbyterian churches, for example, all had downtown missions where they worked among the disadvantaged and the immigrants. Walmer Road Baptist used the Memorial Institute to the same end, and if the church of the Ascension is any indication, Low Church Anglicans seemed to be as engaged as their High Church counterparts in social assistance. Many Catholic parishes had St Vincent de Paul Societies whose members visited the needy in their homes and distributed material assistance to those deemed "deserving." The Toronto Hebrew Ladies Aid Society, loosely connected with Goel Tzedec Synagogue, performed similar functions among Toronto's Jews. Historians over the past forty years, articulating the values created by the postwar Welfare State, qualified such efforts as intrusive, condescending, arbitrary, and ineffectual. But these services were never intended to change society. They were seen instead as short-term measures to assist those who through no fault of their own found themselves in difficulty. According to this perspective, only religion could truly transform society into a Judeo-Christian commonwealth where justice and brotherhood would reign supreme.

In sum, religion in this period was more shaped by economic forces than it shaped them. It reproduced social divisions as well as ethnic ones, and it did much to develop a consensus around such values as work, family, nation, self-reliance, and social cohesion, while holding out the prospect of a dimly perceived and fairly remote better life to come.

Chapter Three

Fulsome Fellowship, 1880–1920

Industrialization swept away remnants of the old colonial system, ushering in new social classes, such as the patrons of industry who became the new church benefactors. It was because of the wealth they and their workers generated that larger, more costly, more elaborate places of worship graced by stained glass windows and even murals were built. Some of these structures were products of the vision of ambitious parish clergy or leading congregants. Be that as it may, they denoted a turn to more formality and beauty in worship. The religiosity of the camp meeting, so popular in the early history of the province, no longer seemed appropriate in these more elegant and refined settings. But industrialization also attracted to the city an army of rural dwellers from near and far, a number of whom brought with them religious sensibilities and forms of expression different from those of the elite. Revivals and "evangelical services," characterized by vigorous preaching and gospel music, had definite resonance in turn-of-the-century Toronto. Indeed, some church administrators regarded such services as a clear sign of the times, the new norm against which to assess the performance of less successful congregations.

Places of worship mobilized not only financial resources but human resources as well. Most churches were heavily engaged in campaigns for temperance, sabbatarianism, and moral and social reform, issues all generated or aggravated by industrialization. In this regard, some observers have interpreted the Social Gospel as a deviation from proper religious concerns – as a secularization of religion, if you will. But this surely is an ahistorical contention, since throughout history, religion has been engaged with the world around it, moulded by it and seeking in turn to shape it. Religion and the world cannot arbitrarily be separated; they are symbiotically connected to each other.

However brief its history, Bethany Chapel illustrates some important themes of this period: ritualism and its opposing currents broadly categorized as the religion of feeling, as well as the commitment to social reform and missionary activity. One of the chapel's founders and likely benefactors was William Holmes Howland, who was briefly mayor of Toronto (1886–7), as well as an avid prohibitionist, sabbatarian, and social reformer; a successful businessman with diverse interests in the manufacturing, finance, and energy sectors; and a church elder at Bethany just before his premature death in 1893. The minister, John Salmon, left his comfortable charge at Yorkville Congregational and sold his house in order to help cover Bethany's $6,000 cost. His example spurred congregants to contribute to the chapel's construction so that by the time of the inauguration it was entirely free of debt. Attractive in its simplicity and harmony, and eschewing traditional Romanesque and Gothic forms of church architecture, the building was reminiscent, but for the porthole windows on the ground floor, of a Venetian palazzo. The original style spoke to the chapel's ambition to break with centuries-old clerical traditions and create something simple and honest.

Both Salmon and Howland, an evangelical Anglican, were disenchanted with their respective denominations. They yearned for meaningful religion, not an empty vessel veiled in ritual; for a religion that could speak to the unchurched, to those marginalized by industrialization. Even before Bethany's founding, they had worked among the downtown's socially disadvantaged population, and they had become convinced that the religion of feeling and emotion was best suited to their evangelizing efforts. Eventually Salmon became a practitioner of faith healing. Given its size, Bethany's members were involved in an amazingly large number of local and foreign projects. The congregants founded a "home for healing," an orphanage for impoverished boys, and a hospice for homeless men, as well as a mission for the "debauched" and destitute. They distributed Bibles and preached on street corners. Thirteen members, men *and* women, were supported as missionaries to India, China, Egypt, and Argentina. Bethany even housed the first training school for CMA missionaries. Like many other churches, and perhaps even more so despite its fundamentalist positioning, the chapel was deeply involved in the modern world. Men like Howland had an intimate experience of industrialization and capitalism, and religion for

3.1 Bethany Chapel (demolished)
Founded by evangelical Christians unhappy with the increasingly bourgeois character of Toronto Protestantism, it became the mother church of the Christian and Missionary Alliance in Canada, which emphasized an emotional style of religion, faith healing, and social outreach to the surrounding disadvantaged population of St John's Ward. (Toronto Reference Library)

them, just as for an earlier generation, was seen as a vital countervailing force, one that could tame modernity's wildest impulses.

As well as social class, Toronto's places of worship expressed differing notions of the sacred and humankind's relationship to the world around it. On this last question, the mainstream view was that religion should not simply confine itself to the sanctuary; it must also propel members into social action, and it authorized leaders to speak out on the important social and national issues of the day.[1] Religion could claim, borrowing from the classical poet Terence, that "nihil humani a me alienum puto." All things human were, it seemed, within its purview. From this perspective, Christians could, by working to improve the human condition, hasten the arrival of a thousand-year reign of peace that would culminate in Christ's return to earth for the Last Judgment. This was the post-millennial interpretation of eschatology, the study of what would happen at the end of the world. Many of the smaller denominations born out of the Third Great Awakening examined in the previous chapter rejected this position. Theirs was a pre-millennial perspective wherein Christ would very soon return to earth to lead the forces of good in a terrifying battle against those of evil commanded by Satan. In this view, the Last Judgment and the ensuing Armageddon would come before the millennium. Since the end of the world was imminent, all human action geared towards improving society was quite futile. All one could do was pray, and try to convince others to prepare for the Messiah's return.

Cultivating the Whole Person

Someone today unfamiliar with church interiors might assume that they simply enclose a sanctuary where people gather for prayer. However, in the past, almost all places of worship had a Sunday school. In fact, Church leaders and administrators often used Sunday school as a strategy for getting a congregation started. But places of worship were not conceived to accommodate a student population, which within a few short years often exceeded the total number of congregants. That is why many parishes and congregations, after becoming financially secure, established special facilities for religious education. Infants and younger children who attended Bible class were grouped together and separated from school-age pupils. Sunday school staff included volunteer teachers, administrators, and librarians, among others, representing on average around 10 per cent of enrolments.[2] In 1899, Wesley Methodist was reputed to have the largest Sunday school in the country, with more than 1,300 students and staff, as well as a library holding 1,000 books.[3] A decade later, nearby Dovercourt Presbyterian claimed to have the biggest Sabbath school of its denomination in the Dominion, with 1,000 youngsters enrolled and 800 attending regularly.[4] In the same period, Walmer Road, the largest Baptist congregation in Canada, had 600 children attending its Sunday school, which was housed in the original church building on Lowther Avenue. St George the Martyr boasted two Sunday schools in the 1880s: besides the parish one, there was one created to reach out to disadvantaged "unchurched" youngsters through the Church Army, Anglicanism's self-described "dignified and orderly" response to the Salvation Army.[5]

Evidently some churches took seriously the dictum "mens sana in corpore sano," an aphorism coined by the Classical author Juvenal, who linked healthy physical activity to a sound spiritual life. In the 1880s, boys in the parishes of St Thomas and St Stephen-in-the-Fields practised calisthenics in the church building. Just before the First World War, St Anne's Brockton and other larger places of worship built halls offering such amenities as swimming pools, gymnasiums, bowling alleys, manual training, and household sciences classes. Boys at Knox Presbyterian even helped build their parish hall by carrying bricks and cement to the worksite.[6] Girls now became targets of physical instruction in their own right. The Young Ladies Missionary Circle at Timothy Eaton Memorial arranged weekly gym classes for immigrant teenage girls at the Dufferin Street Italian mission.[7] Some churches organized sports teams. St Thomas Anglican, for example, had a cricket club, while Knox Presbyterian's soccer team, known as the Britannia Football Club, was coached by a church elder devoted to youth work.[8] In keeping with its higher social standing, Parkdale Presbyterian had tennis and lawn bowling courts. At the other end of the spectrum, some congregations and parishes ran summer camps for socially disadvantaged mothers and children.[9]

Many places of worship created societies promoting temperance, which for some advocates was practically synonymous with Christianity. Alcoholism, an especially prevalent form of dependency in the nineteenth century and one difficult to eradicate because it was rooted in everyday life, work, and leisure, undermined not only one's physical health but also, more importantly for the churches, one's spiritual well-being. Evangelicals took the initiative in this campaign, but it was not long before Catholics got involved as well, although Brian Clarke points to the very erratic existence of temperance societies in the West End's Catholic churches.[10] Ironically, one of the Toronto movement's most prominent members was William Gooderham Junior, a fervent evangelical and son of the founder of the distillery.[11] In some cases, temperance actually fostered the creation of places of worship. Historian

Varpu Lindström has shown that the Finnish Presbyterian Church in Toronto began as a temperance society. Clinton Street Methodist, located north of College (demolished), was born out of the cottage prayer meetings held at the home of A. Farley, whom Champion has called the father of the temperance movement in the West End. When Farley moved away from the neighbourhood, several of his associates decided that the time had come to form a congregation. The church, seating 800 people, was built just opposite his former residence.[12] Some West End congregations established the Band of Hope, an organization founded in Leeds, England, in 1847 to promote total abstinence among working-class children. Membership began as early as age six. Many Methodist churches used Temperance Sundays as a vehicle to reach congregants who were not members of formal societies.

In time, however, people began to doubt that private initiatives alone would eliminate the blight of alcoholism. They began to agitate in favour of total prohibition, calling on the coercive power of the state to effect lasting change in society. By virtue of the Canada Temperance Act (or Scott Act) of 1878, localities were allowed to hold referendums on prohibition. Such a campaign was successfully conducted in West Toronto Junction in 1904. There the local Ministerial Association, a loose non-denominational coalition of Protestant pastors, took a leading role in the victory of those opposed to the sale and public consumption of alcohol. Its president was F.H. DuVernet, rector of St John's Humberside and future Anglican bishop of Caledonia in British Columbia. He was seconded by the ministers at High Park Methodist, Annette Street Baptist, and Keele Street Church of Christ, all of whom used the pulpit to sway their listeners in favour of prohibition.[13] An early advocate of the cause was Daniel Webster Clendenan, ironically himself the owner of a popular local tavern.

Cultivating the mind as well as the body was the objective of several places of worship. The still extant Tuesday Literary Club came into existence in 1909 at St Paul's Methodist when a Sunday school teacher invited his class to meet in his home on Tuesday evenings to read essays and book reviews, take part in debates, and hear guest speakers. When the club moved out of the church in 1922, the minister led the congregation in a special service of farewell.[14] St Francis Catholic had a similar group known as the Literary and Athletic Association, founded in 1914 by Walter Charles Cain, Ontario's future Deputy Minister of Lands and Forests.[15] For its part, the Men's Association of College Street Presbyterian held monthly supper meetings to discuss current affairs under the direction of knowledgeable men. For example, in 1915, Robert Franklin Sutherland of the Ontario High Court of Justice spoke on "Our Debt and Duty to the Motherland" at a time when English Canada was riding a wave of intense wartime patriotism.[16] Parkdale featured a Men's Presbyterian Parliament that must have served a similar function. At St Patrick's, the American Redemptorists who took over the parish in 1888 became carriers of innovation. They founded the first non-devotional association dedicated to literary pursuits. Named after the order's founder, St Alphonsus Liguori (1696–1787), the society inaugurated the practice of having members elect their own executive. So successful was this initiative that a similar society for young women was established a short time later.[17] When in 1913 the order took charge of the adjacent Italian parish of Our Lady of Mount Carmel, it created a kindred organization called *Circolo Colombo*, in honour of Christopher Columbus; its members were upwardly mobile immigrant young men fiercely opposed to socialism and strongly attached to such values as law, order, family, and nation.[18]

As for the churches of eastern European immigrant groups, they served as veritable community centres. Osyp Boyarczuk, pastor of St Josaphat Ukrainian Catholic, set up a choir and drama society and himself directed several of the plays performed there. The church also hosted Ukrainian language, culture, and religion classes for children; English-language instruction was provided to the immigrant generation. Such services mimicked already existing ones created by a Baptist minister named John Kolesnikoff. St Stanislaus Polish Catholic Church boasted a brass band as well as a branch of Sokoł (Falcon), a gymnastic movement launched in the nineteenth century among the Slavic peoples of the Austro-Hungarian empire to promote greater national awareness. In contrast to St Josaphat, heritage language and culture classes for the children at St Stanislaus were poorly attended, perhaps because the parents were confident that the home environment was sufficient to ensure cultural continuity in the second generation.[19]

But the primary goal of places of worship was to nourish the soul. Organized by gender and age, associations dedicated to enhancing spiritual and religious life met regularly in church venues. Some of these specifically targeted young people, encouraging them to engage in proper Christian pursuits. For Presbyterians, Baptists, Congregationalists, and members of the Church of Christ, the Christian Endeavour Society, established in Portland, Maine, in 1881, pursued this task. At Hope Congregational, members of the association worked among the neighbourhood's underprivileged people.[20] Methodists promoted the Epworth League, founded in Cleveland, Ohio, in 1889 and named after John Wesley's birthplace in Lincolnshire. The chapter at the Westmoreland Avenue Church started open-air Sunday evening services and was credited with the creation in 1914 of the Dufferin Street Methodist Mission to Italians.[21] St Cyprian's and St Thomas Anglican each had a chapter of the Brotherhood of St Andrew to encourage men to pray together daily and bring at least one new person per week to church or Sunday school.[22]

As a result of the devotional revolution promoted under Pius IX, Catholic confraternities acquired new vitality. Although meant for the laity, it was the clergy who picked their leaders and set their course of action. Three confraternities – the Children of Mary, the Sodality of the Blessed Virgin Mary, and the Apostleship of Prayer – were especially popular in Toronto parishes, attracting a massively female membership. According to Brian Clarke, participation conferred upon women a moral authority and power in the household, where the Victorian ideal of separate spheres for the sexes was highly prized. Men were far less active in such groups. To engage them more deeply in devotional life, the clergy in a number of West End parishes established the Emerald Benevolent Association, a self-help and recreational organization that, despite the name, welcomed members irrespective of ethnic background. Men were encouraged to take the sacraments together as a group and to attend vespers following their quarterly general meetings. This strategy was apparently successful: men at the turn of the century became more involved in such organizations as the Holy Name Society, a confraternity devoted to fulfilling the Second (or Third) Commandment: Do not swear falsely by the name of the Lord.[23] According to historian Mark McGowan, St Helen was, at 26 per cent, the parish with the highest proportion of men enrolled; the overall average stood at 15 per cent.

Women Workers

As noted earlier, women were the backbone of parish and congregational life. They comprised the bulk of Sunday school teachers as well as its reserve army when enrolments suddenly expanded or contracted. Their various associations were among the very first to be organized, and they covered a wide spectrum of activities: canvassing and conducting surveys door-to-door in the early years to identify the faithful;

distributing tracts and parish or congregational publications; catering and hosting church events; bringing moral and material assistance to needy members; and, perhaps their most important function, fundraising. Women routinely planned, supplied, and staffed bazaars, bake sales, and other money-making events to help reduce the church's debt, pay for improvements, or support missionaries and their families. The Women's Auxiliary at St Mary Magdalene's, for example, helped sustain three First Nations schools in Ontario and Saskatchewan. The three-hundred-strong Women's Missionary Society of Timothy Eaton Memorial financially supported Dr Anna Henry's work in Chengdu, Sichuan Province, China.[24] Often at the initiative of the minister's wife, women came together to sew clothes that, together with the toys and books they collected, were packed and sent to missionaries at home or abroad. During wartime, parcels, often accompanied by letters of encouragement, were dispatched to Canadian soldiers overseas. In Catholic and Anglican parishes, women formed altar or chancel societies to ensure that all the requirements of worship were met, such as candles, altar cloths, flowers, and sacramental wine. They oversaw as well the embellishment of the sanctuary.[25]

Some female religious orders contributed significantly to parish life. The Sisters of St Joseph and the Institute of the Blessed Virgin Mary (Loreto Sisters), for instance, taught in a number of separate public schools, each of which was parish-based. Apart from the academic curriculum, they dispensed religious instruction and prepared children to receive the sacraments. These teachers were committed to a Christian ideal of education: the acquisition of knowledge, while important, was nevertheless subordinated to moral formation, the objective being to turn out principled young men and women. Schools were also vehicles for the devotional revolution mentioned in chapter 1. Sisters trained their pupils to participate in the major feast days of the Christian calendar such as the Christmas and Easter seasons, the month of May dedicated to Mary, and Corpus Christi, a celebration of medieval origin emphasizing the real presence of Jesus in the Eucharist.[26] The Carmelite Sisters of the Divine Heart, a multiethnic community based in Milwaukee, were brought to Toronto by Archbishop Neil McNeil to offset the Protestant proselytizing of Catholic immigrants. From their convent on Harrison Street at Ossington, the sisters replicated a number of services dispensed by Protestant missions and settlement houses, including a kindergarten credited with bringing Catholic children into the separate school system. The pastor of St Agnes parish nevertheless complained to the archbishop in 1915 that many Italian youngsters were still frequenting public schools. He urged the prelate to hire women whose task would be to accompany schoolchildren to the proper establishments.[27]

An Anglican women's order founded in Toronto in 1882, the Sisters of St John the Divine, also played a prominent role in the West End. The community opened its first convent on Euclid Avenue and Robinson in the parish of St Matthias, the only one in the city willing to accept them. They soon established a small hospital nearby and performed various other tasks, including teaching Bible school, bringing food to invalids in their homes, providing meals twice a week to the poor, and running a clothes distribution centre. They founded a home for the aged, initially situated in the parish of St George the Martyr. The sisters soon centralized their activities in the parish of St Stephen-in-the-Fields, opening a thirty-bed hospital named after their patron St John in a two-storey brick building designed by Frank Darling on Major Street above College. Nearby they set up a home for forty elderly women and a kindergarten for more than thirty children.[28]

The Sisters were crucial to the creation of the parish of St Cyprian. The Anglicans of Seaton Village had been left in somewhat of a lurch when their church, St Thomas, was literally taken away from them and moved south of Bloor Street. As a result, the vicar, John Charles Roper, who was also the Sisters' chaplain, asked them to staff a small mission house situated in Seaton. Two of their members performed invaluable work among resident immigrant labourers from England, Scotland, and Newfoundland who had suddenly been thrown out of work by the depression of the 1890s that killed the building boom. The dispensary, staffed by doctors and surgeons from St John's Hospital, treated 2,000 people in one year. Clothes, books, and linens were distributed to those in need, while the sisters set up mothers-and-children sewing classes that proved to be very popular. By creating a sense of community among Seaton's ill-fated workers, the Sisters laid the groundwork for St Cyprian's. They remained in the parish until the First World War, when their work took them to the East End. Accomplished and sophisticated seamstresses, the Sisters turned out altar frontals and rich vestments for a number of parishes such as St Barnabas on Givens Street at Halton and St Michael and All Angels.[29]

At their annual conference in 1882, the Mennonite Brethren in Christ created what were designated as approved ministering sisters. These women did not take vows, nor did they live in communities as did Anglican and Catholic sisters, but they had to be unattached and recommended by their ministers. Enjoying a similar status to the latter, although not ordained, they were full-fledged members of the annual conference and were credited with founding many new missions, including a short-lived one to Jews created after a pastor who had converted from Judaism preached in Toronto in 1903. Later known as city mission workers, they played a prominent role at annual camp meetings, two of which were held in Dufferin Grove Park in the early years of the new century. In 1914 they inaugurated a rescue mission and home for women known as *Berachah*, from the Hebrew word for "blessed."[30]

The office of deaconess, created in the early Christian period and revived in nineteenth-century Protestantism, was brought to Canada from the United States by the Methodists in 1887.[31] St Andrew's Institute, whose origins lay in the social activism of a female Sunday school teacher at Toronto's premier Presbyterian church, provided the neighbourhood's disadvantaged population with a variety of outlets and activities. A three-storey brick edifice built in 1891 included a gymnasium, swimming pool, auditorium, library, and class and meeting rooms, as well as a savings bank that boasted six hundred depositors. A deaconess was hired and lived on the premises. Part social worker, part evangelist, she played a crucial role: "It is she who most of all brings the home-life of the needy, the suffering, or the depraved of the district in contact with the beneficent forces of the Institute."[32] Besides a Sunday school, the institute organized mothers' meetings, sewing lessons, and evening classes that young boys were required to attend regularly in order to have access to the gymnasium. St Andrew's became the prototype for similar programs of Christian "social uplift" in the city. Meanwhile, the deaconess at College Street Presbyterian worked closely with the parish's Women's Association, organizing English-language classes for Chinese and Ukrainian immigrants and supervising the Business Girls' Club, which offered meals and activities for young working women at noontime.[33] At Bloor Street Presbyterian, the newly installed minister, George Pidgeon, hired a deaconess just after the war to help in his work with single women. The job description of the deaconess at Chalmers Presbyterian was quite simply astonishing. Hired in 1914, she was expected to act as secretary, telephone operator, and home visitor, as well as run the parish's employment, relief, and information bureaux.[34]

A number of other social initiatives in the West End are worth mentioning. In 1912 some women at St Thomas decided to set up a facility for unwed mothers, the first of its kind under Anglican auspices. Called

Humewood House, the building had been the residence of former Liberal leader Edward Blake. Because this ample country estate had orchards, residents were expected to cultivate fruit, grow vegetables, and look after chickens. Volunteers helped run the home, besides assisting mothers and their newborns, who lived on the premises for several months after the delivery.[35] In some cases, individuals – as opposed to religious communities or lay groups – initiated projects of social improvement. At Knox Presbyterian, Dr Emma Lelia Skinner Gordon, wife of architect Henry Bauld Gordon, founded the Baraca Club, which provided activities for "incorrigible" boys and later took charge of the soccer team mentioned above.[36] At Parkdale Presbyterian, Andrew Logan Geggie, the Scots pastor, assisted recently arrived compatriots living on the outskirts of the city who were having trouble getting settled. With the $25,000 he successfully raised, he created an "Old Country Club" to welcome and help out newcomers "from the Homeland … to develop a clean, intelligent British Canadian citizenship."[37] A large plot was purchased at Prospect Cemetery to provide a decent burial for Scots immigrants without resources, family, or friends.

As the social problems associated with corporate capitalism became more acute and complex, the need for coordination among parishes and congregations manifested itself. In the Anglican parish of St George the Martyr, the rector, Robert Moore, founded the Downtown Church Workers Association in 1912. The women associated with this social agency, which was overseen by six parishes, worked with female factory workers, immigrants, and the disadvantaged. In addition to handing out welfare, they visited the sick and organized outings for mothers and children.[38] In the same year, the Presbyterian Church established a social agency called St Christopher House on Bellevue Place (now Wales Avenue) in the Kensington Market area. George Pidgeon, whose knowledge of modern industry was, according to the renowned political economist Harold Innis, unsurpassed among Toronto clergymen, initiated a close relationship between his church and this institution, paying the salaries of its female workers.[39]

On the whole, women occupied subservient positions within places of worship and only on the rarest occasions was the pulpit open to them. Still, one woman achieved such notoriety that she was in great demand in Toronto churches. Her name was Nellie McClung. In a sense, she represented the model Protestant woman: mother of five, long-time temperance advocate, activist in the postmillennial struggle to improve the social and living conditions of women and children, suffragist, gifted orator, and successful writer. At the age of thirty-seven, the author of the bestselling novel *Sowing Seeds in Danny* (1908), which sold 100,000 copies, gave a public reading of her book at Bathurst Street Methodist and addressed the Sunday School Institute of St Alban's/North Parkdale Methodist on the theme of "The Call of the Child." Five years later, the by now noted public figure spoke from the pulpit of Timothy Eaton Memorial, attracting one of the largest audiences ever seen there.[40]

Missions at Home and Abroad

True to their stated objectives, evangelical congregations were particularly committed to domestic and overseas missions. Evangelization by English-speaking Protestants began in the late eighteenth century in response to the rise of empire and the horrors of the French Revolution. The movement was strengthened by the revivals that shook Great Britain and the United States in the latter half of the nineteenth century, prompting students especially to enlist as missionary workers. English Canadian Protestants and French Canadian Catholics were caught up in this North Atlantic fever, making a notable contribution to the cause, although English-speaking Catholics seemed less involved in it.[41] And this interest was not confined to the Women's Missionary Societies mentioned earlier. Proselytizers were often invited on Sundays by Toronto congregations to talk about their personal experiences or the overall achievements of the denomination in the field. Good speakers were sure to draw a large audience and were therefore slotted into the Sunday evening service. In 1895, Charles Samuel Eby addressed the congregations of Bathurst Street and Trinity Methodist. By all accounts a very engaging orator, he spoke about his lengthy service in Japan with the Canadian Methodist Mission, then in its twenty-second year.[42] At St Andrew's, R.A. King, principal of Indore College, lectured on Canadian Presbyterian work in central India begun in 1877.[43] Small denominations too featured foreign missionaries. The Christian Workers hosted the pastor of a Gospel church in Cleveland who had served in the Congo.[44]

In some churches a particular Sunday was set aside yearly to raise awareness about proselytizing. The Foreign Missions Day at College Street Baptist was dedicated one year to the Canadian denomination's activities among the Telugu speakers of southern India, which had started in 1874.[45] At times such talks were vehicles for the theatrical or the exotic, eliciting a voyeuristic response from audiences. The *Evening*

Telegram announced that at Clinton Street Methodist, a Mrs Bunhill had dressed in the "costume of a native Hindu priestess [who] will tell her unique story of Hindu life."[46] Missionary activities within Canada were also considered important. In 1915 the head of Presbyterian Church's Home Missions, A.S. Grant, spoke at St Andrew's and at Covenant on his board's work with French Canadians, immigrants, and First Nations people.[47] And a Methodist missionary addressed the Euclid Avenue congregation on his labours among First Nations peoples on Vancouver Island, where the denomination had been active since 1859.

In a variety of ways, congregations eagerly supported missions. Convinced that awareness of their importance started at an early age, Walmer Road Baptist and Erskine Presbyterian formed clubs for young people called mission bands. At the latter site, every second meeting was devoted to "business, missionary intelligence, and the reading of essays written by members on different missionary subjects, both foreign and home fields."[48] At particular congregations such as Annette Street Baptist and Western Congregational, one Sunday collection per month was reserved for overseas missions.[49] Knox Presbyterian provided funds for a chapel to be built in Macau, the Portuguese outpost in southeastern China. One congregant, architect Henry Bauld Gordon, worked for three years at his own expense in northern China and Korea with the Presbyterian Mission Board of Canada.[50] Bloor Street Presbyterian was one of the first in Canada to maintain a missionary overseas: James Menzies was sent to Henan in northern China in 1895 after being trained in both medicine and theology. A few years later some wealthy congregants financed the construction of his hospital there.[51] A short time later the College Street church underwrote the cost of two missionaries: the first in the Canadian West, the second in Rutlam, central India. It later sponsored a third proselytizer, a woman this time, also sent to Henan.[52] Only ten years after its establishment, High Park Baptist supported a female missionary in India, at a cost of $600 a year.[53] Even small congregations collected significant sums for such work. In 1914 the Cecil Street Church of Christ raised $1,500, an amount roughly equivalent to three times an unskilled worker's yearly wage, to help support Mary Lediard in Japan. The daughter of a Church of Christ minister serving in a Peel County town, she went to Tokyo in 1905 as a young unmarried woman, and spent sixteen years there as a missionary and teacher in a girls' private school.[54]

Nor were attempts to convert recent immigrants ignored. Of the large denominations, Presbyterians were the first off the mark, targeting the

Chinese. In 1895 workers armed with tracts and Bibles were urged to visit newcomers in their homes and shops. They had to convince the Chinese to attend the English classes being offered at the West End YMCA (now the Great Hall) located on Queen Street at Dovercourt. According to a 1901 report, close to two hundred men, three-quarters of those identified, were attending five such classes, most of them given in West End churches. Ten years later the number of students had more than doubled and the number of church sites had more than tripled. Initially no attempt was made to reach the few Chinese women living in the city, supposedly for lack of qualified female missionaries. English-language instruction was labour intensive, involving one teacher per group of two to four students, and was basically focused on the alphabet and a core vocabulary, as well as a few simple hymns and scripture lessons. The Chinese showed great enthusiasm for learning English but were less keen on the religious aspect. "Chinese work," as it was called, was aided by the arrival in 1905 of Timothy Kiang Wou Ma from Guandong. After graduating from Toronto Bible College, he was ordained in 1909 and took charge of an embryonic congregation. One of his tasks was to raise funds for the Chinese Young Men's Christian Institute. The aim of the institute was both religious and political: it sought to undermine the nationalist and socialist tendencies of Toronto's Chinese.[55]

The first organized efforts to convert Jews were made around the same time. Begun in 1894, the Toronto Jewish Mission was soon in the hands of Henry Singer, recently converted to Christianity in Boston. It is not clear who paid the yearly cost of $800 to run his operation.[56] But Singer later associated himself with Grace Church Evangelical Association. Housed in a plain brick building with Gothic accents erected in 1903, it was located at the corner of Gore Vale Avenue and Dundas. This English-speaking congregation was the offspring of ethnic German ones situated south of Guelph and was affiliated with an American denomination called *Evangelische Gemeinde* (Evangelical Association), which combined Wesleyan and Mennonite features and emphasized proselytism. Its congregants were probably rural migrants to Toronto in the early years of the twentieth century.[57] When Singer left the city in 1919, the mission was left without direction. The Presbyterians, for their part, joined the fray in 1908. Shabtai Rohold, the son of a Jerusalem rabbi, was brought in from Glasgow to head the Hebrew Christian Synagogue to the east of our area. Anglicans soon followed suit, founding in 1916 the Nathaniel Institute just south of St Stephen-in-the-Fields. Since the surrounding neighbourhood was becoming heavily

Jewish, Nathaniel volunteers distributed New Testaments to the area's homes and tried to enrol youngsters in Sunday school. The institute offered immigrants evening classes and English-language instruction. This kind of proselytism was certainly less intrusive and offensive than the open-air preaching in Yiddish practised by Singer and Rohold on busy thoroughfares frequented by Jews. But it remained manipulative in that it disguised religious instruction as language teaching. Few were fooled, and fewer still converted.[58]

The Methodists, for their part, occupied the "Italian field." Three missions, including two in the West End, were directed by a native-speaking Italian minister. However, in the absence of a resident clergy-man at each mission, English Canadian female volunteers proved to be crucial to day-to-day operations. Soon after his arrival from Italy, Michael Di Stasi was taken by his father, an early convert, to hear the minister, Mansueto Scarlata, speak. He recalled how effectively Scar-lata communicated to the small working-class congregation using a clear, simple, and direct idiom and how the stories he recounted were drawn from everyday life and commonplace experiences, in sharp con-trast to the pompous homilies of Italian Catholic priests. The Dufferin Street Mission began as a kindergarten. An unassuming church was soon built that instituted a full program of Sunday and weekday activi-ties. The Sunday school was superintended from nearby Westmore-land Avenue Methodist, the congregation responsible for the mission's creation.[59]

Baptists claimed the Slavs as their territory. As noted earlier, John Kolesnikoff, a Shtundist from Kherson in southern Ukraine who had immigrated to Scranton, Pennsylvania, before coming to Toronto, was an active evangelizer. He launched a series of initiatives, publishing a hymnbook in Ukrainian that he himself had translated from English; preaching at street corners in the Junction and in downtown areas of Slavic concentration; and penning missionary tracts and pamphlets. Kolesnikoff also promoted cultural activities. He established a local branch of *Prosvita* (Enlightenment), the literary movement at the heart of the Ukrainian national revival in nineteenth-century Galicia, whose reading room contained Ukrainian-language newspapers and maga-zines. Courses were mounted for women in cooking, sewing, and dress-making. Free language classes were offered to adults and children. The Baptist Home Mission Board's decision to centralize all Slavic work at the Beverley Street church doubtless displeased the more nationally con-scious non-Russian members they were trying to woo.[60] Kolesnikoff's

3.2 Keele Street Church of Christ
Daniel Webster Clendenan, property developer and first mayor of West
Toronto Junction, was a member of this small congregation. He campaigned
vigorously in favour of total prohibition in his municipality, a policy that was
only recently overturned. (Toronto Refernece Library)

death in 1918 created a vacuum that prompted Presbyterians to set up
their own Ukrainian mission station in the Junction.

The Catholic Church did not engage in active proselytizing as such,
but it did insist that the offspring of religiously mixed marriages be
brought up Catholic. Nevertheless, a community of priests dedicated to
the conversion of North America did arrive in Toronto in 1910. Established by men who were themselves converts, many of whom were
influenced by the Oxford Movement, the Missionary Society of St Paul
the Apostle was the first male North American foundation. Suspected
in Rome of being carriers of the Americanist heresy, a body of ideas
condemned by Leo XIII (1878–1903) that emphasized the peculiarly
American character of the Catholic Church in the United States and its
relative autonomy from Rome, the order still managed to retain the confidence of the US hierarchy. Their methods of evangelization focused

on the polite engagement of ideas rather than on street preaching, col-
portage, or door-to-door visitations. They created the Catholic Truth
Society, wrote articles for the press, published their own magazine, and
welcomed public debate on theological or religious issues. Four years
after settling into the city, Archbishop McNeil assigned them the parish
of St Peter. Right from the start, their presence sparked controversy. The
very year of their arrival, the pastor of Parkdale Methodist preached a
sermon titled "'The Charms of Roman Catholicism' an Answer to the
Paulist Fathers."[61]

Embellishing Places of Worship

Parishioners and congregants, either singly or collectively, spent significant sums of money decorating their churches. For some, this was a
tangible manifestation of personal or collective wealth that reflected the
city's increasing prosperity. For many others, adornment heightened
the sense of solemnity and awe of sacred spaces. Although originating in the Middle Ages, stained glass was not the exclusive preserve of
Anglican and Catholic churches. In fact, denominations strongly associated with evangelicalism such as Knox Presbyterian, made use ofi it,
as did Low Church establishments such as Redeemer, St Margaret's,
and Ascension. However, the large window that dominated the latter's
chancel represented abstract patterns, in keeping perhaps with Protestantism's (and Judaism's) abhorrence of figurative representations in
sanctuaries. Be that as it may, St Anne's Brockton, a Low Church parish,
featured windows depicting each of the twelve Apostles and Jesus. The
Keele Street Church of Christ also had stained glass windows, perhaps
as a testimony to its aspirations for growth and social respectability.

Stained glass was often associated with wealth. According to historian Stephen Speisman, Goel Tzedec Synagogue had such amenities
as stained glass windows and electric lighting in order to hold on to
well-off congregants who might otherwise be tempted to join the more
prestigious Holy Blossom Temple. Ten stained glass windows graced
St Paul's Methodist, whose congregants included financier Edward
Rogers Wood, a founder of Dominion Securities and Dominion Steel,
Timothy Eaton at the end of his life, and William Gooderham.[62] The
Good Samaritan window above the pulpit at St Andrew's Presbyterian dominated the church's interior. By contrast, some wealthy con-
gregations, such as Walmer Road Baptist, shunned such adornments.
At nearby Trinity Methodist, among whose members were Timothy

Eaton in mid-life, the publisher William J. Gage, and successful lawyer Thomas C. Robinette, the windows had plain geometric patterns in the palest of colours.[63] Conversely, stained glass windows adorned churches in less well-heeled neighbourhoods.

Two local firms dominated the production of stained glass: Joseph (later Robert) McClausland, founded by an Ulster-born immigrant, is the oldest studio on the continent; Napoleon Theodore Lyon was started by an Irish Catholic immigrant who had apprenticed with McCausland. These two firms merged many years later. The first made windows for St Stephen-in-the-Fields, St Thomas, and Bonar Presbyterian, among others. The second received a number of important commissions. The largest in the West End undoubtedly came from St Francis: twenty-one windows, four of which, depicting the life of St Francis of Assisi and designed just before the war by Georg Boos's internationally known glass studio in Munich, were executed by Lyon.[64]

Such works were sometimes commissioned by better-off members as memorials to deceased dear ones or to significant individuals in the life of the community. At St Mary's Catholic, two windows were installed depicting St Lawrence and St Elizabeth, figures celebrated for their devotion to the poor, an attribute the donor obviously intended to associate with the parents being commemorated. The parish priest donated a window in memory of John Walsh, his predecessor, who later became archbishop of Toronto. The central window at Redeemer Anglican, produced by N.T. Lyon, commemorated the first rector, Septimus Jones. It shows Jesus on his way to Emmaus, where he was to reveal himself as the resurrected Christ to the two disciples accompanying him.[65]

In rare circumstances, churches hired artists to paint murals. The best-known example of this is the second St Anne's. Its single-minded rector, Lawrence Skye, had a vision for the projected new church, which was erected in 1907. As an evangelical, he sought to break free of Roman traditions of church architecture and to return to Christianity's primitive Eastern origins. After visiting Constantinople's sixth-century Church of Hagia Sofia (then a mosque), he produced a Greek Cross design for the church. Once completed, however, the structure looked positively cavernous. In the words of Group of Seven member J.E.H. MacDonald: "The walls were of brownish concrete colour, so dull that they gave no indication of the true architectural form. It was impossible, for instance, to appreciate the higher curving of the dome. To look up into it was just to look into a brown hole." Having met MacDonald at the Arts and Letters Club, where they both were members, Skye persuaded him to decorate the church with the help of colleagues Frederick Varley and Franklin Carmichael. Varley did the panels representing the major Prophets, while MacDonald and Carmichael painted various scenes relating to the early years and public life of Jesus.[66]

But St Anne's was not the first church to call upon artists. A young painter recently immigrated from Germany was commissioned in 1890 by Edward Rogers Wood and W.K. Doherty, superintendent of the Sunday school, to decorate the ceiling of St Paul's Methodist church. Aged twenty-four at the time, Gustav Hahn produced delicately fluid Art Nouveau depictions of angels holding lilies that climbed towards the vault, the figures separated by gracefully curving vines. Tragically, his work was lost in a fire of suspected criminal origins that destroyed the edifice in 1995. In the Junction, James Power Treacy, pastor of St Cecilia Catholic for thirty-three years, hired an obscure artist by the name of P.C. Brown in 1917 to decorate the church. Covering the sanctuary, ceiling, gallery, and upper walls of the nave, his paintings depicted the triumphant figures of Jesus, Mary, and the Holy Spirit, as well as scenes symbolizing Christian virtues. As evidence of the utter disregard often shown by pastors and ecclesiastical administrators for this artistic heritage, some of his work was whitewashed in later years.[67]

Formalizing Worship

Music, whether vocal or instrumental, had pride of place in Toronto's sanctuaries. Churches often competed with one another for the type of musical program offered during services, especially at Christmas and Easter. Newspaper advertisements listed selections from the classical repertoire as well as the names of featured soloists. At St Thomas, the parish's sixty-man choir and orchestra performed such works as Charles Gounod's *St Cecilia's Mass*, while the music at St Matthias elicited the following remark by John Ross Robertson: "it [is] at once evident that the musical culture of this congregation [is] of a superior nature to that usually known in Protestant churches."[68] By now all large congregations had organs costing in the thousands of dollars. Whatever doubts stemming from tradition or doctrine might have existed about their use were swept away in the quest for more formal worship and social prestige. Indeed, the Carnegie Foundation offered churches grants to help them purchase an organ. One of these was the comfortable but working-class Westmoreland Avenue Methodist, which spent

$3,200 to acquire one. At Epiphany Anglican the subsidy covered half the cost of the organ. [69]

Wealthy congregations tried to attract reputable musicians as regular staff. In 1892, Erskine Presbyterian paid its organist the very respectable sum of $500 a year; fifteen years later, the cantor at Chevra Tehillim Synagogue was enticed from New York by a salary of $1,000 exclusive of perquisites offered by individual congregants. He formed a choir of twenty-six voices composed of four men and twenty-two boys.[70] A talented fifteen-year-old named Ernest MacMillan was appointed organist at Knox Presbyterian, holding the position for two years. MacMillan would later become a distinguished Canadian conductor and composer, the pre-eminent English Canadian musical figure of his time.[71] Canadian-born William Reed, who was organist at Keble College, Oxford, where he studied on a scholarship, was hired by St Andrew's Presbyterian at the same time as he taught at the Toronto (later Royal) Conservatory of Music (TCM). After only one year at this post, however, he moved on to Quebec City.[72] At Trinity Methodist, composer and TCM teacher Ada Kent served for a decade as organist, while the choirmaster for eighteen years was Richard Kirby, a founder and vice-president of the Toronto Mendelssohn Choir. Kent often accompanied the choir, which included James Wilson Gray, architect of Knox Presbyterian, as a lifelong member.[73] Timothy Eaton Memorial Methodist appointed an Englishman as both organist and soloist when it opened for worship: baritone Dalton Baker was somewhat of a celebrity because he had sung at Windsor Castle at the behest of Edward VII at a concert to mark the state visit of the monarch's brother-in-law, King George I of Greece. Baker held this position for five years, teaching voice as well at TCM. He was succeeded by Ernest MacMillan, who had just been released from a German internment camp, where he spent the war years.[74] Chevra Tehillim's cantor was reputed to be the best tenor on the continent, and its choir included a TCM medallist.[75]

Whether led by the organist or by a distinct director, choirs were commonplace in places of worship. In Anglican and Catholic churches and in large Orthodox synagogues, they were composed of boys and men only. From the time of its founding, however, Epiphany Anglican had instituted a mixed group, a practice common in most evangelical churches.[76] Repertoires were neither uniformly classical nor traditionally liturgical. Some congregations experimented with gospel music. Euclid Avenue Methodist, for example, featured John Whyte, described as the "sweetest Gospel singer."[77] By the turn of the twentieth century,

Whyte was a celebrity outside his native Paris, Ontario, having published five volumes of such music. At nearby Crawford Street/Berean Methodist, the gospel Stringer Sisters were the highlight of Sunday evening gatherings. Meanwhile, in an effort to offer an evangelistic service with popular appeal, the vestry at Dale Presbyterian gave the minister a free hand in selecting gospel soloists and recommending the types of music the choir should sing.[78]

By the end of the nineteenth century, Euclid Avenue Methodist, Crawford Street Methodist, and Dale Presbyterian were facing the "downtown problem." Because the lower West End was becoming more distinctly industrial and working class, new strategies to attract and hold potential congregants had to be devised. According to musicologist John Beckwith, gospel music was strongly identified with revivalism and temperance; like them, it was personal, immediate, and emotional, if not downright sentimental. Tunes were simple, unadorned, and straightforward, often using marching rhythms to create a mood of triumph and euphoria. Newer denominations readily incorporated such patently popular musical forms in their worship. Those who were attached to a more traditional liturgy dismissed such music as vulgar, strident, and tasteless – in other words, low class. For this reason, gospel songs did not easily find their way into traditional denominational hymnbooks, and when they finally did, they were placed in a separate back section. Beckwith cites a passage from the Anglican *Book of Common Praise* (1908) that seeks awkwardly, almost painfully, to justify their inclusion: "It was felt that in railroad construction camps, in lumber camps, and in similar surroundings ... these hymns could be found use [*sic*] and necessary ... They may not be found necessary in every parish, or under all circumstances."[79] In any event, Methodists and Presbyterians who sensed they were in competition with the newer denominations adapted some of their forms, including musical ones, in order to keep up with the changing tastes of congregants, a number of whom had been exposed to gospel music in the Ontario towns from which they originated and where the Salvation Army, for one, was active.

A musical incident involving Goel Tzedec is worth mentioning here because it illustrates deep-seated ethnic stereotypes in the receiving society. Toronto newspapers were fond of characterizing eastern European Jews as innately and stubbornly litigious, perhaps because such depictions confirmed images of the Pharisees found in the New Testament. Reading the local press, one gets the impression that Jews were constantly in litigation before the courts. In any event, two members of the synagogue choir, one of whom was thirteen years of age, sued the cantor and president for breach of contract and demanded financial compensation. They alleged that, although the choir was at full complement one Sabbath, the precondition for payment, they were dismissed without having sung or being remunerated. The older of the two complained that he was rudely knocked down during the service after inquiring about when they could sing. The dispute seems to have found an amicable resolution.[80]

Music showed that wealthier congregations at least had developed a marked taste for more formalized worship. Assistant rabbi Julius Price sought to achieve more decorum at *Goel Tzedec* by urging congregants to adopt prevailing North American norms in their worship.[81] At Redeemer Anglican, 150 parishioners impatiently demanded a vested choir for the Christmas service in 1905. Although similar requests had been rejected out of hand in the past, the petition met with not the slightest opposition. St Andrew's Presbyterian sought to stem the tide of decline by altering the church interior: the amphitheatrical seating plan was replaced by a central-aisle arrangement allowing for proper processionals and recessionals, as well as calling attention to Sunday offerings that were solemnly brought to the front of the church by ushers. Not surprisingly, the new minister, Thomas Crawford Brown, freshly recruited from St Giles cathedral in Edinburgh, instigated the change. The chancel was now richly decorated and the choir, entering in formal procession, was gowned, an innovation in Canadian Presbyterianism. By contrast, Bloor Presbyterian scrapped its central aisle plan in favour of an amphitheatrical one in response to its changing social composition. Once solidly comprised of well-to-do families, by the end of the war the congregation included conspicuous numbers of white-collar workers, boarders, and students. Known for his skills as a preacher, George Pidgeon had found a solution tailor-made to his talents and the congregation's changing fortunes. [82]

The turn towards more formalistic worship was an indirect result of the Oxford Movement, although some congregations would have been horrified to be associated with what they regarded as crypto-popery. By continually raising the liturgical stakes, High Church parishes in Toronto shifted the balance towards greater formality and ritual. It must be emphasized, however that the evolution towards Anglo-Catholicism was neither linear nor gradual; rather, it was somewhat intermittent

3.3 Trinity Methodist
The amphitheatrical interior so popular in North American Protestant
churches of the period fostered a sense of community with its focus on the
pastor's pulpit. (Toronto Reference Library)

and erratic. Liturgical innovations might be allowed to lapse for several years before being reintroduced, the process often involving a tacit negotiation between a determined priest and his parishioners. Priests at St Matthias, St Thomas, and St Mary Magdalene were decisive in finally making these parishes Anglo-Catholic.

For example, St Thomas's departure from Seaton Village had predictably resulted in a precipitous drop in attendance. In a vain effort to draw back these parishioners, rector J.H. McCollum brought in modest

3.4 St Thomas Anglican
The rood (crucifix) screen separating the chancel from the nave, the sacred
from the profane, the clergy from the laity, recalls a feature common in medieval Western European churches and still found in Eastern Orthodox ones,
where the rood screen is known as the iconostasis. (Toronto Reference Library)

innovations in 1883–4, such as the surpliced choir and altar frontals. The
church's fortunes markedly improved only after English-born, Oxford-
educated John Charles Roper was appointed vicar in 1888. Roper
wasted no time in instituting a Eucharist-centred liturgy as then practised at St Matthias and later at St Mary Magdalene. This entailed liturgical vestments for the celebrant, as well as altar cloths, candles, and
bells that were rung at that point in the Eucharist when the priest raised
the consecrated bread and wine above his head. The faithful, for their
part, genuflected, crossed themselves, and knelt at appropriate inter-
vals in the liturgy.[83] Such changes were regarded as dramatic departures
by local Anglicans and clearly marked these West End parishes off as
"ritualistic," an expression commonly used at the time. Their priests
began calling themselves and being called father rather than reverend
or mister. Soon the practice of the reserved sacrament was introduced:

the bread and wine not consumed during the liturgy were set aside or "reserved" and later brought to the housebound and the dying of the parish or used for veneration, practices that had fallen into disuse in Anglicanism since the time of Edward VI (1537–53). Incense appears to have made its appearance in the early years of the century. A solemn Eucharist, or high celebration as it was then called, which required three celebrants in hierarchical order of priest, deacon, and sub-deacon, was first observed in 1906 at St Thomas. Incense was used then and at festivals such as Corpus Christi, which was inaugurated at the church in 1916.[84]

Such liturgical innovations scandalized many Protestants. But Frank Hartley, rector of St Matthias, created a veritable furor in 1901. "Take Sins to Priest," read the headline in the *Toronto Daily Star*, while below it one could read: "An Episcopalian Clergyman in Toronto Comes Out Strongly for the Confession and the Granting of Absolution." Appearing at the top right-hand corner of the front page and taking up two columns, the article reported on the rector's sermon at the Sunday evening service, which was a commentary on one of the Beatitudes described by Jesus in his Sermon on the Mount:

> The audible naming over of a man's sins to a priest makes them so hideous in that man's eyes that he will not commit them again, having heard how hideous they sound. His sins audibly confessed, and audibly put away from him, a man is ready to receive and be filled by that life and grace that Christ has promised to them that hunger and thirst after righteousness.

Just below this article, a second one was titled: "Bold Beliefs for Anglican: Rev. Father Davenport in St Thomas' Church Preaches on the Presence of Christ in the Sacrament." The reporter informed his readers that, because the vicar had spoken in favour of the confessional in the previous Sunday's sermon, on that day "the church was crowded in the expectation of hearing something out of the ordinary and the worshippers were not disappointed." Davenport proclaimed his belief in the real presence of Jesus in the Eucharist, later telling the newspaperman that he felt it necessary publicly to affirm this article of faith because people (read some Anglicans) kept on denying it.[85]

This convergence of doctrine and practice with Roman Catholicism provoked incidents of intimidation in late-nineteenth-century Toronto. According to Hannah Grier Coome, founder of the Sisters of St John the Divine, the Orange Order threatened to burn their convent down when it was inaugurated. Sisters were regularly harassed by youths chanting: "Teeter-Tauter, Milk and Water, Sprinkle Catholics every one" when they processed from the convent to St Matthias for daily worship.[86] Coome claimed that it was only after they had returned from the Northwest where they had gone to nurse wounded soldiers during the second Riel Uprising that they found some acceptance in Toronto. St Thomas Church meanwhile was the scene of three separate attacks in less than ten years. In 1893, vandals targeted those features that set the parish apart: the crypt chapel, doubtless associated with secrecy and obscurantism; the sacristy, where priests put on their liturgical garb; and the altar. Three years later and on three successive occasions, church vestments were trodden in the mud and the reserved sacrament and the altar frontals were stolen. There can be no doubt that hooligans knew exactly what they were doing since they went after precisely those elements that caused Protestants the greatest anxiety. In 1901, perhaps in reaction to Frank Davenport's sermon on the real presence, windows were shattered in the rectory and the sacristy, while anti-Catholic diatribes were distributed to parish households.[87]

These incidents occurred against a backdrop of heightened ethno-religious tensions in Canada as a whole, the possible consequences of which clearly alarmed Protestant opinion. Many in this camp had an ethnocentric and homogenized view of the country and its future. Louis Riel's uprisings threatened their dream of a British nation from sea to sea by creating what they saw as special privileges for Catholics and French speakers on the prairies. Later demands by French Canadians that Louis Riel's death sentence for treason be commuted reinforced such fears. When, in the wake of the Métis leader's hanging, the Quebec government adopted the Jesuit Estates Act, Protestant anger reached the boiling point. The legislation designated the pope to arbitrate the age-old question regarding Jesuit lands confiscated by the Crown after the Conquest of 1759. In the eyes of many Protestants, this was an unprecedented and intolerable abrogation of British sovereignty. What is more, the new premier of Quebec, Honoré Mercier, was gallivanting around Europe and North America, pretending to be the head of a separate French and Catholic state.

Unsuccessful calls for the federal government to repeal the act led to the formation of very popular, militantly Protestant organizations such as the Equal Rights Association and the Protestant Protective Association. While in Ontario the Conservative opposition demanded the abolition of separate Catholic schools in the province, the Manitoba government took action in this regard. Its law provoked drawn-out legal battles ending in the final judgment of the highest court in the Empire, the Judicial Committee of the Privy Council – further proof, if any were still needed, according to militant Protestants, that Catholics somehow viewed themselves as above British law. In such overwrought circumstances, many Protestants could only regard Anglicans behaving as Catholics as a dangerous fifth column at a time when the need for Protestant unity was uppermost.[88]

Considering that at the time, Catholicism was the largest Canadian denomination, comprising over 40 per cent the country's population, one might well be taken aback by the strength of such opinion. This question in fact speaks to Canada's fundamentally asymmetrical nature. Two-thirds of all Catholics were in the province of Quebec. In neighbouring Ontario, the most populous province in the Dominion, they were fewer than 20 per cent of inhabitants and tended to live on its northern and eastern fringes. By contrast, in the industrial heartland, the most vital, dynamic, and progressive part of the country, the number of Catholics was below the provincial average, and in Toronto it stood at a mere 12 per cent. As a result, Quebec was for militant Protestants a blind spot, an unacknowledged reality, a mental blank when they were articulating their vision of the country. All of this reflected their local reality, which they wanted writ large. Be that as it may, the focus on the local is important for a fuller understanding of "the national."

While more formalized and elaborate styles of worship characterized a number of congregations, revivals in evangelical ones, although still occurring, seemed to be less frequent. One of them did sweep through Toronto in 1890–1.[89] As already noted, guest preachers were at times brought in to ignite the spark of religious feeling. Two Irish evangelists, the McCombe brothers, conducted services every day for three weeks, even instituting ones for men only; these culminated in an open-air rally at Clinton Street Methodist. Five years later the duo were back preaching every evening for an entire week at Queen Street Methodist.[90] The church also featured John Hunter, who together with Hugh Crossley formed a peripatetic team of Canadian evangelists celebrated throughout North America for their theatrical conversion crusades.[91] On different occasions, both Crawford Street and New Richmond Methodist advertised in the press special "evangelistic services" held every evening of the week.[92] Once the fervour of these campaigns subsided, however, it was difficult to maintain the commitment to spiritual

3.5 Forester's Hall on Brunswick Avenue
The building housed small congregations such as the Mennonite Brethren in
Christ, who occupied it from 1906 to 1944. Emphasizing a personal and emotional
religion, it was influenced by Methodism and distinguished itself from traditional
Mennonitism. In 1945 the building became First Narayever, a hometown-based
synagogue taking its name from the town of Narvayev in the Austro-Hungarian
Empire. It describes itself today as egalitarian and orthodox. (Gabriele Scardellato)

rebirth in mainstream congregations, whereas in smaller ones, such as
the Mennonite Brethren in Christ, the Christian Workers, the Pentecostals, the revivalist mystique remained very much a living reality.

Religion in Public Life

Agitation over prohibition clearly demonstrated that religious leaders
did not hesitate to use the pulpit to express opinions on public issues.
The evangelical clergy went into high gear again over the question

of allowing streetcars to run on Sundays; this led to three successive
and ultimately successful referendums in the 1890s. The Toronto Ministerial Association called public meetings, made representations to
City Council, and spearheaded petitions against the measure, which
congregants were asked to sign. Some West End clergy were in the
vanguard of the action: the president of the Ministerial Association
was Reformed Episcopal Bishop T.W. Campbell, minister at Christ
Church, while D.J. Macdonnell of St Andrew Presbyterian and A.M.
Phillips of St Paul Methodist spoke publicly and lobbied vigorously
in favour of sabbatarianism. The latter stated his opposition to the
very idea of a referendum on the question. In words reminiscent of
the Quebec clergy often accused by Protestants of meddling in politics, J. Mutch, pastor at Chalmers Presbyterian, expressed fears that
voters could not be trusted to vote the right way. The clergy's stance
was founded on one of the ten commandments enjoining respect for
the Lord's Day. Campbell certainly expressed the fear that permitting
streetcars to run on Sundays would put Toronto on a slippery slope
that would lead to bars being open on that day. Still, the arguments
used were not invariably nor narrowly religious. Macdonnell, for
instance, stated: "Sunday is the one great humanitarian institution
which provides for the needs of man's spiritual being as a child of
God, showing that he has not only got a body." Others, in an obvious
appeal to trade unions, spoke of the working person's need for a leg-
islated day of rest, even accusing the private interests that ran public
transportation of a cash grab.[93]

Places of worship were also platforms for proclaiming a congregation's loyalty to constituted authority. Ministers were natural spokes-
men for articulating such sentiments. Special services were held in
Toronto on the occasion of Edward VII's coronation in August 1902,
allowing Torontonians to exhibit their fierce attachment to the monarchy. S.D. Chown, minister at Broadway Tabernacle/Spadina Avenue
Methodist, a rising star in the church and its future superintendent, was
one of many ministers who preached a special sermon that day. Groups
whose loyalty was considered in some way dubious by the wider society made especially sure to flaunt it publicly. St Thomas Anglican was
heavily draped in black for the high celebration following the death of
Queen Victoria in 1901. At the cornerstone-laying ceremony for the new
Goel Tzedec attended by Mayor Emerson Coatsworth, the congregation
offered prayers to the king, the Royal family, and the Governor General. The guest speaker, a rabbi from Montreal, contrasted the freedom

to practise their religion enjoyed by Jews "under the folds of the British flag" with the repressive measures current in other countries. Such sentiments still did not prevent the local press from speculating about possible charges being brought against the synagogue for breaching the Lord's Day Act, since the cornerstone had been laid on a Sunday! At the building's inauguration the following year, the congregation closed the ceremony with the singing of "God Save the King."[94] This was the same synagogue that had prayed for the restoration to health of Czar Alexander III (1845–1894), brother-in-law by marriage to the Prince of Wales and a monarch not known for his Jewish sympathies. In the event, the czar died a few days later.[95]

Torontonians were not only committed monarchists but avid imperialists as well. In the decade-and-a-half before the First World War, Britain keenly felt the pressure to maintain its imperial pre-eminence against not only old foes such as France but also new ones such as Germany. The mother country therefore called upon the former settler colonies within the Empire to do their part to help it keep its global supremacy. The first crisis arose in southern Africa, where Britain was seeking to extend its authority over the mineral-rich territories occupied by the Boers, descendants of seventeenth-century Dutch-speaking settlers. Annexing these lands was strategically important, for it would create an uninterrupted British corridor through the heart of Africa stretching from Cairo to the Cape. Toronto clergy expressed their congregations' unflinching support for such territorial ambitions. For Elliott Rowe, minister at Euclid Avenue Methodist, Britain's cause was one of liberty and individual opportunity. Canadians were therefore duty-bound to place all of their possessions at the mother country's disposal. His colleague at Queen Street Methodist, C.O. Johnston, predicted the Boers' certain defeat because their position had no foundation in reason. As chaplain of the 48th Highlanders, D.J. Macdonnell of St Andrew Presbyterian told his troops at a special service held in their honour that he prayed for British victory in a war he regarded as necessary. Britain, whose rule was the most beneficial known to humankind, was battling the forces of slavery in southern Africa as it had done in the Sudan during the Mahdist Revolt a few years earlier. It was therefore imperative that British law be extended to all areas of southern Africa. Opposition to British imperialism in Quebec prompted William Hincks, minister at Broadway Tabernacle/Spadina Avenue Methodist, to preach an evening sermon on the topic "Quebec Nationalism versus True Nationalism."[96]

Besides expressing loyalty to the monarchy and the empire, Jewish leaders were early and ardent Zionists. *Goel Tzedec* was the venue of an address given in 1904 by a rabbi from Rochester to the United Toronto Zionists.[97] Four years later, a Montreal rabbi named Meldola De Sola argued in the same venue that for Jews, Palestine was the fatherland, whereas imperial Britain was the motherland: devotion to the two was not, in his mind, mutually exclusive. At a time when recent pogroms in Russia were still fresh in people's minds, he warned that prosperity in the West should not make Jews insensitive to Zionism. Synagogues were also sites where horror and outrage could be expressed at the violence committed against Jews elsewhere in the world. A mass meeting was held at Chevra Tehillim, chaired by Premier James Whitney (1843–1914) of Ontario and Mayor Thomas Urquhart (1858–1931) of Toronto, to protest against the Kiev pogrom of 1905 in which scores of Jews had been killed. West End ministers such as Alexander Gilray of College Street Presbyterian, Joseph Wild of Zion Congregational, and Andrew Geggie of Parkdale Presbyterian attended the event as a gesture of solidarity. The following month a memorial service was held at Chevra Tehillim for the victims of the rampage.[98] Synagogues could also be used by community members to draw attention to their cause. After a fire destroyed the offices of the National Matza and Biscuit Company, employees locked themselves in Chevra Tehillim with the firm's secretary, demanding that he pay compensation to the wife of a worker who died in the blaze.[99]

Socially prominent Jews, while strongly committed to Zionism, also began showing a marked interest and involvement in Canadian politics. During the 1904 federal election, a community meeting was called by the president of Goel Tzedec to express support for Thomas C. Robinette, who was running as a Liberal candidate in the riding. Well-known figures, many of them members of the synagogue, spoke in Yiddish at the gathering, praising Wilfrid Laurier's party, notably its achievements in uniting "the races," while criticizing the Conservatives for their denigration of foreigners. The meeting made clear that these Jews, at least, were well aware of their immigrant group's political strength. One speaker boasted that Jews were numerous enough to decide the outcome of the election in York Centre. For his part, insurance agent Louis Gurofsky, who would later run for alderman, underscored the accomplishments of his community in Toronto: Jews represented 3 per cent of the city's population but paid 15 per cent of its property taxes; their children were at the top of their class in the public schools. Similar arguments were invoked at a meeting of Polish congregations called at Goel Tzedec to promote a Jewish candidate for alderman in the municipal elections of 1906.[100]

Congregational Tensions

Relations between clergy and their congregants were not always harmonious. In 1905, twenty-nine year-old Oliver Horsman left his charge in New Jersey to take up an appointment – a short-lived one as it turned out – at the well-heeled Walmer Road Baptist. Less than a year later, he submitted his resignation after a congregant openly called him a heretic during a Sunday sermon. On that occasion, Horsman had questioned whether the world had been created in literally six days, understanding the term "day" figuratively to mean "epoch." It must be remembered that the founding pastor of this congregation, Elmore Harris, a leading evangelical, was constantly fulminating against the doctrinal liberalism being taught at the Baptist McMaster University. Evidently the elder pastor had retained a faithful following after leaving his charge in 1895 because of ill health. But Horsman too was popular, taking with him seventy-five congregants when he left. Together they formed a new congregation, calling itself Independent Tabernacle Baptist.[101] At Chalmers Presbyterian, meanwhile, a bitter dispute of unexplained origin erupted involving the pastor, Samuel Ross MacClements, appointed in 1897 from a parish in Pittsburgh. The conflict went to the ecclesiastical courts for resolution. In any event, many members left the church, as did MacClements himself after only eighteen months in Toronto to take up a charge in the United States.[102]

Conflicts between pastors and faithful were especially common among immigrants in the early years of settlement. Recruiting qualified clergy who spoke the newcomers' language was not always easy. Aspirants at times came to Toronto without proper authorization, some even escaping doubtful situations back home. A few clergymen found the transition to immigrant life stressful, especially when it came to leading an often illiterate or poorly educated congregation. To complicate matters, issues of class and regionalism often intruded. Almost all of the priests appointed to serve Italian-language parishes were from northern Italy. Trained in high-blown rhetoric in the seminaries of the home country, they were hard pressed to express themselves in a simplified idiom understandable to illiterate, dialect-speaking peasants, a class universally reviled by educated urbanites. Priests considered them not just ignorant, but miserly as well. To shame parsimonious parishioners, the pastor of St Clement's/Our Lady of the Angels, Luigi Scafuro, published an almanac containing a list of their names together with the sum of yearly offerings. Congregants fought back, accusing Scafuro of a string of sexual and financial improprieties.

By the turn of the century, tensions at Goel Tzedec were not so much class based or regional as they were generational. The children of immigrants had been socialized in North America and wanted worship to reflect cultural values considered by them to be modern and progressive as opposed to those of their parents, which they dismissed as backward and old-fashioned. Many were irritated by Rabbi Gordon's heavily accented English, of which he had an imperfect command, as well as by his exclusive use of Hebrew in worship and Yiddish on most other occasions. Born in Lithuania and trained in the yeshiva of Valozhyn, Belarus, Gordon was twenty-seven when he took up his post in 1904. An English-speaking assistant was finally found for him in 1914 after some strenuous lobbying. The congregation's youth predicted that "he will be a great boon to the uplifting of the moral tone of the Jewish circle in Toronto." Brought up in Worcester, Massachusetts, and educated at the New York Hebrew Theological College and Columbia University, where he received his master's degree, Julius Price was also twenty-seven years of age when he arrived. He wasted no time in instituting weekly sermons at Goel Tzekec, an innovation for this Orthodox synagogue that prompted a walkout by outraged traditionalists. Be that as it may, Price struck exactly the right chord with younger members. Of the older generation, the rabbi stated in an interview: "When they come to America they imagine they have the right to make laws to suit themselves. If the parents insisted upon their children studying Judaism and Jewish history and religious principles under modern methods the Jewish race would be holding a more exalted position in the eyes of the English-speaking world."[103] This impatient appeal to forsake the old ways in favour of the new, to adapt, to fit in; this testy insistence that immigrants were somehow the authors of their own failure to progress and their own exclusion; this imperative need to measure up "in the eyes of the English-speaking world": these were sentiments that resonated with his young audience. Price also displayed a typically modern North American clergyman's ambition to make religion relevant to young people's interests and daily life. He was a founder of the Young Men's Hebrew Association, which aimed to amalgamate all Jewish athletic and social clubs.[104] His European-trained colleagues would surely have considered such an accomplishment frivolous and entirely outside of religion's purview.

Modernity intruded on Toronto's places of worship between 1880 and 1920. The concept of modernity is as nebulous as it is multifaceted. It is connected with a number of phenomena that are themselves interrelated, chief among which is industrialization – that is, the production and distribution of goods in factories for mass consumption, and the technological innovations it has caused in industry, transportation, and communication as well as in social and domestic life. Modernity is therefore closely related to urbanization – that is, the growing trend of people to live in cities where, as we have seen, space is reorganized and rationalized with an eye to industrial efficiency. The concept also denotes the formal participation of ever larger numbers of people in the political process, whether they be women, youth, or workers without property. In its simplest form it means voting for candidates running for public office, but also organizing civil society to mimic such practices through structured meetings, platforms, decisions taken by majority rule, and techniques of mass persuasion. Modernity generates collective forms of expression, often along class, gender, and ethnic lines, in response to industrial and urban life, such as mutual aid societies, trade unions, business and ethnic associations, movements of reform, and all manner of leisure and sports activities. Associated with all of this is the expansion of civil rights, most notably the notion of the rule of law. In terms of the arts, modernity connotes the reaction of creators to the industrial and urban world around them. In painting, for example, it can take the form of the nostalgic Pre-Raphaelite movement in industrial England or pioneering Cubism in Continental Europe.[105]

Modernity in the West End expressed itself in many different ways: a society in a Catholic parish electing its own executive; an association formed to channel the energies and interests of young people; a regular English-language sermon given in a synagogue. The emergence of women as active participants in the parish or congregation was another manifestation of modernity's presence. Whether called deaconesses, city mission workers, sisters, or nuns, they performed a variety of tasks as home visitors, fundraisers, welfare and health care workers, teachers, hostesses, nurses, cooks, and bakers, as well as caregivers and administrators in facilities for preschool children or the elderly. The fact that some deaconesses also acted as secretaries to pastors is an indication that women's role was becoming more complex and varied, reflecting in turn religion's ambitions in this age of exuberance. Even Protestant proselytizers were carriers of modernity, serving as bridges between the old world and the new. They spoke English and knew how to navigate the perilous waters of the receiving society. They were conversant with contemporary technological tools of persuasion: the typewriter and the printing press. They offered immigrants services outside of their customary networks of family and kin – impersonal ones in that they were being provided by strangers and the native born. For a small minority, proselytizers embodied individualism, a sense of adventure, and the freedom to break with kinship and community.

Modernity's key figures came mainly from the United States, from organizations such as the Christian Endeavour Society and the Epworth League. They included Carmelite nuns who worked with immigrant families, Redemptorists who took over the parishes of St Patrick and Our Lady of Mount Carmel, and Paulists cloaking Catholicism in a North American idiom. They were men like Rabbi Price and his followers, who were anxious to give Judaism an American face and eager to engage in Canadian politics. They were composers and singers of gospel music born of camp meetings, nourished by temperance crusades, performed in work camps across the continent, and expressing the essence of the religion of experience. They were evangelists such as Hunter and Crossley, who appropriated the techniques of persuasion developed and patented by their American counterpart, Dwight Moody (1837–1899), when he was a shoe salesman in Boston: the tone had to be upbeat but provocative; the language, plain and direct with liberal use of humour, folksy anecdotes, and especially melodrama. The overall effect was highly emotional. As historian Kevin Bradley Kee correctly observed: "These were not the apparently spontaneous outpourings of the Holy Ghost that had marked the early 1800s; these were planned and controlled religious events, in keeping with the rational spirit of the late nineteenth century."[106]

In what way, might it be asked, were followers of the Oxford Movement harbingers of modernity? They were like architect Eden Smith, artist Franz Johnston, and sculptor Frances Loring, all of whom had been inspired by modern artistic currents such as the Arts and Crafts movement and Expressionism. Although enthralled by a medieval model of Christianity, they were responding to the social and moral conditions of their time: the dehumanization of work, the stratification and segregation of urban life, the material and cultural impoverishment of entire segments of the industrial population. They yearned for community in the face of the ethic of rugged individualism, for craftsmanship in answer to mechanistic mass production, for order and ritual in an age of social chaos and regimentation, for beauty and solemnity amidst the pervasiveness of the utilitarian and the ugly. In other words, they were not living in a medieval time warp.

Missionaries working with immigrants were especially keen to bring "their people" into the twentieth century. At the start of settlement, they were often among the first encounters newcomers had with the receiving society in their own language. Bibles and tracts were made available to them in an idiom they could understand, but so also was valuable information about health and child care, language classes, and social assistance. For example, the very first Ukrainian-language publications to appear in eastern Canada were those of the Baptist missionary Kolesnikoff. That proselytizers played a pivotal role in early settlement can be seen in how seriously the Catholic Church and Jewish leaders took the threat they represented to group cohesion. Ultimately, however, Protestant missions to immigrants were fatally flawed. As historian Enrico Cumbo demonstrated for Italians, newcomers were quite pragmatic and utilitarian in their dealings with missionaries, gratefully accepting services offered free of charge but rejecting accompanying religious forms and world views judged to be too alien.[107] Most could discern attitudes of cultural condescension conveyed by notions "of a clean, intelligent, British Canadian citizenship," emanating not so much from the ministers themselves as from their Canadian assistants, the very ones providing the practical assistance needed in immigrant settlement. One might be tempted to say that newcomers preferred the well-known cultural superiority displayed by the clergy of their denomination to the unfamiliar superiority of Protestant mission workers. Be that as it may, conversion did entail a fairly radical break with family and community that few were willing to make. In the end, immigrants fashioned their own compromises with modernity.

Not a single woman led a West End parish or congregation at the time; all of them occupying subordinate positions. As in the household, their work was invisible and most often unacknowledged: dinners appeared, events happened, socials occurred, funds materialized, children and the elderly were cared for, parish affairs were coordinated, and clergy were assisted. It would be intriguing in this respect to compare the salary of the live-in deaconess at St Andrew's Institute with that of the pastor of St Andrew, doubtless the best-paid clergyman in the city. Within their parishes and congregations, women were nevertheless acquiring experience as organizers, managers, supervisors, and even administrators. Their knowledge extended beyond the household to specific categories of people lacking autonomy, to groups requiring social assistance in unknown parts of the city, to those in Canada and abroad needing to hear the "word of God." Such knowledge may have been rudimentary and coloured by class, ethnic, and racial biases, but it was a start. Ultimately, when Nellie McClung, homemaker, temperance activist, social reformer, and defender of women's rights, spoke from the pulpit of Timothy Eaton Memorial Methodist, it was a prelude of things to come. Whatever position was taken with regard to modernity, the issue had to be confronted and negotiated.

Chapter Four

Ecclesiastical Musical Chairs, 1920–1960

The continued flight to the suburbs by the downtown's established residents, and the move westward out of St John's Ward of its non-British population, together with a new wave of European immigrants, had a powerful impact on the West End. The disjunction temporarily created between existing places of worship and the area's new inhabitants quickly vanished as sacred structures traded hands, assuming new ethnic or religious identities. But change was not only demographic; it was also denominational. The founding of the United Church of Canada, a major split within Baptist ranks, and the demise of the Christian Workers were markers of shifting religious allegiances. For example, whether Presbyterian congregations joined the United Church or not, dissidents within them were assigned to other places of worship. Meanwhile, Church Union led to a rationalization of sacred spaces. Choices had to be made when Methodist, Presbyterian, and Congregational churches were in close proximity to one another regarding which would remain open and which would close, and this required further transfers of people. Despite these changes, religion continued to show unmistakable vitality, as indicated by the construction of new religious buildings. Yet some contemporary observers thought otherwise. The birth of the United Church generated high expectations that what was now the largest Protestant denomination in Canada would generate heightened religious fervour and commitment throughout the country. In the West End, however, the facts on the ground told a different story, one of church closings and transfers to non-Protestant groups. Even as a number of Protestant congregations reached their peak in the 1930s, clerical leaders expressed glum forebodings of religion's impending decline.

Queen Street West Methodist expressed the hopes and disappointments of the period. Created in the 1840s, the West End's oldest congregation merged with its Euclid Avenue counterpart in 1923 as a result of intensified commercialization in the area around Spadina, which had depleted its ranks. Ecclesiastical administrators thought it sensible to transfer the remaining members to the nearest Methodist place of worship, ten short blocks to the west. As often happened in neighbourhoods in transition, the vacated building was rented out to a Pentecostal group whose success confirmed the vitality of the religion of experience in spite of the simultaneous disappearance of the Christian Workers.

The United Church conducted a survey of the area and found that thousands of immigrants were without access to spiritual services in their first language. According to officials, Protestant churches were making no effort to reach out to these people, leaving them entirely on their own. So it was decided to reoccupy and restructure the old building and rename it the Church of All Nations. Distinct congregations were set up for a number of groups, each headed by a pastor speaking their language, all worshipping separately under one roof. This was an innovative experiment in immigrant outreach, and the practice of offering newcomers a variety of spiritual and material services continued, proving especially welcome during the Great Depression. What also persisted was the determination to turn these foreigners into true Canadians – that is, to wean them away from "alien" ideologies such as communism. The emphasis was thus on integration, tolerance, and good citizenship. The missionary activities conducted at the Church of All Nations by the United Church, which defined itself as the quintessentially Canadian denomination, brought to the fore issues of entitlement and identity, of who was in and who was out, of who defined the pace and scale of integration and who was constrained by these. More generally, those activities spoke to the important role played by the churches in determining English Canadian identity. At the same time, however, the objective of mass conversions among immigrants never came close to being achieved.

Up until 1951 a casual observer might think that Toronto was holding steady on its path to becoming the economic capital of Canada. Everyone acknowledged its wealth and power. Its control over the country's manufacturing, wholesaling, and retailing was undisputed. An important hub as well of finance, transportation, and mining, it was poised to overtake Montreal as Canada's great metropolis. By 1911, Toronto boasted more head offices of branch plants than its Quebec rival. In 1934 the merger of the Toronto Stock Exchange and the Standard Stock and Mining Exchange created the largest such trading centre in the country. Some twenty years later the city would wrest from Montreal its leadership in the field of insurance. But the phenomenal population growth observed up to 1920 seemed to be a thing of the past. The city in fact grew by a mere 30 per cent in the following three decades, reaching a peak of 676,000 in 1951 and actually registering a slight decline after that so that it stood at 672,000 inhabitants in 1960. And despite high levels of immigration, the city's British and Protestant character remained basically unaltered.[1]

Appearances, however, were deceiving. In tandem with the city's unspectacular demographic growth, there was an explosive increase in the suburban population, which stood at 440,000 inhabitants in 1951, doubling again by 1961. Reflecting the decentralization of manufacturing and other economic activities, this new phase of industrial development restructured yet again Toronto's urban space, as geographer Richard Harris would so clearly demonstrate.[2] The suburbs maintained a more distinctly British character than did Toronto proper, where people claiming that ancestry accounted for under 70 per cent of the population in 1951, compared to 85 per cent thirty years earlier. Overall, people of British ancestry comprised 73 per cent of the Metropolitan Toronto population.[3] The statistics on religion told basically the same story: Protestants still represented about 70 per cent of the city's population in 1951 (74 per cent in the metropolitan area), down from about 80 per cent in 1921.[4] But the huge wave of immigration in the 1950s would substantially alter the face of Toronto.

The Demographics of Migration

Internal migration and immigration from abroad continued to contribute significantly to Toronto's population increase. The city drew its Canadian labour force chiefly from the southwestern Ontario hinterland. But its range now extended to other regions, especially Manitoba and Saskatchewan, where agriculture was recovering only slowly from the body blow dealt it by the Depression and where prospects for farmers' non-inheriting sons were few. The pull effect was especially felt during the war, when jobs in industry were plentiful and local manpower was scarce. Canada received a substantial number of immigrants from continental Europe in the five short years between 1924 and the Wall Street crash of 1929, and most of them settled in Toronto or other Ontario cities. The prairies were not as attractive as they had once been because the good land was already occupied and the cities there had reached a temporary economic plateau. The proportion of foreign-born in Toronto remained unchanged in 1931 at 38 per cent. That figure, the highest on the entire continent, had dropped to 31 per cent in 1941. The Depression with its high rates of unemployment hit unskilled and non-British workers the hardest. A number of them may have sought opportunity elsewhere.

The 1950s were a turning point for the ethnic structure of the city as immigrants began arriving in torrents in response to Canada's manpower needs. By the end of the decade, 42 per cent of Torontonians were foreign-born.[5] The percentage of people claiming British ancestry fell to 52 per cent (60 per cent in the entire metropolitan area).[6] Until 1951, Jews had been the largest non-British group, although their share of the population had declined slightly after the war to 6 per cent. Ten years later that figure had plummeted to less than 2 per cent (over 3 per cent in Metropolitan Toronto).[7] Italians were now over 11 per cent of the city's population, and three-quarters of them were recent arrivals.[8] Taken together, people of central and southern European origin were 35 per cent of the population. Some of these newcomers were refugees from DP camps or were fleeing political crises such as the Greek Civil War (1946–9) or the Hungarian Revolution (1956). Toronto now had the largest concentration in Canada of most immigrant groups, displacing cities of early settlement such as Montreal and Winnipeg.

More dramatic still were changes in religious affiliation. From an all-time low of 12 per cent in 1921, Catholics almost doubled their share of the population by 1951; a decade later, Catholics were 37 per cent of the population and the largest single denomination in the city.[9] Over the same time span, mainstream Protestants fell markedly from 76 to 47 per cent. The sharpest drop occurred in the 1950s, at the beginning of which they had still accounted for just under two-thirds of the population.[10] The largest Protestant body in the city was the United Church, whose adherents totalled 19 per cent of Torontonians, followed very closely by Anglicans at 18 per cent. Presbyterians who refused to join the new church came next at 7 per cent, while Baptists stood at only 3 per cent. While the Presbyterians' share of the population was cut by two-thirds, Baptists fell by almost half. Suburbanization had caused some of this decrease. Anglicans, Presbyterians, and members of the United Church had higher proportions in the metropolitan area than in the city. The reverse was true of Catholics, who had a lower percentage in the suburbs. New non-Christian groups, such as Buddhists and Muslims, made their appearance, although they comprised an infinitesimal part of the population.

ST. CLAIR AVE. W.
DUNDAS ST. W.
KEELE ST.
DAVENPORT RD.
AVENUE RD.
DOVERCOURT RD.
CHRISTIE ST.
DUPONT ST.
RONCESVALLES AVE.
DUFFERIN ST.
BLOOR ST. W.
BATHURST ST.
SPADINA AVE.
OSSINGTON AVE.
COLLEGE ST.
DUNDAS ST. W.
QUEEN ST. W.
UNIVERSITY AVE.
Methodist/United
Presbyterian
Pentecostal
Catholic
Jewish
Other
0   500   1000 m
N
Boundary of the
City of Toronto,
1834-1998.
MAP AREA

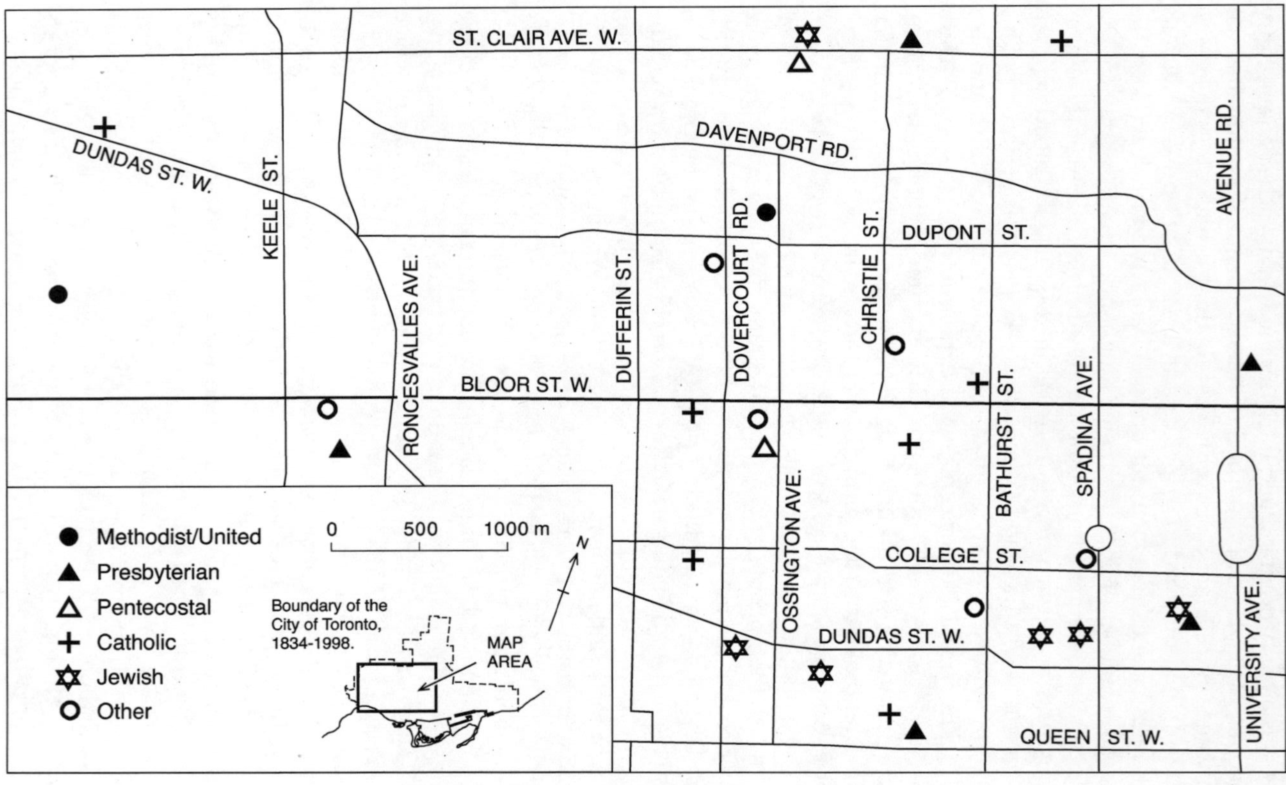

Map 4.1

Immigration transformed the Catholic Church from a solidly Irish Canadian institution into a multiethnic one. Already in 1931 about one-third of the city's Catholics were of non- British origin.[11] By contrast, the non-British members of the major Protestant denominations did not exceed 5 per cent of the total, and persons of French origin formed an important component of that figure. In the postwar era, Catholicism's multiethnic character was further accentuated, while the fundamentally British nature of Protestantism remained unaltered. The West End became a major immigrant reception area after the First World War. It is there that Jews and Italians were concentrated until the 1950s and that postwar immigrants initially resided.

A Changing Environment

Seventy-two new places of worship were erected in this period. They were on the whole smaller structures than had been built in the past, and less identified with well-known architects and major Protestant churches. There was in fact a marked proliferation of denominations in the West End. A simple fact highlights this reality: while Catholics had the largest number of new buildings, eleven in all, thirteen denominations, including new ones not seen before in the area, erected one place of worship each. Nine new synagogues dotted the West End, including the showcase Polish *shul*, *Beth Jacob*. Presbyterians and Baptists built seven churches, while the Anglican and United churches were not far behind with five each. In addition, Brethren constructed six gospel halls. The years of most intense activity were those marked by prosperity: thirty-three buildings went up in the 1920s and twenty-one others in the 1950s. Catholics led the pack in both periods. Jews, by contrast, concentrated their efforts in the years before the Second World War. See table 4.1 for the cost of some places of worship and their year of construction.

The United Church welcomed seven major West End Presbyterian congregations into its fold: Bloor Street, College Street, Covenant, St Columba (Wychwood), Western, High Park/Erskine, and the newly built Alhambra Avenue. Dissidents within these congregations had to transfer to the nearest Presbyterian church or wait for a new place of worship to be built. Three such churches were erected within a dozen years after Church Union. The largest of the three, High Park on Boustead Avenue, had seating for 650. The other two were Central (Avenue Road at Lowther Avenue) and Wychwood (on St Clair Avenue). In

Table 4.1. The cost of some sacred spaces, 1920–1960

	Cost ($)	Year
Men of England Synagogue	156,000	1921
Beth Jacob Synagogue	156,000	1921
Ostrovtzer Synagogue	20,000 (+30,000 renovations)	1921
Holy Rosary	175,000	1926
High Park Presbyterian	85,000 (lot and building)	1926
Dormition of the Theotokos Ukrainian Catholic	24,500	1928
St John's Evangelical Lutheran	72,000	1929
Christ the Saviour Russian Orthodox	8,500	1930
Finnish Pentecostal	3,500	1937
Wychwood Presbyterian	50,000	1937
First Hungarian Presbyterian	12,500 (lot and building)	1938
Hungarian Baptist	7,000 (+ 5,000 repairs)	1943
St Wolodymyr Ukrainian Orthodox	106,000 (lot and buildings)	1947
Shaarei Shomayim Synagogue	500,000	1949
First Baptist (second)	100,000 (lot and building)	1955
Resurrection Lithuanian Catholic	360,000 (lot and building)	1955
First Ukrainian Pentecostal	82,000	1957
Nativity of the Theotokos Slovak Catholic	70,000	1959

the intervening years, congregants of High Park and Wychwood had to endure considerable disruption. Worship for the first was at held the Revue Cinema and in a disused school, for the second, at the Christie Theatre and in a former Baptist church. It was only because of a bequest of $25,000 from a deceased member that this congregation was able to build a new church.[12]

The fate of Western Congregational became a source of controversy and anxiety. Its pastor, the well-connected Bertram Nelles, son of a prominent Grand Trunk Railway official, proposed in 1921 that because of declining numbers, the building be sold and the congregation merge with Dale Presbyterian, whose minister he would then become. Nelles's predecessor, James Pedley, strongly opposed the move. It was Pedley who at the beginning of the century had turned the church's fortunes around, even managing to burn the mortgage. A fervent advocate of Church Union, he led a dissenting faction that held services at the now empty Cecil Street Church of Christ nearby, and he would be damned if the money from the sale of his church ended up supporting, as he put it, the dissenting Presbyterians. The prospect that Western Congregational would be purchased by Jews caused further disquiet. As a *Globe* editorialist put it:

"St James' with its endowment may soon be the only Protestant church below Queen Street. There is talk of even St Andrew's moving north."[13] In the event, Nelles won out, while Pedley's group was forced to occupy the former College Street Baptist.[14]

Disruption within congregations also resulted from a major split within Baptist ranks. In 1928, T.T. Shields, pastor of the Jarvis Street church, was expelled from the Baptist Convention of Quebec and Ontario and formed a fundamentalist group later known as Fellowship Baptists. Four of the fourteen West End congregations followed Shields: Dovercourt Road, High Park, Annette Street, and Runnymede Road. A fifth congregation calling itself Grace and later Central occupied a building on Ossington Avenue just south of Hallam.

It was in the West End that architects of non-British origin produced the greatest number of places of worship. Beth Jacob, on Henry Street at Cecil, was the work of Benjamin Brown. Born in Lithuania and educated at the University of Toronto, where he obtained his degree in 1913, he was one of the first Jews to practise successfully in the city.[15] Rodfei Sholom Anshe Kiev (commonly known as the Kiever), on Denison Square in Kensington Market, was designed by Romanian-born Benjamin Swartz.[16] A compatriot of his, Harold Kaplan,[17] and partner Abraham Sprachman, born in Honchariv, Bibrka County, eastern Galicia, conceived plans for Anshei Minsk, inaugurated on the site of the previous synagogue on St Andrew Street, also in Kensington Market. Kaplan and Sprachman were the architects as well of the imposing Shaarei Shomayim (Gates of Heaven) on St Clair Avenue near Winona. These men are, however, best remembered for their commercial ventures, such as the cinemas they designed.

Also in the West End, just north of Bloor Street at Dundas West, was a short-lived French Canadian parish named Sainte-Jeanne-D'Arc, built by a Quebec-born architect. An Ottawa-based firm headed by a native German was chosen for the new St John Evangelical Lutheran on Concord Avenue just south of Bloor; it replaced an older, smaller structure a few blocks away. First Hungarian Presbyterian Church on McCaul Avenue north of Baldwin was the work of its pastor, who never completed his architecture degree at Temple University, opting instead for the ministry. St Cyril and Methodius Slovak Catholic Church on Robinson Avenue at Claremont was designed by an architect evidently of German descent who was responsible as well for the harmonious St Wolodymyr Ukrainian Orthodox on Bathurst Street north of Dundas (although Yuriy Kodak, a Hamilton-based architect of Ukrainian Orthodox churches in North America, is also connected with the building).[18] A South Slav was selected to design Our Lady Help of Christians

4.1 Beth Jacob Synagogue
One of the few West End places of worship actually to have been built as a synagogue, it housed Beth Jacob, erected in 1922 by Benjamin Brown, the city's first Jewish architect. It was the premier synagogue for Polish Jews, who formed Toronto's largest Jewish contingent. In 1966 it became the Church of the Holy Trinity, the second Russian Orthodox parish, serving postwar displaced persons who rejected the other parish as too assimilated and too well-disposed to ecumenism. (Gabriele Scardellato)

Table 4.2. Architects of West End places of worship, 1920–1960

Architects	Year	Place of Worship
A.J. Barclay	1925	High Park Baptist
Benjamin Brown	1922	Beth Jacob
J. Francis & Francis Bruce Brown	1925	Runnymede Baptist
	1926	High Park Presbyterian
	1937	St Olave Anglican
	1950	Farmer Memorial Baptist
	1950	Runnymede Presbyterian
Murray Brown	1928	Third church Christian Science
W.C.V. Chadwick	1922	Christie Street Tabernacle
James Michael Cowan	1936	Our Lady of the Angels
Peter Dimitroff	1954	Our Lady Help of Christians
Gordon & Helliwell	1923	Christ Ch. Reformed Episcopal
James Haffa	1941	Sts Cyril & Methodius
	1947	St Wolodymyr
Arthur Holmes	1920	St Anthony
	1926	Holy Rosary
	1927	St Thomas Aquinas
James Patrick Hynes	1925	St Peter Catholic
John MacNee Jeffrey	1922	Hillcrest Church of Christ
Harold Kaplan & Abraham Sprachman	1930	Anshei Minsk
	1946	Shaarei Shomayim
Arthur Laurin	1920	Ste-Jeanne-D'Arc
John Mah	1960	Chinese Presbyterian
R.B. McGiffin	1927	Runnymeded United
William John Miller	1923	St Paul's Runnymede
George & Moorhouse	1956	Trinity College chapel
George, Moorhouse & King	1928	Erskine United
	1931	Community of Christ
Frederick Noad	1937	Wychwood Presbyterian
Noffke, Morin and Sylvester	1929	St John Evangelical Lutheran
Andrew Sharp & Herbert Horner	1922	Alhambra Presbyterian/United
Charles Steinmetz	1938	First Hungarian Presbyterian
Benjamin Swartz	1926	Rodfei Sholom Anshe Kiev
Wickson & Gregg	1924	St Clair Avenue Methodist
George Yamazaki and Roy Matsui	1955	Toronto Buddhist church

Slovenian Catholic on Manning Street north of Harbord, while two Japanese Canadian architects were awarded the contract for the Toronto Buddhist Church on Bathurst Street north of Barton.

For many of the older architects, the 1920s marked the sunset of their career (see table 4.2). Arthur Holmes still managed to design three West

End Catholic churches. Gordon and Helliwell, and Wickson and Gregg, each produced plans for one place of worship. For their part, J. Francis Brown, who had been active since the 1890s, and his son Francis Bruce, chalked up five churches in Bloor West Village.

A Profusion of Synagogues

In the interwar years, the "downtown problem" referred to a much broader area than before, extending south of Bloor Street and east of the CN/GO Transit railway tracks. A publication of College Street Presbyterian described how the surrounding area had been affected by it: "Only a few years ago this same church was in the heart of a quiet residential district but today the factory has made its inroad, carrying in its wake the boarding-house, the over-crowded apartment house, the cinema with its lurid signboards, the poolrooms and the public dance hall."[19] These symptoms of structural change were thought at the time to have caused the flight of the middle classes to the suburbs. The expression "downtown problem" had class connotations but also ethnic ones, in that it encompassed immigrants. In any event, the phenomenon triggered a multitude of church transfers and a smaller number of constructions and demolitions (see table 4.3).

Table 4.3. Changes to West End places of worship before 1960

	Change	Year
Cecil Street Church of Christ	Ostrovtser Synagogue	1921
Crawford Street Methodist	demolished	1921
Western Congregational	Men of England Synagogue	1921
Royce Avenue Gospel hall	Polish Baptist	1922
Robert Street Christian Workers	First Holiness Pentecostal	1923
Adventist Christian	Chiesa apostolica Italian Pentecostal	1923
Christ Church Reformed Episcopal	Western Congregational/United	1923
First Church Christ Scientist	demolished	1925
Grace Evangelical Association	St John the Baptist Lithuanian Catholic	1928
Christian Workers Missionary Tabernacle	Dormition of the Theotokos Ukrainian Catholic	1928
Cowan Avenue Presbyterian	Parkdale Tabernacle	1928
Broadway/Spadina Avenue United	demolished	1929
Dewi Sant Welsh Presbyterian	Christian Standard Tabernacle	1929
Reorganized Church of Latter-Day Saints	African Methodist Episcopal	1929

Table 4.3. (continued)

	Change	Year
African Methodist Episcopal	Church of God and Saints of Christ	1929
St Paul English Evangelical Lutheran	Christ the Saviour Russian Orthodox	1930
Brunswick Ave. Gospel Mission Hall	Shomrai Shabot Synagogue	1930
Clinton Street Methodist	Mogen Abraham Synagogue	1930
St Mark Carlton Anglican	merged with Calvary Anglican	1930
Western United	First Holiness Pentecostal	1931
First Christian (Disciples)	church of Spiritual Love/Grace Spiritualist	1932
First Holiness Pentecostal	St Paul's Italian United	1935
Parkdale Tabernacle	First church of the Nazarene	1935
Adventist Christian	Crawford Street Congregational	1935
Covenant Presbyterian	Avenue Road Tabernacle	1935
Grace Spiritualist	Springdale church	1939
Avenue Road Tabernacle	Avenue Road Church of the Nazarene	1941
Bathurst Street Disciples of Christ	Adath Israel Anshei Romania	1942
St Paul's Italian United	Apostolic Church	1943
Apostolic Church	First Hungarian Baptist	1943
St Philip's Anglican	St Elizabeth of Hungary	1944
Maranatha Hall for the Deaf	closed	1945
Western United	Torah Chaim Synagogue	1947
Christie Street Alliance Tabernacle	United Jewish People's Order	1948
Ukrainian Presbyterian/United Mission	demolished	1950
Central Church of Christ	West End Gospel	1950
Dale Presbyterian	St Nicholas Ukrainian Catholic	1951
Britten Memorial Spiritualist	Veterans' Hall	1951
First Church of the Nazarene	St John Polish National Catholic	1954
First Baptist	building demolished; congregation moves to Huron Street	1954
Brothers of Jacob Synagogue	Beth Israel	1956
Springdale Church	demolished	1956
Adath Israel Anshei Romania	First Ukrainian Pentecostal	1957
Apostolic Church	St George's German Evangelical Lutheran	1957
Wesley United	destroyed by fire	1957
Olivet Church of the New Jerusalem	demolished	1958
Memorial Baptist	Ukrainian Baptist	1959
West End Gospel	St Cyril of Turov Belarusan Autocephalous	1959
Chevra B'nai Israel Synagogue	Nativity of the Mother of God Slovak	1959

4.2a and 4.2b (above and opposite) Before and after
Western Congregational, a Gothic-style building erected in 1888 on Spadina Avenue
near D'Arcy, became the Men of England Synagogue (demolished). After a fire
ravaged the building in 1926, its architectural design was altered to reflect a more

The "downtown problem" in fact had a distinctly Jewish physiog-
nomy. Roughly fifty synagogues sprang up in this period. A handful
of them were housed in new buildings; others were acquired from
Protestant congregations; others still were *stiblach*. In any event,
they were so closely clustered together that twenty of them could
be found in the area between Beverley Street and Spadina Avenue
from below Dundas Street to College Street. An equal number were
located in a larger space west of Spadina to Clinton Street between
Queen and Bloor. Within this perimeter, the legendary Kensington
Market, popularly regarded as quintessentially Jewish, contained
only six synagogues. The new buildings included the ones mentioned above as well as the plain but pleasing Chevra B'nai Israel
(Congregation of the Children of Israel) on Shaw Street below Dundas, the modest First Moldovia Congregation of Romania Tifferes
Israel on Augusta Street in Kensington Market, and the utterly functional Mach Zikei B'nai Israel (Upholders of the Children of Israel)
on Dovercourt Road below Dundas.

Some former churches were substantial structures. Men of England
(also called the Londoner *shul*) had its architectural style altered after

Eastern influence. Despite its name, the synagogue was composed of Russian and Polish Jews who had spent some time in England before finally settling in Canada. A second fire caused by lightning gutted the interior in 1960. The congregation moved to North York, and the building was demolished. (Toronto Reference Library)

a disastrous fire caused considerable damage to it in 1926.[20] The original neo-Gothic design, judged to be too Christian, was changed to Byzantine/Romanesque. The rabbi, Meyer Levy, an early immigrant from Augustów, Suwalki *gubernia*, in Russian Poland, was described as "a one-man welfare board and employment agency," helping newcomers find jobs through personal visits to factories and shops.[21] Just up the street, Tiffereth Israel Bikur Cholim Anshei Ostrovtze (Israel's Glory Visitors of the Sick Men of Ostrovtze) also modified its facade and entrance. The Ultra-Orthodox Torah Chaim (Torah Life) Synagogue and *yeshivath* purchased Western United, built on College Street at Montrose in 1912. Other congregations moved into more modest buildings.

Many synagogues were founded by *landsleit*; many grew out of *landsmanshaftn* (see table 4.4). At least nineteen synagogues explicitly incorporated a hometown or country affiliation in their name.[22] More than half of these referred to towns within a 60 kilometre radius in the Kielce and Radom *gubernias* of Russian Poland. In Toronto, seven of these buildings were within three blocks of one another and a stone's throw from the Polish flagship, Beth Jacob.

4.3 Koil Yankov Anshei Emes Synagogue
This typical *stiblach*, that is, a synagogue housed in an apartment, was
established in 1927 on Brunswick Avenue just above College. It survived as
an intimate place of worship until recently. (Gabriele Scardellato)

Table 4.4. Synagogues named after hometowns in Kielce and Radom Gubernias, Russian Empire

	Location	Town of Origin
Bikes Cholim Anshei Kielce	Dundas/Huron	Kielce
Tiffereth Israel Bikur Cholim Anshei Ostrovtze	Cecil/Spadina	Ostrowiec
Linas Hatzedek Anshei Drildz	Huron/Baldwin	Dar Ilza
Stashever	Dundas/Beverley	Stashów
Anshei Shidlov	D'Arcy/Spadina	Szydłów
Chevra Ezras Israel Anshei Apt	Beverley/Cecil	Opatów
Beth Radom	Beverley/Cecil	Radom
Holy Fellowship of the Company of the Community of Israel of the Men of Lagov	Euclid/College	Łagóv
Anshei Chmelnik	Huron/Dundas	Chmielnik
Chevra B'nai Yankov Anshei Beizetchin	D'Arcy/Huron	Bodzentyn
Knesses Israel Anshei Slipia	Oxford/Augusta	Nowa Słupia

An eighth, Chevra B'nai Moshe (Congregation of the Children of Moses), on D'Arcy Street at Beverley, is said to have been the creation of *landsleit* from Iwaniska, a town some 50 kilometres southeast of Kielce.[23] These findings confirm the importance historians of immigration give to hometown networks, not only in settlement but in the successful insertion of newcomers into the receiving society.

Most synagogues were *stiblach*, some of which were very much identified with a founding rabbi, as we saw with Torah Emeth in chapter 2. Moses (Morris) Langner, who settled in Toronto in 1921 from Stratyn, Berezhany County, Galicia (hence his title "Strettiner rebbe"), founded Chevra Mishnayes (Congregation of the Mishna) on Cecil Street near Huron. He was the descendant of a long line of rabbis stretching back to the very foundation of Chassidism, an eighteenth-century movement of eastern Galician origin characterized by mysticism, joy, and the assurance that God's immanent presence infused meaning in daily prayer, study, and good works performed by individuals. (There are remarkable parallels here with the birth of Methodism in eighteenth-century England.) Within this tradition, spiritual leaders, who formed veritable dynasties, were venerated as powerful intermediaries between God and the faithful. Langner joined followers established in the city at the beginning of the century. At forty-four years of age, he

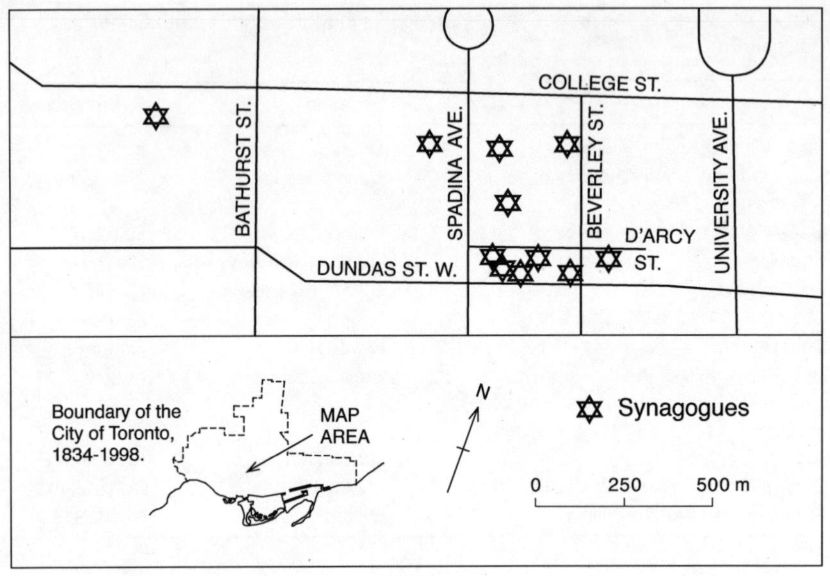

Map 4.2

was accompanied by his family, which included four sons, all of whom became rabbis:[24] Shlomo served at the Kiever, Shaarei Tzedec (Gates of Justice) on Markham Street and Ulster, and First Narayever on Huron Street near Dundas (incidentally, Naraiv was about 10 kilometres from Langner's hometown); Mordechai (Marcus) was rabbi at Knesseth Israel, Shomrai Shabot Anshei Oistreich Minhag Sfard (Guardians of the Sabbath Men of Austria Using the Sephardic Prayer Book), and Beth Mordche (House of Mordechai) on College Street and Manning; Isaac succeeded his father at Chevra Mishnayes; Abraham was not associated with any particular synagogue. Another descendant of Chassidic rabbis, Zvi Yehuda Kelman, came to Toronto in 1928. He had a long association with B'nai Israel Husyatiner Kloiz (Children of Israel of the Husiatyn Cloister), at first situated on Ulster Street at Borden and later one block east of there on Brunswick Avenue. The synagogue's name refers to Husiatyn, a town not far from where Kelman was born.[25]

Besides origins, synagogues could express other Eastern European realities. Agudath Israel Anshei Sforad (Union of Israel of the Men of the Sephardic Prayer Book)[26] on Palmerston Avenue just below Dundas was part of a religious response to the Tenth World Zionist Congress held in Katowice, German Poland, in 1912. Embracing a secular vision of Zionism inspired by left-wing or liberal ideologies, the congress rejected calls for the granting of financial backing to religious schools. As a movement, Agudath Israel opposed this decision, as well as the very idea of a Jewish state, espousing the traditional notion that Israel was wherever Jews happened to be – hence the insistence on support for Orthodox religious institutions. In time it became a political party represented in the Sejm (Polish Parliament). By contrast, Torah V'avodah (Study of the Torah and Labour) on Markham Street at Ulster was the expression of Poale Mizrachi, the labour wing of a Zionist current that placed religion at the core of a future Jewish state. In Palestine it became a political party, but its roots were in Poland, where it was also influenced by progressive ideologies such as Marxism.[27] Nachman Shemen served as its rabbi on a volunteer basis. Born in 1912 near Chodel, Lublin *gubernia*, Russian Poland, he was a close associate of Yehuda Leib Graubart, regarded as the leader of Polish Jews in Toronto.[28]

Synagogues also appeared outside the area of dense Jewish settlement. The beginnings of Chevra B'nai Israel date back to the First World War. Two houses bought on the edge of Trinity Bellwoods Park on Shaw Street were converted into a place of worship and a Talmud Torah. The members who requested a provincial charter were clearly better off; they included a furrier, two merchants, a real estate agent, and a teacher at the synagogue. The houses were later demolished and replaced by a solid brick building.[29] The congregation never hired a full-time rabbi, although they sometimes called on Joseph Weinreb of Shomrai Shabot. A split developed within this congregation just after the First World War. Dissidents calling themselves Machzikei B'nai Israel (or Independent Chevra B'nai Israel) built a hall-like, structure of plain brick on Dovercourt Road. A third congregation, Bais Yahuda (House of Yehuda), was founded by a manufacturer, two Bloor Street businessmen, and two "gentlemen."[30] This congregation was at first located on Ossington Avenue; it later moved to Sovereign Hall on Dovercourt Road and Northumberland.

Farther north, along St Clair Avenue, Jewish shopkeepers began to appear after a streetcar service was inaugurated in 1915. By 1951, one-third of businesses on this thoroughfare were Jewish-owned.[31] Brothers of Jacob Synagogue was opened on Mackay Avenue in the home of Louis Rasky, a grocery store owner and *shochet* (ritual butcher), provoking the short-lived ire of neighbours on this residential street. A large delegation went to City Hall, where the local alderman, named Mac-Gregor, expressed their concerns. Using rather faulty logic, this politician claimed that there was no need for a synagogue in the area because it was solidly English, Irish, or Scots.[32] When the building required urgent repair, Rasky persuaded a group of young men to take it over and undertake the work. As a result of their improvements, the congregation soon began to expand. Wanting at this point to take charge again, Rasky provoked a split. His opponents left to found what would become Shaarei Shomayim. Although a property on St Clair Avenue was soon purchased, depression and war left the congregation bitterly divided. The building was formally opened in 1949 in the presence of the Lieutenant-Governor, the Premier of Ontario, Judge Sam Factor, MP David Croll, the Mayor of Toronto, and President Sidney Smith of the University of Toronto. In 1975, Brothers of Jacob amalgamated with it, putting an end to a long separation.[33]

Neighbourhoods with a strong Jewish presence were also sites of Christian missions to the Jews. On Major Street just south of Harbord, a prayer house was opened by Henry Bregman, an English convert to Christianity who, after arriving in Toronto, was for a time associated with the Presbyterians' Christian Synagogue. Sponsored by the Christian and Missionary Alliance, the mission, called Beth Dor'she Emeth (House of the Seekers after Truth), had signage in Yiddish, while Bregman wore a *kippah*. The evangelist did not wait for people to drop in, but went out into the highways and byways to win converts. This ex-rabbi preached and sang Gospel hymns in Yiddish at the corner of Dundas and Spadina, in the very heart of the Jewish district, receiving police protection for good measure.[34] His son Frederick continued this work into the 1930s and 1940s. Meanwhile, the Toronto Jewish Mission, originally headed by Henry Singer, acquired a new lease on life when the preacher briefly returned to Toronto after a prolonged absence. On his initiative a storefront was opened at Dundas and Augusta, called Peniel Hall after the biblical site where Jacob met God, and later at College and Delaware. In the early 1960s, its operations were transferred to Downsview. Baptists too established a mission, this one in a modest cottage on Maria Street in the Junction just down the street from Knesseth Israel. For several years previous, A.A. Holzer, another convert to Christianity, had been in charge of Baptist evangelization to the Jews.[35]

Perhaps the best-known convert was Morris Zeidman. Born in Częstochowa, this young man began to frequent the Christian Synagogue after arriving in Toronto unaccompanied. After completing his studies at Knox College, he became a Presbyterian minister and was soon made director of the Christian Synagogue, renamed the Scott Institute. He would occupy that position until his death in 1964. In 1948, the institute, which in the meantime had become non-denominational after severing its affiliation with the Presbyterian Church, acquired two attached houses on Spadina Avenue above College. The Scott Mission, as it was popularly known, promoted an essentially fundamentalist Protestant vision: Zeidman in fact felt a certain affinity with Pentecostalism. At the same time, he displayed a strong social commitment, providing emergency accommodation for immigrant families after the war, as well as distributing food and clothes to the needy.[36]

The 1950s saw the start of a long process of synagogue closings that resulted in amalgamations and relocations uptown. With the coming of postwar prosperity and the easing of housing restrictions, Jews in large numbers left their crowded neighbourhoods along the Bathurst Street corridor for neighbourhoods north of Eglinton Avenue where larger single-family dwellings abounded. Twelve synagogues shut down during this decade, including the two biggest ones, Goel Tzedec and Chevra Tehillim, which merged to form Beth Tzedec. After this, the trend accelerated. Among the seven that quickly followed suit were Adath Israel Anshei Romania (1958), Chevra B'nai Israel (1959), and Anshei Kielce (1959). Not even the institutions founded by the Langners survived. Some time after the untimely death of Mordechai in 1948, Beth Mordche closed its doors. As for the trademark Chevra Mishnayes, it ceased operations a few years later after Moses died.

The Downtown Tower of Babel

Although relatively few in number, other immigrant groups left their mark on the West End. The hardships of the Depression made it difficult for them to organize their collective religious existence and to attract and maintain clergy. On the whole, their priests and ministers were young and inexperienced. Many were themselves recent immigrants facing very high expectations from congregants, who wanted help integrating into Canadian life. Women, whether as deaconesses or members of religious orders, often played key roles in bringing these groups together.

Lithuanians, Hungarians, and Slovaks

The archdiocese acquired Grace Church Evangelical Association for Lithuanian immigrants, then numbering several hundred. The parish had its origins in a mutual aid society, whose members were, however, divided over its secular character. The religious faction founded its own association named after St John the Baptist and held meetings at the nearby churches of St Agnes and St Francis. Meanwhile a Lithuanian priest living in the United States visited the community every Easter. The new parish took its name from the mutual aid society's patron saint. During the Depression, volunteers dug a basement where Lithuanian language and culture classes were held for the immigrants' children. Beset by severe financial difficulties, which possibly resulted in a rapid turnover of priests, the parish was entrusted to an English-speaking pastor in a concerted effort to reduce its debt. At the same time, the archdiocese allowed the more numerous Hungarians to share the building. These unpopular arrangements lasted several years.[37]

Religious services for the 1,000-strong Hungarian Catholics began when a young seminarian recommended to the archbishop by the Primate of Hungary arrived in Toronto. A report at the time stressed the need to organize social activities for Hungarians because "in Toronto the[se] people live very much scattered."[38] The seminarian therefore rented a series of sites serving simultaneously as a place of worship, a community centre, and temporary lodgings for needy immigrants. The young man also visited local factories to try to find work for his charges. After he left, parishioners found it hard to find a replacement. A change of fortune occurred with the arrival of two nuns. Members of the Sisters of Social Service, a Hungarian order originally sent to Canada to work among compatriots in Saskatchewan, they proved crucial to community-building efforts, visiting families, running a Hungarian-language school, and helping organize associational life. A member of the order succeeded in raising $10,000 from Hungarians in North America; together with a matching grant from the archdiocese, this made it possible to acquire St Phillip's Anglican. Renamed St Elizabeth of Hungary, the church was blessed by Archbishop James McGuigan (1934–74).[39]

Services for Calvinists meanwhile began at the St Andrew's Institute. A student from the Princeton Theological Seminary was appointed pastor of a congregation totalling 140 in 1932. Soon dismissed because of congregants' exasperation at his inability to find them jobs or organize community activities, he was replaced by Károly Steinmetz, an insurance salesman who had come to Toronto from the United States. Steinmetz married Bernice Bernath, a part-time deaconess who brought new vigour to the congregation by organizing the Sunday school, Women's Association, and the Young People's Society. A church choir was also formed.[40] The minister and his wife worked tirelessly, "seeking the newcomers, interpreting, transcribing letters and documents, making addresses in our respective Canadian Churches."[41] A cottage was purchased on McCaul Street, and when Steinmetz was finally ordained, congregational revenues trebled. The new church, of which he was the draftsman, foreman, and chief carpenter as well as architect, was inaugurated in 1939. Jock Inkster, the pastor at Knox who had led the forces against Church Union, turned the first sod; John Wanless laid the cornerstone. The highlight for this congregation was the visit by Austrian Archdukes Otto and Felix Habsburg during the war.[42]

A Baptist congregation got started in earnest in the wake of the Congress of the Baptist World Alliance, held in Toronto in 1928. A Hungarian-language service at College Street Baptist attended by delegates from Hungary and the United States resulted in a mission being entrusted to a student at the Baptist Seminary in New Jersey. Hired on a part-time basis so that he could complete his studies at McMaster University, Gyorgy Balla preached at street corners and published a Hungarian-language newspaper called *Light*, subsidized by the Home Mission Board. The congregation, totalling less than one hundred, bought a small church on Robert Street, half the amount coming from members and the other half from the American Hungarian Baptist churches. A loan from the Church Edifice Board covered the cost of repairs and furniture. The Hungarian Baptist Silver Band from Buffalo played at the opening in 1943.[43]

Like their Hungarian counterparts, many Slovaks were young sojourners confronting the rigours of the Depression. They founded a mutual aid society called the First Slovak Catholic Union with branches all over North America, as well as a Sokol gymnastic group. Worship took place at St Stanislaus Polish Catholic. With the arrival of Michael Shuba, a Slovak priest from Ohio, a regular congregation took shape.[44] St Paul's Slovak Lutheran parish followed pretty well the same pattern, sharing space with a German-speaking congregation at the YMCA building that been Ascension Anglican.[45]

Germans, Russians, and Maltese

The multiethnic Redemptorist Order at St Patrick's took charge of the 7,000-strong German-speaking Catholics in 1929, one-third of whom came from Germany, and another third from Czechoslovakia and Austria. The rest were Danube Swabians from the ethnically varied Banat region now divided between Romania, Serbia, and Hungary. Their pastor was Daniel Ehman, a Redemptorist born in Saskatchewan and trained in New York. Although worship began in the basement library, the congregation soon moved upstairs.[46] Besides a fledgling Baptist group organized in 1930 and based at the College Street church, Germans formed a New Apostolic congregation and erected a place of worship on Dupont Street near Albany. New Apostolics (*Neuapostolische Kirche*) traced their origins to the schism of 1863 within the German branch of the Catholic Apostolic movement, one of the many expressions of nineteenth-century millennialism. Catholic Apostolics in fact were already present in nineteenth-century Toronto, their most famous member being George Ryerson, eldest brother of Egerton.[47] Although retaining the Catholic Apostolics' complex hierarchical ecclesiastical structure, New Apostolics had a less elaborate liturgy.

The Russians who had lost their church in the Junction found strength when a few refugee families arrived after the war. A house on Clarence Square was purchased in 1923 and converted into a church thanks to the free labour of parishioners. The mastermind behind the purchase was apparently Catherine de Hueck, who solicited donations for this purpose from businessmen. A member of the minor Russian nobility who had fled the Revolution, she converted to Eastern Rite Catholicism in London before reaching Toronto with her philandering husband.[48] The building's upper floors had rooms to accommodate refugees and the resident priest's family. Language, religion, and culture classes, organized by the priest's wife, were held here for the children of immigrants. When the building burned down, the congregation acquired St Paul's English-language Lutheran Church on Glen Morris. Christ the Saviour Russian Orthodox Cathedral was thus consecrated by Archbishop Platon of New York in 1930. To help pay off the mortgage, the choir, led by Nina de Gedeonoff, a former singer with the Russian Opera, performed at various local Anglican churches. In fact, there developed a close and cordial relationship between the Anglican Church and the congregation, which included in its ranks Count Pavel Nikolayevich Ignatiev, who for a short time had been education minister in the wartime government of

4.4 Christ the Saviour Russian Orthodox
Following a merger, the English-speaking congregants of St Paul's Evangelical Lutheran sold their church to Russian speakers in 1930. The new occupants included Count P.N. Ignatieff, briefly a minister of education in the czarist regime in Russia, and Grand Duchess Olga, sister of Nicholas II, after she settled in Canada in 1948. The building was vacated in 1966 when Christ the Saviour acquired the former St Cyprian Anglican. The building then ceased to be place of worship and became a theatre of the University of Toronto. (Gabriele Scardellato)

Czar Nicholas II, as well as the czar's own sister, Grand Duchess Olga, who joined at the end of the Second World War.[49] During the Depression a Russian–Ukrainian Pentecostal congregation took shape, buying a garage at the corner of Dovercourt Road and Queen and turning it into a place of worship under the name Slavic Pentecostal.[50]

Immigrants from the Mediterranean island of Malta began arriving in Toronto just before the First World War. It is estimated that in 1917 there were four hundred of them settled in the downtown and the Junction. Like other newcomers, they at first had to content themselves with the occasional visits of a Maltese priest, usually at Easter. After the war they created the Maltese Society of Toronto, which lobbied hard for a pastor and a separate parish. Archbishop McNeil responded to their request by appointing an Augustinian priest, Alphonse Cauchi, to that charge in 1929. Although the community was divided over the site of their church, those favouring the Junction won out because of the lower cost of land there. During the Depression, parishioners contributed their labour to erect a place of worship dedicated to St Paul, the apostle who had sojourned on the island before ending his days in Rome.[51]

Already Established Groups: Italians, Poles, and Ukrainians

Older ethno-linguistic parishes achieved a measure of stability in the interwar period. This was because Catholic ones were taken over by religious orders of priests, a trend followed in later years as well. Franciscans from New York took charge of Our Lady of the Angels from a somewhat paranoid northern Italian pastor who had a low opinion of his parishioners of peasant origin. They also accepted St Agnes parish after the faithful accused the previous pastor of misappropriating funds.[52] Such conflicts led some parishioners to become Protestant. The very act of immigrating sometimes loosened attachment to the ancestral religion. Pentecostalism proved to be attractive because the congregation could exercise control over the clergy and was not answerable to a higher ecclesiastical authority, such as a bishop or a presbytery. An Italian Pentecostal congregation was formed in 1921, taking over the Adventist church in Little Italy. Like some fellow members, the presiding elder, Luigi Ippolito, had come in contact with Pentecostalism in Hamilton as a result of the revivals preached by evangelist P.W. Philpott. However, a schism soon divided the nascent group. Originating in Chicago, the split revolved around the interpretation of a passage in the Acts of the Apostles concerning the eating of blood products. Leading the rigorist camp, Ippolito left the College Street church, taking his followers with him. In time, however, the rift was healed. Ippolito joined his rival, Ferdinando Zaffuto, as co-pastor of a reunited congregation. The following year an overarching body, called the Christian Church of Canada, was formed by Italian Pentecostals in Canada. This association was separate both from its American counterpart and from the Pentecostal Assemblies of God, the largest Canadian organization of this kind, created in 1941.[53]

As at St Agnes, the discord at the Polish parish was probably fuelled by class differences. The parishioners, largely of peasant background, criticized Jozef Dekowski, an urbane, multilingual, and decorated former army colonel, for disdaining his role as an ethnic pastor. He allegedly refused to attend to their immediate material needs. In fact, associational life in the parish all but died out under his charge. The crisis deepened when Dekowski, who was also accused of embezzling parish funds, refused to administer the sacraments to his critics. A schism then rocked the parish, his opponents leaving to join the Polish National Catholic Church (PNCC), a body formed in United States at the end of the nineteenth century by ethnically conscious Polish immigrants in bitter conflict with the Irish American hierarchy. The PNCC affiliated itself with the Old Catholic Church, a body rejecting the doctrine of papal infallibility and headquartered in the Dutch city of Utrecht. Followers retained the Catholic liturgy and ecclesiastical structure, although mass was said in Polish. Worship in Toronto initially took place at St Matthias Anglican. A building was then purchased on Queen Street just opposite the Polish National Hall to house the newly erected parish of St John. In 1952 the congregation moved to the old Cowan Avenue church in Parkdale, which was elevated to the status of cathedral with its own bishop.[54] The schism was what finally prompted James McGuigan to dismiss Dekowski and replace him with Oblates.[55] Again as at St Agnes, the solution favoured by the archdiocese was to replace a troublesome secular priest with a religious order.

Ukrainian Catholics living downtown acquired the Missionary Tabernacle on Bathurst Street. The church later became the second Ukrainian parish dedicated to the Dormition of the Theotokos (Assumption of the Blessed Virgin Mary). That same year a Ukrainian order of teaching nuns, the Sisters Servants of Mary Immaculate, arrived from the prairies and began making a significant contribution to parish life.[56] Orthodox faithful were brought together by John Humeniuk, the first lawyer of Ukrainian origin to practise in Toronto. The liturgy was initially held at St John the Evangelist Anglican. Numerically weak (numbering only about five hundred), they were finally able to buy the Odd Fellows Temple on Bathurst Street at Nassau, site of their future church, where the liturgy began to be celebrated on a regular basis.[57]

The Ukrainian Presbyterian congregation, headed by Pavlo Krat, adhered to the United Church in 1925. But Presbyterians refused to allow the new denomination to monopolize outreach to Ukrainians and recruited Michael Fesenko, a student at the Princeton Divinity School. Fesenko was also courted by Krat, although the latter could not promise a secure position that would allow him to pursue his studies.[58] Ordained a Presbyterian minister, Fesenko began open-air preaching on Queen Street, assisted by his future wife, Julia Maystrowych, a graduate of the Missionary and Deaconess Training Home (now Ewart College) in Winnipeg. Throughout the 1930s, worship was conducted in storefronts, where Fesenko performed weddings and funerals free of charge as a means of attracting new members. Krat, whose congregation was now less numerous, accused his competitor of harbouring communists, a charge apparently investigated and rejected by the Presbyterian Church. The Home Mission Board and the Women's Missionary Society finally advanced funds for a small plain brick place of worship, to be built on Claremont Street at Robinson.[59]

Experiments in Canadianization

The United Church and Convention Baptists each embarked in these years on an original experiment in immigrant outreach: different ethnicities would share the same church in the expectation that cohabitation would foster Canadianization. Queen Street West Methodist and Beverley Street Baptist were designated as centres of these missionary efforts. A report commissioned by the United Church revealed that the area south of Dundas Street between University and Bathurst was home to 10,000 immigrants speaking thirty different languages. Queen Street was described as a great non-Anglo-Saxon thoroughfare, especially around Spadina Avenue.[60] To reach out to these people, old Queen Street Methodist was renovated to house three distinct chapels, the first two having a seating capacity of three hundred and the third, forty. Each had a separate front entrance and was to be used by a different group on Sunday mornings, afternoons, and evenings. The United Church's strategy assumed that cohabitation would lead to collaboration, interaction, and integration based on ideals of "Christian citizenship." This objective was symbolized by a yearly two-day International Fair held at the church from 1929 until 1957, where European and Asian products "unknown to Canadians" were sold. To further this goal, a compendium of European and other favourite folk songs, titled *All Nations Song Book*, was published with a cover designed by a Hungarian-born artist, Nicholas Hornyansky. As well, sports competitions were organized during the war between teams of enemy backgrounds. For example, Chinese confronted Japanese in a game of basketball. The United Church expected that the immigrant congregations it created and fostered would wither away after the first generation because children would be socialized in English-language Sunday schools, further hastening integration into regular churches.

Inaugurated in April 1928, the Church of All Nations initially encompassed Dutch, Scandinavian, Hungarian, and Finnish groups (the latter being the original Finnish Presbyterian Mission).[61] These congregations tended to be unstable, because they were too small, or too dependent on the person of their pastor, or too independent-minded when it came to church policy on integration. The Dutch were under the care of J.G. Perold, a South African lecturer in economics at the University of Toronto, who founded the first Protestant church-based credit union in Canada. Shortly after his death in 1944, the congregation disbanded. The Hungarians had Ambrosius Czakó, a former Dominican priest and published philosopher, who later returned to his faith of origin, becoming a Jesuit and a professor at St Mary's University in Halifax. By the end of the war, that congregation was practically moribund, but it was revived again thanks to postwar refugees. The Finns, whom church officials seemed to regard as clannish, insisted that their Sunday school be run in their native tongue. When told that this ran against church policy, most of them placed their children in Lutheran schools. The Ukrainian congregation, although it was formally part of the Church of All Nations, continued to meet separately at their old site on Dupont Avenue under a long-serving deaconess and a succession of ministers until its demise in 1953.

Two new congregations were added in the 1940s. The Czechoslovak one proved difficult to sustain. The Czechs were better off than most newcomers, some of them even founding successful wartime industries, and they were dispersed throughout the city. The Japanese congregation was composed of people who had been forcibly removed from their West Coast homes during the war and relocated to Toronto. As for immigrants who were too small in numbers to form viable congregations, they were invited to the "international service" held every Sunday evening.[62] The most enduring groups at the church proved to be the Hungarians, the Finns, and the Japanese. The latter moved out in 1950.

Baptists too were actively engaged in outreach to newcomers. While the Home Mission Board expressed an unambiguous preference in the

1920s for British immigrants, it accepted the challenge of turning others into good Canadian citizens, "civilizing" them through the Gospel.[63] Also, it was argued that if these immigrants had, for some reason, to return to their country of origin, they could be effective ambassadors of the new religious, moral, and political values acquired in Canada. So the board inaugurated separate language missions to Finns, Chinese, Germans, Czechs, Swedes, Poles, and Estonians. Like the United Church, Baptists insisted that children of immigrants always be addressed in English and ministered to as much as possible in that language.[64] Although these proselytizing efforts produced few converts and tiny congregations, the board considered this work important "from the standpoint of the New Canadians themselves, our Country, and the Kingdom of God."

Always attentive to the costs of evangelization, however, the Home Mission Board pursued policies of retrenchment and consolidation in the later 1920s, closing feeder stations and merging missions.[65] Part-time or student ministers were hired at salaries that were a fraction of those paid to regular pastors. Even then, these wages were cut in an attempt to get congregations to assume more of the operating expenses. In 1937, consideration was even given to moving immigrant outreach out of the Beverley Street church, which was thought to be too close to the Church of All Nations, and to cooperating with the United Church in downtown evangelization; ultimately, though, there was found to be little overlap in the groups being targeted. Even so, questions continued to be asked about how "to further Anglicize our New Canadian missions" and whether these missions were not overstaffed. Tensions developed between, on the one hand, English-speaking congregations that believed precious resources were being wasted on a futile effort, and, on the other, immigrant ones that viewed themselves as second-class citizens or at least objects of misunderstanding and indifference. At the insistence of the Women's Baptist Home Mission Board, to oversee relations between the two types of congregations, a board was created on which immigrants were represented.

In any event, a Finnish Baptist church was formally recognized in 1926 but was soon "plagued by the inroads of Pentecostalism."[66] Led by two women, evangelist Liida Myyra and her assistant Mrs Anton Salo, the Pentecostals first met on the second floor of the former St Margaret Anglican Church. In 1937, two houses were purchased on Beverley Street north of Queen and transformed into a church seating more than

150 congregants. Truck driver Matti Hamalainen, who had been converted in Toronto by a friend, the pastor of a Free Church in Finland, took over from Myyra. Despite this setback, the Baptist Convention of Quebec and Ontario formally recognized Russian, Czechoslovak, and Hungarian congregations in the early 1940s. By that time, the first group had welcomed a new minister as well as members from Saskatchewan, who had come to take wartime jobs in Toronto.[67] Similarly, a number of Czech families who had settled in the city from Manitoba were able to form a congregation when a compatriot from Winnipeg, businessman and publisher Frank Dojacek, guaranteed the pastor's salary.[68] As for the Poles, two missions were set up, the first operating out of the Memorial Institute downtown and the second out of the vacant Royce Avenue Gospel Hall in the Junction. Although the two groups merged in 1944, separate worship was maintained. The Estonians started their congregation during the war, and their numbers increased thanks to the DP migration after the war.

Conjunctural Changes

The Depression of the 1930s

The interwar years in Canada were marked by the government's inability to shelter workers and their families from unemployment and destitution; by its laissez-faire stance on non-British immigrants, who were basically left on their own in times of crisis, forced to rely on the meagre resources of their families and ethnic communities; and by the activism of the Communist Party in putting forward concrete solutions to meet the needs of those in distress. This was a time of ideological polarization. Communism was especially associated in the public mind with immigrants and foreigners. Police Chief Dennis Draper employed strong-arm tactics to intimidate protesters, who were regarded as communist agitators, and to break up demonstrations by unionists, strikers, the unemployed, and the homeless. He used spies to monitor public meetings and was the driving force behind a municipal by-law that made it illegal to hold such gatherings in languages other than English. West End congregations, especially immigrant ones, were allies in this war on communism, which was regarded as a dangerous competitor of religion. The Baptist Board of Home Missions observed that proselytizing work among New Canadians had become increasingly difficult because of the rapid spread of communism, which was accompanied by atheism and scepticism and which posed a grave threat to home, church, and nation.[69] In this regard, the motto of the Church of All Nations was highly revealing: "For a worthy Canada and a truly Christian Internationale" – an allusion to the socialist anthem "The Internationale" composed by Eugène Pottier after the Paris Commune of 1871.

In this context, a number of churches replicated the facilities provided to the unemployed and the destitute by communist organizations. Since transience and homelessness were major problems for those thrown out of work, the Church of All Nations created a postal box service for congregants that was still in operation towards the end of the war. The church gymnasium afforded shelter for eighty homeless men, while 250 warm meals were distributed there daily. At Beverley Street Baptist, soup kitchen tickets were given out at services, thus achieving the double objective of helping out the immigrant needy and enticing them to attend worship.[70] An annual report on the Hungarian Presbyterian Church revealed that, although there were at least eight hundred coreligionists in Toronto, "the majority of them are lost to Christian influence because they are carried away with the tide of Communism from their childhood faith to no faith."[71] Ten years later, a summer camp inaugurated in Grimsby was attended by thirty-one mothers and their children. That year's report stated: "We are getting back to our church in ever growing numbers people who were communists, atheists, and decided enemies of the Church. We have a number of such individuals, two of whom now are serving as able and loyal elders."[72] Good works alone, however, seemed not to suffice. Historian Carmela Patrias indicates that a Presbyterian theological student and a Lutheran minister monitored the activities of communists and presumably reported on them to the police.[73]

The Redemptorists of St Patrick considered the Vojvodina Germans who arrived in the late 1920s either as unattached singles or as young couples to be especially prone to communism because they lacked the structured environment that an extended family would have fostered. In 1931 a lay woman provided German instruction to the children of immigrants. That same year the Sisters of Service, an English Canadian order specializing in the care of immigrants (not to be confused with the Hungarian Sisters of Social Service), were brought in to set up a Catholic Settlement House on Dundas Street around the corner from the church. The sisters, later replaced by the multi-ethnic Felician Order of nuns, opened a kindergarten and after-school programs to assist working families, especially working mothers. To counter the influence of the nearby communist reading room, a library was set up with the help of the wife of a mining engineer who had put one together in her home parish of St Peter. Sewing and cooking classes were offered to young women. A hall hosted theatrical works, musical performances, and dances. During the war, the parish purchased a farm in Richmond Hill, which was soon equipped with a lodge, swimming pool, dance hall, tennis court, and baseball diamond in order to prevent young people in particular from being "lost to Communist clubs and to intermarriage with non-Catholics."[74]

A similar experiment in the adjacent parish of St Mary proved in the end to be not so successful. The pastor, Campbell James, seemed quite content to manage his flock according to tried and true ways, impassive to the terrible plight of downtown immigrants. Or so Catherine de Hueck thought. She felt the urgency of combating communism through the precepts of Catholic social action, recently reiterated by Pope Pius XI (1922–39) in his encyclical *Quadragesimo Anno* (1931). Multilingual, she felt that she was especially well positioned to confront the arguments of local ideologues in their own language. Inspired by Dorothy Day, an American convert to Catholicism, social activist, and promoter of worker communes, de Hueck instituted Friendship House in a disused meat market on Portland Street, a stone's throw from St Mary's church. She did this without consulting or informing James, but apparently with the tacit support of Archbishop McNeil. Following the Franciscan rule of poverty and complete availability to those in need, de Hueck and her associates provided the services found in other settlement houses. She also visited immigrants in their homes and distributed issues of Day's newspaper *Catholic Worker* to strikers on the picket line. In 1935 she opened a boys' home complete with carpentry shop, artist's studio, and game room, further alienating James, who accused her of replicating existing parish services. When in 1934 James McGuigan became archbishop, he seemed more concerned than his predecessor that de Hueck's unorthodox practices be governed by canon law, which gave primacy to the clergy over the laity and to men over women. He instituted a commission of inquiry composed of three priests, including Stanislaus Puchniak, the Oblate pastor of the nearby Polish parish of St Stanislaus. Following their recommendation, he ordered de Hueck's facilities to be closed down, despite the strong support she received in some clerical circles.[75] As a result, de Hueck left Toronto for New York, where she worked among the African Americans of Harlem.

Attempts to combat communism took different forms. In 1934, leaders of the German Workers Society at St Patrick's instituted Celebration of German Days (*Feier des Deutschen Tages*) in order to stir up nationalist feelings among parishioners. Ehman, the pastor, opposed this initiative, stating that "German is our tongue, not our belief," and inaugurated instead *Katholikentage* (literally Catholics' Days), a lay organized festival of faith first held in Mainz, Germany, in 1848. Meanwhile, in Italian parishes there developed a close relationship between fascist consular authorities and a compliant clergy – most of them Catholic, but some of them Protestant – for whom fascism was synonymous with patriotism. The signing of the Lateran Treaties between Pius XI and Benito Mussolini in 1929, which accorded special status to the Catholic Church in Italy, strengthened this identification. The pastors at St Agnes and Our Lady of the Angels blithely graced patriotic events with their presence and made halls available for fascist festivities, as well as for meetings of fascist-controlled organizations. At the same time, Catholic schools hosted Italian-language classes, which were conceived by Mussolini's government as vehicles for indoctrinating youth.[76] The minister of St Paul's Italian United, for his part, held high office in the fascist-directed Order Sons of Italy and actively solicited funds for the establishment of the Casa d'Italia, a fascist-inspired community centre, today the seat of the Italian consulate in Toronto. Conservative Ukrainians, meanwhile, were heartened when in 1937 Danylo Skoropadsky visited St Josaphat Ukrainian Catholic Church. A leader of monarchist forces, he was the son of Pavlo, who briefly ruled Ukraine towards the end of the First World War following a coup supported by the German army that toppled the socialist administration set in place in the wake of the Russian Revolution.

The Second World War

In places of worship, the Second World War brought to the surface questions of loyalty and solidarity originally confronted in the first conflict twenty-five years earlier. These questions were raised either in purely religious or in ethnic and racial terms. Pacifist congregations were once again put to the test. The Brethren at the Brock Avenue Gospel Hall were split fairly evenly between those who refused to compromise on their antiwar principles and those who accepted non-combatant service.[77] Moved by similar principles, the Russians at Beverley Street Baptist asked the Board of Home Missions to forward their request for military exemption to Ottawa. The board declined to do so, evidently demonstrating a different understanding of the tenets of their faith.[78] At the end of the Phoney War in May 1940, when conscription became a serious option for the government, J.B. Thompson, minister at Dufferin Street Presbyterian, condemned Quebec's opposition to the measure, expressing a view commonly held by fellow clergymen: "Is it fair," he asked rhetorically, "that Protestant boys who volunteer to fight Canada's battle, should leave Roman Catholic boys to take the jobs? It is a shame. It is not British."[79]

Parishes and congregations showed little hesitation in lining up behind the Canadian war effort. In a number of them, women were mobilized to prepare Red Cross packages for soldiers on the front lines or in Britain. The Maltese Canadian Society of Toronto used their church to rally members around campaigns to provide relief to their war-torn island homeland.[80] Meanwhile, Sunday school students wrote letters of encouragement to Canadian troops abroad. At Walmer Road Baptist, a war services committee was struck to keep in touch with enlisted congregants, in response to serious concerns voiced by the Home Mission Board about the moral impact that exposure to drinking, smoking, prostitution, and gambling would have on their boys. In the board's view, the men and women "returning with knowledge of great sins" after the war would need to be the focus of particular attention to ensure that the church became key to their salvation.[81]

For immigrants from Axis countries, the war proved to be a difficult time. Archbishop McGuigan assured the German speakers of St Patrick's of the Church's support, provided they remained loyal. They in turn assumed a low profile, exercising great caution when speaking German in public. Sermons continued to be delivered in that language but were now monitored by the RCMP. Although generally parish life continued, some public activities, such as the annual pilgrimages to the Jesuit Martyrs' shrine at Midland and parish missions, were curtailed. In 1943–4, the pastor deplored the fact that relatively few Germans were attending church on Sundays.[82]

Unlike during the First World War, the Canadian government made a concerted effort to win over non-British immigrants, whom it had largely neglected before then. It helped found the Ukrainian Canadian Committee (UCC), a pan-Canadian umbrella organization excluding Communists, whose task it would be to rally Ukrainians to the war effort. The president of the UCC's Toronto branch was Theodor Humeniuk, a founder of St Wolodymyr Ukrainian Orthodox. He was also a noted Ukrainian nationalist who in 1934 had protested the visit to Toronto of Sholem Schwarzbard, the Jewish revolutionary who had assassinated Ukrainian political and military leader Symon Petlura in Paris in 1926. The Canadian government also subsidized a newly created Italian-language weekly, *La Vittoria*, one of whose editors, Augusto Bersani, a Montreal-based minister, had once led a revival at St Paul's Italian United Church. The controversial anti-fascist clergyman, whom some accused of supplying the RCMP with the names of those to be interned as security risks, came to Toronto expressly to direct the short-lived newspaper.

Among the six hundred Italian Canadian men interned at Camp Petawawa during the war were Settimio Balò, the Franciscan pastor of Our Lady of the Angels, and Libero Sauro, the minister of St Paul's Italian United. Although the latter's confinement turned out to be brief, the United Church decided in 1943 to sell his church on College Street at Lippincott to a Pentecostal group calling itself the Apostolic Church. It is unclear why this decision was taken. Perhaps it was because thirty-four members of the church were then serving in the Canadian armed forces, thus draining the small congregation of its vitality. Be that as it may, the rest were compelled to conduct services in a large room at Western United, farther west along College Street.[83] A dozen parishioners at St Patrick (out of a total of eight hundred Germans interned) were confined in a camp at Gravenhurst, and although Daniel Ehman had opposed expressions of German nationalism in the 1930s, he felt it was his duty to visit them at least once. Towards the end of the war, he also called on German prisoners of war who were being held in a camp at Cooksville, saying mass for them and attending to their religious needs.[84]

Some of the more than 20,000 Japanese Canadians removed by the government from their homes on the west coast following the Japanese attack on Pearl Harbour started life anew in Toronto. Slowly they began to organize religious services. The Japanese group at the Church of All Nations was started by retired missionary Mary Scott and C.J.L. Bates, former president of Kwansei Gakuin University in Tokyo. They were later replaced by Kozaburo Shimizu, who was allowed to visit the small congregation on a number of occasions from the camp at Kaslo in the BC Interior, where he was being detained.[85] Two years later, Japanese Anglicans began to worship at St George the Martyr, later moving to the Church of the Redeemer.[86] Toronto's first Buddhist congregation was established when a Nisei priest, Kenryu Tsuji, visited southwestern

Ontario from the Slocan camp. A small house acquired on Huron Street in the heart of the Jewish district served as place of worship, a Sunday school, and a priest's residence.[87]

The war actually encouraged some inter-faith dialogue. As early as the 1930s, a few ministers had been sensitive to the plight of Jews in Nazi-controlled central Europe. At a rally held at Maple Leaf Gardens to protest *Kristallnacht*, the orgy of violence unleashed against synagogues in Nazi Germany on 9 November 1938, the rector of St Stephen-in the-Fields, J.E. Ward, spoke in the name of the Anglican Primate of Canada. In 1939 during Holy Week – a time when the gospels of Matthew and John especially remind the faithful of the role played by the Jews in the death of Christ – the chaplain of Trinity College, W.J. Gilling, affirmed: "Truly the Jews have little cause to love us Christians. The blood-stained record of Christian cruelty should fill our hearts with shame." As a convert *and* minister, Morris Zeidman considered that he had a double responsibility with regard to Jews: to bring them the Gospel, but also to combat anti-Semitism among Christians. Some clergymen, such as fellow minister Jock Inkster of Knox Presbyterian, nevertheless continued to expound traditional views, maintaining that Jews were guilty of unbelief and the denial of Christ and therefore did not deserve the sympathy of Christians for events such as *Kristallnacht*.

As a result of working together on the Community Chest, a forerunner of the United Way, Gordon Domm, minister of Bathurst Street United, asked Reuben Slonim, a Canadian-born, American-trained rabbi at *Chevra Tehillim*, to speak to his congregation. This was the first time an Orthodox rabbi had preached in a Toronto church. In his address, Slonim contended that the depiction of Judaism found in the New Testament, particularly of the priestly caste as narrowly legalistic, rigid, and superficial, was unreliable. The rabbi would address the congregation on a number of other occasions; however, the invitation was not reciprocated because Slonim believed his synagogue's executive was too hidebound. Still, as a result of these contacts, Domm delivered a sermon at Bathurst Street United in which he denounced as anti-Semitic the opponents of a more liberal refugee policy towards Jews.[88]

After the war, congregations and parishes turned their attention once again to commemoration. Stained glass windows and bronze plaques were common expressions of this need to remember. Among the churches unveiling new windows were St Michael and All Angels

Anglican; Western (Parkdale) Baptist, where nine congregants had been killed out of the 109 who served in the armed forces; Epiphany Anglican, which recorded sixteen deaths out of 240 enlistments, and Wychwood Presbyterian, where six lost their lives out of the 100 serving, notably the minister, Gordon Rintoul, who died of a heart attack while in uniform.[89] Messiah Anglican inaugurated a second chapel as a war memorial in its south transept. A new communion table and a memorial tablet were installed at Ossington Avenue Baptist.[90] *Adath Israel Anshei Romania* dedicated a cornerstone to the congregants who had served. At this synagogue and at Epiphany Anglican, victory dinners were held in their honour, the proceeds of the former event going to aid Romanian Jewish refugees.[91] Latvians who came to Toronto after the war from DP camps set up a Latvian Relief Society to care for disabled war veterans.[92] The Women's Association of St Wolodymyr Ukrainian Orthodox supported relief efforts in the DP camps where Ukrainians found refuge after the war.[93]

The Glorious Thirty

The first decades after the war – termed by some historians "the Glorious Thirty" because of the sustained economic growth experienced between the war's end and the first oil crisis of 1973 – saw many important social and economic transformations, including the emergence of a strong consumer culture. But it took some time before the effects of this change were fully felt. By contrast, the massive wave of immigration that rolled over Toronto in the immediate postwar years was felt instantly. The non-British immigrant cohort was different from the one that had preceded it: better educated, more nationally conscious, and in general more numerous, it was also less likely to go back home. But the receiving society had also changed. For one thing, the British identity of the past was being discarded in favour of a more distinctly Canadian one, as already suggested by the new Citizenship Act, which took effect in 1947. Once they became citizens, newcomers could, with the gradual founding of the welfare state, look forward to an increasingly broad range of social services to help them in case of need. This rendered the mutual aid societies of the past obsolete. Together with the Canadian-born, these new immigrants rode a wave of prosperity that had evaded previous generations. What did *not* change was the receiving society's expectation that the new arrivals fit in as quickly as possible.[94]

SLAVS AND JEWS

Aware of their demographic weight and their distinctiveness in relation to the previous cohort, many new immigrant groups wasted no time in creating separate congregations. Ukrainian Catholics, for example, at first attended the Dormition of the Theotokos but soon demanded their own space. Mostly originating from the *oblasts* of Ternopil and Ivano Frankivsk (formerly Stanislaviv) in western Ukraine (formerly eastern Galicia), they took over the old Dale Presbyterian in 1951, renaming it St Nicholas. Land for a second postwar parish, to be called Holy Protection of the Mother of God, was purchased in 1959 on Leeds Street just east of Ossington. A new Orthodox church named after St Andrew was created in 1953 in the Junction on Dupont Street at Edwin.[95] Baptists, who like their Catholic counterparts originated in western Ukraine, purchased the Memorial building on Tecumseth in 1959, much to the dismay of their Polish coreligionists, who had hoped to make it their own. These Ukrainians disdained the established Slavic congregation, where Russians and Ukrainians were thrown together.[96] Similarly, Pentecostals split off from the Slavic church on Queen Street, wanting to worship in their own language. They purchased Adath Israel Anshei Romania Synagogue in 1957 and renamed it First Ukrainian Pentecostal.[97] Two years later, their pastor, Michael Derkatch, left the congregation to open a storefront called Christian Mission Tabernacle on Dundas Avenue in the Junction because he wanted to serve second- and third-generation Ukrainians who preferred English-language services.[98]

Postwar Jews from the Carpathians in eastern Europe gathered around Meyer Grunewald, like them a recently arrived immigrant, who before the Shoah had been spiritual head of the Jews of Técsö, Czechoslovakia (now Tyachiv, Zakapattia *oblast*, western Ukraine). This Ultra-Orthodox congregation rejected the perceived compromises and permissiveness of the modern world. They worshipped at Machzikei Torah (Upholders of the Torah), which occupied a spacious house on Markham Street south of Ulster. Only men who strictly observed the Sabbath were permitted to read from the Torah, hold office, and receive honours. One member of this synagogue's executive was a postwar refugee born in Vienna of parents originating in Beled in northwestern Hungary named Paul Reichmann, who went on to become a real estate magnate.[99]

A second Russian Orthodox parish, this one dedicated to the Holy Trinity, was formed by fifty DP families and a smaller number of émigrés who had been living in Yugoslavia since the October Revolution. They had turned away from Christ the Saviour Cathedral partly because of its wartime support of the Soviet Union and partly because it was thought to be too assimilated. Worship initially took place in a rented space in the Church of All Nations.[100] Meanwhile a group of recent Russian and Ukrainian immigrants calling themselves evangelical Christians rejected the already existing congregation at Beverley Street Baptist. In 1952 they built a two-storey brick place of worship on Carr Street at Denison, calling it Russian-Ukrainian Church of Evangelical Christians. Many years later they would join the Baptist Convention of Quebec and Ontario. A third Polish-language church, named after St Casimir and entrusted to the Oblates, was erected in 1954 on Roncesvalles Avenue at Garden to accommodate postwar arrivals. A parish hall built on the same site a few years earlier thanks to the labour of parishioners had served as a temporary church.[101] Meanwhile, Baptists lost their historic place of worship in the Junction when it was demolished in the early 1950s. For more than a decade, they shared facilities at Ossington Avenue Baptist.[102] Slovaks, for their part, purchased Chevra B'nai Israel Synagogue in 1959 and created a Byzantine Rite parish called the Nativity of the Mother of God, placed under the care of Redemptorists.[103]

New immigrant groups not represented in the city before the Second World War were also quick to establish their own places of worship. Although few in number, Belarusians founded two Orthodox parishes, a consequence of distinct migration movements that made their way to Toronto a year apart from each other. Temporarily situated in a storefront on Dundas Street facing Trinity Bellwoods Park, St Cyril of Turov was created in 1954 by veterans who had fought with the Polish Second Corps and settled in the city six years earlier. Grouped together as the Byelorussian National Alliance, these men were loyal to the government-in-exile headed by Mikola Abramchyk, whose *I Accuse the Kremlin of the Genocide of My Nation* was first published in Toronto in 1950. The second parish, St Euphrosinia of Polatsk, was established by DPs from UN Refugee Relief Administration camps. Unsympathetic to Abramchyk, whom they viewed as too closely connected to the Polish government-in-exile and the Vatican, they split from the Alliance, forming the Byelorussian National Association. In 1957 they established their own church in a reconverted cinema on Dovercourt Road north of Hallam. These two places of worship answered to separate Orthodox higher religious authorities.[104]

LITHUANIANS, HUNGARIANS, AND SOUTH SLAVS

Feeling little kinship with their peasant and left-leaning prewar compatriots, recently arrived Lithuanians founded the Parish of the Resurrection on College Street at Havelock, which was entrusted to American Franciscans. When Canadian banks refused to advance a mortgage for their church, the order turned to American institutions instead, using properties in the United States as collateral. An equivalent amount was raised from donations by parishioners. A hall was built in 1956 that had a church on the upper floor. In 1947, their Lutheran compatriots, who numbered only about five hundred, erected a small rustic-style structure named Redeemer on Bloor Street at Indian Road. But they were hampered by splits over which higher authority, if any, should govern them and who should be named pastor. An appointment was finally made in 1953. Meanwhile, St John Evangelical Lutheran provided a wide array of religious and secular services to DPs from the Baltic States.[105]

In 1949, thanks once again to the Sisters of Social Service, Jesuits who had arrived in the wake of the Communist takeover of Hungary became pastors of St Elizabeth.[106] The parish thus became yet another immigrant one, led by a congregation of priests. The Hungarian Uprising against the Soviets in 1956 mobilized compatriots in Toronto. St Elizabeth became the site of the Hungarian Canadian Relief Fund, which offered assistance to refugees in transit camps after Warsaw Pact troops invaded Hungary. The parish also housed a temporary reception centre for exiles arriving in Toronto. According to the *Telegram*, around three-quarters of those landing at the airport at the time were met by volunteers, who took them to the church, where they received clothing, food, and temporary housing. The Hungarian congregation at the Church of All Nations suddenly quadrupled in size as a result of this influx.[107] A report prepared for the United Church traces an interesting portrait of this refugee cohort. Half of them were well educated, skilled, and well qualified. The other half were factory workers and labourers. Almost all of the women found jobs in Toronto in offices or factories or as house cleaners. They evidently had high expectations of their new country, aspiring to a well-furnished home, a summer cottage, and a motorboat. They were on the whole a cultured cohort with a marked preference for the theatre and classical music. Since they were not especially regular churchgoers, their contribution to the life of the congregation was judged to be moderate. From a moral standpoint, they were neither orthodox nor traditional. In fact, 25 per cent of them were divorced, a figure considered very high at the time, when divorces in Canada were hard to get and involved long and complex legal procedures.[108] Among the newcomers were 5,000 Jews. A conservative congregation calling itself Beth Hazicharon (House of Remembrance) was organized in 1958 at the Associated Hebrew Schools on Brunswick Avenue under Zoltan Zagon, a rabbi who had escaped from Budapest with his wife and daughter.[109]

The first Yugoslav group to establish a permanent place of worship after the war were Slovenes, who comprised two regional subgroups: the *Prekmurci*, from the extreme northeastern part of the country near the Hungarian border, who tended to concentrate in Etobicoke; and the *Primorci*, from the Adriatic coast adjacent to Croatia and Italy, who located mainly in Parkdale. For a time, religious services were held at Our Lady of Mount Carmel, where associational life got started. Our Lady Help of Christians, seating five hundred, was consecrated in 1954 by James Cardinal McGuigan. This parish, the first of its kind in Canada, counted 260 families or almost 1,300 members. Its pastor, Jakob Kolarič was Slovenian born and educated. In the early years, parishioners took their religious obligations very seriously. Less than 5 per cent of them failed to fulfil the minimum requirement of confession and communion at Easter.[110] Albanians, most of them from Macedonia and Kosovo, settled in the Junction area along Dundas Street in the 1950s, forming the Muslim Society of Toronto, comprised of twenty or thirty families. They used the facilities of West Toronto Baptist, a new church built by its pastor-architect, H.H. Kent.[111] They then rented a space nearby on Dundas Street at McMurray that in effect became the city's first mosque.

GERMANS AND ITALIANS

A second German Lutheran congregation (the first dating back to the mid-nineteenth century and situated to the east of our area) was founded in 1954 under the name St George. Three years later, they bought the Apostolic Church on College Street at Lippincott, becoming the seventh congregation to occupy the building since its erection in 1873. A Danish Lutheran group briefly shared these facilities. Around the same time, twenty-nine German Baptists started a congregation affiliated to the North American Baptist Conference rather than a Canadian body. In 1955 they purchased and renovated Achdus Israel Umberchoz Harav (Unity of Israel), a *stiblach* on Euclid Avenue north of Dundas.[112] German-speaking Catholics who settled in Toronto during these years seemed content to frequent St Patrick's, which was especially solicitous in their regard. As a result of their presence, the number of Sunday masses with German sermons jumped from one to three over the next few years. Baptisms and weddings reached an all-time high in the latter half of the decade, representing a sixfold increase over the previous peak of the early 1930s and highlighting the demographic impact of the postwar cohort.[113]

The number of Italians more than quadrupled in the city of Toronto as a result of the massive immigrant wave of the 1950s. Most of them came from southern Italy, with smaller numbers from the northeastern regions of Friuli and Veneto. Most of these newcomers were unskilled, and of peasant background, and had basic elementary school education. They quickly found work in the city's booming economy, chiefly in the building trades and in factories. Married women and older children worked outside the home to boost the family's earnings. The Archdiocese of Toronto responded to this massive influx cautiously. Existing Italian parishes faced serious overcrowding: "It often happens," commented one dismayed priest, "that [parishioners] are out in the vestibule and standing on the steps leading into the main body of the church." In the late 1950s, ten Sunday masses, with sermons in Italian or English, were said at St Agnes, while at Our Lady of the Angels a mass was even added on Sunday evenings in the auditorium to relieve the overcrowding in the morning. In 1958 alone, 763 baptisms and 310 weddings were performed at St Agnes. Finally, in 1958, the adjacent territorial parishes of St Francis of Assisi and St Clare were authorized to celebrate one Sunday mass with an Italian sermon.[114]

Immigration also revivified St Paul's Italian United. After the war, Libero Sauro began a campaign to build a new church. Congregants donated most of the money. An additional sum came from outside supporters, including the Orange Lodge. Land was purchased on Ossington Avenue north of Dupont, and a brick church was constructed in 1957. After suffering a stroke in 1948, Sauro was replaced by Michael Di Stasi, who had grown up in the congregation. The new minister received a yearly salary of $1,500 in addition to a car allowance of $200 and a manse.[115] Expanding membership due to immigration encouraged Italian Pentecostals to replace their small church, built at the beginning of the century, with a larger, modern-looking one, which now faced College Street rather than Montrose. A significant donation was made by Elio Madonia, a Sicilian convert to Protestantism who immigrated in the 1950s and had become a successful soft-drink manufacturer. A second congregation was created, and in 1956 a brick hall was constructed on Ossington Avenue south of Bloor to accommodate it. Meanwhile, Italian Brethren began an evangelizing campaign out of the Bracondale Gospel Hall on Arlington Avenue at the corner of Benson.[116]

If gauged by West End places of worship, religion was hardly static in the forty years after the First World War. More than seventy new buildings went up, most of them north of Bloor Street and in the comfortable neighbourhoods of High Park, Swansea, and Runnymede – a testimony to suburban growth in the metropolitan area and to the continued importance of religion. By contrast, the concentration of gospel halls in the Junction and adjacent industrial districts highlighted the working-class character of those areas. Religious buildings were also constructed in neighbourhoods diagnosed with the "downtown problem," reflecting the expansion of Jewish and Catholic places of worship serving first- and second-generation immigrant congregations. At the same time, another forty or so structures (storefronts, houses, or religious buildings) accommodated new linguistic or denominational groups, emphasizing the passage of people through the West End.

It was easier for Jews to set up a congregation than it was for most other groups. Given their demographic weight, Polish Jews were often able to organize themselves by town of origin, underscoring their strong bonds of kinship and solidarity. Other coreligionists would form congregations by country of birth, by political or ideological orientation, by allegiance to a particular rabbi, or, for those living outside the core of Jewish settlement, by Toronto neighbourhood. This, however, did not prevent conflicts within congregations based on personality or ideology, nor did it always dampen competing ambitions and traditions. Like Jews, fundamentalist Protestant groups, such as Brethren and Pentecostals, had few prerequisites for worship and tended to gather in small groups. By contrast, non-British Catholic and mainstream Protestant immigrants had to find clergymen willing to serve them as well as means to support them. Such parishes and congregations had to be larger, often bringing together people of different regions in the originating country and possibly of competing religious traditions. Historian Robert Harney recounted how two southern Italian hometown groups at Our Lady of Mount Carmel vied with each other over sponsorship of the feast of St Roch, a fourteenth-century French saint popular throughout the Western Mediterranean who happened to be the patron of both towns. Given the scarce resources in the early years of settlement, it is not surprising that tensions also surfaced between congregants and poorly paid clergymen.

The concentration of foreigners in the downtown core disturbed many Torontonians. The image evoked by the *Globe* reporter of a vast alien territory stretching from Lake Ontario to Bloor Street where venerable religious institutions harkening back to a glorious past had either shut their doors or seriously contemplated moving resonated with the native-born. Just as disquieting was the depiction of Queen Street, running through the very heart of the city, as a great non-Anglo-Saxon thoroughfare. Newcomers were often associated with social unrest and communism. They, however, had to rely on the scarce resources of kin and community in case of need, for in the interwar years, requesting government welfare often led to deportation. The Communist Party of Canada effectively filled this vacuum, defending the interests of the unemployed, the homeless, unorganized workers, and the economically vulnerable. Governments responded to social unrest with repression. In this context, the churches proved willing to collaborate with the authorities, spying on suspect individuals but more importantly providing the same services as the communists offered.[117] The Church of All Nations, the Catholic Settlement House, the Scott Institute, St Christopher House, and many other institutions all did their part in fighting communism, while offering a measure of assistance to the needy.

Just as in the previous period, a spirit of condescension marked such efforts: it was as if immigrants were incapable on their own of learning such supposedly indigenous values as fair play, open-mindedness, intercultural encounter, and dialogue. They were thought to require the mediation of knowledgeable Protestant social agents. For all the evident goodwill behind much missionary work, such didactic techniques told immigrants they were inferior. This message was reinforced by ambivalent Church policies that, while stressing the need to evangelize, continuously cut the budgets of Home Mission Boards, paid ministers of non-British origin a fraction of what regular clergymen received, and generally had immigrants gather in spaces, such as basements, halls, or former residences, not originally conceived as places of worship. Doubtless such measures were justified for reasons of economy and congregational size. Even so, newcomers were left with the distinct impression that they were second-class. Ultimately, mass conversions did not occur, however good the intentions of some Protestants.

The ancestral faith mattered to immigrants – perhaps not to specific individuals, who may not have been observant or who did not practise their religion, but certainly to the group as a whole. For this reason, conversion was generally regarded as a betrayal and an aberration. In light of this, Italian Protestants felt an acute need to exhibit their *italianità* by recalling Protestant contributions to Italy's Risorgimento and by taking part in patriotic festivities. In any event, places of worship were among the first enduring establishments immigrants set up in the country of adoption, whatever their ethnic background or denomination. The beginnings of such institutions may have been arduous and unsteady, but these pioneers gave generously of their time, money, and labour to ensure success. The example of First Hungarian Presbyterian well illustrates the fact that once the minister had been ordained – that is, once stability had been achieved – there was a general rallying around the church, and parish life flourished.

But newcomers were not like so many empty vessels waiting to be filled with religion, as the Protestant missionaries often assumed. At their peak, immigrant congregations numbered in the thousands, in most instances far outstripping the big Protestant ones of the interwar period. The faithful attended church in large numbers on a fairly regular basis and were serious about fulfilling their religious obligations. They also contributed money, time, and effort in building, remodelling, and beautifying places of worship, which often served as centres of community life. But they also had expectations: clergymen had to help them find jobs and intervene on their behalf with Canadian officials; and church facilities had to provide facilities where their children could learn their language and culture of origin, and that could serve more generally as the focal point for leisure activities. The dismissed pastor of the Polish church, Jozef Dekowski, had paid for ignoring such expectations. Many Catholic immigrant parishes achieved stability when male and female religious communities were brought in to serve them. The contributions of female orders, while vital in this respect, have on the whole been ignored in the scholarly literature. Similarly, ministers' wives and deaconesses proved vital to congregational cohesion. With stability came respectability. Members' energies could be channelled more effectively into religious and other activities under parish or congregational sponsorship. The divisions of the past were set aside as behaviour conformed more closely to North American patterns. What immigrant evangelists sought to attain through didactic and manipulative techniques was realized naturally over time and with the provision of adequate resources.

Chapter Five

The Empire of Full-Orbed Religion, 1920–1960

The formation of the United Church might be seen as emblematic of changing times. It would be more correct, however, to view it as the culmination of a long process of collaboration between Methodists and Presbyterians, especially on the prairies, where financial resources were scarce. The forty years following the First World War were marked more by continuity. The ideal of the local congregation or parish as the expression of a full-orbed religion remained firmly entrenched for Torontonians of British origin and was gradually accepted by immigrants of various backgrounds, including Jews, as congregations became more affluent and adapted themselves to North American standards. Experiments geared towards attracting specific cohorts, notably the young, continued, and despite the Great Depression and the war, a consensus on the importance of regular attendance persisted (whether individuals did so or not is another question). So too did the trend towards more formalized ritual. Individuals, families, and congregations expended energy and money to adorn their places of worship with stained glass, marble, and carved wood, but equally to make them functional in order to serve various community-based activities. Music was an important component in both endeavours. Qualified musicians and singers were hired to enhance worship; they also used sacred spaces for concerts directed to a broader public. Strong links were thus created between congregations and artists trained or working at institutions such as the Toronto/Royal Conservatory of Music, the Ontario College of Art, and the Royal Ontario Museum. Substantial change did not occur in this period, but rather in the subsequent one, as later chapters will show.

St Patrick's was perhaps exemplary of an immigrant parish fully subscribing to the model of a full-orbed Christianity. Its German-speaking parishioners could benefit from an intense social and religious life. Famed as preachers, the Redemptorists instituted parish missions stretching from several days to a fortnight and culminating in alternate Sunday communions for fathers–sons and mothers–daughters. At the same time, an English-language mission was inaugurated for immigrants' children. Parishioners took part in processions to mark the feasts of Corpus Christi and All Souls, as well as pilgrimages to the Jesuit Martyrs Shrine at Midland, Ontario. Many pious associations were created, such as the Rosary Society, the Holy Name Society for men, and the Children of Mary for girls. There was even one for young couples under the tutelage of St Gerard Majella, an eighteenth-century Italian Redemptorist and patron of expectant mothers. The association's goal was "to honour mothers and the unborn." A youth choir was established whose repertoire included German and English music, and the first of a series of passion plays was performed in German.

Since most parishioners were immigrants in early adulthood, St Patrick's offered them a wide range of social activities to help them with their transition to the new environment. Blending Old and New World influences, dances were especially popular and frequent, capping off traditional seasonal celebrations such as Carnival, *Trachtenfest* (usually held in early summer and characterized by the wearing of traditional costumes), *Weinfest* (coinciding with the grape harvest in early fall), *Kirchwei* (an annual fair in November marking the consecration of the village church), St Catherine's day (25 November), and New Year's eve, all featuring familiar *Blechmusik* (brass band music). But typically North American festivities were also observed, including Valentine's Day, Mother's Day, and Halloween. Christmas, as opposed to St Nicholas Day (6 December), became the day on which children received presents. In the summer months, informal get-togethers were preferred, such as picnics at Old Mill. Women created a *Kaffee Kränzchen* (coffee circle) and were the mainstay of frequent bazaars. Like English-speaking parishes and congregations, St Patrick's had hockey, baseball, softball, bowling, and wrestling teams. Plays specifically targeting children or adults (where the admission charged was higher for men than for women), as well as concerts, were performed regularly.

5.1 St Patrick's Catholic
Built for parishioners of Irish origin after they ceded their church to Italians
in 1908, this substantial stone edifice became an important centre of German
Catholic life from 1929 until the 1960s. Immigrants from central Europe came
to Toronto in two waves during the interwar and postwar periods. Masses are
still said in German. (Gabriele Scardellato)

Services meeting immigrants' immediate material necessities were also provided. The adjacent Catholic Settlement House distributed beds, mattresses, used clothing, and linens during the Depression. In addition to the kindergarten and after-school programs set up by the Sisters of Service, a German-language school with an enrolment of almost 250 children allowed parents to better balance the exigencies of work and home. The sisters also offered English-language courses for adults, as well sewing and cooking classes for young women. A hall built with parishioners' volunteer labour (but still costing $18,000) hosted theatrical works, musical performances, dances, and meetings of church groups, as well as a kindergarten. A mutual aid society and a credit union were created because newcomers had little to no access to financial aid in the event of a breadwinner's sudden death or to banking services in general.

Volksdeutsche, who arrived after the war and clearly outnumbered their interwar compatriots, gave new impetus to parish life. The many and varied religious and secular activities of the 1930s were revived, such as the men's choir, which sang Franz Schubert's *German Mass* (D872) at the University of Toronto's Convocation Hall. Meanwhile, new organizations, such as the Kolping Society, were created. Begun in mid-nineteenth-century Germany, the association took its name from founder Alfred Kolping, a priest in the diocese of Cologne, who sought to help rural Catholic artisans establish themselves in cities and to shelter them from the ills of urban life. The St Patrick's branch functioned as a mutual aid society, helping new arrivals find work and housing. It also worked to maintain group cohesion by sponsoring social activities as well as monthly communion breakfast meetings at the church. St Patrick's instituted marriage preparation classes, mirroring the postwar era's concerns for youth and family stability as well as the rising marriage rates in the parish during the 1950s. As many as twelve weddings were celebrated some Saturdays. Catholic Action for Youth (*Christliche Arbeiterjugend*), a movement organized along gender lines aiming to train Catholic leaders in various walks of life, also made its appearance in the parish.[1]

Decorous Devotion

Two Anglican churches, St Mary Magdalene and St Thomas, continued to be in the vanguard of the trend towards more dignified worship. The curate of the first parish, Henry Hiscocks, was an unapologetic, indeed adamant Anglo-Catholic. He insisted on sporting a biretta, a three- or four-peaked black cap topped by a pom-pom worn by the Catholic clergy since the Middle Ages. It is doubtful, however, that any Catholic priest in Toronto would make a public display of it for fear of the negative response it would provoke, its use being generally reserved to church precincts. The strong-willed Hiscocks introduced in the parish's liturgical calendar a series of new Marian feast days such as the Immaculate Conception, the Purification, the Annunciation, and the Assumption, each with appropriate devotions. His controversial innovations became the focus of another front-page article in the *Toronto Star*, which quoted him urging his parishioners "to pray for bad men and bad women who come to spy on us, who make mock of us … who would stop us worshipping God." The article depicted the anomalous rituals of this parish, including the recitation at the end of the mass of three Hail Marys, "which," the journalist asserted, "are not legal in Church of England services here."[2] Responding to the furor, for which he held Hiscocks personally responsible, Bishop James Sweeny urged him to stop making himself the object of controversy, even though it was Wycliffe College that had brought the issue into the public domain by publishing a pamphlet censuring the curate's liturgical innovations. Undeterred, Hiscocks invited the Sisters of the Church, an Anglican order founded in England half a century earlier, to establish a convent next to his church. The following year he tried to bring the Society of St John the Evangelist (commonly known as the Cowley Fathers) to the parish as a gauge of its Anglo-Catholicity. Established in 1866, it was the first male religious order to be created in England since the Reformation. Ever allergic to controversy, Bishop Sweeny vetoed the move.

At both St Mary Magdalene and St Thomas, feast days now became occasions for the regular rather than occasional use of incense. This practice caused disquiet not only among Toronto Protestants in general,[3] but also within these very parishes. The vicar at St Thomas, Cecil Stuart, introduced incense only after instructing parishioners on several successive Sundays on its function in worship, evidently leaving some of his flock distinctly sceptical, if not outright hostile. In line with the emphasis on Eucharist-centred worship, fasting was introduced before the taking of communion, a practice observed in both Catholic and Orthodox traditions: food and drink were prohibited beginning at midnight before communion was received.[4] In 1938 he also inaugurated a devotion after Sunday Evensong "to adore our Lord in his

Sacrament," which was modelled on the ritual observed at the same time of the day in Catholic churches. Stuart took pains not to advertise this change in order to avoid the controversies that had bedevilled Hiscocks.

Taken together, St Thomas and St Mary Magdelene were the parishes holding the greatest number of religious services yearly in the diocese of Toronto: 540 for the first, and 460 for the second, compared to the average of 145. Among the celebrations at St Thomas were those marking the fiftieth anniversary of the founding of the Sisters of St John the Divine and the centenary of the Oxford Movement. The latter festivity saw the guest celebrant, the Bishop of Algoma, vested in a red cope and mitre, accoutrements absolutely shunned by Bishop Sweeny. A further innovation was the very discreet introduction of women in the choir: they were kept behind the rood screen in the choir stalls while their male colleagues processed with the celebrant and his entourage.[5]

Influenced by Anglican ritual as a result of her frequent trips to England, Flora McRea Eaton single-handedly advanced the trend towards more formalized worship at Timothy Eaton Memorial. From 1922 until her death in 1970, she was a formidable presence on the Board of Trustees, which included members of the Eaton family as well as company executives. Trevor Davies, the minister whose appointment she arranged, was successful in his request to wear a gown during services, a practice prohibited in Canadian Methodism since 1906. Medieval hymns such as the *Te Deum* were inserted into the Sunday morning service. In 1929, Flora Eaton wanted to have formal processionals and recessionals accompanying worship, a proposal the Quarterly Official Board considered impractical because of the building's amphitheatrical structure. As a memorial to her husband John, whose death in 1922 was marked by the closing of city shops and businesses as well as the suspension of the sitting of the legislature, she proposed that the chancel be lengthened to allow for the addition of a central aisle, as at St Andrew's Presbyterian. Also, the communion table, now an elevated altar of Indiana limestone, became the central focus of the church, dominating the sanctuary. The pulpit and reading desk were placed on either side of it, diminishing somewhat the strong emphasis placed on the word in Protestant churches. Kneelers were also introduced at each pew to encourage prayerful devotion. When a candelabra suddenly appeared on the altar, a lifelong Orangeman and one-time secretary of the Board of Trustees had it removed on the

5.2 Timothy Eaton Memorial United

In memory of the deceased founder of the Eaton's department store, his family donated the land and the building of this church. Located in Toronto's comfortable northern suburbs, it had a wealthy and socially conscious congregation. At the urging of Lady Flora Eaton, Timothy's daughter-in-law, who dominated all aspects of church life until her death at the age of ninety, the interior of the building was altered from an amphitheatrical to a central aisle plan. The church was an important focus of musical culture in the interwar years, thanks in part to its organist and choirmaster Sir Ernest MacMillan. (Toronto Reference Library)

grounds that it was "too Popish." Brooking no opposition, Flora Eaton ordered its immediate return.[6]

Music was integral to the formalization of worship. It was Hiscocks who in 1921 brought English-born composer Healey Willan to St Mary Magdalene. Willan, like Hiscocks an ardent Anglo-Catholic, was given free rein in musical matters, and he would serve the parish faithfully as organist and choirmaster for nearly half a century.

He wrote perhaps his most important compositions for the church, favouring plainsong and polyphonic music as those best suited for its style of worship. His considerable output, which included masses, motets, hymns, and works for choir and for organ, were both mystical and intensely personal. He had a number of talented students, including composer Walter MacNutt, organist and choirmaster at St Thomas, Weldon Kilburn, organist and choirmaster at St Alban the Martyr, and David Ouchterlony, who served at St Andrew's Presbyterian for a decade before moving to Timothy Eaton Memorial, a position he occupied until his death. Ouchterlony's successor at St Andrew's was the composer Gerald Bales, founder of the St Andrew's Singers, who performed several oratorios by George Frederick Handel on CBC radio in the 1950s.[7]

Whether accompanying services or not, music was a vital part of Timothy Eaton Memorial, linking it to pre-Reformation traditions. A succession of talented musicians were hired as organist-choirmasters, including Ernest MacMillan (1920–25), whose Oxford doctorate earned him the handsome salary of $1,800, Albert Jordan (1925–32), Thomas Crawford (1932–46), and David Ouchterlony (1946–87). MacMillan assembled the orchestra and conducted the first Toronto performance in the church of J.S. Bach's *The Passion According to St Matthew*, as well as George Frederick Handel's *Messiah*. His successors built on this experience, directing major works in the classical religious repertoire, including Antonin Dvořák's *Stabat Mater*, Felix Mendelssohn's *Elijah*, Joseph Haydn's *The Creation*, and Handel's *Judas Maccabeus*.[8] Timothy Eaton Memorial boasted such well-known soloists as contralto Eileen Law (1923–36), a first-rate oratorio performer, and Jeanne Pengelly (1930–74), whose operatic career began auspiciously in 1933 at the Teatro San Carlo in Naples; she made her Metropolitan Opera debut three years later, the first fully trained Canadian singer to do so.

The competition for beautiful music involved other churches, especially during the Christmas and Easter seasons. Dorothy Allan Park was a soprano soloist at the Church of the Redeemer for a dozen years before moving on to First Church of Christ Scientist. Trinity United featured the internationally renowned soprano Lois Marshall. It was there too that Ernest MacMillan gave a gala solo recital in 1941 to inaugurate the church's Casavant organ. After the war, conductor Mario Bernardi served as an organist at St Vincent de Paul Church as a means to support his studies at the Royal Conservatory of Music. For

5.3a and 5.3b (above and opposite) Morningside Presbyterian
A modest frame structure typical of suburban churches was replaced in 1916
by an architecturally designed stone edifice, announcing the neighbourhood's
elevated social standing. The congregation of High Park Presbyterian merged
with it in 1970. (5.4a, Toronto Reference Library; 5.4b, Gabriele Scardellato)

her part, Nina de Gedeonoff, choirmaster at Christ the Saviour Russian Orthodox, gave private voice lessons to soprano Evelyn Gould and cantor Esther Ghan. [9]

Morningside Drive Presbyterian took the formalist turn somewhat later. In 1958 the church inaugurated a new chancel, designed by the architectural firm of Bruce, Brown and Brisley (founded by J. Francis Brown), at a cost of $50,000, an amount entirely absorbed by a handful of congregants. The central space was occupied by a carved wooden altar (called a communion table in the documents), whose importance was heightened by a tall, sculpted canopy (known as a reredos) standing behind it, which was flanked by wood panelling running along the

lower part of the chancel walls. On either side of the communion table were pews with carved fronts, resembling choir stalls, closed off by richly decorated lecterns for the reading of the epistle to the right and the gospel to the left. Architecturally, the chancel replicated the space found in medieval churches rather than Reformation ones (especially of the Calvinist type, where the pulpit dominated) and was in complete harmony with the building's Gothic style. The morning and evening inauguration ceremonies were accompanied by the music of Bach, Handel, Mozart, Schubert, and Franck.[10]

It would be incorrect to conclude from these examples that questions of more dignified worship concerned only bourgeois congregations. Historian David Greig has established from baptismal records that in the interwar period, 60 per cent of St Mary Magdalene's parishioners were blue-collar workers.[11] Also, immigrant congregations were involved in this process. Among Jews, for example, respectable behaviour became a concern in the large downtown synagogues. This was a product of two phenomena: upward social mobility, and incorporation into North American life. As early as the 1910s, assistant rabbi Julius Price was critical of the lack of decorum at Goel Tzedec. He would have been pleased to learn that congregants later rejected as crassly commercial the practice of making financial pledges during the reading of the Scriptures. Five years after Price's departure, English speakers were regularly appointed to assist the resident rabbi. They normalized the use of English sermons during Sabbath services. This constituted a significant shift in conceptions of the rabbi's role from eastern European ones focused on the interpretation of the scriptures and arbitration of community disputes to North American ones centred on pastoral care. Separate Friday evening services and special activities were instituted for young people in order to ensure generational continuity and to combat declining rates of affiliation, especially defections to Holy Blossom, which was regarded as more affluent but also as more Canadian. In the 1930s, women were allowed to sit on the ground floor of the sanctuary, albeit in designated areas on its margins. Congregational singing and a uniform prayer book were also instituted.[12]

Sermons in English began at nearby Chevra Tehillim in the 1920s, but only on high holidays. Not until 1937 did the *shul* finally appoint a Canadian-born rabbi; it was the first in the city to do so. Twenty-three-year-old Reuben Slonim of Winnipeg was impatient for change, as the following passage from his memoirs well illustrates:

> For years before my arrival [the] rabbi [Jacob Gordon] was a man of the
> old school, learned and saintly but unaware of the problems faced by a
> generation in transition from the Russian-Polish milieu. He spoke Yiddish
> from the pulpit and from a traditional perspective that insisted nothing
> was so wrong which could not be remedied by a stronger devotion to the
> Torah and its commandments. But the young people were not listening.
> They wanted a message couched in the language of the integrated society,
> not the ghettoized shtetl.[13]

Shortly after his appointment, the young rabbi made front-page head-lines. "Does Not Believe Moses Mere Pen in God's Hand," read the title of the article. The subtitle, "Rabbi Slonim Wants Modern Tinge and Flavor to McCaul St. Synagogue," was in part a quote from his expressed heartfelt ambition to attract young people to Chevra Tehillim. Slonim sought to make Judaism more appealing to them, arguing that the Bible had to be interpreted in light of the findings of modern science and archaeology.[14] The synagogue executive reacted immediately, calling the rabbi before the board, a body he later described as an Inquisition that at times disintegrated into fistfights. The president, Solomon Breslin, a manufacturer born in Talačyn, Mogilev *gubernia*, in present-day Belarus, who always wore a top hat at official functions, was so angered by Slonim's remarks that he sought to humiliate the rabbi publicly during the service by having his chair removed from the sanctuary.[15]

Unconcerned, Slonim instituted regular English sermons, delivering only the occasional one in Yiddish. To standardize worship, he introduced a common prayer book as at Goel Tzedec. Decorum was in his mind the key to a smooth generational transition in the synagogue. But the battle was an uphill one, pitting the immigrant cohort's established ways and cherished traditions against North American notions of religious practice viewed by Slonim as modern. For example, on feast days, congregants would arrive en masse at the synagogue for *Yizkor*, the prayer recited for one's dead parents. Just as suddenly as they appeared, they would leave for work a few minutes later, thus disrupting regular worship. A similar pandemonium broke out yearly when one-third of the synagogue's seats were offered for sale to the unaffiliated. Slonim likened the event to "bargain day at Eaton's."[16] To the rabbi, the *beth midrash* or study hall further illustrated his point. Young people were conspicuously absent from it, and except for needle workers from the Spadina factories, who attended first thing in the morning to hear the explanation of a Talmudic passage, achieving a quorum was proving to be increasingly difficult. The hall was in the hands of a tiny coterie of *Litvaks* (Lithuanians), who "stood erect and still, like boards in a picket fence" when they prayed, and *Galizianers* (Galicians), who instead "swayed like trees in a storm."[17] Despite their many differences, the two factions were united in their Old World beliefs and practices, which Slonim largely viewed not only as superstitious, but also as positively bibulous.[18] In the end the rabbi prevailed, but not without completely alienating the old-timers.

Slonim was impatient with what he termed his congregants' irrational behaviour. Many *shtetl* Jews, for example, believed that a marriage could not take place if the bride shared the same name as her prospective mother-in-law, for this would be tempting fate – one of the many demons that populated the universe could mistakenly take it out on the one instead of the other.[19] Such beliefs and traditions harkened back to the rural religion practised in the *shtetl*, which had little resonance with the generation brought up in a large urban environment. The point here, however, is not to stigmatize *shtetl* Jews or their Judaism as premodern, irrational, and vaguely amoral, as did Slonim, but to highlight the fact that this kind of religion was destined to wane because the rural or peasant world from which it sprang could not survive in a North American urban-industrial setting.[20] Priests and ministers trained in North America doubtless fought similar battles with their immigrant congregations in the name of modernity, which they claimed legitimately to represent as members of the second generation.

Standardization, regulation, and adaptation were also the order of the day at *Shaarei Shomayim*, following the appointment in 1944 of Judah Washer, an American-educated rabbi: the sale of *aliyahs* or calls to read from the Torah scrolls was eliminated, and young men were given greater opportunities to perform this function; men *and* women were seated on the ground level, albeit across the aisle from each other; a common Hebrew prayer book with concurrent English translation was adopted; and men were encouraged to wear *kippahs* rather than hats during services.[21]

Inspiring Interiors

Parishioners and congregants continued to spend considerable sums to adorn their places of worship. In the early 1920s St Thomas's was fitted with a small, wood-panelled Lady chapel in honour of Mary, designed by parishioner William Rae. Architect and artist Scott Carter executed the plan, including a richly ornamented coffered ceiling. Together with sculptor Edward Watson, they went on to enrich the existing oak reredos behind the high altar with the addition of nine carved and painted wooden figures of saints. St Mary Magdalene's introduced stations of the cross or representations of episodes from Christ's Passion, which since the Middle Ages had been objects of silent meditation by the faithful. They were produced at the mother house of the Sisters of the Church in England. The church inaugurated its own a Lady chapel, also designed by William Rae, and decorated by Sylvia Hahn, staff artist at the Royal Ontario Museum and daughter of painter and teacher Gustav. These examples highlight the association between ambitious parish rectors and the small community of Toronto artists gravitating around the Arts and Letters Club, the Ontario College of Art, and the Royal Ontario Museum, as well as the close collaboration between the latter and artisans associated with the Arts and Crafts tradition in Britain.[22]

Following St Anne's early lead, other evangelical Anglican parishes were fitted with stained glass windows. Between 1927 and 1952 a dozen of them of unknown manufacture were acquired by the Church of the Messiah, including the large sanctuary one showing Christ breaking bread with the disciples of Emmaus.[23] The new church of St John's Humberside, erected in 1923, boasted fifteen stained glass windows produced over many years by the firms of N.T. Lyon and Robert McClausland. One of these reproduces British painter William Holman Hunt's famous *The Light of the World*.[24] In 1937, Sextus Styles, rector of St Olave's, commissioned Trinidad-born Yvonne Williams, a graduate of the Ontario College of Art, where she had won the Governor General's Award, to create windows for the baptistery. One of these depicted Jesus holding a child (Williams's niece), and another, the Children of the World. In the 1950s, Williams produced twelve other windows for the church.[25]

After the Second World War, two United Church congregations commissioned unique stained glass windows that featured important figures in Canadian Protestantism. Following the fire that in 1954 entirely destroyed the sanctuary of Bloor Street United, the architectural firm of Bruce, Brown and Brisley was hired to carry out restorations costing of $430,000. Nine stained glass windows were placed in the narthex or lobby of the church, produced by Celtic Studios of Swansea in Wales and commemorating pastors, missionaries, and administrators

5.4a and 5.4b (above and opposite) St Anne's Anglican Church
The original Gothic-inspired church in suburban Brockton was replaced in
1908 by the current Byzantine-like structure very loosely modelled on
Hagia Sofia in Constantinople. The ambitious rector of this evangelical
Anglican parish chose an architectural style he thought predated Roman
Catholicism. His connection with the Arts and Letters Club ensured that
the building would be decorated by the top Canadian artists of the day.
(5.4a, Toronto Reference Library; 5.4b, Gabriele Scardellato)

historically connected with the three denominations that formed the
United Church.[26] The same company created twelve other stained glass
windows for the nave of Runnymede United: the first six, depicting
various forms of Christian ministry, used biblical subjects drawn mostly
from the New Testament; the remaining six were scenes or figures
highlighting the expansion of Protestantism in the different regions of
Canada.[27] The windows were planned in 1960 and installed later in the

decade. The first of these was donated by John Pickup, former Chief Justice of the Appeal Court of Ontario, who had played a prominent role in raising funds for the erection of the church in 1927 and in its early governance.

Catholic churches too were objects of artistic endeavour. Built in 1922 at a cost of $160,000, St Anthony, a Romanesque-style brick edifice, featured a recently rediscovered and restored Arts and Crafts fresco above the apse by an unknown artist. It depicts an enthroned Christ as priestly king holding an orb and sceptre, flanked by symbols of the four evangelists, themselves surrounded by swirling acanthus leaves. Beneath the figures are seven stylized palm trees that nicely highlight the six stained glass windows illustrating the life of St Anthony.[28] The same firm of N.T. Lyon created the other windows in the transepts, nave, and façade, where a smallish rose window is displayed. Built five years later at a similar cost, Holy Rosary, a perpendicular Gothic stone church, was inaugurated with a solemn high mass featuring nineteenth-century Lichtenstein-born composer Josef Rheinberger's *Mass in A*. A large, richly decorated stained glass window of Mary holding the child Jesus, executed in Birmingham, England, rises above the altar. The Basilian pastor, Michael Oliver, was responsible for the subject of this window, as well as those of the nine others lining the nave. Designed by artist Marjorie Naser and executed by the Toronto firm of Pringle and London, they represent saints of both sexes from various centuries and ethnicities.[29]

The windows of another West Toronto parish, St Cecilia's, were manufactured by N.T. Lyon, mostly in the interwar period. If the church's decoration is any indication, pastor J.P. Treacy was well connected. The statue of St Rita was a gift from Rafael Cardinal Merry del Val, Apostolic Visitor to Canada (1897), Secretary of State to Pius X (1903–1914), and prefect of the powerful Holy Office until his death in 1930. Merry del Val's long-time rival, Mariano Cardinal Rampolla del Tindaro, Secretary of State under Leo XIII (1878–1903), for his part, donated the statue of St Cecilia. White marble altars were purchased in the late 1920s for the sanctuary and side chapels, while marble statues of St Patrick and St Anthony decorated the spaces between the altars.[30]

Central and eastern European immigrants were avid supporters of church decoration. In 1930 the Russian Orthodox congregation built its own iconostasis, later beautifully adorned by Russian-born artist Julia Gerikova. The one at St Wolodymyr was completed by architect

Yuriy Kodak in 1955. The icons and the interior decoration of the church were the work of Mykhailo Dmytrenko, Ivan Kubarsky, and Wolodymyr Balas, members of the Ukrainian Association of Artists, which was founded in German DP camps after the war. Around this time, the first pastor of St Nicholas Ukrainian Catholic, Bohdan Lypsky, conceived of plans to turn his church into an authentic expression of Byzantine worship and art, spending $120,000 to achieve his aim.[31] The rebuilt apse was closed off by an imposing and finely crafted iconostasis produced by Vladimir Barac, a Montenegrin-born woodcarver recently arrived in Canada. Iconographers Ivan Dyky, a native of Kharkiv, eastern Ukraine, and Igor Suhačev, from Yugoslavia, where both artists' parents settled after the Russian Revolution,[32] created the sumptuous frescoes adorning every corner of the edifice as well as the iconostasis. Especially noteworthy are those above the apse of the traditional figure of Christ Pantocrator (the Almighty) and, below him, Mary the Mother of God (Theotokos), flanked by deferential figures of the archangels Michael and Gabriel. Candelabras hang from the ceiling, including the imposing central one with its outer crown ornamented inside and out with small icons. Our Lady Help of Christians Slovenian had ten stained glass windows installed depicting scenes from the lives of Jesus and Mary in a modern geometric design. The reputable Slovenian American artist, Franc Gorše, whose works are displayed in churches elsewhere in North America, produced statues, reliefs, and Stations of the Cross as well as a nativity scene. The crowns for Mary and Jesus were fashioned by Ted Kramolc, a painter, architect, writer, and interior designer and a graduate of the Ontario College of Art, which he attended shortly after arriving from an Austrian DP camp in 1948. A painting of the Virgin produced in 1927 by a Franciscan friar in Slovenia was prominently displayed in the sanctuary. Outside the church, above the entrance, a mosaic of Mary was produced by the Hungarian Sisters of Social Service, who also created the indoor and outdoor mosaics at St Elizabeth of Hungary.[33]

Some synagogues too had decorated interiors. Above the elaborately carved *Aron Ha-Kodesh* in Beth Jacob, the main Polish synagogue, were stained glass windows with symbolic representations of the twelve tribes of Israel. Along the walls on the main floor were paintings portraying scenes of the Holy Land, while on the balcony were found depictions of the signs of the zodiac. A large, semicircular stained glass window graced the facade. Symbols of the zodiac decorate the ceiling above the women's gallery in the intimate, much less imposing interior

5.5 St Nicholas Ukrainian Catholic
In 1951, Ukrainian Catholic DPs who arrived in Toronto after the war purchased
the former Dale Presbyterian Church, erected in 1916. Gifted artists specializing
in the Byzantine style utterly transformed the building's interior so that no one
today would guess its denominational origins. (Gabriele Scardellato)

of the Junction's Knesseth Israel. Naïf-style murals surround the *Aron
Ha-Kodesh*, depicting, on the one hand, musical instruments, and on the
other, animals, the latter all in reference to the verse from a Mishnaic
tractate: "Be as bold as a leopard, light as an eagle, swift as a deer and
strong as a lion to do the will of your Father in Heaven." The walls
of the interior are painted to look like marble, and the pale blue ceiling with clouds and stars recalls the firmament. The imposing *Shaarei
Shomayim* had a black Italian marble *Aron Ha-Kodesh* and stained glass
windows representing Jewish holidays and festivals. One of these windows, doubtless outside the sanctuary, celebrated the recent rebirth of
Israel, with pioneers holding an Israeli flag beside a tractor. [34]

The Religion of Feeling

Greater formality characterized the worship of many Toronto congregations. But premillennial ones were more inclined to spontaneity and expressiveness. In 1921, Oswald Smith, a graduate of the Toronto Bible College founded by Elmore Harris, took charge of the Christian and Missionary Alliance's Parkdale Tabernacle, quickly reversing its decline. Smith had been associate pastor of Dale Presbyterian, where he had offended a number of congregants with his fundamentalist tendencies, revivalist style, and gospel music.[35] His stay at Parkdale Tabernacle was short-lived. He left to build the Alliance Tabernacle on Christie Street just north of Bloor. With a seating capacity of 2,700, the building clearly spoke to Smith's ambitions. Revivals here were a common occurrence: Welsh evangelists Fred Clark and George Bell conducted a twice-daily one in the late summer of 1925. Women were also frequent guest preachers there. One of them was the granddaughter of William and Catherine Booth, founders of the Salvation Army.[36] Smith relinquished his charge in 1926 in somewhat obscure circumstances after being appointed superintendent of the Christian and Missionary Alliance in Eastern Canada.[37] Within two years, he had gone on to found the People's Church, which is outside our area of inquiry. Smith's itinerary is reminiscent of that of earlier evangelists examined in Chapter 2. The Alliance Tabernacle was not the same after Smith's departure, but it managed to survive for two more decades, at which point, in 1948, the building was taken over by the United Jewish People's Order, a secular, left-wing Jewish organization.

Meanwhile, Parkdale Tabernacle affiliated itself with the Church of the Nazarene, taking over the former Cowan Avenue Presbyterian, whose ranks had been depleted after Church Union. It was in the Nazarene congregation that evangelist Charles Templeton's mother, a single parent with five children, found religion. Shortly thereafter, her son, who had resisted its call, came home late one Saturday evening overwhelmed by a crushing sense of guilt that left him

> numb, speechless, immobilized, alone, tense with a sense of expectancy. In a moment, a weight began to lift, a weight as heavy as I. It passed through my thighs, my belly, my chest, my arms, my shoulders and lifted off entirely. I could have leaped over a wall. An ineffable warmth began to suffuse every corpuscle. It seemed that a light had turned on in my chest and its refining fire had cleansed me. I hardly dared breathe, fearing that I might end or alter the moment.[38]

5.6 Parkdale Tabernacle
Formerly Cowan Avenue Presbyterian, the building was taken over in the
interwar years by a Nazarene congregation, one of whose members was the
mother of evangelist Charles Templeton. In 1954 it was acquired by Poles who
had broken from St Stanislaus to form St John's Polish National Catholic Parish. Raised to cathedral status, the church is affiliated with the Old Catholic
Church, whose seat is in Utrecht, Netherlands. (Toronto Reference Library)

A high school dropout who until then had worked as a cartoonist and
sports journalist for the *Globe*, Templeton went on to lead the Avenue
Road Church of the Nazarene, filling its 1,600 seats to capacity every
Sunday evening. He added a second service called Songfest aimed specifically at young people, who came from all over the city to hear him.
At the war's end, Templeton began his Youth for Christ rallies, which
increased his fame.

Charles Price, one of Oswald Smith's associates, decided after leading an evangelistic campaign at Massey Hall in 1924 to rent the then vacant Queen Street Methodist Church. He teamed up with Pentecostal preachers Willard and Christine Pierce, who were in Toronto on a healing mission, and the three evangelists conducted a two-and-one-half-year revival, as we saw at the beginning of Chapter 4.[39] Their faith-healing sessions drew publicity and big crowds (6,000 people attended one service, according to the *Star*). A sceptical reporter gave a highly gendered account of one such meeting: "Scores of patients, mostly women have fainted away at the touch of [Pierce's] hands upon their heads, which in some cases is a part of the ceremony anointing them. Some remain in a state of semi-unconsciousness from fifteen to twenty-five minutes." Citing a local doctor, the journalist added: "The unconscious desire in women for sympathy and publicity ... was to a large extent responsible for the fact that they fainted in churches and other public places and if a woman makes up her mind to fall unconscious, nothing on earth will prevent her from doing so."[40] A few months later, the church hosted evangelist Mae Eleanor Frey, the first woman to be ordained a Baptist minister in New York State. Her travels to "Mohammedan lands" apparently authorized her to compare Christianity and Islam. The title of her evening lecture was "Fire-Eating Dervishes."[41]

As in the previous period, exoticism proved to be an effective means of captivating congregants' imaginations and generating financial support for missionary activity in "heathen lands." At the Queen Street congregation, lantern slide shows and skits were common events. At one such presentation, a woman missionary recently returned from northern India and "dressed in the Indian 'Sari' spoke to the whole assembled congregation as tho [sic] she were an Indian woman who had been saved, telling how the gospel had brought her joy, light and peace." At the same meeting, two white women missionaries back from southern China performed a skit in which "a native Chinese Bible woman and a heathen Chinese woman portrayed to us vividly how the Gospel is carried to the home of the heathen woman. They both spoke in Chinese." The English translation was provided by a third proselytizer, also white.[42]

First Holiness Pentecostal, a congregation led by a former Christian and Missionary Alliance minister, took over the former Christian Workers church on Robert Street. Membership increased as a result of special events, including revivals, missionary conventions (such as those attended by Della Lageer in Chapter 2), and district conferences, which were usually directed by pastors from the United States. At one revival, "the church [was] packed to the doors and the spiritual atmosphere attending this service was very precious and encouraging."[43] We lose sight of this congregation in 1935. But three new ones sprang up around the same time. The first of these briefly occupied the former Avenue Road United before moving to a new building called the Stone Church, on Davenport Road outside of our area. The second, named Glad Tidings Tabernacle, was created by the minister H.R. Pannebecker and his wife. The congregation then moved to facilities on St Clair Avenue near Winona. The building's cornerstone was laid by the chairman of the Assemblies of God in Great Britain. Reporting on a two-month-long revival led in 1938 by two women, in which "many were slain of the Lord at every service," Pannebecker captured the spontaneity and expectancy of Pentecostalism's mindset: "Our Evangelists came to us from the Lord not having previously made arrangements for this meeting, but we left ourselves open to the leading of the Spirit as they did also and God was able to work in His own way."[44] The third, known as West End Pentecostal, originated in the Stone Church and then moved into a renovated fire hall in the Junction.[45]

The Standard Church of America came to Toronto at the end of the First World War, probably with the arrival of rural migrants from the Ottawa Valley. Founded by Ralph C. Horner in Brockville, the denomination was the result of a split within the Holiness Movement Church, which Horner himself had created. At issue was the evangelist's autocratic style, in particular his inability to work with younger colleagues. As a young man, Horner had been converted to Methodism at a camp meeting. He claimed to have later received a tongue of fire from the Holy Spirit that empowered him to preach. He was deposed as minister for refusing to conform to the discipline of the Methodist Church and for his unqualified championing of old-time revivalist religion with its shouting, thrashing, weeping, and swooning. Throughout the 1920s the Standard Church had various worship sites in the West End along Ossington Avenue and Queen Street. The following decade, it opened a storefront on Dundas Street West, which it occupied until 1961.[46]

Although these denominations claimed few followers, it would be unwise to dismiss them. The mass revivals held at Massey Hall and other large venues demonstrate that they had a capacity to mobilize far beyond their numbers. Just as High Church parishes exerted influence beyond their narrow circles, indeed beyond their denominations, so too did these small congregations have an impact on Protestantism in general, albeit in the opposite direction: towards an expressive, spontaneous, and enthusiastic worship, where the clergy's training, respectability, and gender were of little consequence. The mainstream congregations may have rejected premillennialism's positions on female ministry and on the relative unimportance of clerical education, but some shared their emotive religiosity. This was true of Baptists who followed T.T. Shields and of Presbyterians who rejected Church Union. At High Park Baptist, for example, the spontaneous public confession of a congregant triggered a month-long revival in 1924 that included day and night prayer meetings and new baptisms. A congregant at Bonar Presbyterian recently reminisced in rather unsympathetic tones that "in the forties and fifties, the fundamentalist gang from Bob Jones College with their flannel-board demonstrations invaded what had been a very Scottish Presbyterian church ... Their unscholarly tone pervaded the Sunday School for years to come. Even the CGIT [Canadian Girls in Training] had a somewhat evangelical flavour."[47] By contrast, George Pidgeon deplored the fact that the creation of the United Church had not ignited a national revival – not, of course, the kind championed by premillennialists, but one responding to the real spiritual hunger he felt existed in Canada.

Disquiet on the West End Front

Pidgeon's thinking reflected a sense of unease that had begun creeping into downtown churches in the interwar years. Generational continuity, discussed earlier in this book in the context of synagogues, was also an issue for Christian congregations, even those considered invulnerable. With a membership of 1,500 by 1927, Timothy Eaton Memorial was a model of success. Yet three years later, an internal report confirmed that young people were leaving that congregation for other churches.[48] Places of worship were feeling the competition for young people from premillennial denominations, but also from secular agencies offering specialized and well-funded programs of social improvement.

Notwithstanding Pidgeon's views, churches had not been idle in the 1920s. He himself had launched a junior congregation at Bloor Street Presbyterian in 1920 and had experimented with visual aids to captivate the minds of youth. He had also opened a kindergarten on the premises so as to bind young families more firmly to the church. Timothy Eaton Memorial offered a range of highly gendered youth-centred activities, enlisting young men freed up at the war's end to direct its "boy's work." The Canadian Standard Efficiency Training (CSET) Program,[49] promoted by the YMCA and embraced by the United Church, spawned new, age-specific boys' clubs such as Tuxis and Trail Rangers, which organized intellectual, artistic, social, and sporting events. Debates and lectures were held, plays were performed, baseball and hockey games were arranged, and social assistance was provided to inner-city youth. These organizations participated in annual Boys' Week parades, which were held in the spring. In 1923 the church sponsored a delegation to the Provincial Boys' Parliament. By contrast, girls' groups, such as CGIT[50] and the Explorers, seemed more focused on personal and spiritual development, although they too were involved in small outreach and missionary projects. Leisure was centred on gendered activities such as baking, cooking, and playing games.[51] Be that as it may, the congregation implemented the main recommendation of its internal report by appointing a young assistant minister. Although he stayed only one year, this cleric apparently succeeded in turning things around. At the same time, under the tolerant gaze of the Eatons, young people's organizations began to host dances at the church, an activity frowned upon in the past. Another pastime once denounced by Methodists, card playing, discreetly made its appearance shortly thereafter.

Sports were regarded as especially effective in drawing young men to places of worship. Timothy Eaton Memorial had a fully equipped bowling alley in the basement, as well as outdoor tennis courts and lawn bowling greens. At Davenport Road Methodist/United, a hockey rink and a tennis court were installed at the rear of the building. St Helen's, the biggest Catholic church after the St Michael's Cathedral, offered interwar youth activities such as boxing, bowling, hockey, and euchre. Matches featuring bantam and lightweight boxing champions were held in the adjacent church hall. It was there that Walter Newton got his start as a boxer. A member of the Canadian team at the Antwerp Olympics of 1920, he went on to pursue a professional career in Chicago. Queen Street United underwent extensive renovations costing close to $100,000, which made it "one of the most modern institutional churches in Canada." The building included a four-lane, regulation-size bowling alley and a gymnasium with showers. Meeting rooms were described as bright and airy, club rooms as inviting.[52]

New media were also explored for their outreach potential. In 1924, Timothy Eaton Memorial became one of the first in Toronto to accept the *Toronto Star*'s offer to broadcast services monthly on its radio station. Although a reluctant Trevor Davies expressed fears that the new format might actually encourage some of his congregants to stay home, the argument that it would reach shut-ins and others unable to attend services finally prevailed. This program came to an end a decade later when the station went off the air. Morning services at Bloor Street United began to be transmitted after George Pidgeon resumed his pastoral duties following his election as first moderator of the United Church.[53] Other large congregations, such as Dovercourt Presbyterian, Western Baptist, Bathurst Street United, and Knox Presbyterian, followed suit. At St Thomas a shortened version of evensong was relayed throughout North America in the 1930s. Even relatively small congregations were given air time. St John's Evangelical Lutheran, a member of the English District of the Missouri Synod, broadcast services in English from 1938 to 1940.[54] During the same decade the Radio Kings of Harmony, a gospel group associated with the Afro-American First Baptist congregation, were also featured on radio.[55] Catholics, for their part, ignored the new medium: worshippers were required to be physically present at Sunday mass. It was not until the 1950s that the Catholic Information Centre – founded and directed by the Paulist Frank Stone, and comprising offices, classrooms, a library, and a broadcast studio adjacent to St Peter's parish – aired its own radio program.[56]

These various initiatives apparently did little to quiet the turmoil caused by the Wall Street Crash of 1929 and the Second World War. Congregations responded differently to these events. Some remained tied to the past. Avenue Road Presbyterian, for example, declined a request by its Young People's Society to mount a Bible drama on a Sunday for fear of offending congregants' sabbatarian sensibilities. Unwavering in its attachment to tradition, it allowed the Ulster Defenders of the Loyal Orange Lodge to use the church and hall for their 12 July parade celebrating the victory of William of Orange over Catholic forces at the Battle of the Boyne. At the war's end the church had to be sold because of declining membership and the resulting inability to meet mortgage payments. The congregation survived another two decades only by merging with nearby Olivet Congregational. While the above-mentioned decisions did not in themselves cause the demise of the church, they were symptomatic of a deeper malaise: the inability to adapt. Other congregations made shallow

5.7 First Baptist

Founded in the early nineteenth century, this African American congregation built its church in 1907 on University Avenue. It is here that in the interwar years a gospel group called the Radio Kings of Harmony sang. The congregation moved to its current location on Huron Street after the war when University Avenue was taken over by large institutional buildings. (Toronto Reference Library)

attempts at change. At Walmer Road Baptist, where membership peaked at just under 2,000 in 1929, the minister, H.H. Bingham, introduced travelogues and pastor's parties to halt the slow decline over the following decade.[57]

George Pidgeon's methods were more substantial as well as more orthodox. After failing to launch a Canada-wide evangelization campaign sponsored by the main Protestant denominations, he turned to the Oxford Group (not to be confused with the homonymous movement in nineteenth-century Anglicanism). This international organization of British origin promoted intimate encounters in which participants, led by trained teams, spoke openly of their experiences and sins. The exercise was somewhat reminiscent of nineteenth-century

Methodism's class meetings, but also of modern-day premillennial movements. The assembled group would first seek to be wholly possessed by the spirit. This was followed by individual testimony that sprang from self-criticism and exchange. The experience was meant to be personally and collectively transformative. In contrast to the Social Gospel, which explicitly posited social reform as the key to personal salvation, the emphasis here was wholly on the individual. The Oxford Group reinforced a commonly expressed idea during the 1930s that the Depression was a sign of a moral rather than economic failure, and could be remedied not so much by structural changes to society but through personal moral regeneration. So is it surprising that the Oxford Group's campaigns showed a marked predilection for the rich and powerful, an association it unabashedly publicized? Critics denounced the Oxford Group's high-pressure tactics, later adopted by Alcoholics Anonymous, in the course of which the group could effectively exert control over individuals' thinking and behaviour. This tendency would become more apparent in the Moral Re-Armament movement to which the Oxford Group gave birth.

Be that as it may, early on Pidgeon invited Oxford Group teams to Bloor Street United. Some congregants became prominent in the organization, and he himself made its group-centred techniques a hallmark of his ministry. Pidgeon led teams to other churches in the city and around the country in order to propagate the Oxford Group's methods of evangelization. He also became one of its apologists, publicly countering criticisms of it as they appeared in the press.[58] Trevor Davies of Timothy Eaton Memorial was also enthusiastic about the organization. On his initiative, a group of ten couples from the congregation met regularly for a number of years.[59] Inspired by the Oxford model, the rector of St Anne's, Noel Palmer, an Englishman who may have had contact with the group in his home country, initiated fellowship meetings after the evening service on Sundays where congregants spoke freely about their personal religious experiences.[60]

The Challenge of Secular Social Agencies

Congregations previously engaged in "works of social uplift" now faced stiff competition from social agencies and service clubs. During the Depression, the activities of the Victorian Order of Nurses and Big Brothers, for example, forced Walmer Road Baptist to cut back on the extensive services it had been offering through the Memorial Institute, which included English, first aid, craft, and music classes, a men's social club, a women's sewing circle, a children's play group, and a well-baby clinic (the district had the highest infant mortality rate in the city). It must be said that the area surrounding the institute had changed markedly over the years: industries had moved in, the recently demolished stock of houses had not been replaced, and residents of British ancestry had given way to eastern European immigrants. By 1944, Walmer Road Baptist had withdrawn entirely from Memorial, which now served the Russian-Ukrainian congregation.[61]

Just one block away, Queen Street United faced the same predicament. A report commissioned by the United Church in 1944 concluded that the renovated church had not succeeded in reaching out to the community, where people of British origin now made up scarcely one-tenth of the population. The church had been built to accommodate 1,200 worshippers; the new sanctuary seated one-third that number, the rest of the space being used for rooms and offices. Even so, only seventy worshippers regularly attended on Sunday mornings and about twice that number in the evenings, among whom were "quite a few" African Americans and their children. Overall, only one-quarter of the 160 members were "in vital touch" with the church. This core group was described as aging, British, and deeply attached to the church's traditions, although lacking leadership abilities. It was they who ran the Sunday school, where two-thirds of the attendees were of non-British background. To rejuvenate the membership, the report's authors recommended a more evangelistic Sunday evening service, which was the one considered most likely to attract outsiders. They noted that the minister, Fred Smith, had strong organizational skills, worked hard to draw in new congregants, and showed resourcefulness in his use of music, drama, and other devices. But, as Smith himself admitted, he was not suited to evangelical preaching.

The same report criticized the minister for throwing open the church's facilities, including the bowling alley, to Big Sisters and Kiwanis. With their considerable financial resources, specialized staff, and advertising, these bodies organized weekly and even biweekly activities, quite independently of the church, drawing away members from congregational associations such as the Young People's Union, which had an average weekly attendance of only twelve.[62] The document had no quarrel with the work being done by these groups, but did note that religion was conspicuously absent from it. Meanwhile, the church's own youth services were woefully inadequate. It was therefore proposed that the church hire a full-time specialized youth worker, especially for boys. The report also deplored the absence of a day nursery.[63]

Similar tensions developed over St Christopher House. It was founded in 1912 when philanthropist Sir James Woods purchased three adjacent properties in the Kensington Market area. These buildings were then connected and a gymnasium installed. Two downtown churches became closely involved with this work. Bloor Street Presbyterian made substantial financial contributions over and above the monies given by the denomination's missionary board. As well, the church initially supplied almost all of its head workers. The minister at College Street Presbyterian, whose territory encompassed the settlement house, chaired the board of management, a deaconess acted as a staff member, and the boys' worker operated at both the church and the house. Woods insisted that St Christopher House be in the hands of a self-appointed board of trustees, independent of the church, who would hold legal title to the building. With Church Union the special relationship linking St Christopher House to the Presbyterians devolved to the United Church.

The minister of College Street United later became dissatisfied with the arrangement. The deaconess, who was paid out of the church budget, was working entirely on her own, isolated from both supervisors and colleagues. The boys' worker had relinquished his duties at the church, including Sunday school teaching. When the minister tried to bring about greater collaboration between church and settlement workers, he discovered to his surprise that their goals were fundamentally at odds. A former head worker articulated this difference by insisting that her personnel be qualified and trained by the Social Service Department at the University of Toronto, adding that she "didn't see the need for Church connection. The only type of Christian work she was ever interested in … was improving people socially and brightening their lives and preparing them, through social ministries, for good citizenship." The minister, for his part, emphasized the centrality of religion, pointing out that "no person was prepared entirely for good citizenship unless they had known the influence and fellowship of the Christian Church."

In the end, the Federated Budget Committee of Toronto, a body coordinating fundraising appeals for various social agencies, agreed to subsidize St Christopher House in exchange for representation on its board. Because its yearly grant and salary scale were higher than those of the United Church, staff workers were better paid. The denomination accordingly considered severing its ties completely with the settlement house and turning College Street United into a home mission. "With a strong evangelistic preacher in the pulpit and an adequate staff of social workers, [it would be possible] to do from the corner of Bathurst and College Streets all the work that the United Church could be expected to do in the way of community betterment and the extension of the Kingdom of God in the life of the people of the area."[64]

Knox Presbyterian faced its crisis much later, in the 1950s, having reached a peak of 1,700 members in the worst years of the Depression. Although a day nursery was opened in 1942 and open air services inaugurated after the regular Sunday evening worship, activities targeting young people had fallen off considerably over the following decade as a result of the war and weak clerical leadership. In 1956 two youth workers were finally hired, the first in connection with the congregation and the second with ties to the community at large. Ian Rennie, a student minister and former staff member with the Inter-Varsity Christian Fellowship, an association of fundamentalist university students founded in 1929, organized "uncompromisingly evangelistic" youth rallies every month. Special days dedicated to prayer were held at the church, as were half-nights of prayer. In 1957 the church sponsored a major youth weekend led by a well-known British evangelist. Meanwhile, a skilled athlete took over the sporting activities at the Baraca Club, while keeping a watchful eye on young people's spiritual welfare.[65]

Young people were also a major concern for Gedalia Felder, a distinguished rabbi born in Ustrzyky Dolne, Lwów voivodeship, Poland, and trained at Toronto's Torah Chaim *yeshiva*. Shortly after assuming the pulpit of Mach Zikei B'nai Israel, he and some senior members launched a junior congregation headed by a twenty-one-year-old engineering student, which had its own services on Friday evenings and weekend mornings. The basement of the synagogue was transformed into a club room housing bowling and floor hockey teams, a choir, and a small orchestra. An engaging and gifted teacher, Felder left an indelible mark on the young people with whom he came in contact.[66] *Bais Yahuda* too inaugurated youth Sabbaths, with young men taking complete control of the service, a practice perhaps inspired by Felder, who was the principal of the synagogue's Talmud Torah. Other innovations included post–Bar Mitzvah classes and father–son breakfasts. Meanwhile, up the hill at Shaarei Shomayim, the proposed construction of a facility to house its varied youth activities met with intense criticism from a number of members because of the high costs involved. Shortly after the centre

5.8 Bathurst Street United

In the 1940s and 1950s, the minister promoted Jewish–Christian dialogue, invited spokespersons of progressive social forces, and fought against juvenile delinquency. After the congregation moved to Trinity–St Paul's United in 1975, a gay congregation called Metropolitan Community Church temporarily worshipped here. The building is now home to the Bathurst Street Theatre. (Gabriele Scardellato) was completed in the mid-1950s, the synagogue executive voted to pull up stakes and follow the northward movement of Jews.[67]

While some men of the cloth may have frowned on service clubs using church facilities for youth work, in 1948 Gordon Domm actually invited Kiwanis to run a boy's club out of the basement of Bathurst Street United. Open most afternoons and evenings, the Midtown K Club organized craft activities, games, and floor hockey, which was played in its gymnasium. Movies were shown one night a week, and a subsidized camp at Lake Muskoka made it possible for young people to enjoy a summer holiday in the countryside. The Ladies' Auxiliary sponsored an annual Christmas party where presents were distributed in the presence of a celebrity, usually from the world of sport. Domm took this initiative following a brawl that broke out at Wasaga Beach on Georgian Bay, resulting in dozens of arrests of members of a West End gang called the Beanery Boys. The minister decided to hold a community forum on juvenile delinquency – a much debated and publicized concern in the postwar era – as a result of which the church was made available to the gang. In a *Toronto Star* interview given a few years later, the minister reformulated the message of the Social Gospel in up-to-date terms:

> There is a great opportunity here for combining religion with work and play. Here we have a democratic wholesome program without respect for race or creed and a place where humans can gather. Our church is in the centre of a mobile community whose members can't be reached in the usual way of churches. We must reach them where they are. And there is a special challenge in young people's work among boys and girls of all races, all religions and none. [68]

At St Paul's–Avenue Road United, a church that had narrowly avoided closing by a vote of its members in 1959, the newly inducted minister, Stewart Crysdale, extended a hand to the Ramsden Park Gang, whose name was derived from that of the nearby park. Known as greasers because of the copious quantity of lubricant they put in their hair to hold it back, these feisty working-class teenagers were involved in petty crime in the neighbourhood. For this reason, they were reviled by local businessmen and largely ignored by the area's churches. Historian Stuart Henderson has justly underscored the conflicting values to which greasers subscribed. On the one hand, they wanted to appear cool, tough, and set for kicks. On the other, they aspired to respectability, as was evident in the importance they placed on the clothes they wore and in their deference to certain forms of authority. Besides taking a number of them to his summer cottage, Crysdale agreed to their request to create a club where they could feel they belonged. Twice weekly, more than one hundred young people turned up in the church basement to hang out to the sounds of rock'n'roll. Because alcohol was often smuggled in, complaints emanated from the neighbourhood about street fighting, swearing, revving motors, and squealing tires. Reports were also made of break-ins and vandalism. In the long run, however, this work apparently produced positive results for the church: over the following decade, a number of gang members settled down and became congregants, together with their families.[69]

Politics and the Pulpit

Churches that were responsive to the religion of feeling with its focus on the individual's relationship with Jesus tended to be politically conservative and avoided taking public stances on the issues of the day. In general, pastors were less politically involved than in earlier times, when sabbatarianism and the Social Gospel were openly and strongly espoused. Nevertheless, in 1923 a group of progressive clergymen, including Salem Bland of Broadway Methodist Tabernacle and Lancelot Minehan of St Vincent de Paul parish, ruffled Tory feathers by publicly supporting the appointment of J.A. Dale, Professor of Social Science at the University of Toronto, as head of the Public Welfare Branch of Toronto's Health Department. British-born and educated, Dale considered himself a Christian socialist, although termed a "parlour Bolsheviki" by the Conservatives, who succeeded in blocking his nomination, which had been made by Premier Ernest Drury's United Farmers of Ontario government.[70] Shortly after this incident, Minehan was accused of sympathizing with the Irish Republican organization Sinn Fein. Determined to fight back, he wrote a letter to the editor inviting the electorate to

> mark where booze and brass, prevaricators and plunderers … journalistic humbugs and hydrophobiacs, are ranged … Ask yourselves how many of the candidates appealing for your votes have shown any appreciation of the serious social issues confronting us or paid the slightest tribute to what has been recently done in the field of social betterment. If you have even moderate powers of observation you should not find it hard to decide as to the side on which your vote and influence should be cast.[71]

Some ministers and congregations lobbied the government to open Canada's doors to interwar refugees. Their efforts failed. As secretary of the Armenian Relief Fund, A.J. Vining, pastor of College Street Baptist, championed Armenian immigration to Canada in the wake of the widespread and horrific massacres occurring in the Ottoman Empire during and after the First World War. The government classified Armenians as Asians and therefore as inadmissible; Vining argued that they merited special consideration because they were Christians and had supported the Allied cause during the war. Aware of the government's preference for agriculturalists, he advocated rural settlement as the solution for these prospective newcomers. Jews too regarded farming as an effective means of advancing the cause of immigration for their coreligionists to Canada.[72] A mass meeting was called to this effect at *Goel Tzedec* with the support of its rabbi, Jesse Schwartz, and Ferdinand Isserman of Holy Blossom. The Federated Jewish Farmers of Ontario, an organization recently established at the instigation of Morris Saxe, a successful businessman, purchased the old Eaton farm in Georgetown in order to teach farming techniques to young Jewish immigrants and help them get settled.[73] In the event, seventy-nine orphans from Międzyrzec Korecki in interwar Poland (now Mezhirichi, Cherkasy *oblast*, Ukraine) received training at the Georgetown facility, which was closed in 1933. Towards the end of that decade, at a time when central European Jews under Nazi control were the targets of extreme civil rights abuses and physical violence, the Ladies' Auxiliary of St Paul's United followed the lead of the denomination's higher bodies in urging the government to be more generous in admitting refugees.[74]

St Mary Magdalene's was the site of a number of socially progressive causes. In 1924, Henry Hiscocks once again made headlines when, cautioning striking postal workers against all acts of violence, he urged them nevertheless "to stick it out to the end." In a further gesture similar to Canon Lionel Groulx's 1949 appeal during the Asbestos Strike in Quebec, he recommended that the strike committee send a circular to the city's clergy asking them to have their congregants pray for social justice.[75] During the Depression, rector Gordon Graham, an active member of the Co-operative Commonwealth Federation, set up a "sociology group" to hear lectures and discuss socially significant topics, much as his Low Church counterpart, J.E. Gibson, had done at the Church of the Ascension (see Chapter 2). Another priest, Reginald Thomas, became chairman of the "Friends of the Mackenzie–Papineau Battalion" and the unofficial chaplain to the pro-Republican veterans, whom he met at Union Station when they returned from combat in the Spanish Civil War. Finally, during the Second World War, his colleague, Charles Fielding, advocated worker participation in the control of industry (much as the Quebec hierarchy did in their pastoral letter of 1950), as well as fair treatment for Japanese Canadians.[76]

During Gordon Domm's twenty-year pastorate, Bathurst Street United was also identified with progressive causes. The church boasted a membership of 750, with well over twice that number of people frequenting it weekly. As we have seen, social service organizations regularly used the facilities. During a strike by Toronto milkmen in 1951, union meetings were often held there. That same year, the civil liberties sections of the Congress of Industrial Organizations (CIO) and the Canadian Congress of Labour (CCL) – industrial union federations in the forefront of the fight for legislation banning discrimination in housing, employment, and public services in Ontario – also met there.[77] But it was Domm's perceived relationship with communists that got him into trouble. In 1944 the minister initiated Sunday evening forums at which invited guests expressed their views on current affairs. One such speaker was James G. Endicott, son of a former United Church moderator and himself a missionary, having served in China for twenty-two years with the support of Timothy Eaton Memorial's Sunday school. On his return to Canada in 1947, Endicott made headlines by denouncing Nationalist leader Chiang Kai-shek's regime as oppressive and calling for its overthrow, an act he deemed democratic and progressive. In 1949, Bathurst Street United hosted the founding convention of the Canadian Peace Congress, which was attended by three hundred delegates, at which Endicott was elected president. In the face of the Cold War and American expansionism in Asia, as well as growing Western hostility to national liberation struggles, he promoted citizen mobilization for peace.

Domm fully supported his colleague, signing a petition against the sale and shipment of arms to Chiang Kai-shek. He also threw open church doors to organizations such as the Congress of Canadian Women and the Canadian–Soviet Friendship Society, much to the dismay of the United Church Session. At the height of McCarthyism, the church's governing body adopted a resolution prohibiting a Canadian Peace Congress local from meeting there without prior approval. At the same time it strongly criticized Domm for his liberal views. Some congregants, viewing such organizations as communist fronts and suspecting the minister's own political orientation, called for his resignation. The minister's response clearly was not intended to appease them. Domm declared that he would exclude no one from his fellowship. Jesus did not disregard truth because it came from unpopular sources, he asserted. The Christians' program for social action was just as daring as that of the communists and the two should therefore make common cause against social injustice. Indeed, there was "something of a brotherhood between them," their objectives being "to a degree" the same. "My Christ," he concluded, "goes along with communism, but my Christ goes beyond communism, and my Christ goes beyond Christians."[78]

At *Chevra Tehillim*, Domm's friend Reuben Slonim also ran into difficulties with the congregants over an international question. At issue for him were the laws on marriage and education in the newly founded state of Israel. At the invitation of the *Toronto Telegram*'s publisher, the rabbi penned a series of articles on the theme "Freedom Crisis in Israel" in which he denounced the absence of civil marriage, an educational system that separated Jews and Arabs, and the monopoly on marriage that had been awarded by law to the Orthodox rabbinate. The series caused a furore among a Jewish population that had long been strong supporters of Zionism and that regarded criticism of the fledgling state as an act of perfidy, especially when expressed before a Gentile audience. Long perceived as a maverick and an outsider, Slonim began to receive threats by mail and phone. When the synagogue board met to consider the question, he stuck to his position, telling the members: "Israel has a special duty and role to promote freedom of conscience. The Jews suffered too much over the centuries from lack of it. In a sense, this is a family quarrel, and Israelis have to work it out for themselves. But the outside world deserves to know about it because it touches Christians and because the restriction of freedom anywhere affects people everywhere."[79] By majority vote, the board declined to endorse their rabbi's views, but nevertheless upheld his right to express them.

Places of Worship in the Lives of Immigrants

The Interwar Years

Places of worship were invested with great importance even by the religiously lukewarm or indifferent. They were often the first concrete manifestations of an immigrant group's institutional life. Their sacred spaces offered a sense of belonging and community that transcended the individual and the family. Newcomers also founded secular organizations, such as the Ukrainian Farmer Labour Temple Association and the United Jewish People's Order. But in Toronto at least, these institutions did not become focal points of community life, any more than the multiethnic experiments undertaken by the United and Baptist Churches. Immigrant congregations were especially important in the early years of settlement. Indeed, it is striking how soon after their arrival in the city newcomers of all faiths and denominations set up religious structures. The beginnings of such institutions may have been arduous and unsteady, but the newcomers gave generously of their time, money, and labour to erect places of worship, or renovate them, and adapt them to the various uses to which they would be put. By offering members a variety of services that transcended the purely spiritual or religious, places of worship more closely followed the North American model of a full-orbed religion than their counterparts in the countries of origin.

Taking their cue from the Redemptorists of St Patrick's, the newly arrived Oblates breathed new life into St Stanislaus parish. The Polish-language school that had been closed for thirteen years was reopened, plays were performed weekly, and the Catholic Youth Organization was set up. A credit union was founded in 1945 that today claims to be the largest parish-based one of its kind. A Polish order of nuns, the Felician Sisters, who had come to North America in 1874 to serve their compatriots, arrived from Buffalo to establish a day care centre. This order was also active in Sts Cyril and Methodius Slovak parish and at St Patrick's, where, besides taking over the kindergarten, they instituted music classes for children.[80]

Some places of worship championed particular ideologies or political currents associated with the immigrants' homeland. For example, one association behind the founding of Sts Cyril and Methodius parish was the Slovak Canadian League, a promoter of self-determination for Slovakia, then part of the Czechoslovak Republic created in 1918 when the Austria-Hungary was dismembered. St Wolodymyr parish was, like Ukrainian Orthodoxy in general, closely identified with the Ukrainian Self-Reliance League, a moderate liberal nationalist organization founded in 1927 and opposed to the authoritarian nationalism represented by the Organization of Ukrainian Nationalists, a group committed to the armed liberation of Ukraine.[81]

The Postwar Years

On the whole, pastors and rabbis were attuned to the needs of wartime refugees. Some became champions of their cause, while others provided much-needed assistance in Canada. Throughout the war, both Christ the Saviour Russian Orthodox and St Wolodymyr Ukrainian Orthodox sent relief supplies to camps in Europe where compatriots were being held.[82] For his part, Abraham Price, rabbi of *Chevra Shas* and founder of *Torah Chaim* yeshiva, spearheaded a campaign to release fifty young Jews who had been transported and interned in Canada because they were considered enemy aliens by birth. He was also responsible for bringing over some fifty yeshiva students from Prague.[83] In the postwar period, Ernest Marshall Howse, minister at Bloor Street United, was a conduit for money and supplies reaching DPs in German camps, which he personally visited, establishing contacts there.[84] Parishes and congregations sponsored refugees to Canada.[85] The pastor of St Patrick's, Daniel Ehman, lobbied the federal authorities by letter and in person to allow the relatives of parishioners into the country, even though the UN's International Refugee Organization (IRO) excluded *Volksdeutsche* from refugee status, considering that Germany had an obligation to repatriate all ethnic Germans. In any event, Ehman vowed to engage every Redemptorist in the country in his drive to achieve success.[86] The pastor of St John Evangelical Lutheran kept his congregants informed about recently announced government programs to stimulate immigration through family reunification and labour contracts in farming, forestry, mining, and domestic service.[87] At the same time, letters were arriving via denominational channels from persons seeking help to immigrate. Donald Ortner, the American born and trained newly appointed assistant pastor, spent much of his time answering questions regarding housing, work, and children's schooling.

Parishioners and congregants volunteered to meet refugees at Union Station, while clergymen tried to respond to the latter's immediate wants. Ortner became a pivotal figure in the settlement of Baltic refugees, endorsing applications by prospective employers for farm labourers and domestics, writing letters of reference that spoke to job seekers' moral, political, and personal character, as well as their physical appearance, and intervening on behalf of those who had broken their labour contracts and, as a consequence, faced deportation. As chief coordinator of the Lutheran Labour scheme in the city, Ortner collaborated closely with the labour department's National Employment Service, the personnel offices of large companies, and the Canadian Overseas Garment Commission. He had an especially good working relationship with the YWCA, given that he and they were intent on redirecting some refugees' interests away from the Communist Party "into church and traditional social activities." The agency supplied lists of young women temporarily boarding with them so that Ortner might contact and counsel them. Meanwhile, St John's Evangelical Lutheran gave emergency food and shelter to refugees who had failed to find work upon arrival.[88]

The rectory of Christ the Saviour Parish became a temporary shelter for recently arrived Russian speakers. Used clothing was collected and distributed to those among them in need. The pastor, John Diachina, himself a native of Volhynia *gubernia*, who as a young man had immigrated with his parents to the prairies, accompanied men to factories in search of work. His wife Mary did the same with the women. "In some cases," she claimed, "I had to be an interpreter and show them how to operate the machines for some weeks. Some bosses took the new immigrants on condition that I would be with the[m]." Meanwhile, the church choirmaster, Nina de Gedeonoff, used her contacts with prominent Anglican families for those seeking jobs as domestics.[89]

Some refugees were or became clergymen who went on to lead Toronto parishes and congregations.[90] Before the War, Bohdan Lypsky of St Nicholas Ukrainian Catholic had been a professor of moral and dogmatic theology at the Seminary in Lwów. Bishop Mykhail (Khoroshy), who headed the newly created Ukrainian Orthodox *metropolia* of Toronto, had spent several years in Russian camps in the 1930s and the previous six in Munich serving the Ukrainian community there. Arnold Lusis, future archbishop of the Latvian Evangelical Church in exile, was recruited in 1949 directly from a German DP camp for the fledgling congregation worshipping at St John's Evangelical Lutheran. His colleague, Oscar Puhm, who served the Estonian group at the same church, had been chaplain to the Estonian and Finnish armies allied with Nazi Germany against the Soviet Union. Their Lithuanian counterpart, Leonas Kostizenas, had been brought over from Germany by the Missouri Synod to head Grace Lutheran, a German-Lithuanian bilingual parish. Charles Kamber, pastor of Our Lady Queen of Croatia Catholic, had served as chaplain to the Ustače army allied with Nazi Germany and Fascist Italy.[91] Michael Rusnák, founder of the Nativity of the Mother of God Slovak Byzantine Catholic, had just been released from jail by the Communist authorities in Czechoslovakia. The American-born, Slovak-trained clergyman's US passport proved to be his key to freedom. His compatriot, Paul Jamnicky, also a refugee, led St Paul's Slovak Evangelical Lutheran for a time. Former concentration camp inmates Meyer Grunewald and Benjamin Hauer were appointed rabbis. The latter, a recent graduate of *Torah Chaim* yeshivath, was at twenty-six years of age the youngest rabbi to serve at Beth Jacob.[92]

New arrivals, whether they were refugees or economic migrants, had an enormous impact on structures of worship in the city. This was certainly the case for newcomers from central, eastern, and southern Europe, although less so of Jews and visible minority groups, whose immigration rates were relatively low in the quarter-century after the war. Where old and new immigrants of the same ethnicity shared a common place of worship, relations were not always cordial because of differences between the two cohorts (discussed in the previous chapter). Tensions predictably emerged at First Hungarian Presbyterian, where, according to a report, the older group "resents the coming into leadership of recent comers to Canada, and complain that younger members of the congregation who, the [*sic*] assert, contribute little to the [financial] support of the Church, wish to have a greater say in the conduct of the work and worship of the Church."[93] Relations were also strained in the first years after the war at St Wolodymyr Ukrainian Orthodox. Originating in Galicia, many prewar parishioners had actually been converts from Catholicism, and they brought with them "their own particular state of mind, culture and ritual." Postwar compatriots, by contrast, came from either Volhynia or eastern Ukraine; having grown up in the Soviet Union, they had little familiarity with the church. Some had lived through the trauma of the 1933 famine. In time, however, these differences were overcome as the church grew rapidly after being raised to cathedral status and seat of an eparchy in 1951.[94]

Immigrant Community Life

For postwar immigrants too, places of worship became a focus of intense community life, although this was less true of Italians than of central and eastern Europeans. In any event, the Franciscans at St Agnes sponsored a number of sports and other activities for youth, including bowling, boxing, and hockey, in addition to devotional societies.[95] But what distinguished the central and eastern European parishes was the range of their community involvement.

Places of worship nurtured organizations with tenuous connections to religion. Our Lady Help of Christians was the birthplace of the

Slovenian Sports Federation (*Slovenska Telodavna Zveza*), whose gymnastic events directly supported the church building fund. Similarly, there was the Ausra Sports Club at Resurrection Lithuanian Catholic.[96] As we have seen, some organizations pursued political objectives. The *St Michaelwerk Verband Katholischer Donauschwaben* at St Patrick's lobbied to obtain compensation for members whose property had been confiscated by communist regimes back home. Postwar refugees at St Wolodymyr established the Ukrainian Association of the Victims of Russian Communist Terror to fight against what they saw as Soviet expansionism and to raise awareness of the Ukrainian famine of the 1930s, denounced as a premeditated act, like the Holocaust, but perpetrated by Joseph Stalin. An association of refugees from Volhynia was also formed to gather and publish materials on their region "because contemporary works ... published under Soviet control, are falsified by Communist doctrinaires."[97] The parish was closely associated with efforts by the Ukrainian government-in-exile to unite various political factions abroad in order to convene a pre-parliament, a potential rival institution to the parliament in Soviet Ukraine. Such action was premised on the doubtful view that Ukrainians abroad constituted a compact diaspora integrally living their culture of origin in their lands of adoption. As for Belarusians, the religious divisions besetting them reflected the political split within the Byelorussian National Alliance over the government-in-exile.

These examples would seem to confirm that places of worship were faithful replicas of Old World culture. But in fact, they were hybrid institutions that in many ways eased the integration of newcomers to the new society. In the postwar era, as married women entered the workforce in unprecedented numbers, parishes and congregations offered families invaluable assistance in their pursuit of the Canadian dream. Day care facilities, after-school or Saturday classes in the ancestral language and culture, youth activities ranging from Scouts and Guides to sports, summer camps, and easy access to credit were provided in most of the larger central and eastern European places of worship. The latter two services merit closer attention.

Placing children in a structured, safe, and familiar environment outside of the school timetable was psychologically important for parents as well as a crucial strategy in the immigrant family economy. The long summer holidays were especially problematic. In the earlier part of the century, a number of Protestant churches and missions had set an example by acquiring or supporting summer camps in the Toronto countryside for mothers and children. In the same decade that St Patrick's purchased a fully equipped leisure space for youth, First Hungarian Presbyterian inaugurated a summer camp in Grimsby attended by mothers and children. In the 1950s, newer immigrant congregations equally anxious to retain their youth followed suit. St Elizabeth's bought a property near Streetsville and named it after József Cardinal Mindszenty, the imprisoned Primate of Hungary. The parishioners dug out a riverbed to create a swimming area for children. Holy Trinity Russian Orthodox established a summer colony at Jackson's Point on Lake Simcoe. St Wolodymyr Ukrainian Orthodox acquired a hundred-acre farm near Oakville. Christened Camp Kiev, it hosted hundreds of young people for up to four weeks. Estonians and Latvians at St John's Evangelical Lutheran had separate facilities: the former secured a farm along the Nottawasaga River; the latter, a three-hundred acre site in the Hockley Hills. The Lithuanians of Resurrection parish purchased a smaller camp on Georgian Bay. Our Lady Help of Christians Slovene parish deviated somewhat from this pattern, offering families the possibility of camping or renting cottages on a farm near Alliston. The parishioners built a pool and pavilion for common use.[98]

A second problem for non–English-speaking immigrant households was access to credit. From the start, commercial banks regarded newcomers as a high risk, and operating hours were unsuited to their working lives. The first unchartered church-based credit unions catering to immigrants were founded during the Depression.[99] Exponential growth ensued with the arrival of the postwar cohort. The Hungarian credit union proved attractive because it offered cheap loans and high interest rates on savings. Membership in the So-Use Ukrainian Orthodox credit union tripled in just five years; by 1955, its assets had reached $3.5 million. Its Slovenian counterpart, although serving a smaller group, grew tenfold in seven years, with membership standing at just under 1,200 and assets close to $1 million. The institution was open weekday evenings and weekends, including Sundays. It was slow to pursue customers – as many as 25 per cent of the total – who were in arrears or default. Nor were written agreements scrupulously adhered to; some debts in fact were repaid on terms differing from those explicitly outlined in the contract.

Fragmentary evidence from secondary sources suggests how and why immigrants used credit unions. One-third of Toronto's Ukrainians, for example, belonged to one compared to one-tenth of the Ontario population as a whole.[100] Immigrants were twice as likely to borrow from credit unions as the native-born, and Ukrainians three times more likely.[101] Canadians called on such institutions to obtain short-term loans to purchase a car, for example, whereas newcomers sought longer-term arrangements, typically to buy or build a house or to renovate or repair it. Statistics compiled on Ukrainians in the late 1950s indicate that 90 per cent of the loans they received were for such purposes. This figure had slipped only slightly by the end of the next decade.[102] At a time of sustained economic growth and low unemployment, a number of credit unions were founded under church auspices that funnelled the savings generated by newcomers. This proved to be a precious collective resource that served individuals' needs besides benefiting particular communities as a whole.

Is there anything new under the sun? Protestant churchmen certainly thought so, and their sentiments, oscillating between high expectations and glum forebodings, have influenced our understanding of this period. The founding of the United Church raised hopes of a great Canadian religious revival. When this did not happen, euphoria gave way to unease and even despondency, states of mind that were then aggravated by the Great Depression and the Second World War. The causes of these negative feelings were not new. The "downtown problem" that forced the closing of more places of worship in the interwar years had manifested itself in an earlier period. The belief nourished by religious leaders that immigrants living compactly in the eastern portion of the West End would convert en masse to Protestantism and thereby rejuvenate downtown churches was unfounded. Newcomers would instead give religion a new face, one that Protestant churchmen did not recognize because all they saw was the dismaying decline of Protestantism in an area occupied by foreigners who were indifferent to it. This caused them anxiety.

So too did the youth question. Complaints about religious apathy among young men were commonplace in the late nineteenth and early twentieth centuries, as historian Lynne Marks has well documented. Notwithstanding church administrators' predilection in the interwar years for "bright evangelistic services,"[103] it is clear that there existed no single antidote for these ills (if indeed any antidote was available to the growing commercialization of the downtown core). Fundamentalism and the preaching associated with it clearly appealed to young people. This was implicitly recognized in the report prepared for Timothy Eaton Memorial and was plain for all to see in Charles Templeton's

Youth for Christ campaigns, which packed Massey Hall on Saturday evenings during the war. Toronto had in fact the distinction of being the city with the largest among the thousands of such events held on the continent. This chapter, however, has shown that other approaches to attracting youth were also effective: hiring young clergymen, giving youth a space they could call their own, using a captivating idiom when engaging with them, and creating religious, community, and leisure activities led by or targeting youth.

Selective evidence tells a different story from the flawed one told by Protestant clerical officials. In solidly residential neighbourhoods there was no imminent mass desertion of places of worship. It is true that many congregations reached their peak in the 1930s, but after the hiatus caused by the war, most managed to bounce back despite the great postwar exodus to the suburbs. Was decline in the downtown core then a sign of secularization? If so, how do we explain that people still flocked to church on Sunday mornings or evenings? This was especially true of immigrant congregations, a fact largely ignored by both Protestant clergymen and historians of religion. While it is undeniable that service clubs and settlement houses with their better-trained staff and greater financial resources were slowly eroding the older ideal of a full-orbed religion, that model was being reinvented in immigrant congregations. From the perspective of the pew, it would be more correct to say that this period witnessed an incipient secularization, rather than a fully formed one.

In time and often with the help of North American–trained clergy, immigrant congregations achieved stability and respectability, adopting North American norms of worship. And what were these norms? Places of worship in Toronto had dignified interiors with stained glass windows, carved wooden furniture, ornate lighting, and choral singing. Clergy, choirs, and soloists wore attire that set them apart from congregants, who nevertheless dressed up for the occasion. Worship, structured around an order of service that the faithful could follow in uniform prayer books, was characterized by formality, dignity, and order. This standard applied to Catholic churches as well, where, despite more elaborate interiors, including candles, altar cloths, and statuary, low mass on Sundays was the norm for most parishioners. High masses, requiring three celebrants, the use of incense, Gregorian chant, and six rather than two candles on the altar, were reserved for feast days and were by no means universal. Only fundamentalist Christian places of worship and the smaller Jewish synagogues deviated from this norm. There, interiors were plain and unadorned. Services were marked by greater spontaneity, informality, and freedom. Leaders of worship were distinguished from ordinary congregants neither by dress, nor by education, nor by training. It is undoubtedly for this reason that in many fundamentalist Christian denominations, women were able to make a breakthrough, assuming positions of clerical leadership. Despite its attraction, however, fundamentalism remained distinctly a minority phenomenon.

On the whole, places of worship met the challenges that confronted them in the interwar and postwar years by turning to new media of communication, strategies for engaging youth, worship satisfying congregants' tastes, and activities that stimulated people physically, intellectually, and culturally. The ideal of a full-orbed religion maintained its hold, although it was evolving. Crisis would characterize the later decades, but that term cannot be applied to the entire period, which ended on an optimistic and self-congratulatory note.

Chapter Six

To Every Thing Turn! Turn! Turn!
There Is a Season, 1960–2000

Qoheleth 3:1
Smash hit by The Byrds (1965)

Just as religion in late-nineteenth-century Toronto was shaped by the broad socio-economic currents of industrial capitalism, so too was it profoundly marked almost a century later by the consolidation of consumer capitalism in Canada and other Western societies. Admittedly this latter phenomenon was in evidence earlier – in the 1920s, for instance, or even before that. But it was only with the wealth generated during the "Glorious Thirty" years after the Second World War that it fundamentally altered human relationships – specifically, the paternalistic family economy that had been a pillar of industrial capitalism and the mainstay of working-class life. Under that earlier system the family had chiefly been an economic unit in which the interests of individual members were subordinated to the good of the whole. The insecurities of the job market, relatively low wage levels, and the absence of a welfare state brought members together in the struggle against economic adversity, ill health, and sudden death. Yet in the end, working-class families had few material possessions to show for their efforts.

The social and economic policies pursued by Western governments, including Canada, during and after the war created job and labour market stability, as well as higher earnings. In contrast to the Spartan living conditions of earlier times, working-class households began to display signs of this new wealth: domestic appliances, television sets, cars, motorboats. Unlike in the past, when people often organized their own entertainment in the form of picnics, dances, sporting events, and theatre performances (as novelists Michael Ondaatje and Steven Hayward so vividly remind us),[1] leisure and sports activities increasingly became purchasable commodities in the postwar era. Because the primary breadwinner could now bring home a decent wage, other family members had disposable incomes for their own use, and this fed the economic growth and consumerism that were hallmarks of this period. The individual consumer and her or his purchasing power were now front and centre. In this context, new social movements arose that catered to specific categories such as women and youth. These groups began to demand the liberalization of the highly restrictive laws on divorce, contraception, and prostitution, as well as the decriminalization of abortion, homosexuality, and drug consumption. The long 1960s became a period of sexual experimentation and self-affirmation.

In this climate of heightened individualism, religion could no longer serve as the glue that supposedly bound together family, community, and nation. It came to be perceived more as a force of division than of union, as narrowly sectarian instead of broadly tolerant. Clerical leaders had once been spokespeople for collective aspirations; now, they felt as if they lacked the authority to speak on behalf of a wider public. When they did so, they were likely to be openly contradicted by fellow clergymen.[2] Even after the Anglican Church was disestablished in 1854, religion had occupied a prominent institutional space in Ontario, at least until 1960. After that year, institutions such as universities, hospitals, and other care facilities traded their denominational affiliations for provincial government funding, as did the Protestant public schools and boards of education. Prayers and religious exercises were removed from those schools' curricula. Religion, in other words, was largely relegated to the private sphere.[3] Even the clergy began to feel that the churches' many social and institutional commitments had distracted them from their properly spiritual mission.

The story of Centennial–Japanese United captures this turn of events. In the 1930s the white middle-class congregation numbered 1,800 and its Sunday school had 1,400 pupils. Thirty years later the school's enrolment had plummeted to 230, while church membership had dropped by half. Because of its declining fortunes, Centennial invited a Japanese congregation to share its facilities. A separate chapel for English-speaking Nisei designed by architect Raymond Moriyama was built on the top floor of the building. Centennial had reached its peak membership in the 1930s; the Japanese achieved theirs in the 1970s, boasting associations for all age groups as well as a range of religious and social activities. However, a generation after the Japanese congregation settled into the church, with its Sunday school enrolment dropping yearly, it decided to merge formally with Centennial's original congregation. In 1993, when the last minister of Japanese origin departed, the

6.1   Centennial–Japanese United (condominiums)
Established in 1891 to mark the centenary (hence the name) of the death
of John Wesley, Methodism's founder, the congregation expanded under
the pastorate of Edwin Pearson, father of Canadian prime minister Lester
Pearson. A larger building was erected in 1908. In the postwar period, a
congregation founded by Japanese expelled from their west coast homes
during the Second World War shared the church, eventually merging with
the original occupants. (Gabriele Scardellato)

congregation had an average attendance of less than one hundred and
a Sunday school attendance of fourteen. Of the active members, 94 per
cent were of Japanese background and half were retired. The building
was sold in 2007 and converted into condominiums.[4]

Some commentators have recently wished for or anticipated the return
of religion,[5] but this is unlikely to happen, for its decline is what Émile
Durkheim once called a social fact. A nineteenth-century founder of modern sociology, Durkheim defined this concept simply as "des manières

d'agir, de penser et de sentir, extérieures à l'individu, et qui sont douées d'un pouvoir de coercition en vertu duquel ils s'imposent à lui."[6] Social facts are independent of what an individual might wish or be aware of; they can change only as a result of significant transformations in society. At the same time, they have the ability to shape an individual's way of behaving and thinking (*s'imposent à lui*). In other words, the decline of religion is a historical trend unrelated to the consciousness, actions, or desires of individuals, be they popes, princes, or paupers. It is not a blip, but a long-term phenomenon alterable only through profound social change.

In the past half-century, Toronto has become the country's largest city as well as its undisputed economic and financial capital. In the early part of this period, manufacturing was the motor of the city's economic growth, attracting high levels of domestic and foreign investment as well as large numbers of workers. In these years of prosperity, the city's highly productive industrial workforce grew faster than the provincial average. By 1970, 40 per cent of the province's manufacturing jobs were concentrated in the Toronto Metropolitan Area. As time went on, the service sector overtook the manufacturing sector to become the city's largest employer, reflecting the shift in Canada to a post-industrial economy. Toronto attracted the head offices of the top financial institutions, half the headquarters of foreign-owned companies, and roughly 40 per cent of its top five hundred corporations.[7] Its economic activities included medical research, aerospace, engineering, telecommunications, and leisure industries. Its stock exchange now ranks third on the continent and seventh in the world in terms of market capitalization (a combination of the number of stocks traded and their prices).

Toronto's boundaries have been reconfigured over the years. In 1967 a number of the smaller municipalities surrounding the old City of Toronto were amalgamated into five larger units, forming a two-tier metropolitan structure. Key services, such as municipal borrowing, public transit, and regional planning, were centralized at the top level of local government. Former Ontario premier John Robarts (1961–71) credited this structure with Toronto's unique development: "Unlike many large American cities, rapid growth in the suburbs has not brought a deterioration of the central core." Many industries moved to the periphery, where land was less expensive; meanwhile, the city's office towers, including the head offices of the five major Canadian banks, all built between 1967 and 1988, were concentrated in the downtown core, where they provided jobs not only for professionals but also for the unskilled.[8] Some thirty years later, Toronto's metropolitan structure was eliminated and the six municipalities were joined into one. As a result, the city's population climbed to 2.5 million in 2001. However, the Census Metropolitan Area (CMA) of Toronto, extending from Oshawa to Hamilton, is home to twice than many people, a clear indication that suburbanization has continued and intensified.

Because of its central role in Ontario's economy, and in Canada's, Toronto attracted the most immigrants of any Canadian city – almost half the total – making it the country's most racially and ethnically diverse city. However, the population of the old City of Toronto peaked in 1971, at 710,000 people, 44 per cent of them foreign-born. Over the next decade, that number fell, largely because postwar immigrants were moving to the suburbs. But it slowly rose again to reach 676,000 by 2001, 41 per cent of whom had been born abroad (compared to 44 per cent for the CMA as a whole).[9]

Catholics were the single largest religious group within the old city limits, with 208,000 adherents, or 31 per cent of the population (34.5 per cent in the CMA). This was a numerical and proportional decrease from their high point of 40 per cent, reached in 1971. The next most important group was the 175,000 people claiming no religious affiliation, who were 26 per cent of the total (17 per cent in the CMA), a cohort steadily growing during this period. Some data suggest that this category includes visible minority immigrants and their children. Sociologist Reginald Bibby analysed 1991 census statistics for Canada as a whole and found that 27 per cent of Asians born outside the country and 42 per cent of all those born in Canada of non-European ancestry declared that they had no religious affiliation.[10] In Toronto this category was heavily concentrated in the Kensington–Chinatown neighbourhood, with significant pockets in the Annex, Palmerston–Little Italy, and Trinity Bellwoods.[11] The religiously unaffiliated were numerically more significant than all Protestants combined, who numbered less than 160,000, or 24 per cent of old Toronto's inhabitants (28 per cent in the CMA). At 34,000, Jews made up another 5 per cent (3.5 per cent in the CMA). Although well below the peak of 49,000 established in 1941, this figure represented a reversal of the downward trend that had begun in 1951 with the mass movement of Jews to the suburbs. Just below them were Muslims, with 27,000 faithful, or 4 per cent of Toronto's residents (5.5 per cent in the CMA), followed by 25,000 Orthodox Christians, who were another 4 per cent (3.5 per cent in the CMA). Buddhists, with 22,000 adherents, formed 3 per cent (2 per cent in the CMA), while Hindus, with 13,000 followers, represented another 2 per cent (4 per cent in the CMA) of the total.[12]

ST. CLAIR AVE. W.
DAVENPORT RD.
JANE ST.
DUNDAS ST. W.
DUPONT ST.
KEELE ST.
BLOOR ST. W.
LANSDOWNE AVE.
S. KINGSWAY
DUNDAS ST. W.
RONCESVALLES AVE.
Humber R.
THE QUEENSWAY
QUEEN ST. W.
GARDINER EXPWY.
LAKE SHORE RD. W.
KING ST. W.
Lake Ontario
Catholic
Pentecostal
Other
MAP AREA
Boundary of the City of Toronto, 1834-1998.
N
0   500   1000 m

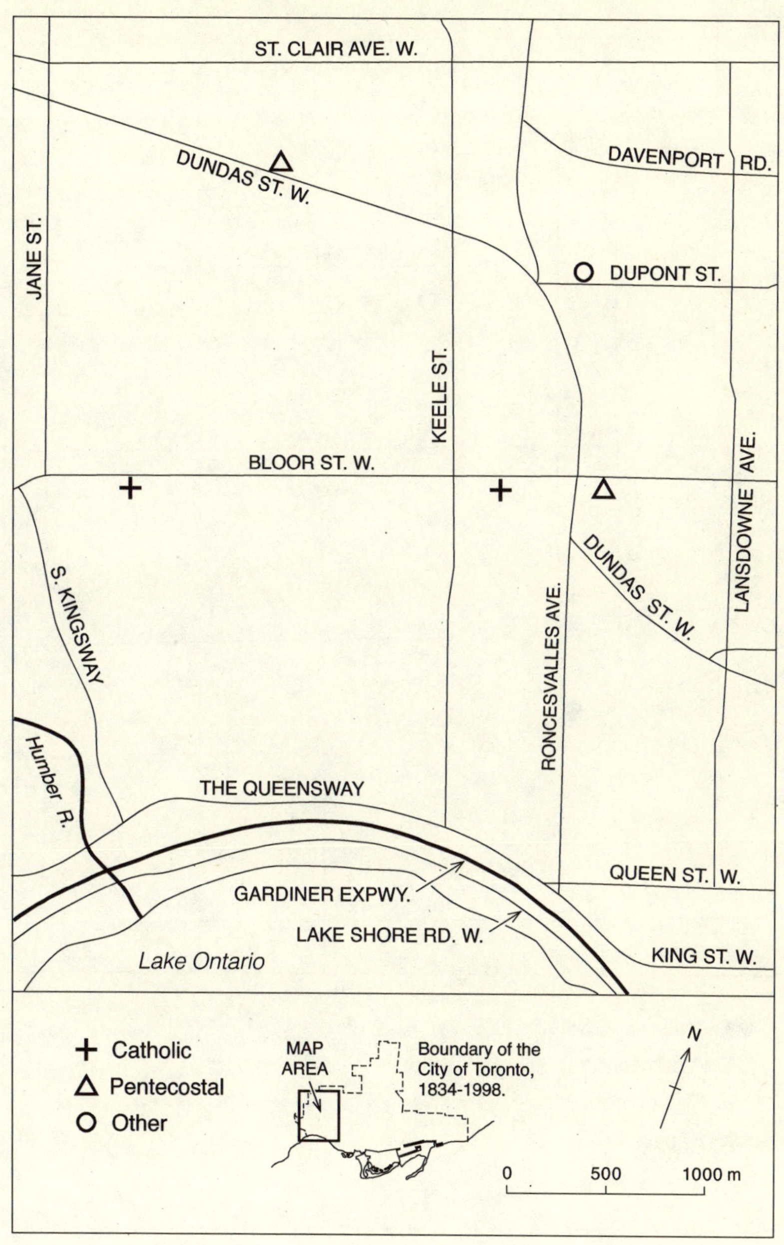

Map 6.1

ST. CLAIR AVE. W.
DAVENPORT RD.
DUPONT ST.
DUFFERIN ST.
OSSINGTON AVE.
CHRISTIE ST.
DOVERCOURT RD.
BATHURST ST.
SPADINA AVE.
AVENUE RD.
BLOOR ST. W.
COLLEGE ST.
DUNDAS ST. W.
UNIVERSITY AVE.
QUEEN ST. W.
KING ST. W.
Methodist/United
Presbyterian
Catholic
Baptist
Synagogues
Buddhist
Other
Boundary of the
City of Toronto,
1834-1998.
MAP
AREA
N
0   500   1000 m

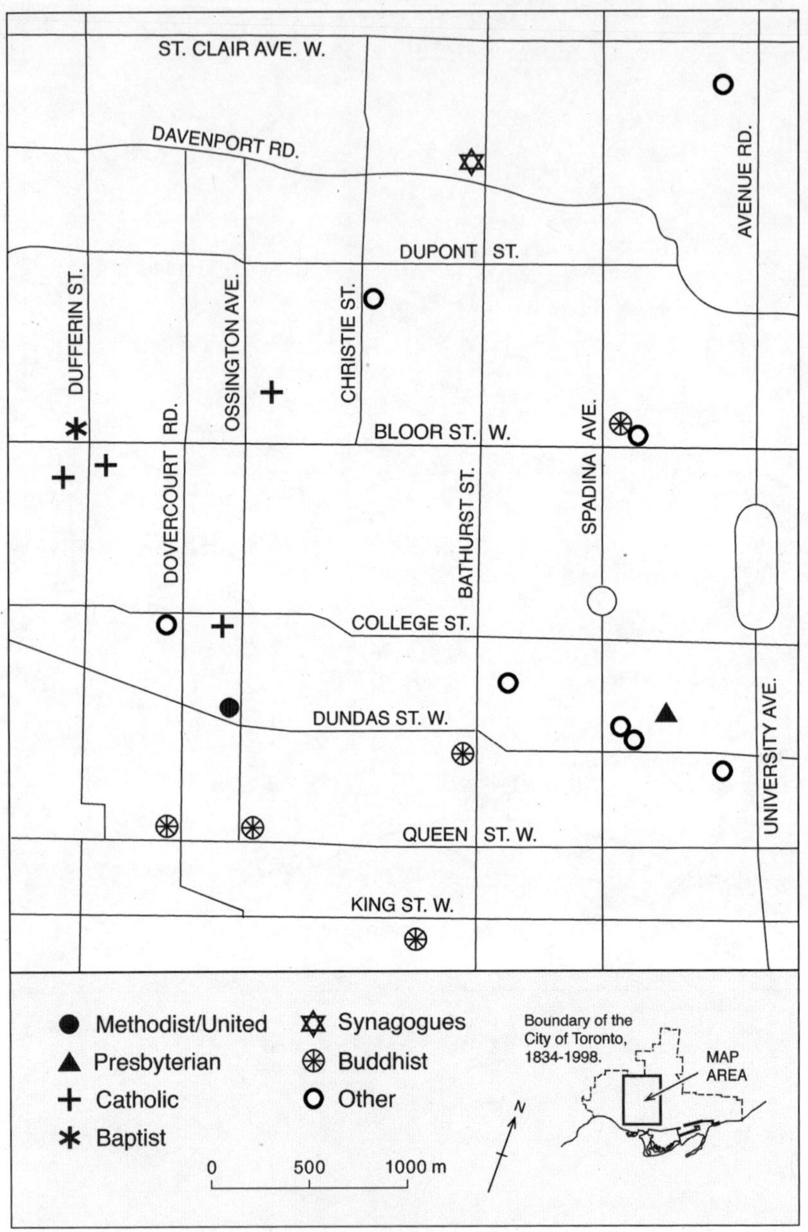

Map 6.2

The precipitate decline of Protestants during these years is truly remarkable. In 1961, mainstream denominations claimed 320,000 followers and accounted for slightly less than half of Toronto's citizenry. Over the next forty years their numbers fell by more than half, until in 2001 they were only 21 per cent of the city's inhabitants. Catholics too were less numerous, but their decline was less dramatic. Part of this drop can be explained by suburbanization, given that the proportion of both groups to the overall population was higher in the CMA than in the old city. But it is also clear that the people who swelled the ranks of the religiously unaffiliated, which more than trebled in thirty years, had once belonged to mainstream Christian denominations. Even so, just under 60 per cent of Torontonians defined themselves as Christian (66 per cent in the CMA), and they far outnumbered non-Christians, who were 14 per cent of the population. So while the city was more religiously diverse than ever, it had retained a solid Christian core.

The Changing Environment

In large measure this diversity was the result of changes to Canada's immigration policy. In 1967 the federal government introduced a points system for immigrant recruitment whereby skill, education, and knowledge of English or French trumped race and place of origin. In the past, various barriers had been set up to restrict severely, if not prohibit entirely, the entry of visible minorities. But as Europe's importance as a source of immigration dried up in the 1960s, the country was forced to cast its net wider. At the same time, a series of political crises worldwide produced flows of refugees seeking asylum. This was the case following the Soviet invasion of Czechoslovakia (1968), the expulsion of Asians from Uganda (1972), the military coup in Chile (1973), and the end of the Vietnam War (1975). Up to that point, Canada had no refugee policy as such. For instance, the 165,000 DPs who made Canada their home after the Second World War had been admitted as immigrants according to existing if somewhat relaxed criteria. It was only in 1976 that the government finally devised a policy for asylum seekers, recognizing them as a category in their own right. Specific targets were later set for their admission. As a result of all these changes, Asia and the Caribbean became prime sources of immigration.

The primary objective of Canada's immigration policy remained the age-old one of serving the country's economic needs. The points system's emphasis on skills, training, and education revealed a desire for highly qualified people who could meet the challenges of the post-industrial economy. In 1978, Ottawa created a new category of independent immigrants – the business class. These individuals were expected to invest substantial sums of money in the country and to stimulate economic growth as well as job creation. During these years, politicians even tried to reduce the number of family-sponsored immigrants, arguing that the vast majority of them were unskilled, and apparently ignoring the fact that these newcomers were willing to fill many lower-paying jobs disdained by Canadians.[13]

Religion in Toronto mirrored these changes in immigration policy and patterns, as well as calls for change that were becoming more insistent in the late 1950s and early 1960s. In his bestselling book *The Comfortable Pew*, commissioned by the Anglican Church's Department of Religious Education and published in 1965, journalist Pierre Berton argued that religion had to become more relevant, more meaningful to the average person, more in tune with the times. The church, he argued, had become ossified in meaningless ritual, byzantine dogma, bureaucratic routine, and social convention. It was failing to lead, to shake up existing structures, to assume daring positions on such issues as social justice. It needed to once again assume its prophetic role in society and to make the pew less comfortable for those faint-hearted Christians who were the bulk of worshippers; otherwise, Berton warned, the institution would die out.[14] Pope John XXIII (1958–63) made similar pronouncements, albeit more gently. It was time, he affirmed, to open the windows and let in fresh air; Catholicism was in need of *aggiornamento*, of being brought up to date. The Second Vatican Council (1962–5) that he convened brought to Rome more than 2,000 prelates from around the world to study proposals for reform.

The council's pronouncements had a profound impact not only on Catholicism worldwide but on other churches as well. To start with, they enunciated a new vision of the Church. Previously the emphasis had been on authority, hierarchy, and clerisy. Taken to its extreme, this view regarded the laity as unquestioning followers, silent subordinates, and simple spectators. The document *Lumen Gentium* (The Light of Nations) embraced a more encompassing vision, that of the Church as the people of God, in which laymen and laywomen would be active collaborators. *Dignitatis Humanae* (Human Dignity), for its part, affirmed the Church's regard for individual conscience as well as for the principle that persons must not be coerced to act against conscience. *Gaudium et Spes* (Joy and Hope) stated that the Church was of and in the world, thus reversing the view of it as a besieged fortress standing outside and above the world, a perspective forcefully expressed by, among others, Pope Pius IX. This change of stance opened up the possibility of dialogue with non-Catholics, non-Christians, and secularists.

These new perspectives necessarily had an impact on liturgy. Clarity became a guiding principle of proposed reforms. The twofold structure of the mass, divided into the liturgy of the word and that of the Eucharist, was highlighted. *Sacrosanctum Concilium* encouraged greater use of vernacular languages, especially in scriptural readings of the epistle and gospel. In a few short years, Latin virtually disappeared from parish worship in order to make the liturgy better understood by the faithful and to encourage their more active participation. Gregorian chant dating back to the Middle Ages was replaced by approved contemporary music. Also cast off were priestly vestments such as the chasuble, stole, and maniple that traditionally went over the alb, a garment that now became the focal point of liturgical dress. Because it had been worn by celebrants in the early days of Christianity, it was considered to be authentic. The priest now faced the people instead of turning his back to them, making his actions at the altar visible and transparent. Repetitive gestures in the saying of the mass, which some believed confirmed notions of Catholic worship as strange and superstitious, were eliminated. The involvement of the laity in worship was encouraged through the collective recitation of prayers and the singing of hymns.

Another important innovation was ecumenism, which sought to foster greater understanding and collaboration among the religions of the world. The siege mentality that for centuries had governed relations with non-Catholics was lifted. In particular, the ideal of unity among Christians was affirmed, and dialogue was initiated with a number of churches in order to attain that goal. As a first step, Protestant and Orthodox representatives were invited to the Vatican Council as observers. In 1964, Pope Paul VI (1963–78) travelled to Jerusalem to meet the Greek Orthodox Patriarch of Constantinople, Athenagoras I (1948–72), the first such encounter in five hundred years. The two primates later rescinded the excommunications their predecessors had pronounced against each other, that had marked the Great Schism of 1054. Two years later, the pope got together in Rome with Michael Ramsey, Archbishop of Canterbury (1961–74). Both prelates regarded the historic meeting as the first step towards full unity. The Catholic Church no longer viewed Protestants as enemies, but as separated brethren. *Lumen Gentium* affirmed that they were part of "the people of God" with whom the

Catholic Church felt bound by many common links. As for the Jews, *Nostra Ætate* emphasized that neither they nor their ancestors living at the time of Christ could be held responsible for his death, a belief commonly held by Christians, especially since the Middle Ages. The document also condemned anti-Semitism in its many guises.[15]

The West End's Changing Face(s)

The West End mirrored the international, national, and regional changes of the period. Although the area had lost its status as the main reception area for non-British immigrants by the 1970s, it retained a degree of vitality: being so close to the city centre, it continued to attract newcomers. Europeans continued to settle there in large numbers well into the decade. It is useful to remember that close to half of postwar Italian immigrants arrived in the 1960s. For postwar Greeks, that proportion was even higher, while for Portuguese it reached 86 per cent.[16]

Visible minority immigrants tended to settle in the suburbs, although they were also relatively well represented in the West End. Large numbers of Chinese, most of them from Hong Kong but some from the People's Republic (PRC), arrived between 1985 and 1994, doubling their numbers in Toronto. After 1997, PRC Chinese surpassed those from Hong Kong and included a higher proportion of business immigrants.[17] South Asians, three-quarters of whom hailed from the Indian Subcontinent and the rest from East Africa, the Caribbean, Great Britain, and Fiji, followed a similar temporal pattern. Immigration caused their numbers in Canada to triple between 1980 and 2000.[18] Newcomers from the Caribbean, mostly of African ancestry and overwhelmingly from Jamaica, Guyana, and Trinidad and Tobago, had a steadier pattern of growth: they comprised about 10 per cent of the total yearly intake of immigrants to Canada between 1970 and 1990. As a result of all this, 30 per cent of the old City of Toronto's population was classified in 2001 as belonging to a visible minority (compared to 37 per cent for the CMA), the largest groups being Chinese 64,000 (CMA 260,000), black 35,000 (CMA 204,000), South Asian 31,000 (CMA 254,000), Filipino 17,000 (CMA 86,000), Latin American 13,000 (CMA 54,000), and Southeast Asian 11,000 (CMA 34,000).

The decline of Protestantism is evident in the number of churches – sixty-two in total – that were closed, demolished, or transferred to other congregations (see table 6.1). The United Church topped the list with sixteen, followed by Presbyterians with ten; Anglicans and Baptists, eight each. Almost all of the area's gospel halls, except for the one on Brock

Table 6.1. Changes to West End places of worship before 2000

Name	Change	Date
Dewi Sant Presbyterian	St Paul Slovak Evangelical Lutheran	1960
Men of England Synagogue	destroyed by fire	1960
Torah Chaim Synagogue	Demolished	1960
West Toronto Free Methodist	Polish Baptist	1962
St Alban's Parkdale United	St Mary Annunciation & Dormition Greek Orthodox	1962
West End Full Gospel Tabernacle	Congregazione pentecostale italiana	1962
Markham Street Brethren	Demolished	1963
St John Garrison Anglican	Demolished	1963
Central Baptist	Christadelphian	1964
Apostolic Faith	St Michael the Archangel Serbian Orthodox	1966
Christ the Saviour Russian Orthodox	Theatre	1966
St Cyprian Anglican	merged with St Mary the Virgin; Christ the Saviour Russian Orthodox	1966
Beth Jacob Synagogue	Holy Trinity Russian Orthodox	1966
Shaarei Shomayim Synagogue	Hungarian community hall	1967
Ostrovtzer Synagogue	St Francis Xavier Chinese Catholic	1967
Shomrai Shabot Synagogue	Petah Tikva Anshei Castille	1967
St Columba United	St Alphonsus Catholic	1967
Carman United	St Sebastian Catholic	1967
Second Church of the Nazarene	San Nicola di Bari	1967
Bonar Presbyterian	church closed; merged with Parkdale	1969
Royce Avenue Presbyterian	merged with Victoria; demolished	1969
St Paul Presbyterian	Demolished	1969
High Park Presbyterian	Jami mosque	1969
Alhambra United	merged with High Park United; Lithuanian Hall	1970
Howard Park Avenue United	Howard Park Avenue Italian Pentecostal	1970
St Paul Slovak Evangelical Lutheran	Holy Trinity Greek Orthodox	1971
St Barnabas Anglican	Toronto Church of God	1971

(continued)

Table 6.1. (continued)

Name	Change	Date
Door of Hope Mission	Slavic Evangelical Baptist	1971
Petah Tikva Anshei Castille	congregation moves to North York	1972
Grace Evangelical Lutheran	St Paul Slovak Evangelical Lutheran	1973
Perth Avenue United	Perth Avenue Seventh-Day Adventist	1973
Davenport Road Presbyterian	Toronto Korean Presbyterian	1973
Olivet Gospel Hall	Evangelische Gemeinde	1973
Dovercourt Road Baptist	Santa Cruz Portuguese Catholic	1974
College Street Baptist	Portuguese Seventh-Day Adventist	1974
West End Revival centre	Church of God of Prophecy	1974
Queen Street United	merged with Grace United	1974
Beverley Street Baptist	Toronto Chinese Baptist	1975
Bathurst Street United	chapel at Trinity United; Metropolitan Community church; Worship centre Ruwach	1975
Annette Street Baptist	Czechoslovak Baptist	1975
Avenue Road CMA	Temple of Krishna Consciousness	1975
Parkdale United	demolished; chapel in new building	1975
St Edmund's Anglican	St Nektarios Greek Orthodox	1977
Torah Emeth Synagogue	Church of God/Sabbath Keeping	1978
Chalmers Presbyterian	Closed	1978
Church of All Nations United	Demolished	1978
First Hungarian Presbyterian	Holy Word Chinese Evangelical	1979
Humberside Road Baptist	Newgate Korean Presbyterian	1979
Fern Avenue Church of Christ	Hindu Prartana samaj	1979
Lippincott Street Salvation Army	First Filipino Bapitst	1979
Congregazione pentecostale italiana	Zion Apostolic Church of Jesus Christ	1980
Davenport Gospel Hall	Apostolic Church of God/ Newborn Church of God	1981
Mach Zikei B'nai Israel	Graciosa Portuguese community centre	1982
St Dunstan's Anglican	Ghandi Bhawan	1983

Table 6.1. (concluded)

Name	Change	Date
Grace & Truth Mission hall	Toronto Korea Pray house; cathedral church of Christ the King	1983
St Paul's United	merged with Trinity	1983
Western Baptist	Demolished	1983
Salem Gospel Hall	Bibleway Pentecostal Church of God Apostolic	1983
West Toronto Gospel hall	Hallelujah Filipino Baptist	1984
St Elizabeth of Hungary	Demolished	1984
Epiphany Anglican	Our Lady of Lebanon Maronite	1984
Beth Israel Synagogue	Hungarian Free Reformed (United)	1985
Epworth United	East Toronto Korean Presbyterian	1986
Ukrainian Presbyterian	Grace Chinese Baptist	1986
Calvary Assembly	Church of God of Prophecy	1986
College Street United	demolished; chapel in new building	1986
Westmoreland Avenue United	Korean Central Presbyterian	1988
Grace-Carman United	Toronto Korean Bethel Evangelical	1990
St Andrew's Japanese Anglican	Chapel of Royal St George's school	1991
Sts Cyril & Methodius Slovak Catholic	Condomiums	1993
Grant African Methodist Episcopal	Assemblea de Deus de Toronto	1994
Dufferin Street Presbyterian	Hope centre Full Gospel	1995
Westennial United	Closed	1997
Toronto Church of God	Demolished	1997
Glad Tidings Tabernacle	Cornerstone Baptist tabernacle	1997
St Jude's Anglican	parish closed in 1983; demolished	1997
Toronto Korean Presbyterian	Galilee Presbyterian	1997
Bracondale Gospel Hall	Faith Believers' Gospel Apostolic	1998
Resurrection Lithuanian Catholic	Demolished	2000
Assemblea de Deus de Toronto	Demolished	2000

Avenue, which survived until 2009, were shut down. Twenty-seven places of worship have been torn down.[19] The congregations of Parkdale and College Street United continued to worship in spaces provided by the residential developments that had replaced their demolished churches. Dovercourt Road Baptist was not razed but abandoned, its congregants deciding to erect a senior citizens' tower at Bloor Street West and Dufferin, adjacent to which a modern brick chapel was built for their use.

By contrast, the demographic rise of Toronto's Catholics can be discerned in the eight churches that were opened in the area, five of which had been Protestant. Later in the period, as the percentage of Catholics in the overall population began to fall, two were demolished and one was closed. This trend points to the suburbanization of postwar immigrants. The continuing movement of Jews to the suburbs led to the closing of twenty-eight synagogues, almost all of them in the 1960s. The last one to close, *Mach Zikei B'Nai Israel*, became a Portuguese regional community hall; this left only seven synagogues in the West End. The brief appearance of Moroccan Jews hardly affected this pattern. Arriving in the wake of their home country's independence, which had placed power in the hands of Arabs, they soon followed the movement of their coreligionists northward. In 2000, Jews by single or multiple origin were a significant presence in only two West End neighbourhoods: they were 17 per cent of the population in Casa Loma (neighbourhood 96), and 11 per cent in the Annex (95).[20]

Only thirteen places of worship were erected after 1960, almost all of them in that same decade (see table 6.2).

Two of the six Catholic ones – the utterly functional St James on Annette Street near Jane, and the eye-catching St Joan of Arc on Bloor Street at Indian Grove – served English speakers and replaced buildings that had been torn down, the latter to make way for the Dundas West subway station. The other four were intended for older and new immigrants. After being ravaged by fire in 1964, St Josaphat Ukrainian Catholic was reborn as a plain edifice with modern accents. The property's small size restricted the style of architecture. By contrast, the imposing Holy Protection of the Mother of God Ukrainian Catholic was built in modern Cossack Baroque style.[21] Another brick modern building, remarkable for its windowless walls, was dedicated to Our Lady Queen of Croatia, replacing an older structure destroyed by fire. Finally, Our Lady of Good Counsel occupied a three-storey red-brick office building on College Street at Concord, housing a church and offices for Afro-Caribbeans.

Of the remaining new churches, five were Protestant and earmarked for immigrants. First Chinese Presbyterian, a modern structure of rough

Table 6.2. The cost of some places of worship, 1960–2000

	Cost ($)	Year
Congregazione pentecostale italiana	25,000	1962
Our Lady Queen of Croatia Catholic	240,000	1965
Slavic Evangelical Baptist	55,500	1969
Chinese Gospel (first property)	17,000	1970
Chinese Baptist	105,000	1975
Unification Church	330,000	1978
Fu Sien temple (two lots and renovations)	800,000	1985

stone on Beverley Street at Baldwin, was designed by architect John Mah, son of the first Chinese minister. It replaced the Chinese Christian Association, which had been demolished to make way for office blocks. Dedicated by Lieutenant-Governor Keillor Mackay, the church represented the culmination of efforts to make the congregation self-sustaining.[22] Chinese Gospel, a square brick building, replaced Anshei Kielce Synagogue on Dundas Street at Huron; it was conceived by architects Stephen Cheng and Simon Ng. The congregation was founded when two former medical missionaries to China began working among Hong Kong students in Toronto. They purchased the synagogue and occupied it until the new church was built.[23] Up the hill, on Balmoral Avenue at Poplar Plains, St John Latvian Evangelical Lutheran, a bold, bright A-frame structure of white brick and stained glass with adjacent steeple, was erected by architect Egils Tannis to serve a congregation that had previously met at St John's Evangelical Lutheran. In the Junction, the unassuming Christian Mission tabernacle replaced the storefront that had served English-speaking Ukrainian Pentecostals. Finally, in 1960, the utterly serviceable Westennial United replaced Wesley United, which had been destroyed by fire.

Two other places of worship appeared in the West End: St Andrew's Ukrainian Orthodox, a rather plain red-brick building designed by architect Hryhorij Khoroshyj, replaced an earlier structure that had served successive groups since the late nineteenth century.[24] The Toronto Bahá'í centre, an austere but harmonious modern construction of red brick on Bloor Street at Huron, is part of a universalist denomination founded in nineteenth-century Persia that emphasizes the unity of religion and humankind. To these buildings can be added two Buddhist temples that required extensive renovations of existing facilities.

6.2 Toronto Bahá'í Centre

A rational and egalitarian religion stressing the unity of humankind, Baha'i originated in nineteenth-century Persia. Its Canadian headquarters are in Toronto. In the late 1960s, a Bahá'í group met briefly on Brunswick Avenue. This site has been occupied since the mid-1990s. (Gabriele Scardellato)

Ching Kwok on Bathurst Street below Dundas West completely altered the appearance of the former Ukrainian Labour Temple. The two-storey brick structure has a decorative overhanging yellow clay-tile roof with a prominent middle section. The overhang above the entrance is made of the same material and extends the entire width of the building; the facade's four red columns stretching from the ground to the roof define the edifice and its access. In the end, though, Ching Kwok pales when compared to Fu Sien Tong on Niagara Street south of King West, where a modest working-class home has been transformed into a striking Chinese shrine. The ornamented two-tiered sweeping roof with its elevated central portion is made of green clay tile. The building itself, faced with bright red tile, has a slightly protruding second floor and a windowless third floor with an image of Buddha at its centre. Both temples are associated with Pure Land Buddhism and serve Cantonese speakers from the Cholon district of Ho Chi Minh City in Vietnam, who arrived in Canada as refugees after the collapse of South Vietnam.[25]

6.3 Fu Sien Tong Chinese Buddhist
Two adjacent homes were purchased and transformed into this beautiful temple inaugurated in 1985. Congregants are overwhelmingly Cantonese speakers from Vietnam. (Gabriele Scardellato)

New Wine in Old Wineskins: European Immigrants

Instead of putting up new places of worship, the vast majority of congregations preferred to either take over existing ones or (more often) move into commercial, institutional, and residential spaces. In the first instance, transferrals between and within denominations all involved transactions between non-immigrant and immigrant congregations, with only one exception: Central Baptist was sold in 1964 to Christadelphians. In the second instance, sixty commercial or residential sites became places of worship, although many more were briefly occupied by newly constituted congregations looking for more suitable permanent facilities. Not all such locations were cheap. For instance, Covenant Christian, an evidently affluent group associated with the Canadian Fellowship of Churches and Ministers, bought Osler Hall on Huron Street above Bloor from the Academy of Medicine. The mortgage was paid off in ten years. By contrast, Britten Memorial, a spiritualist congregation that had to abandon its church after the war, moved into a storefront on Lansdowne Avenue below Bloor, where it remained until recently. In general, sites tended to be inexpensive –for recently arrived immigrants, a crucial consideration in the early and uncertain phases of settlement.

Italians, Portuguese, and Greeks

In light of the West End's changing demographics, the Archdiocese of Toronto assigned a number of existing churches to particular linguistic or racial groups. Italians at St Agnes were given the nearby and more capacious St Francis. Similarly, Our Lady of Mount Carmel ceased being an Italian parish because few compatriots lived in the vicinity any more. Farther west, however, three former Protestant churches were set aside for their use. Located along the St Clair and Dufferin corridors, the new parishes of St Alphonsus, San Nicola di Bari, and St Sebastian marked clusters of Italian immigrants. The archdiocese also designated churches where masses would be said regularly in one or more languages other than English. Those offering Italian services were St Clare (1959), St Peter (1960), St Anthony (1964), St Helen (1967), and, for a brief time, St Patrick (1970).[26] This perimeter, bounded on the west by Lansdowne Avenue, on the east by Bathurst Street, on the north by St Clair Avenue, and on the south by Dundas Street, neatly delimited the broad area of postwar Italian settlement in the West End. Today, Italians are heavily concentrated in only one neighbourhood – Corso Italia–Davenport (#92), where they are 30 per cent of the population. In adjacent Weston–Pellam Park (#91) and Wychwood (#93), they are over 10 per cent of the population.[27]

Meanwhile, Italian Pentecostals left their College Street church for the former Howard Park United. At the inauguration of the church, Phil Gaglardi, a Pentecostal minister and Social Credit cabinet minister from British Columbia, was the guest of honour, together with an Ontario cabinet minister and the Toronto mayor. Music was provided by the Scarborough temple choir and band.[28] The *congregazione pentecostale italiana*, which was affiliated with this group, acquired the building near Old Weston Road and St Clair previously belonging to the English-speaking West End Full Gospel Tabernacle. Headed by Michele Sauro, a postwar immigrant from the region of Molise who had converted to Pentecostalism while living in Montreal, the congregation occupied this site for over fifteen years before moving on to Downsview.[29]

The Portuguese who settled in the downtown core in Alexandra Park and Kensington Market began frequenting St Mary's, where masses and other services were now provided in their language. The church was set aside for their exclusive use in 1969. From the Italians they acquired St Agnes, where they had worshipped for a time in the church basement. The parish later came under the care of the Missionaries of the Holy Spirit (also known as Spiritans), many of whom had served in Angola prior to the decolonization movement triggered by Portugal's Carnation Revolution of 1974. The Portuguese also acquired the former Dovercourt Baptist Church, which was renamed *Santa Cruz* (Holy Cross). St Helen's and St Sebastian's, which included among their parishioners newcomers from the Azorean islands of São Miguel and Terceira, soon had pastors from Portugal. Meanwhile, Portuguese-language masses were regularly celebrated at other sites, such as St Anthony's, a multilingual parish entrusted to the Congregation of the Missionaries of St Charles (also known as Scalabrinians), a community founded in late-nineteenth-century Italy for the care of Italian immigrants. A Brazilian pastor of Italian origin instituted a separate "Brazilian" mass there. As the Portuguese moved northward along the Dufferin Street corridor, Our Lady of the Angels began catering to parishioners mostly hailing from northern Portugal.[30] Finally, St Peter's offered Portuguese masses for two decades until 1995. Clearly, the area of Portuguese settlement overlapped with the Italian one, but was not contiguous with it, as the former stretched farther south to King Street. By the same token, the shift in language use clearly highlights the retreat of Italians from the area. Over time, the Portuguese migration to the suburbs, notably Mississauga, has led to a drop in the number of parishioners at St Agnes, St Helen's, and St Sebastian's.[31] Today the Portuguese are demographically concentrated in five adjacent neighbourhoods, the most important being Little Portugal (84), where they comprise almost half the population. In Dufferin Grove (83), Trinity Bellwoods (81), Dovercourt–Wallace Emerson (93), and Weston–Pellam Park (91), one in three inhabitants is Portuguese, while in Palmerston–Little Italy (80), the proportion is one in five.[32]

A Portuguese mission was established at the Church of All Nations under Vernon Kimball, a former missionary in Angola. The minister reported that his fledgling congregation was wracked by dissension rooted in diverse denominational, regional, and linguistic backgrounds. Most of the twenty or so families who received pastoral and other assistance, including information on health care, workmen's compensation, and employment, lived in Scarborough and worked on Sundays, which severely hampered congregational life. Around the same time as this mission began, a more forthrightly evangelical, but unaffiliated, congregation began meeting at various West End sites. A building on Lippincott Street at Nassau belonging to the First Portuguese Club was purchased, remodelled, and opened for worship under the name First Portuguese Evangelical. Adventists, for their part, took over the imposing College Street Baptist Church, occupying it for thirty years. Portuguese speakers also had their own services at Baptist, Presbyterian, and Jehovah's Witnesses places of worship.[33] Small Pentecostal congregations were formed, often in storefronts in the Dufferin–Dundas West area. Some of these groups, of recent origin, are affiliated with large denominations originating in Brazil.[34]

Postwar Greeks, originating mostly from Macedonia, the Peloponnese, and Cyprus, initially formed two clusters of settlement, the primary one being in the West End. By 1970, however, the secondary one along Danforth Avenue had supplanted it, becoming in effect Greektown. By then, Greeks were moving out of the downtown in a northeasterly direction towards Scarborough.[35] The choice of Parkdale as the site for the Greek Orthodox cathedral reflects the early phase of settlement. St Alban's/North Parkdale United became the Cathedral of the Annunciation and the Dormition of Mary, consecrated by Metropolitan

6.4 Santa Inês Portuguese Catholic

Opened in 1902, the parish, originally called St Francis, was English speaking. A dozen years later, it was renamed St Agnes and became the second Italian-language parish in the city, serving Italians who were moving into the area from the Ward, where the housing stock was being depleted. Reflecting changing population movements, the parish was turned over to the Portuguese in 1970. Meanwhile, Italians took over St Francis church just to the north on Grace Street. (Gabriele Scardellato)

Athenagoras Kokkinakis of Eleia. When a fire severely damaged the structure in 2000, it was restored to even greater splendour.[36] Unlike the cathedral, the two small churches of Holy Trinity on Clinton Street and St Nektarios Cathedral on Dovercourt Road are not under the authority of the Patriarch of Constantinople and follow the Old Calendar.

Slavs

Numerically smaller and more dispersed European groups chose worship sites according to criteria other than residential concentration. As automobiles became commonplace in the postwar years, distance was no longer an obstacle to worship, except for people who could not afford them.[37] Slavic groups were very active in acquiring new sites. The Russian Orthodox Cathedral of Christ the Saviour moved into the more spacious St Cyprian Anglican. The rival Holy Trinity Russian Orthodox took over the former Beth Jacob Synagogue. A congregation comprised of Russians, Ukrainians, and Russian speakers of mixed heritage offered to buy Beverley Street Baptist, where they had worshipped since the First World War, but were rebuffed by the Department of Canadian Missions. The building, they were bluntly told, was not for sale, and even if it were, they would have to pay the full market price for it. Undaunted, they purchased the Door of Hope mission on Gladstone Avenue above Argyle, which became the Ukrainian Evangelical Christian and Baptist (now Slavic Evangelical Baptist).[38] Czech Catholics acquired a two-storey brick commercial structure off Gladstone Avenue just south of Bloor, where they installed the church of St Wenceslaus. The parish priest, who had served as a missionary in Peru, invited local Peruvians to worship there in the 1980s. Every year these parishioners observed the feast of the Señor de los Milagros with a procession in the streets around Dufferin Grove Park. Slovak Lutherans, for their part, settled into Grace Lutheran, a church housing Polish coreligionists as well. Finally, Czechoslovak Baptists shared the Parkdale church with the English-speaking congregation before moving to Annette Street Baptist, which they soon purchased.

Yugoslav churches were a reflection of their homeland's troubled recent past. In 1961, parishioners at Our Lady Queen of Croatia were keen to celebrate the twentieth anniversary of the proclamation of Croatian independence following the invasion of Yugoslavia by Nazi Germany and Fascist Italy in 1941. A puppet regime had been installed in Zagreb under Ante Pavelić, founder of Ustaša (Insurgency), a movement

that had advocated independence by violent means. That the commemoration took place is not surprising in light of the church's membership, which was described by the pastor, Charles (Dragutin) Kamber, as
comprised of former soldiers in Pavelić's army and refugees fleeing the
collapse of his regime in 1945. To these the cleric added a younger generation who had grown up in Marshal Josip Broz Tito's Yugoslavia, who
were religiously lukewarm and morally dubious despite their fierce
anti-communism, and who now embraced North American materialism
with a vengeance. The pastor described the latter group as rather crude,
misogynist, and violent, as well as mentally and emotionally unstable.
They did not hesitate to beat up parishioners, even in the church vestibule, who were judged to be insufficiently patriotic. *Bratstvo I Jedinstvo*
(Brotherhood and Unity), an organization committed to the Yugoslav
government's policy on inter-ethnic harmony, strongly condemned the
commemoration by recalling the massacre of Serbs, Romani, and Jews
by the Pavelić regime.[39] In the aftermath of the celebration, the Croatian
church burned to the ground. Kamber, a US citizen, publicly accused
local Yugoslav Communists of arson, claiming that they had it in for
him because he had served during the war as chaplain in the Croatian
army and because some of his parishioners had earlier protested against
the Yugoslav government in front of the consulate. Privately, however,
he told a very different story, laying the blame on the emotionally and
psychologically troubled elements in his parish.[40] After his death in
1969, Kamber was succeeded by Josip Gjuran, the long-serving pastor
who later admitted in an interview: "Our people were sympathetic to
Pavelić's state and I was serving those people as church leader. I wasn't
a political activist. I would have been stupid to fight against my own
people."[41]

A few blocks away, the former Apostolic Faith Church became home
to a dissident Serbian Orthodox group. Named after St Michael the
Archangel, the parish was largely composed of Chetniks, members of
a Serb nationalist movement ardently loyal to the monarchy that had
fought against both Nazi occupation and Marshal Tito's partisans. As
the latter accumulated military successes, the Chetniks were marginalized, ironically becoming a Nazi collaborationist militia armed by the
Reich. The parish was the product of a schism with origins in the Cold
War that split Serbian Orthodoxy in North America and Toronto's East
End parish of St Sava. The West End group claimed allegiance to Dionisije Milivojevich, bishop of the North American Serbian diocese since
1939 and organizer of a highly visible and coordinated campaign to

protest Marshal Tito's official visit to the United States in 1963. The following year, the prelate was defrocked for misconduct by the Serbian Orthodox Church in Belgrade.[42] In retaliation, Dionisije convened his Diocesan National Assembly, which proclaimed him metropolitan of the Free Serbian Church in North America – free, that is, of Communist control.[43] St Michael the Archangel became a hotbed of Serbian nationalism, briefly publishing its own newspaper, *Slobodna Srpska Crkva* (Free Serbian Church), and then establishing organizations and cultural activities dedicated to the cause.

Hungarians and Germans

With Hungarians moving to the suburbs, both First Hungarian Presbyterian and St Elizabeth of Hungary had to relocate within a decade of each other. However, congregants at the Church of All Nations were reluctant to leave their Queen Street site despite strong pressures from the United Church. When they finally did so, they moved into the former Brothers of Jacob Synagogue.[44] Although Germans too were moving to the suburbs, religious services in their language continued downtown. A small independent congregation, the *Evangelische Gemeinde,* related to the English-speaking group that had established Grace Church Evangelical Association earlier in the century, took up quarters in the former Olivet Gospel Hall on Ossington Avenue. Composed of equal numbers of *reichsdeutsche* and *volksdeutsche,* all were converts from other faiths. Deaconesses from Kitchener, performing their traditional role of "congregation planting," had come to Toronto to initiate home-based Bible study classes. After a while, the pastor, a resident of Kitchener, decided to make Toronto his home. A frequent visitor to the *Marburger Bibelseminar,* a fundamentalist and charismatic institution in Germany where he had been trained, the minister also took continuing education classes at the Ontario Bible College during his tenure. A decade after its creation, the congregation was losing members due to suburbanization.[45]

New Wine in Old Wineskins: Visible Minorities

Sephardim

Visible minorities too preferred to use existing facilities rather than erect new ones. Moroccan Jews, for example, established a Spanish-language Sephardic congregation named *Petah Tikva Anshe Castille*

(Opening of Hope Men of Castile). With the assistance of the Jewish Immigrant Aid Society (JIAS), they had come to Toronto from Tangier, an international port city that was also a Spanish protectorate where Jews made up one-quarter of the inhabitants. Numbering more than six hundred families, they purchased the former *Shomrai Shabot* in 1968, thanks to the fundraising activities of the Sisterhood.[46] Two years later, Yehudah Edery, a native of Tangier who had studied in England and the United States, was appointed rabbi. Within six months of his installation, however, he had generated dissention and division, largely because of his financial transactions on behalf of the community. After being repudiated by his congregation, he founded a new Sephardic synagogue to the north of our area, taking with him a number of families who remained loyal to him. Around the same time, a second split left Petah Tikva with only two hundred families. The congregation bought land in Downsview and moved out of the Brunswick Avenue building.[47]

Tension also marked relations between the congregation and community agencies controlled by Ashkenazim. The synagogue's president, Leon Osiel, accused the latter of doing nothing for elderly Sephardim, most of whom were being left to languish in their homes without support. "If we are not regarded as second class, then why don't we get proper help from the community?" he pointedly asked. His position was supported by Mitchell Serels, the new rabbi, who stated, "There is a lack of respect for the dignity of the Sephardic community," and who added that the JIAS had "done a good job in bringing over families and supplying them with immediate needs, but in terms of social, cultural, and religious adjustment, they have not provided the help." Osiel concluded: "We want to be part of the community yet preserve ourselves as Sephardim."[48] Perhaps it was this feeling of being on the margins that impelled the congregation to invite rabbi Meir Kahane as a speaker in 1971. A follower of Vladimir Jabotinsky, the right-wing founder of the Irgun, a clandestine military organization dedicated to achieving the goal of Eretz Israel (Greater Israel) through violence, Kahane established his own paramilitary Jewish Defence League in New York in 1968. Like Irgun, this organization used intimidation and violence to uphold Jewish rights. Shortly after his talk in Toronto, the rabbi immigrated to Israel, where he founded the Kach Party, whose main ambition was to rid Eretz Israel of its Arab inhabitants.[49] The invitation made it clear that leading Petah Tikva members sympathized with extremist right-wing Zionism.

Chinese

Toronto's Chinese began moving from Queen Street to Dundas Street after the departure of downtown Jews; later, they established other enclaves outside this core area of settlement. Presbyterians among them were the first to build a proper church in Chinatown. Congregations were later formed by Chinese from Hong Kong, many of whom were students who had overstayed their study visas. Thanks to an amnesty granted by the immigration minister, they were able to remain in the country. Educated and urbanized, they saw themselves as different from previous immigrants, most of whom were barely literate peasants from Taishan region in the Pearl River Delta, just west of the British colony. Mandarin speakers from the PRC and Taiwan would later join many of these new congregations. Because Protestant missionaries in China did not call attention to their denominational affiliations, often simply referring to themselves as Christian, a number of Chinese churches in Toronto did the same. This was the case with Chinese Gospel, with Holy Word Chinese Evangelical, which took over from First Hungarian Presbyterian, and with the Church in Toronto, a group that developed rapidly in the suburbs of Willowdale and Scarborough before buying a house for worship on Cecil Street.[50] The True Jesus Church, for its part, occupied a commercial space on Harbord Street that had been vacated by Hungarian Pentecostals. Affiliated with the similarly named denomination begun in 1917 in Beijing, this group worships on Saturdays, rejects major Christian holidays because of their pagan roots, baptizes only in bodies of water, and practises footwashing and glossolalia (speaking in tongues). They left the downtown for Scarborough in 1997.[51]

The archdiocese created the Chinese mission of St Francis Xavier, housed in the old Ostrovtze Synagogue and named after the Jesuit missionary to the Orient who died near Taishan in 1552. On its inauguration, a lion dance was performed from St Michael's Cathedral to the new site, which was blessed by the Archbishop of Nanjing. Soon after, Our Lady of Mount Carmel Parish was reserved for their use. Its pastor, a native of the Portuguese colony of Macao across the Pearl River Delta from Hong Kong, was assisted by a Chinese sister. Baptists established a congregation recognized by the Convention of Ontario and Quebec and soon acquired the Beverley Street church. Membership shot up very quickly, reaching 1,000 within a few years. Like their Catholic compatriots, the Baptists opened a new church in Scarborough because theirs was bursting at the seams.[52] A Mandarin-speaking congregation was later started and initially met in the Afro-Americans' First Baptist church in Chinatown. After securing a mortgage from the Department of Canadian Missions, they moved into a church, originally belonging to Ukrainian Presbyterians, now renamed Grace Chinese Baptist.[53] The Pentecostal Living Water Assembly was begun by a young Hong Kong immigrant, David Ko, who had converted after arriving in Canada. Following studies at the Pentecostal Eastern Bible College and ordination, Ko held services at First Ukrainian Pentecostal for almost a decade before occupying a reconverted garage on Claremont Street.[54]

Chinese non-Christian places of worship began appearing in the West End in the 1980s. The Taoist Tai Chi Society was founded by a monk from Hong Kong who wanted to take Taoist arts out of their monastic setting and make them accessible to a broader public. After visiting the city in 1970, he set up his society in a building behind City Hall. A decade later it moved to the current facility on Bathurst Street below St Clair. Since the founder travelled regularly between the British colony and the Queen City, congregants offered him a residence on D'Arcy Street in Chinatown in the former Szydlower Synagogue. The building doubled as a temple called Fung Loy Kok, attracting non-Chinese participants from different Judeo-Christian traditions. Renovations, including the acquisition of an adjacent property, were completed in 1995.[55] Another Taoist place of worship, Ming Sing Tao-Tak, affiliated with the Heavenly Way temple movement founded in southern China a century ago, occupies an entire office building on St Patrick Street north of Queen. Services are conducted in Cantonese and Mandarin, with the occasional lecture in English, usually about interpersonal relations in light of the teachings of the great world religions. The temple stresses the commonality between the moral precepts of Buddhism, Confucianism, Taoism, Christianity, and Islam. Some members even attend both the temple and a Christian church.[56] The Hong Fa Buddhist Temple moved from the suburbs where it was founded into a larger and more accessible brick commercial site on Bloor Street just west of Lansdowne subway station. Named after a Hong Kong temple, the structure has its main shrine on the first floor, a chanting and meditation space on the second, and a library on the third. In addition to the original core of Hong Kong immigrants, the temple has welcomed Sino-Vietnamese, as well as Chinese from the PRC and Taiwan. Members are drawn from all over greater Toronto; very few of them live nearby. The Chuen Te Buddhist Society, for its part, acquired a former University of Toronto

6.5 Fung Loy Kok Taoist

Standing on the site of the former Anshei Szydłów Synagogue (1914–64), the property was purchased in 1995 for the spiritual leader of the Taoist congregation. After his death, it was frequented mostly by Hong Kong immigrants, although non-Chinese also attended. (Gabriele Scardellato)

6.6 Toronto Church of God (demolished)
Reflecting the downtown's shrinking white Protestant population, St Barnabas
Anglican on Halton Street at Givins was taken over in 1971 by Afro-Caribbeans
affiliated with the Church of God branch of Pentecostalism, established in the
early twentieth century in Tennessee. The church was demolished in 1998.
(Gabriele Scardellato)

student residence on Beverley Street at Cecil. Its director lives on the
premises, and it relies entirely on volunteers and donations to serve a
community of 1,000 members. In line with the society's emphasis on
humility, minimal structural changes have been made to the building.
Nor are religious services and community outreach programs in any
way advertised. Fundraising and collections are rigorously prohibited.[57] Two other Buddhist societies occupy Victorian houses on nearby
Cecil Street.[58]

Christian, Buddhist, and Toaist places of worship clearly demarcate the
Chinese presence in the West End. Chinese are highly concentrated in the
Kensington–Chinatown neighbourhood (78), where they are 43 per cent

of the local population, but they are also a strong presence in adjacent Trinity–Bellwoods (81) to the west and in University to the north (#79), where one in five residents is Chinese. In Little Portugal (84), Palmerston–Little Italy (80), and Dufferin Grove (83), the proportion is one in ten.[59]

Afro-Caribbeans and Africans

Fairly scattered in the West End, Afro-Caribbeans joined existing congregations or founded new ones. Although only one church was built expressly for them, they became a conspicuous presence in six others: Ossington Avenue Baptist, Toronto Spiritualist Temple, St Mark and the Epiphany Anglican, St Michael and All Angels Anglican, and St Matthew United, as well as Christ Church Afro-Community, where in the 1960s the minister offered Caribbean domestics special activities on their afternoons off. About one-quarter of St Matthew's members are from Jamaica; a smaller number are from the eastern Caribbean.[60] Afro-Caribbeans also took over nine churches, all of which became fundamentalist, most of them belonging to the variety of Pentecostal denominations active in the Caribbean but founded in the United States, such as the Church of God, founded early in the century in Tennessee, and the Church of God of Prophecy, which split from the first.[61] While these buildings were all substantial, Afro-Caribbeans also took over three smaller gospel halls.[62] All of these churches were in a distinct West End area roughly bounded by Shaw Street to the east, Dundas Street/Davenport Road to the south and west, and St Clair Avenue to the north.

Within these boundaries, Afro-Caribbeans also rented commercial spaces adjacent to railway tracks, where property was cheaper.[63] Fully one-quarter of the sixty such sites were in the hands of Afro-Caribbeans. Oakwood Wesleyan, for example, moved into the old Brandon Avenue Hall, scene of many Italian Canadian events, including union meetings during the troubled construction strikes of the early 1960s.[64] Its congregants evidently preferred to maintain their established allegiance to Methodism rather than join the United Church. Spiritual Baptists, a group once banned in Trinidad and Tobago and whose syncretic practices combined Catholic, Anglican, Baptist, and African traditions, formed two congregations in the West End, the most enduring one being St Ann's in a storefront on Dupont Street near Christie.[65] Founded by an immigrant from St Vincent who later became an archbishop, it was composed of people sharing ties of kinship and immigration. Most adherents were former Catholics who wanted to renew their African roots. Worship involved shouting, twisting, the ringing of bells, and

6.7 Oakwood Wesleyan
The former Brandon Hall hosted meetings of Italian construction unions
during the famous strikes of the early 1960s. The building has since
1982 served an Afro-Caribbean congregation that holds true to its
Wesleyan origins. It has declined to affiliate with the United Church
of Canada. (Gabriele Scardellato)

the playing of drums. Great stress was placed on visions and dreams,
which were believed to convey messages from God. Baptism was by
total immersion in a body of water.[66] A similar mix of Catholic and African traditions was found in a congregation calling itself St Peter temple
of IFA or St Peter I am the Divine Halibethian, which briefly occupied
spaces in the Bathurst and Davenport area. The group was founded by a
Jamaican woman, now a bishop, and the buildings' windows displayed
small statues whose identities were simultaneously Catholic and African as in Cuban Santeria. The boisterous worship with its shouting and
drumming angered neighbours, who succeeded in getting the place
shut down.[67]

Although Afro-Caribbeans have been especially active in creating places of worship in the Junction, this area is not one where they are residentially concentrated. In 2001, blacks were a significant presence in only three West End neighbourhoods: Waterfront Communities–the Island (77) at 10 per cent, South Parkdale (85) at 11 per cent, and Weston–Pellam Park (91) at 12 per cent.[68] Yet the greater Junction became for them a kind of congregational incubator. Very often, congregations began with only a few individuals. The minister's capacity to meet the faithful's various needs was often a key factor in expansion, but so was the congregants' ability to involve themselves in its activities. Success often required a move to a larger location; otherwise the place closed down within a few short years.

Africans too were present in the West End, although in much smaller numbers. Egyptian Copts were the first to appear in the area and worshipped briefly in their rite at St Matthias Anglican. Years later, Zerit Yohannes, a Lutheran pastor, came to Canada as a government-sponsored refugee from Eritrea and for five years held services in Tigrinya, the language spoken in northern Ethiopia and Eritrea, at St John's Evangelical Lutheran.[69] A short walk away, at St Mary the Virgin and St Cyprian Anglican, the Coptic Orthodox congregation of St Mary rented the church for its Sunday morning liturgy, which typically lasted three hours. By 1997 they had raised enough money to settle into permanent quarters in North York.[70] Eritrean Coptic Catholics frequented San Nicola di Bari for their Sunday afternoon liturgy, which was said in Ge'ez, an ancient South Semitic language. A Junction storefront first rented by Afro-Caribbean Pentecostals was taken over by the Celestial Church of Christ. A syncretic religion combining Christian and African traditions founded after the war in Benin and now centred in Nigeria, it is active among African immigrants in Europe and North America. Wearing white clothes, men and women sit separately during worship. Women are temporarily excluded when menstruating or after giving birth.

South Asians

South Asians belonging to many religious traditions have left their mark in the West End. In 2001 they achieved a modest degree of residential concentration in four contiguous West End neighbourhoods, where they comprised between 7 and 11 per cent of the local population and where, coincidentally, their places of worship were

6.8 Prarthana Samaj Hindu
The building goes back to 1890 when the Ruth Street Presbyterian mission
was established. From 1913 to 1979 it housed the Fern Avenue Church
of Christ. It is now a Hindu temple whose congregation, formed in 1967,
is the oldest in metropolitan Toronto and one of the oldest in
North America. (Gabriele Scardellato)

situated: Dufferin Grove (83), Dovercourt–Wallace Emerson–Junction (93), Roncesvalles (86), and South Parkdale (85).[71] Sikhs, mostly
from the northern states of Punjab, Harayana, and Uttar Pradesh,
took over a disused school at Old Weston Road south of St Clair
to form their own *gurdwara* (God's house), named Sri Guru Singh
Saba, after having split from the congregation in the East End South
Asian enclave. But the new congregation has itself been riven by
factionalism over the issue of support for Babbar Khalsa International, an organization advocating armed struggle to achieve an
independent Sikh homeland called Khalistan.[72] More recently a Sikh
group has established an ashram on Palmerston Avenue north of

College bearing the name of one its historic gurus, Ram Das. It is dedicated to the teaching of kundalini yoga, made famous in the West by Swiss psychiatrist Carl Jung in the 1930s.

In 1979, *Prarthana Samaj* (Prayer Society) became the first permanent Hindu temple to be established in the Toronto metropolitan area. Located in Parkdale, it was soon joined by Gandhi Bhawan (large house), a congregation partly composed of West Indians. Immigrants from the Caribbean also founded the *Gayatri Mandir*, which moved from its original site in the East End enclave to Dupont Street west of Ossington.[73] Meanwhile, Tamils from Sri Lanka were connected with two churches a short distance from each other: St Anthony's, where Catholic and Hindu compatriots venerated the saint's statue with equal fervour; and St John Evangelical Lutheran, where Tamil refugees fleeing the Sri Lankan civil war found welcome. Although they were members of the Church of South India, a union of Anglican, Presbyterian, and other Protestant denominations, the parish offered them assistance in sponsoring friends and relatives displaced by the war.[74]

South Asians were also among the earliest members of the Jami mosque, the second such establishment in Toronto after the Albanian Muslim Society and the first permanently to occupy a space originally built as a place of worship, the former High Park Presbyterian. The building's interior had to be adapted for Muslim worship: the pulpit was replaced by the *minbar*, from which the imam delivers his sermon; choir stalls gave way to the *mehrab* (semicircular niche), indicating the direction of Mecca, which worshippers must face when praying; pews were removed and a carpet covering the entire floor surface was laid to allow men to stand together in rows for prayer and occasionally prostrate themselves. The stained glass windows depicting human figures were taken down and replaced by non-figurative ones. In the early 1970s the building was almost lost when intense factionalism prevented the faithful from meeting their mortgage payments. Rooted in divergent scriptural interpretations and national traditions of Islam, these struggles for power produced "continuous verbal and at times physical violence on the Mosque premises." As a result, a group split off and established a second mosque, the Islamic Foundation of Canada, in the East End. The remaining members launched an appeal to King Faisal of Saudi Arabia (1964–75), who advanced the funds needed to reclaim the edifice.[75]

6.9 Jami Mosque

Known as High Park Presbyterian until 1969, it was built in 1930 for those who rejected union with the United Church of Canada. Although Albanian Muslims had been worshipping in the West End since the mid-1950s, this was the first ecclesiastical building to serve as a mosque. (Gabriele Scardellato)

Southeast Asians and Latinos

Filipino migration came in two phases: the first involved single professional women admitted as independent immigrants under the points system; the second, based on family reunification, was marked by greater gender balance and less-skilled workers.[76] A mere fraction of these people settled in the West End. At 9 per cent, South Parkdale (85) registered the highest proportion. Elsewhere their ratio varied between a low of 0.5 per cent in Little Portugal (84) and a high of almost 4 per cent in Wychwood (94).[77] Although they would have preferred to form national parishes like other immigrant groups, ecclesiastical authorities, including some Filipino priests, favoured integration into existing parishes.[78] As a result, they worshipped in English-language Catholic churches such as Holy Rosary, St Patrick, or Holy Family. St Anthony was the only West End parish where weekly mass was briefly said in Tagalog, the national language. Convention Baptists founded First Filipino Baptist congregation in a former Salvation Army barrack on Lippincott Street at Bloor, as well as a fledgling one at Western/ Parkdale Baptist mostly composed of Catholic converts. They met regularly in the church basement before finally securing a chapel on the main floor. Later on, they succeeded in buying the former West Toronto Gospel Hall on Pacific Avenue "at half its market value" and established a congregation called Hallelujah. At some point, the congregation left the Baptist Convention and joined the rival Fellowship Baptists. [79]

Other Southeast Asians surpass 5 per cent of the population in only two neighbourhoods: South Parkdale (85) and Weston–Pellam Park (91). The most numerous group in this category, the Vietnamese, have a mission dedicated to the Vietnamese Martyrs operating out of St Cecilia's. At St Pius X, another church in the High Park area, a Sunday mass is said regularly for Indonesians, most of whom in Toronto are Christians of Chinese ancestry.[80] There are also two Buddhist temples: Chua A Di Da (or Amida) on Lisgar Avenue at Queen, and the Linh-Son on Howard Park at Dundas West. The former was established by laymen from North Vietnam belonging to the first refugee wave, who were royalist, anti-communist, and strongly nationalist. They were followers of a prominent monk in their country of origin, who inaugurated the temple and became its spiritual head, visiting it often from his residence in Montreal. The second resulted from a conflict at another temple between clergy and laity. The lay faction, composed of South

Vietnamese professionals, controls Linh-Son's administration; their spiritual head lives in France.[81]

Latin American migration began in the wake of the military coup in Chile that toppled the democratically elected government of Salvador Allende. Political instability and repression throughout the region, especially in the Central American countries of El Salvador, Guatemala, and Nicaragua, as well as in the Southern Cone, brought many refugees to Canada. These were followed by economic immigrants. Hispanics worshipped at the Lithuanian parish of Saint John the Baptist before the church was turned over to them. Regular masses in Spanish were also said at St Alphonsus, St Anthony, and St Peter. A Baptist mission (*Iglesia Bautista Hispana*) began at Dufferin Street Baptist, conducted by two female students of the Ontario Bible College. Grace Church of the Nazarene in High Park established the *iglesia evangélica de el Nazareno* in 1992, composed mostly of Central American refugees.[82] Meanwhile, other small congregations, including Pentecostal and Jehovah's Witness, shared storefronts for the most part with Portuguese speakers or Afro-Caribbeans.[83] Hispanics have attained the greatest degree of residential concentration in the West End neighbourhood of Corso Italia–Davenport (92), where they form over 8 per cent of the population.[84]

Koreans

In 2001, Koreans comprised just over 6,500 of the old City of Toronto's population. The earliest among them arrived in the 1960s as students or independent immigrants who, having found employment, chose to become permanent residents. The most recent ones have included refugees whose families migrated to China after the Japanese occupation of their country in 1910.[85] Many Koreans came from large cities such as Seoul, Daegu, and Busan. A significant number came from North Korea but had spent some time in South Korea before immigrating. In terms of places of worship, Koreans had an importance far beyond their demographic weight: they took charge of five large churches, one of which became Pentecostal and the rest Presbyterian. Koreans also formed separate congregations in at least ten other West End churches, thereby helping pay for their upkeep.[86] The very first congregation, Toronto Korean United, was formed in 1967 with the support of former Canadian missionaries to Korea. Many of its members came either from the North or from the southwestern province of Jeolla. A disproportionate number of them were professionals, reflecting the profile of the earliest wave. The congregation soon shared space at Bloor Street United in order to be closer to the original area of Korean settlement around Christie Street and Bloor.[87]

Virtually from the beginning, Sang Chul Lee (Sang Ch'ol Yi), future moderator of the United Church of Canada (1988–1990), led the congregation. Unshakably progressive in theological, political, and social matters, he followed in the footsteps of his father-in-law, Kim Chai Chun, Princeton graduate, founder of Chosun (now Hankuk) Seminary, and leader of liberal Presbyterians who in 1954 formed the Presbyterian Church in the Republic of Korea, a denomination that ordains women as ministers and elders. Lee was a prominent opponent of Park Chunghee, the military strongman who ruled South Korea from 1961 until his assassination in 1979. He founded the Council for Democracy in Korea, which coordinated demonstrations at the consulate in Toronto and the embassy in Ottawa. He also served as vice-chair of the North American Coalition for Democracy in Korea, an organization partly funded by the World Council of Churches.

During these years, Korean diplomatic officials in Ottawa and Toronto interfered heavily in community affairs in order to build up solid support for the regime among expatriates and their elites. When Lee and other community leaders issued a statement denouncing President Park's declaration of martial law in 1971, one local newspaper refused to publish it. When it finally appeared in another Korean-language organ, the embassy personally attacked both the editor and the minister. Back home, prospective immigrants to Canada were pointedly told not to associate with Lee's church, which was characterized as a hotbed of communism. Fear was strong in the community, whose family members back home were vulnerable to reprisals. Beginning in 1972, this climate of insecurity induced a number of Korean United's members to secede. They constituted, as we have seen, a number of Presbyterian congregations that unanimously deplored Lee's blending of religion and politics for the harmful effects it had on the entire Korean Christian group.[88]

Toronto Korean Presbyterian was the first to separate, taking over the vacant Davenport Road Presbyterian. Almost immediately, three other splits occurred: Central Korean, comprising three hundred worshippers, purchased the former Westmoreland United Church;[89] East Korean occupied Epworth United on Christie Street; and Saehan (later Metropolitan Korean), with some 150 members, established itself in

Scarborough before moving into the former Toronto Korean Presbyterian Church in 1997. Shortly after these rifts, a fifth congregation, calling itself Newgate, was created, purchasing the former Humberside Avenue Baptist and allying itself with the Presbyterian Church in America, a socially and theologically conservative body in the United States that rejects homosexuality and the ordination of women.[90] Most religious leaders agree that these and subsequent splits had little to do with theology or church polity, since the congregants identified themselves as conservative, but were driven instead by loyalty to family and kin networks.[91] Central Korean and Newgate maintained a practice brought over from the home country of holding early morning prayer meetings during the week, in addition to Wednesday evening and Sunday services. Metropolitan Korean, for its part, held Wednesday and Saturday morning worship followed by a breakfast for the older congregants.[92] Most of these congregations celebrated Korean festivities such as the Lunar New Year and a day to honour both fathers and mothers, as well as traditional Christian holidays.

Be that as it may, Korean United, or the "red church" as it was dubbed by its detractors, remained true to its original progressive identity. It became an "affirming congregation," endorsing the full integration of homosexuals into church life and worship, an issue that caused one hundred members to secede in the late 1980s. At the end of the millennium, one-third of its elders were women. As well, there was sympathy in the congregation, many of whose members came from the North, for the regime in Pyongyang. One adherent in fact maintained contact with the government and regularly sent it money. Besides maintaining its distinct identity, the congregation saw itself as comprising the elite among Koreans because of its disproportionate number of professionals and intellectuals.[93]

Korean Catholics attended mass said by a compatriot at Our Lady of Mount Carmel, in what proved to be a difficult cohabitation with Chinese coreligionists. They then shared space at St John the Baptist before finally settling into a new church in Mississauga. Toronto Korean Bethel Evangelical, a Pentecostal congregation, used various sites before taking up permanent residence in the former Grace United on College Street. In 1985 a Korean Buddhist temple called the Nine Mountains Zen Society occupied a commercial space on Queen Street at Ossington. It is astonishing, in light of this intense religious activity in the area and Koreans' historic connection with Koreatown, that they are now virtually absent from the West End. In 2001, only in the Annex (95) did they reach close to 3 per cent of the population.[94]

6.10 Hare Krishna Temple
Completed in 1906, Covenant Presbyterian closed shortly after Church
Union in 1925. The building became famous in the 1940s as Avenue Road
Church of the Nazarene, where Charles Templeton electrified congregants
with his evangelistic services. It was taken over In 1977 by white converts
to Hinduism living communally. The congregation now includes south
Asians. (Gabriele Scardellato)

Lebanese immigrants who came to Canada in the wake of the civil
war worshipped according to the Maronite Rite in Syriac, the language spoken in Palestine at the time of Christ, at St Vincent de Paul
in Parkdale. They then purchased Epiphany Anglican on Queen Street,
renaming it Our Lady of Lebanon. A Lebanese congregation of priests,
the Antonine Fathers, has the care of the parish, which is part of the
Maronite eparchy, whose seat is in Montreal. A second Muslim place
of worship recently opened in a large storefront on Bloor Street west
of Dufferin. The Islamic Information and Da'wah Centre International,

whose mixed congregation includes Arabs, Guyanese, Somalis, South Asians, and converts, actively promotes proselytism.

Converts and Proselytism

While newcomers devoted time and effort to establish and support their places of worship, native-born Canadians, particularly those of the baby-boom generation (including the children of some immigrants), were distancing themselves from Judeo-Christian traditions. Some of these were among the more than 7 per cent of Torontonians listed in the 1971 census as having no religion. Others experimented with new or Eastern religions. The Unification Church, founded in Korea by former Presbyterian Sun Myung Moon in 1954, was one such denomination that claimed to be Christian but held a number of unorthodox beliefs. It established a foothold in Toronto in 1968, targeting young people in the University of Toronto area. Ten years later it acquired a house on Bellevue Avenue that had served as a home for the aged run by the Sisters of St John the Divine.[95] Another highly controversial denomination is the Church of Scientology. This non-Christian religion, established by Ron Hubbard in the United States in 1952, focuses on personal self-improvement through unconventional "scientific" techniques. A residence at Avenue Road and Bernard served as its base of operations for the better part of the 1970s. Created in 1969 and composed almost exclusively of white converts, the International Society for Krishna Consciousness (ISKCON) purchased the Avenue Road Church of the Nazarene in 1975. Sixty devotees moved into the building and shared a communal life. Today, a dozen such individuals reside in the temple. The congregants there now comprise second-generation members as well as immigrants from India. Around the time that the ISKCON site was acquired, another manifestation of Hindu religion aimed at a predominantly white audience got started in Toronto. Founded in India in 1936 and now centred in the northern state of Rajasthan, Brahma Kumaris opposed the caste system and sought to promote women to positions of authority. Like most such centres, the one in Toronto, located on College Street near Dovercourt (now closed), was headed by a Guyanese-born Hindu woman who had received her training in India and Barbados. Stressing inner peace through meditation, service to others, vegetarianism, and celibacy, she held seminars for specific groups such as health professionals.[96]

Those seeking alternative forms of religiosity were also drawn to Buddhism, identifying mainly with its Japanese or Tibetan variants. Like Hare Krishna, the Zen Centre began in the late 1960s at the instigation of an American who had received extensive Buddhist training in Japan. After giving a series of workshops in Toronto, he invited followers to visit his centre in Rochester, with which the Toronto facility maintains close ties to this day. A house was acquired on Christie Street for meetings and meditation. Membership doubled within a few years, reaching one hundred. However, a split occurred after a teacher from Buffalo who had come to Toronto to conduct an intensive meditation session (*sesshin*), usually lasting one or more days, decided to create her own group. Located in the High Park area since the mid-1980s, the Zen Centre has as many members as it did before the split. As with other Buddhist temples, followers included Canadians of British ancestry, northern European immigrants, and second-generation European immigrants.[97] The Dharmadhatu Buddhist Meditation Society, like most other Tibetan religious sites in Toronto, was founded in 1971 following the visit of a monk who encouraged disciples, most of them young American draft resisters, to form a study group. A few years later, the society changed its name and orientation. Called Toronto Shambhala Meditation Centre, it emphasized more secular practices of meditation and awareness, distinct from Buddhism. Occupying commercial spaces in the Bloor and Bathurst area, the facility has more recently attracted Russian Jews.[98]

Four other Tibetan temples were subsequently established. Karma Sonam Dargye Ling was founded in 1976 when the head of the one of the four major traditions in contemporary Tibetan Buddhism visited Toronto. The congregation purchased a house in Parkdale and converted it into a temple that served not only ethnically mixed whites but Tibetans as well. Most of the latter were recently admitted refugees living in the area, but there were also first-wave asylum seekers who in the 1970s had lived in smaller communities such as Lindsay and Belleville, encouraged to do so by the government.[99] Gaden Choling's founding was also linked to the visit of its spiritual head. Located in a house on Christie Street, this small congregation also attracts some Tibetans when a guest lama stops in.[100] Riwoche Pemavajra was founded in the Junction in 1990 and now occupies a space on Heintzman Street in the same area. Meanwhile, Tengye Ling moved into permanent facilities on Madison Avenue in the Annex. From a handful of faithful at its founding, the temple now has thirty-five regular worshippers, many of whom are immigrants from

Eastern Europe, Turkey, and Brazil. Their religious backgrounds include Catholic, Eastern Orthodox, Protestant, and Jewish.[101]

The interest in Eastern religions was in part an outcome of the decolonization movement that swept through Asia and Africa after the Second World War, leading to the break-up of European empires. In the West, the movement provoked a general reassessment of indigenous cultures, earlier regarded as inferior. This is evidenced in the Second Vatican Council's 1965 document *Ad Gentes* (To the Nations) on missionary activity. It invited proselytizers to live among the people they were seeking to convert, sharing their experiences and absorbing their values and cultures: they were to be among, not above or apart from indigenous populations. The emphasis was on service, not dominion. In the past, Christian proselytism had been the handmaiden of European expansionism, and conversion had been deemed a necessary step on the path towards higher forms of civilization and, not coincidentally, towards integration with the imperial centre. Despite this new perspective, the number of Catholic missionaries in the field plummeted in the wake of decolonization, such work being regarded as a vestige of an imperial past best forgotten. But in the 1970s with the spread of liberation theology, that explosive blend of Christianity and Marxism, and the successes of fundamentalist missions in Latin America, Rome once again pushed for missionary activity to be carried out, this time not only by priests but also by the laity.

The impact of these developments could be felt in Toronto as the mainstream Protestant denominations became less and less interested in active proselytizing. Still, change was gradual. In the early 1960s it had been open season on the Italians, who were arriving in the city in huge numbers. The attitude of the Protestant churches towards these newcomers is best captured in a Baptist Church document speculating on the prospects for converting Spanish-speaking immigrants. Although the ethnic group is different, the outlook is the same. Referring to their nominal Catholic background and infrequent attendance at church, the paper observed:

> In part, this low figure is due to the "liberation" that the … person feels as he emigrates. Not only is he giving up his native land, he may also give up the traditional faith that had so little influence and relevance in his life before. For all intents and purposes, he arrives in Canada as a practical agnostic, if still a nominal Catholic. In this vacuum, we believe he is in an excellent position to reappraise his life in relation to Jesus Christ.[102]

In this context, an Anglican mission to "unchurched Italians" was opened in 1960 by a priest and compatriot who used St Edmund's and later St Anne's as his base of operations. St Mary Madgalene's, where church attendance had fallen by half, inaugurated a weekly mass in Italian in the 1980s for Little Italy's residents.[103] Needless to say, it would have been impossible for an Italian attending this church to identify it as Anglican given its interior and furnishings.

Missions to Italians were also started by fundamentalist Christians. The Keele Street Church of Christ put up an Italian sign below its English one in 1959 to inaugurate its postwar immigrant work. Two decades later, outreach targeted Chinese students attending a nearby college, as well as Koreans and Muslims.[104] Around the same time, the Dufferin Street and Ossington Avenue Baptist churches started a joint mission to Italians, the first church offering English-language classes and the second Italian-language services led by a minister brought over from Switzerland by the Home Mission Board. A report dated 1962 estimated that half of the Italian population of Toronto was in active contact with the Baptist Church, which was encouraging them "to become integrated, as quickly as possible, into existing Baptist churches."[105]

As noted above, Convention Baptists regarded Latin Americans as a promising mission field. However, a report noted how difficult it was to reach them. Unlike many other immigrant groups, the document observed, they were not concentrated in any particular part of the city. Often both parents worked outside the home, and if the wife did happen to be in, she often did not open the door to proselytizers because of her inability to speak English. Transiency marked a number of households as newcomers moved in response to new opportunities. One commentator concluded that home visitations were perhaps not the best way to proceed. Stressing the need to hire a Spanish-speaking minister, he pointed to the success achieved in this regard by Jehovah's Witnesses, Pentecostals, and the Portuguese congregation at Olivet Baptist.[106]

A Baptist mission aimed not at a specific ethnic group, but at the condominium dwellers of Harbourfront where there were no worship facilities, was kicked off by a telemarketing-style campaign. As a result, the Quays Community Church was formed and later gathered at the Great Hall on Queen Street at Dovercourt.[107] Pentecostals too targeted newer immigrant groups. A storefront on St Clair held services briefly for Tigrinya speakers.[108] Other outreach initiatives were more discreet than the ones just described. Since 1968, for instance, the Christian Reformed Church, a strict Calvinist denomination of Dutch origin, has run the Lighthouse Community Ministry in a storefront on Bathurst Street. The facility provides refugee and immigrant services in Chinese, Vietnamese, and Spanish as well as children's programs and a food bank.[109]

The retreat of religion from the public sphere is best captured by a raw statistic: twice as many West End places of worship – twenty-seven in total – have been demolished as have been built since the 1960s. This figure leaves out sacred spaces torn down or destroyed by fire and subsequently rebuilt, but does include *stiblach* or synagogues that occupied private residences. Overwhelmingly, these were sizeable structures whose disappearance impoverished the urban landscape. To these twenty-seven, nine others can be added that have been turned into condominiums – that is, from community spaces into private ones. As mentioned earlier, only thirteen new places of worship were erected, most of them in the 1960s, when religion's retreat from the public sphere was just beginning. It can conceivably be argued that we should not expect to see new sacred structures in already built-in areas of the city. The fact is, though, that there has been a great deal of construction in West End Toronto; entire neighbourhoods have recently sprung up on its railway and Massey-Harris lands, yet not a single place of worship can be found in them. The point here is not to bemoan the loss of religion, nor indeed to plead for its resurgence, but to highlight a direct consequence of the consolidation of consumer capitalism that has entailed a fundamental structural change that no amount of proselytizing or pious hopes for the return of religion can singly alter.

Into this individualistic and consumerist culture have flowed massive numbers of immigrants, at first from Europe and later the developing world. Demographically they breathed new life into existing places of worship. Many more preferred to create their own separate entities, some of which were affiliated with higher ecclesiastical bodies outside of Canada. Despite their relatively small numbers, Koreans helped save a number of downtown churches at the time of their arrival. When later they vacated many of them, the effect was immediate: in quick order, Central, Newgate, and East Toronto Presbyterian all fell to the wrecker's hammer.

But the process is more dynamic than what has just been described. It is not simply about a single immigrant group taking over a particular place of worship. It is also about a succession of them occupying the same space. Over the course of less than two decades, Lithuanians,

Koreans, and Hispanics took over the Church of St John the Baptist. Similarly, the Second Church of the Nazarene became an Italian parish in the heyday of postwar immigration and now also serves Eritreans of the Coptic Rite. The Ukrainian Presbyterian church briefly accommodated Portuguese Pentecostals before becoming Grace Chinese Baptist. The midtown Torah Emeth Synagogue was for a short while a Greek Orthodox church before successively accommodating two Church of God congregations of Caribbean origin. Over the last half century, Ossington Avenue Baptist has welcomed Poles, Koreans, and Caribbeans.

Through immigration the West End has become racially, ethnically, and religiously very diverse. Non-Christian groups such as Buddhists, Taoists, Hindus, Muslims, Sikhs, and Bahá'í are firmly implanted there. In fact, Buddhist places of worship now outnumber the area's Anglican, United, or Presbyterian churches. Because some Buddhist congregations are quite small, it might seem unfair to count buildings rather than regular worshippers and not take congregational vitality into account. But even by these criteria it is unclear whether mainline Protestant denominations would fare any better. In any event, Buddhists have achieved a degree of longevity in the area. In 2000 the West End's places of worship were characterized by a high level of denominational dispersion: no one group predominated. Although Catholics comprised a plurality among Toronto's religious groups and, at thirty-eight, had the greatest number of churches in the West End, these buildings only accounted for 15 per cent of the total. Pentecostals were not far behind, followed by Baptists, Buddhists, Anglicans, United Church, Presbyterians, and Christian Orthodox, in descending order. Taken together, all the above-mentioned groups had less than two-thirds of the area's sacred spaces. Meanwhile, as many as fifteen other denominations had one place of worship each.

In some quarters, newcomers are perceived as the key to maintaining a strong religious life in Canada.[110] It is true that in general, each new immigrant wave has brought with it a strong sense of religious tradition or at least has come to regard religion as a means to help cushion the transition to a new life, as something familiar in a strange and alien environment. This has created the illusion of a progressive movement in which immigrants and their offspring have preserved ancestral connections and traditions. In previous chapters this study has shown that the newcomers' religion was not something static; rather, it evolved in contact with the North American environment. This was even more the case for the immigrants' children who wanted their religion to adopt explicitly North American features. This chapter has drawn attention to the profound social changes occurring since the 1960s and to the divergence that has been revealed between the first-generation immigrants' religious attachments and the surrounding society's religious indifference. The question thus arises: what about the second generation? The issue of continuity has become an acute one for places of worship frequented by postwar Europeans. Interviews point to an aging population of mostly female worshippers and refer to an absent younger generation vaguely said to have gone elsewhere. It is true that rising real estate prices have driven young families out of the downtown in search of more affordable housing in the suburbs. It is also true that this cohort's education and overall socialization make them more amenable to Canadian society's individualistic and consumerist values, loosening their ties to their parents' religious traditions. This pattern will likely repeat itself with the offspring of more recent visible minority groups, a proportion of whom are already without religious affiliation. Far from congratulating themselves on the arrival of religiously committed newcomers, observers should be concerned about the effect the Canadian environment is having on the second generation's possible religious development.

Chapter Seven

Fellowship in the Time of the Shopping Centre

Congregational or parish associational life in this latter period did not follow a single form or pattern. One thing was certain, however: the model of full-orbed religion all but vanished. Women, who had been its mainstay in the past, were now employed full-time in the labour market, while carrying out most domestic tasks at home. Youth, who had been a prime target of solicitude, were also working, while at the same time pursuing their studies. Religion's aim to provide for all or most of the community's needs was countered by consumer capitalism's claim that there's nothing money can't buy. Full-orbed religion seemed to flourish briefly in parishes established by refugees from Iron Curtain countries. But with the fall of the Berlin Wall, these too were confronted with the issue of continuity: the second generation was not as invested in maintaining the language and culture of origin. These parishes soon resembled the ones of other immigrant communities after the initial flurry of settlement. On the whole, associational life seemed geared mostly to pre-teenage children and the elderly, and this latter category had been largely marginalized by the loosening of traditional family ties. To differing degrees, parishes and congregations combined support for works of social utility and missions, be it at home or abroad, or both.

St Paul's Avenue Road United highlights some of the themes examined in this chapter. In the 1960s the church pursued the youth ministry begun a short time earlier by Stewart Crysdale (see chapter 5). These efforts no longer targeted greasers, but rather hippies flocking to nearby Yorkville in ever greater numbers. A contact made between a prominent hippie and Jim Smith, director of Christian Education for the Ecumenical Council of Metropolitan Toronto, which was head-quartered at St Paul's, resulted in the church's becoming an important drop-in centre for youth who had left home and were living on the streets without support. The Community Services Organization, with the financial assistance of neighbouring churches, equipped the basement with showers, distributed food, and offered counselling by professionals and peers. A coffee shop called The Grotto, funded by the Addiction Research Foundation and the Metro Toronto government, operated out of the basement, attracting as many as six to seven hundred youth in 1965 and 1966. A hostile minister in the same neighbourhood claimed that St Paul's had become the church that sold dope.

This ministry did not resolve the church's financial woes. After being installed as minister in 1971, Murray MacInnes confronted the question of how to pay for the church's upkeep in light of steadily declining membership. A social activist and former missionary in Angola, he invited like-minded organizations, such as the Toronto Committee for the Liberation of Portugal's African Colonies, the Development Education Centre (a non-profit resource facility specializing in Third World issues), and various arts groups to share space at St Paul's, regarding them as partners in his ministry. One of the church's artistic collaborators was Smile Company, which took musical theatre productions to seniors' residences. All of these organizations replaced the many congregational associations that had regularly used St Paul's as a meeting place in the past. An advocate of liturgical renewal, MacInnes shunned the pulpit, preferring to address his congregants, seated in a semicircle around him, from the floor of the church.[1] A short time after he left, the building was sold and the congregation transferred to Trinity United, with which it soon amalgamated. The new arrivals doubtless felt comfortable with the minister, Bill Phipps. The future United Church moderator, a staunch promoter of liberation theology, social justice, and women's issues, was credited with keeping young people active in the congregation. St Paul's congregants also found themselves in familiar surroundings. The Centre for Faith, Justice, and the Arts brought together a host of community organizations, all of which helped cover the hefty costs of upkeep. As well, two congregations, Bathurst Street United and Christos MCC, rented space there for regular worship. Although a shadow of their former selves, the merged congregations pursued with determination their commitment to gender equality, sexual

7.1 St Paul's United (destroyed by fire)
Built in 1887 at the corner of Avenue Road and Webster, it was where
Timothy Eaton's funeral, one of the largest ever held in the city, took place
in 1907. The interior was decorated by painter Gustav Hahn in the Art
Nouveau style. In response to declining membership, ministers carried on
a youth ministry, also targeting hippies in Yorkville. The church was sold
to developers in 1983, and its congregants were accommodated at Trinity
United, with which they later merged. (Toronto Reference Library)

emancipation, environmental renewal, and social progress at home and abroad.

One effect of the triumph of consumer capitalism has been a sharp decline in weekly church attendance. In the 1950s the figure stood at 70 per cent for Canada as a whole; between 1975 and 1985 it had dropped by more than half, remaining steady at 30 per cent during the decade; by 2000 it had fallen again to 25 per cent. Meanwhile, those claiming never to go to a place of worship rose from 21 to 26 per cent from 1985 to 2000, in that year surpassing the frequent churchgoers. Those declaring that they went less regularly – from once a month to once a year – were unchanged at just under half of the total. The rate of decline in frequent churchgoing affected all age categories but was particularly sharp – twice as great – in the cohort aged forty-five to sixty-four.[2] While some observers interpret the statistic on less regular attendance as a hopeful sign of the return of religion, the point surely is that since the 1960s it has not only vacated the public sphere but has ceased to be a building block of community. This argument needs, however, to be qualified. As seen in the previous chapter, religion still plays a community-building role among many first-generation immigrants, whether Christian, Sikh, Hindu, Buddhist, or Muslim, as well as for a number of larger funda-mentalist congregations. But this is far from a majority phenomenon, and nothing today points to a reversal of this trend.

Worship for the Times That Are a-Changin'

The start of this falling off in churchgoing coincided with the imple-mentation of liturgical reforms especially but not only in the Catholic Church. So the question arises: Were the two phenomena linked in a cause-and-effect relationship? Traditionalist Catholics led by Arch-bishop Marcel Lefebvre certainly came to think so.[3] They denounced the wholesale abandonment of the mass authorized in the sixteenth century by the Council of Trent (the Tridentine mass), and indeed the general "Protestantization" of the Catholic Church brought about by the Second Vatican Council. Whatever they contended, however, it is doubtful that such a causal link actually existed. For one thing, by the time the liturgical changes were formalized in 1969 with the adoption of the new Roman missal, church attendance had already begun to slip. For another, the late 1960s were a time of general moral questioning: clergy, as well as women and men in other forms of religious life, abandoned their calling in droves, many of them forsaking celibacy for married life; traditional notions of sex, marriage, and procreation were being openly challenged; and strictures and practices scrupulously observed by generations of Christians were suddenly rejected as trivial, empty, and conformist. It is in this broader context that declining church attendance should be set.

Reforms in the liturgy required a streamlining of church interiors. Once embodying notions of hierarchy, authority, order, and awe, they now conveyed a sense of community, accessibility, and informality. The space in the apse or sanctuary was reconfigured in order for the priest to face the worshippers. The altar had to be detached from the sometimes architecturally elaborate structure that both framed and highlighted it. Standing on its own in the middle of the sanctuary rather than against the back wall, it now looked more like a table recalling the Last Supper around which the priest could actually move. To break down the separation between clergy and laity, the communion rail dividing the sanctuary from the nave was often eliminated. The pulpit whose steps the priest used to climb to give his Sunday sermon became an ornamental artefact or was done away with altogether, the homily now being delivered from the gospel lectern to the left of the altar. To give churches a modern, clean, and uncluttered look, and to emphasize Christ-centred worship, plaster statuary of saints was often removed and votive candles reduced in number. The terrazzo floor at Our Lady of the Angels, probably the work of Friulian parishioners in the late 1930s, was covered over with wall-to-wall carpeting.[4] Fading frescoes at St Anthony and St Cecilia were whitewashed.[5] Replicating most of the above-mentioned changes, the renovations made in the 1960s to St Mary Magdalene's brought out, according to its rector, the church's "basic and simple" character.[6] By contrast, St Thomas retained the traditional position of the altar attached to the elaborately carved reredos.

Central to liturgical reform was the mass, whose bipartite structure, divided into the liturgies of the word and the Eucharist, was enhanced. Obscuring historical accretions, such as the psalms silently recited prior to the Kyrie, as well as the prayers and reading from the Book of the Apocalypse after the dismissal, were eliminated. To highlight the distinctness of the liturgy of the word, the priest conducted this segment of the mass from his seat on the right side of the apse, rather than at the altar. The prayers just before and after the consecration of the bread and wine were recited out loud by the celebrant. After the Agnus Dei, the faithful were invited to shake hands with their nearest neighbours, wishing them peace. This innovation strengthened the communitarian character of worship, as did the widespread practice of inviting the faithful to meet for coffee in the church hall or basement after the liturgy. Traditional high masses, including those for funerals, were eliminated in Catholic churches. When more than one priest was involved, a more egalitarian model of con-celebration was adopted in which no one enjoyed precedence over the others. Sung masses, which replaced high masses and were more elaborate than the spoken ones, began with a processional in which the scriptures were prominently displayed, emphasizing the Bible's importance in worship.

Greater prominence was assigned to the laity, including women and youth. The former were permitted to read the epistle, the first scriptural selection that precedes the Gospel. Girls became altar servers, despite a temporary ban on the practice in the Archdiocese of Toronto, and lay men and women distributed communion, a function previously reserved for the priest. Communicants stood, instead of kneeling as in the past, and received the wafer in their hands, rather than on the tongue, actions meant to underline the laity's active involvement in "taking communion." In line with the overall social trend towards greater casualness, parishioners gradually stopped going to church in their "Sunday best." Informal attire replaced dresses and hats for women and ties, jackets, dress trousers, and shoes for men. Liturgical vestments too were scaled down and largely standardized. Albs and stoles were quite commonly worn for worship and rites of passage by Catholic, Anglican, Lutheran, United Church, and some Presbyterian clergy. In some churches, altar servers simply wore their street clothes rather than surplices or albs.

With the baby boom generation's coming of age, folk masses featuring hymns or songs derived from the North American folk revival became popular. Much of this music was composed in the style of Joan Baez or Peter, Paul, and Mary by American seminarians such as the St Louis Jesuits, who produced six albums from the mid-1970s to the mid-1980s, one of which sold one million copies.[7] The lyrics, which tried to fuse the contemporary with the traditional, often sounded awkward. One of the earliest compositions, "Here We Are All Together" by Ray Repp, is a good example: "Join we now as friends / to celebrate the brotherhood we share, all as one / keep the fire burning, kindle it with care / as we all join in and sing / Here we are all together as we sing our song joyfully / here we are as we pray we'll always be." "Take Our Bread" by Joe Wise displays the same gaucheness: "We are yours, we are yours / Yours as we stand at the table you set / Yours as we eat the bread our hearts can't forget / We are the signs of your life with us yet / We are yours, we are yours." A pivotal instrument in this movement was the acoustic guitar, which for a time even replaced the organ. Such masses were a regular feature at the Newman Centre, the University of Toronto's Catholic chaplaincy, drawing large numbers of students, young faculty, and professionals. In those heady days of liturgical experimentation, young people even delivered a portion of the homily.[8]

Besides the mass, other religious practices underwent streamlining. Devotions to saints, such as triduums or novenas, in which a prayer was said and a candle lit for three or nine consecutive days in the quest for a special favour or purpose, were relegated to the domestic sphere. Even the communal recitation of the rosary was for a time abandoned in a number of parishes. Missions (or Catholic revivals) gradually fell into disuse. The last one at St Patrick's, the Redemptorist parish, apparently was held in 1971. Retreats, however, continued. Organized by linguistic group, age, gender, marital status, or parish association, they achieved the same degree of religious fervour but in a more intimate and homogeneous setting.[9] Processions proved to be especially problematic for the archdiocese, as immigrants to Toronto sought to perpetuate their home country's cherished regional or local public festivities. Officially, the issue was one of order and even public order: groups from various backgrounds could not simply take to the streets whenever they wished without some kind of coordination on the part of religious and civil authorities. But beneath this concern was perhaps the age-old fear often expressed by the North American hierarchy that such practices confirmed stereotypes of Catholics as idolatrous and superstitious, a concern that undoubtedly underlay some of the Second Vatican Council's liturgical reforms. To control processions as well as pare them down, the archdiocese required organizers to obtain permits. In the end, forty such events were authorized.

The pace of change varied according to parish. The faithful themselves were divided over the issues of timing and substance. Echoing media depictions of how Italy's ecclesiastical hierarchy was at the time resisting liturgical reform, a long-time parishioner at St Clare complained to the archdiocese that the newly arrived Italians who worshipped in her church were inordinately attached to the old ways. She held them responsible for the fact that in 1968 the mass there was still being said in Latin.[10] By contrast, two years earlier, the celebration of the Eucharist at the High Anglican parish of St Martin-in-the-Fields had showcased a popular group called The Creeps, who composed and played the accompanying music on electric guitars and drum set.[11] Music and the use of liturgical language became points of bitter contention at St Mary Magdalene's. A typically Anglican solution was found: a folk mass, held earlier in the day and intended for children, gradually drew the partisans of change because of its informal atmosphere as well as its contemporary language and music; the elaborate three-priest high mass in the Elizabethan liturgical idiom meanwhile continued to attract lovers of tradition. But this compromise was not achieved overnight. At one point, some modernists offended traditionalist sensibilities by going to high mass in casual dress.[12] At Trinity–St Paul's a committee recommended that inclusive language be adopted in Sunday worship in order to strike a balance between male and female images of God. But the practical impact of this on much-loved hymns and biblical passages, and on existing hymnals and Bibles, proved daunting and divisive.[13]

At St Thomas, a defender of the old school tried to put a curate keen on liturgical experimentation in his place by bluntly telling him he was no Archbishop Cramner – a reference to the architect of major liturgical reforms in the nascent Anglican Church under Edward VI. Be that as it may, a folk mass was instituted there on Sunday afternoons in conjunction with "dialogue dinners," for the purpose of attracting young people, especially students from the adjacent University of Toronto. These featured guest speakers on topics of contemporary concern. Media celebrity Patrick Watson, for example, gave a talk on a hot issue of the day: "Sex without Babies and Babies without Sex." But overall, experimentation at St Thomas took place outside of Sundays in order not to upset regular churchgoers.[14] In a similar effort to entice youth, the *Christliche Arbeiterjugend*, a Catholic Action group at St Patrick's, sponsored forums dealing with topics such as "Flirt – Sex – Love" and "In Love – Engaged – Married."[15]

At the other end of the liturgical spectrum, currents of change also stirred within fundamentalism. The growth of such congregations after the 1960s required larger spaces. West End Pentecostal serves as a good example. After occupying a renovated fire hall for more than twenty years, it moved in 1962 to a disused cinema on St Clair Avenue, renaming itself West End Revival Centre. Within a dozen years, this location too proved inadequate, prompting a move to Crossroads Cathedral in the suburbs. Bigger spaces called for acoustical and lighting equipment, such as microphones, electric musical instruments, amplifiers, stage lights, and the like, in order to enhance communication and participation. Such devices were eventually introduced even in smaller facilities, giving evangelicalism an aura of modernity. Writing about his Youth for Christ rallies, Charles Templeton captured the new culture of worship:

> Most [meetings] were held in secular auditoriums, and the emphasis was on informality. The music was more like community singing; rather than hymns, rhythmic gospel tunes and Negro spirituals were sung. Musical groups performed and, at the end, a youthful preacher gave a brief "sermon" that was really a religious talk in contemporary language. The thrust was evangelical and the emphasis was pietistic but the atmosphere was derivative more of show business than church.[16]

This style had been perfected in the 1930s by Ontario-born Aimee Semple McPherson, by then a veritable Hollywood star, at her 10,000-seat Angelus Temple in Los Angeles. In Toronto it was reflected in evangelical church interiors. A carpeted stage with a plain lectern created a modern, sleek, and uncluttered look, replacing the carved wooden pulpits and choir stalls of the past. Preachers increasingly officiated in lay apparel, which the clergyman at the fundamentalist *Evangelische Gemeinde* regarded as a true badge of distinction.[17] Behind the lectern stood the choir, perhaps gowned, perhaps not, as well as a live band playing contemporary music with modern instruments. But while the style of worship had changed, its essence remained the same; it emphasized a highly emotional, expressive, and spontaneous spirituality through personal testimony. At First Ukrainian Pentecostal, for example, the use of a prayer book was rejected by members, who "wish[ed] to be released from ritual. Many people share[d] their thoughts and testimonies during worship. Some women read their poems."[18]

Show business and the 1960s youth movement were fused into a truly contemporary, North American religious phenomenon whose appeal extended beyond the continent to all those aspiring to emulate the American way of life. In 1993 a mission was opened in the heart of Little Portugal begun by the *Igreja Universal do Reino de Deus,* a Pentecostal Church founded fifteen years earlier in Brazil. The combination of intense revivalism and Catholic symbolism (holy water and oil, as well as holy objects) proved to be very appealing. When the congregation moved into an amphitheatrical structure outside our area on Dufferin Street, its reputation for producing miracles attracted Portuguese-speaking parishioners from Our Lady of the Angels, who frequented both places. The parish priest confessed: "They were being nourished somehow. They needed more than just the mass. So we were aware of that, so we provide adult catechism, prayer group [sic], for those that want or need it."[19]

The charismatic movement that burst onto the Toronto scene in the late 1960s was unquestionably influenced by Pentecostalism's focus on the religion of feeling. The movement stressed the startling and explosive power of the Holy Spirit in the material world. Through him, charismatics claimed to be able to speak in tongues and practise faith healing. Already in the spring of 1967, the press was reporting on the movement's popularity in the United States, even pointing to some Anglican and United Church congregations in Toronto that had come under its influence.[20]

One of these was St Matthias Anglican, which had promoted "the ministry of healing with holy unction" in an Easter advertisement the previous year.[21] Its rector, David Moore Smith, who had served the parish since 1948, had a conversion experience that led him to nurture this "special gift." In the early 1960s he began a unique ministry to young people in distress, inviting them to share the rectory with him and his wife. The experience ended tragically a few years later when one of his wards died of meningitis. A coroner's inquest found the priest and his assistant guilty of neglect. Following an ecclesiastical investigation ordered by Bishop George Snell of Toronto (1966–72), the clergymen in question were suspended.[22] The inquiry found that while this "bold experiment in Christian outreach" had been inspired by love and genuine concern for the needy, it had increasingly come to be dominated by glossolalia, shaking and jerking, a reliance on out-of-body voices for guidance, and an abuse of the Eucharist.[23] After undergoing a psychiatric examination, Moore Smith was allowed to resume his priestly functions in 1969.[24] Undoubtedly influenced by the bestselling horror novel *Rosemary's Baby*, published earlier that year and soon turned into an enormous box office success by film director Roman Polanski, the press transformed the story into a sensational one of demonic cults, possession, and exorcism. Instead, though, it was a more banal one of well-meaning but untrained social interveners confronted by complex mental health issues well beyond their insight and experience.

The Catholic charismatic movement began in 1968 in eastern Ontario at Catherine de Hueck's Madonna House in Combermere. It reached Toronto two years later, finding a home in the West End parish of Holy Rosary, where a Basilian priest, James Hanrahan, became one of its ardent promoters.[25] Later, Filipino parishioners especially would be drawn to its intense, expressive, and emotional religiosity.[26] Some of them had already been touched by the phenomenon in their home country through the charismatic Bukas Loob sa Diyos Covenant Community. Other immigrant groups too joined the movement. Such prayer groups did not displace the parish, but functioned alongside it in an uneasy relationship because parish clergy tended to be wary of the accent placed on lay leadership and emotional outpourings.[27] In any event, immigrant charismatic groups emerged at a few parishes, with Hispanics meeting at St James, Lithuanians at Resurrection, Portuguese at St Helen's and St Peter's, and Indonesians at St Pius X.

In these years the Toronto Buddhist church underwent considerable adaptation to its contemporary Western environment, as did the broader Jōdo-Shinshū movement of which it is a part. The largest branch of Buddhism in Japan, Jōdo-Shinshū established itself wherever Japanese immigrants happened to be, unlike Shintoism, which refused to leave the homeland. The priest who served the Toronto Buddhist church, Kenryu Tsuji, wanted his Nisei congregants to develop an intellectual understanding of Buddhism rather than one based on rote memory and ritual. He encouraged relations with Japanese Christian congregations, whose members were welcome to visit his church. Hawaiian-born Newton Ishiura, who succeeded Tsuji in 1958, continued this trend. As a result, religious life at Toronto Buddhist was very much influenced by Protestantism. Communal worship took place on Sundays and involved congregational singing accompanied by an organ playing Western music. It featured a sermon from the pulpit, while the faithful sat in pews and children went to Sunday school. Western-style weddings with their familiar processionals and recessionals to the music of Richard Wagner and Felix Mendelssohn were the norm. To downplay religious and ethnic distinction, equivalent Christian terms were commonly used in the lyrics of hymns. When one head minister objected to such terms to designate key Buddhist concepts, he met with stiff resistance from congregants, who expressed deep attachment to the hymns they sang.[28]

The ideal of ecumenism produced some concrete results in Toronto. At the initiative of the Anglican and United churches and with the collaboration of the Immigration Department, an Interfaith Immigration Committee was created in 1967 following the introduction of a new immigration act. Bringing together representatives of twenty-three religious groups including Hindus, Muslims, and Buddhists, and supported by almost seven hundred parishes and congregations in the Metro Toronto area, the committee put newcomers in contact with a representative of their denomination who could then help them with the settlement process.[29] Although this program involved collaboration among clergy of various religions, it did not in and of itself promote inter-denominational contact at the parish level. In this regard, outcomes were more modest. Breaking with a long-established tradition of discouraging socializing across denominational lines, St Patrick's Catholic and St George's Lutheran decided to hold a joint seniors' afternoon for German speakers in 1969. A few years later an annual picnic was organized for members of both parishes.[30] St Wolodymyr Ukrainian Orthodox and St Nicholas Ukrainian Catholic marked Ukrainian Independence Day with joint prayer service at Camp Kiev.[31] The two denominations also worked together to establish a residence for senior citizens. Runnymede Baptist and Runnymede United collaborated on programs to raise awareness of the dangers of anti-Semitism and to promote Christian–Jewish dialogue.

Gender and Sexuality

The issue of women in the liturgy and in church life generally proved to be a difficult one. Doris Way's story illustrates this point well, She became a minister by chance, not as a life choice. When her husband Charles died in 1957, she agreed temporarily to take over his charge as minister of a tightly knit working-class church, Crawford Street Congregational. Nothing had prepared her for this role. As president of the Women's Auxiliary, she had led such typical fundraising activities as bazaars and the thirty-five-cent hot roast beef lunch put on for the staff of the local schools and the nearby Brighton Laundry on Bloor Street. She had also organized euchre nights and rummage sales as well as soap and Christmas card sales for congregants and neighbours. But as a minister, there was virtually no one in mainstream Toronto Protestantism the forty-year-old widow could turn to as a role model or for professional advice: she was on her own. After unofficially occupying her position for eight years, she was finally ordained in 1965. She went on to serve her congregation until ill health prevented her from doing so forty-four years later.[32]

In the Catholic Church, women continued to be excluded from the priesthood as well as the diaconate, although married men could now accede to that office. At St Thomas Anglican, women were allowed to take part in choir processions only after the Archbishop of Canterbury, Michael Ramsey, pointedly deplored their absence on a visit to

7.2 Crawford Street Congregational
Now Chandrakirti Kadampa Buddhist Meditation Centre, this is where
Doris Way cut her teeth as the West End's first permanent female minister.
Erected in 1923, the building initially housed an Advent Christian congre-
gation. (Gabriele Scardellato)

the church. In the 1980s they could officiate at morning prayer and
Evensong, read the lesson during the liturgy, and distribute communion. Only at the very end of the decade was a woman invited to pre-
side at a special Saturday Eucharist, well after the Anglican Church of
Canada's decision to ordain women as deacons in 1969 and as priests
in 1976.[33] Although the United Church was the first major denomination to admit women to the ministry, it proved extremely difficult for
married candidates, especially those with children, to head a congregation.[34] Following the favourable decision on female ordination given
by the Presbyterian General Assembly, the Wychwood Avenue church
ordained two women as elders in 1970.[35] But elsewhere the issue of

female ministers provoked fierce resistance that took the denomination several years to resolve. Women also found that they had little scope for action at *Evangelische Gemeinde*. Traditionally it had been the deaconesses' role to create new faith communities. But as the congregation grew older and failed to expand, there was nothing for them to do. When in 1997 two board members died, a female was finally elected to the governing body.[36] But this happened by chance rather than choice. Women at Brock Avenue Gospel Hall, a Brethren congregation with a similar orientation but a different ethnic composition (including Caribbeans and South Asians), were required to cover their heads during worship and were banned from the ministry.[37]

Gender had a profoundly divisive effect at First Narayever and even led to a court case. In the 1970s the issue of renewal had become a serious one at the Brunswick Avenue synagogue. As a result of gentrification, young Jews were moving back to the downtown, but they were not particularly interested, as old-time members had been, in joining a synagogue for the burial privileges it conferred. They therefore worshipped in private homes, where women began to play prominent roles in reciting prayers, leading hymns, and reading from the Torah. Nevertheless, an American university student named Stuart Schoenfeld did join First Narayever and, as secretary of the congregation, succeeded in bringing in younger people by having the membership rules relaxed. It was not long, however, before these new recruits complained bitterly about the insignificant role assigned to women in worship. The issue came to a head when Schoenfeld was elected president, replacing Sholem Langner, grandson of the Strettiner *rebbe* and the synagogue's *chazzan* (cantor). Members voted in 1983 to reject mixed seating in the sanctuary but to allow a monthly egalitarian service in the basement, which because of its popularity soon became biweekly. Langner and other traditionalists, however, were not pleased. Contending that their property rights over an Orthodox synagogue were being violated, they took out an injunction against the basement group. The court dismissed their claim, citing the principle of the separation of Church and State, but pointing out as well that the plaintiffs were free to frequent neighbouring Orthodox synagogues.[38] Following a three-week lull in which the sanctuary stood empty, the basement group moved upstairs and has since occupied the *shul*, which proudly proclaims itself Orthodox and egalitarian.

Priestly celibacy, which had become a discipline or rule in the Western church in the eleventh century, came under scrutiny in the climate of renewal promoted by the Second Vatican Council. In 1967, however, Pope Paul VI cut the debate short with his encyclical *Sacerdotalis Caelibatus*, which unambiguously reconfirmed the rule. Disappointed priests in North America and Europe who had expected its relaxation left their clerical offices in droves. In Toronto, celibacy became an especially burning issue for the Ukrainian Catholic eparchy. A long-held tradition in the Ukrainian Catholic Church was that the lower clergy could marry. The eparch of Toronto, Isidore Borecky (1948–98), took advantage of this provision to send married or engaged candidates to Yugoslavia or Ukraine to be ordained. His action, however, went against a Vatican decree of 1894 explicitly banning married Ukrainian clergy from exercising their functions in the Americas. The eparch regarded the decree as illegitimate. As a result, more than half of the seventy-five or so priests under his jurisdiction had wives, the eparch simply ignoring Rome's injunctions against the practice, as well as its subsequent reprimands. According to one of his priests, "he knew that this was part of our tradition, and without married clergy our eparchy would have been in a tremendous shortage."[39]

The question of homosexuality and worship increasingly confronted a number of West End parishes and congregations. In 1973, homosexual Christians who felt excluded from or were forced out of places of worship formed Metropolitan Community church (MCC), occupying in the early 1980s the former Bathurst Street United before moving on to the East End. Almost from the beginning the congregation was led by Brent Hawkes, an outspoken activist for gay rights, who had been born into a fundamentalist Baptist family in New Brunswick. As minister, Hawkes publicly censured the Toronto police over the way they conducted raids of gay bathhouses in the early 1980s. He was also a fervent advocate of gay marriage. By 2000, his church was regularly attracting six hundred Sunday worshippers, while the Christmas Eve service, held at Roy Thompson Hall, drew 4,000.[40] Although MCC's form of worship has tended to be evangelical in spirit, over the years it has also been marked by greater formality, with vested celebrants, altar cloths, and candles. Some time after MCC's founding, a mainly lesbian group left it to form Christos MCC congregation, using a chapel at Trinity–St Paul's.

The question of whether homosexuals could be members of congregations and candidates for ordination caused a schism in the United Church when its General Council approved both propositions in

1988. Individual congregations, however, were left free to determine their own course of action. As a result, six West End ones became gay "affirming" in line with general church policy: Bloor Street, Alpha Korean, Trinity–St Paul, Bathurst Street, Parkdale, and Emmanuel–Howard Park. In the Presbyterian Church, only St Andrew's chose this path. The same issues came to the fore in the Anglican Church when in the early 1990s James Ferry, a priest in the diocese of Toronto, had his licence revoked for being in a homosexual relationship. An official statement issued in 1998 confirmed an earlier decision permitting the ordination of gays, but only if they remained celibate. Meanwhile, ten West End churches welcomed homosexuals as parishioners: St Stephen-in-the-Fields, Redeemer, Messiah, St Mary Magdalene's, St Thomas, St Matthias, St Anne's, St Martin-in-the-Fields, St John's Humberside,[41] and Trinity College. As for Catholics, no West End parish has openly welcomed homosexuals.

Expressions of Attachment to Tradition

Confronted by currents of change released in the 1960s, some faithful remained true to the old ways. This sentiment found different forms of expression and involved such questions as popular piety, respect for church canons, the language of the liturgy, the role of women, and ecumenism. As we have seen, some immigrants who had otherwise adapted to the new liturgy were reluctant to abandon hometown or regional religious festivities, especially processions honouring Jesus or one of his saints. The most famous of these was the one held annually since 1962 on Good Friday at St Francis. Replete with characters involved in Christ's passion, including Roman soldiers and officials, some of whom were on horseback, the procession made its way through the streets of Little Italy, drawing several tens of thousands of devotees and onlookers. St Anthony of Padua, a thirteenth-century Franciscan equally venerated in Portugal where he was born and in Italy where he became a prominent churchman, was another object of procession. The one conducted at St Francis drew the largest crowds, estimated again in the tens of thousands, while at St Anthony's the festivity became a multicultural event bringing together Italian, Portuguese, Tamil, and Filipino parishioners. The Corpus Christi procession at St Mary Magdalene's, once confined to church precincts, took to the streets in 1974, possibly inspired by practices at neighbouring Catholic churches. It is said that as a mark of respect, local residents of Italian and Portuguese origin plucked flowers from their gardens and strewed them along the route of the procession.[42]

Two such rituals, each associated since the early 1960s with St Mary's parish, have been especially dear to Azorean immigrants from the island of São Miguel: *Senhor Santo Cristo dos Milagres*, held on the fifth Sunday after Easter, and *Impérios do Divino Espírito Santo*, on the feast of Pentecost. The first venerates the image of an agonizing Jesus who when he stood before the Jewish crowd prompted Pontius Pilate, the governor of Judea, to remark: Behold the Man. To solemn music, the *Ecce homo* image is carried through the streets accompanied by children dressed as angels and adults wearing the capes of their confraternity. In the second, more festive celebration, a child bearing a silver crown and sceptre, symbols of the Holy Spirit's rule, is escorted in procession from the church along the streets of Little Portugal, which are bedecked with flags of the home country and the Azores. The procession ends at a private residence, where the crown and sceptre are exhibited and venerated. Food and drink are then blessed and distributed to devotees, who visit the makeshift shrine for prayer.[43] All processions like these are enhanced by banners, bands, attired members of devotional societies, and clergy in liturgical vestments.

The language of the liturgy also provoked traditionalist responses. After years of being disallowed, the Latin mass approved by the Council of Trent made its return to Toronto, but through the back door. In 1988, in order to limit the impact of Archbishop Lefebvre's excommunication, Rome permitted its celebration subject to the local bishop's approval. Because Emmett Cardinal Carter resisted, some faithful turned to his colleague, the Ukrainian Catholic eparch, who oddly enough allowed it to be said at the Dormition of the Theotokos, one of the churches under his jurisdiction.[44] The Latin mass according to the 1969 Roman rite (*Novus Ordo)* was permitted after Cardinal Carter assigned Holy Family parish to the Oratorians, a community of secular priests established in Renaissance Italy by Filippo Neri and introduced in nineteenth-century England by John Henry Cardinal Newman. In Toronto the congregation upheld its historic reputation for beautiful liturgy especially through fine music. In 1995 they took over the adjacent parish of St Vincent de Paul, where they would later reintroduce the Tridentine mass (*usus antiquior*).[45]

Generational renewal made the language of the liturgy an issue at the *Evangelische Gemeinde*, where the minister opposed the introduction

7.3 Saint Mary Portuguese Catholic
A Catholic church has stood at this location since 1852. It originally served
Irish parishioners. It was one of the sites of the famous riots of 1875, when
Orangemen attacked an open-air procession of bishops and faithful marking
the Jubilee Year decreed by Pope Pius IX. The current structure was built in
1885. In 1969 it became the first to serve Portuguese immigrants, most of them
from the Azores. It is famous for its *Impérios do Divino Espírito Santo* procession
on the feast of Pentecost. (Gabriele Scardellato)

of English because he had not really mastered the language. Yet the offspring of this small congregation had all married outside their religious community. It eventually became necessary to inaugurate an English-language service on Christmas Eve to allow families to worship together at least once a year. By contrast, the use of English was firmly rejected at St Wolodymyr Ukrainian Orthodox Cathedral after a commission created to study the question asserted: "English language [sic] in our liturgical services would create division among our faithful and would lead to decadence [i.e., decline] in the church." The commission also recommended that no change be made to the Julian liturgical calendar revised by Pope Gregory XIII (1572–85) to conform to a year's actual mean length.[46] At St Josaphat Ukrainian Catholic Cathedral, an English-language liturgy was briefly introduced; however, the parish later reverted exclusively to Ukrainian. Holy Trinity Russian Orthodox, for its part, retained Russian as the sole language of communication in the church, with Old Church Slavonic as the liturgical idiom. This practice was in stark contrast to that of Christ the Saviour Russian Orthodox Cathedral, which inaugurated an English-language ministry for parishioners, as well as for University of Toronto students at the Hart House chapel. At Holy Trinity, non–Russian speakers from ethnically mixed or other Slavic backgrounds used headsets provided by the church. At school, catechism and history were taught in a question-and-answer format in order to help children whose Russian was poor. Concerts, plays, literary readings of Russian classics, and folk dance performances reinforced the attachment to the ancestral culture, as did the annual children's pilgrimage to Holy Trinity Monastery in Jordanville, New York, spiritual centre of the Russian Orthodox Church Outside Russia.[47]

By contrast, English was adopted at another Orthodox parish, St Nektarios Greek Cathedral, although the Julian calendar was retained.

Here, as in Orthodox churches such as Holy Trinity Russian and Holy Michael the Archangel Serbian, the calendar became a lightning rod for opposition to ecumenism, which was viewed as a facile accommodation to error and as a manifestation of the spirit of relativism: Christians, it was alleged, mistakenly regarded all churches as equal and true churches. This was exactly the position taken in the past by Popes Pius IX and Pius X and in the present day by Archbishop Lefebvre when condemning the idea of relativism. These parishes were ill-disposed to the World Council of Churches, founded in Amsterdam in 1948, and to the holding of the Second

7.4 *Evangelische Gemeinde*
The former Gospel Hall built by Brethren in Christ in 1924 was taken over
fifty years later by fundamentalist postwar immigrants who tenaciously clung
to German as the language of the liturgy. The building is now used by Chinese
Pentecostals. (Gabriele Scardellato)

Vatican Council. They also rejected any form of collaboration with
other denominations.[48]

Sacred Interiors

With the trend towards infrequent attendance, the embellishment of
sacred structures largely became an immigrant phenomenon. At the
start of this period, however, a bequest from William Arthur Price, a
parishioner and the owner of the nearby Windsor Arms Hotel, turned
the east transept of Redeemer Anglican into a chapel. Designed by the
architectural firm of Mathers and Haldenby, the space was lined with

oak panelling at the centre of which stood an altar dressed with altar cloth and frontal. Ten of the panels on the back wall bore scriptural symbols chosen by the rector, Owen Pritchard, from the Great Litany of the Book of Alternate Service and executed by Sydney Watson, princi-pal of the Ontario College of Art.[49] Holy Rosary commissioned Yvonne Williams to produce a stained glass window for its Lady Chapel; it had been the only window in the church that remained undecorated. Sculp-tor William McElcheran, a former student of Guvtav Hahn's younger brother Emanuel at the Ontario College of Art and designer for the architectural firm of Bruce, Brown, and Brisely, was chosen to create three panels representing people in modern dress in a Palm Sunday procession.[50] Williams also completed six stained glass windows for the nave of St Michael and All Angels Anglican, a church that had been rebuilt in the mid-1950s. A recent and extensive renovation of First Unitarian allowed Sarah Hall, an award-winning stained glass artist, to enhance the captivating foyer with a large window titled "Radiance, Reflection, and Revelation."[51]

As we saw in chapter 5, postwar immigrants from central and eastern Europe were greatly invested in beautifying their Orthodox and Byzan-tine Catholic churches. The most prolific artists were woodcarver Vladi-mir Barac and painter Igor Suhačev, who had worked together on St Nicholas Ukrainian Catholic Church and who collaborated once more on St Josaphat. Barac produced the elaborate and beautifully ornate ico-nostasis; Suhačev helped decorate the interior. Barac also carved the stunning iconostasis of Holy Protection.[52] Suhačev was in great demand: he adorned the inside of the Dormition of the Theotokos; he remodelled the former synagogue that became the Nativity of the Mother of God Slovak Catholic and executed its murals; he designed the iconostasis, besides painting the icons and interior of another former synagogue, Holy Trinity Russian Orthodox, of which he was a faithful parishioner.[53] Mosaics graced the outside entrances to Holy Protection and Nativity of the Mother of God. Those on the doors of the Slovak church were appar-ently installed by Suhačev's wife, Silvia, although Vincenzo Vanin, a recently arrived immigrant from the province of Treviso in northeastern Italy – an area with a long and rich tradition of mosaic art – claimed to have designed and executed them. As for the mosaic at Holy Protection, it was signed by Vanin.[54]

A number of internationally renowned Ukrainian artists, most of them born in eastern Europe, produced icons and murals for the West End's Ukrainian churches. Sviatoslav Hordynsky, who studied with Fernand Léger in Paris and subsequently decorated Byzantine churches in North America and Australia, painted the icons on the iconostasis at Holy Protection, while those in the sanctuary were done by Ivan Belsky. who had previously worked on a number of churches in Venezuela. Recruited by Bishop Borecky in Venice, where the painter was executing a commission, Belsky did the murals in St Josaphat Cathedral in a modern Western style, nicely evoking Ukrainian immigrants' hybrid identity.[55] Financial constraints delayed the completion of artistic work at both the Dormition of the Theotokos and Holy Protection. The first was done by Pavlo Lopata, born in the Pryashiv region of Slovakia and a graduate of the Ontario College of Art. The second was realized in stages by the celebrated Ontario-born iconographer Heiko Schlieper together with Oleg Valeniuk. Finally, Ivan Denysenko, a well-known painter of icons and murals in churches all over the continent, finished the interior decoration of St Wolodymyr Cathedral. An opulent chandelier was purchased and hung from a central point of the ceiling.[56]

The renovations carried out at St Francis Church in the wake of the Second Vatican Council entailed removing "hundreds" of statues. Vienna-born Czech artist Alex von Svoboda, who came to Toronto in the 1950s, designed a large mosaic titled "The Canticle of Brother Sun," measuring sixty by thirty feet, and supervised its installation behind the new altar of white Carrara marble. The work refers to a hymn of praise composed in the vernacular by St Francis of Assisi reflecting his cosmology, in which animate and inanimate creatures are seen as brothers and sisters of mankind. One million small pieces of mosaic tile manufactured in Venice were needed for its completion. Meanwhile the plaster statuary was replaced by a half dozen wood carvings, including sculptures of saints and a scene of the Last Supper incorporated into the main altar, produced by an artists' studio in Bolzano, Italy. Von Svoboda's first commission dated from 1955, when he was asked to decorate the newly built St Casimir's Polish Catholic Church.[57] In the 1960s, another Trevigiano immigrant, Luigi Nasato, worked with Vincenzo Vanin on the mosaic at St Alphonsus Catholic.[58]

Asian immigrant groups too were enthusiastic about embellishing their places of worship. The Fu Sien Tong Temple received its first statues of Buddha from Macau. The building complex's outer courtyard features incense burners, low-relief sculptures, and a pair of traditional Chinese stone guardian lions. A few blocks away, the main room at Ching Kwok Temple has a richly decorated shrine framed by a brightly coloured overhang and pillars, replicating those of the building's facade. Above the altar are three-metre high, enthroned gilded statues made of Burmese mahogany that recall the three representations of Buddha most important to the Chinese: Sakhyamuni, the historical figure, is flanked on his right by Amida, the sovereign of the pure land to which all faithful aspire, and on his left by Yao Shi Fwo, the master healer. In front of these statues are three others standing more than one metre high on the altar itself. The first one, made of alabaster, depicts Buddha achieving enlightenment under the *bodhi* tree; the two others are of wood and portray the *bodhisattvas* (enlightenment beings), who represent wisdom and compassion. Before them are eight gorgeously executed smaller statues that always appear in the same sequence in Chinese temples. Additional statuary can be found in different parts of the building.[59] The main shrine room at Tengye Ling Temple has a two-metre gilded statue of Buddha and smaller ones of lesser figures, which, on the whole, however, are not as finely executed as those at Ching Kwok. In 1998, Riwoche Pemavarja Tibetan commissioned six large wooden statues from master sculptor Tshevang Dorji, a native of Bhutan who apprenticed and worked in South Asia as well as Europe. These sculptures represent Buddha in both male and female guises, as well as historical figures linked to the founding and development of the religion in Tibet. The statues have gilded bodies; their clothes and accoutrements are brightly coloured.[60] Thanks to the dedication and vision of postwar immigrants, Toronto boasts a rich treasury of religious art mostly unknown to the public at large.

Faltering Fellowship?

Parish and congregational life was greatly affected by declining attendance, which led to successive church closings. In 1967, for example, Carman United on Pauline Avenue shut its doors and the congregation was merged with Grace on College Street, which in turn gave up the ghost in 1981, joining Wesley (renamed Westennial) on Ossington Avenue. In 1988, Westmoreland Avenue United closed down; its congregants were directed to Westennial, which itself ceased operations in 1997. Having to move from church to church and adapt each time to a new environment, if not a different congregational culture, the faithful remnant must have felt dispirited: in one generation, four United churches had stopped functioning in an area of roughly one square kilometre, leaving a single congregation, Centennial

Japanese, which suffered the same fate less than a decade later. The same scenario played itself out in Parkdale, where four out of five United churches were closed between 1962 and 1974. Four Anglican parishes ceased to exist north of Bloor Street between Bathurst and Dundas West. Only St Michael and All Angels survived. In Parkdale, two out of three churches were shut down, leaving St Mark and the Epiphany to serve the local faithful. The Presbyterians lost six congregations north of Bloor between Bathurst and High Park. Wychwood–Davenport was the only church to remain open in this wide expanse of the city.

In this changing context, new forms of religiously motivated social intervention were developed, less encompassing perhaps than the ideal of a full-orbed religion, but all the same both targeted and timely. In April 1974, for example, Premier William Davis of Ontario (1971–85) inaugurated the New Horizons Tower for the elderly on the northwest corner of Bloor and Dufferin streets. This project, which filled an urgent social need, was realized after Dovercourt Road Baptist was sold for $167,000. The congregation then formed a not-for-profit corporation that secured a $2 million loan from the Central Mortgage and Housing Corporation to build the new edifice as well as an adjacent single-storey structure serving as a church. The congregants then conducted an active ministry among the residents of the tower.[61] Three other congregations, those of Parkdale, St Columba, and College Street United, also used the proceeds from the sale of their churches to build high-rise apartments to house the elderly, among others. At the time, some prominent United Churchmen regarded churches as veritable albatrosses around their institution's neck, whose exorbitant costs prevented it from effectively carrying out its mission of social utility. They were only too happy to be rid of such expensive relics.

The economic recessions of 1974–5, 1981–3, and 1989–91 resulted in unemployment, stress, and reliance on public assistance for the economically vulnerable. The situation was aggravated in 1994 when Liberal finance minister Paul Martin drastically cut the government's funding of social services as part of a concerted effort to reduce public spending and the national debt, a move imitated by provincial administrations throughout the country. Ontario's Conservative premier, Mike Harris (1995–2002), for one, hailed this development, claiming that it would reduce the public's reliance on government and restore the role that institutions such as the churches had played before the advent of the welfare state. It was in this climate of social crisis and need that Susan Moran, a sister of Our Lady's Missionaries, and John Murphy, a

7.5a Dovercourt Baptist / Santa Cruz Portuguese Catholic
This church, built in 1887 at Argyle Avenue and Dovercourt, was sold
in 1973 to Portuguese Catholics, who formed the parish of Santa Cruz.

7.5b Dovercourt Baptist Church
Affiliated with the fundamentalist Fellowship Baptists, the original
owners purchased land at Bloor Street and Dufferin, erecting a seniors'
tower called New Horizon as well as a small chapel for worship
and evangelization. (7.5a and b, Gabriele Scardellato)

7.6 College Street United

The bell tower is all that remains of this church, which was erected in 1885. This Presbyterian/United Church congregation had a long and close association with St Christopher's Settlement House, which worked among the area's disadvantaged population. The church was demolished in 1990 to make way for a condominium development, which houses a chapel for congregants. (Gabriele Scardellato)

Basilian priest, began the Out of the Cold program in 1987. Their initiative was prompted by the death of a homeless person named George who had succumbed one winter night to the bitter cold in the playground of St Michael's College School. From there it developed into a multi-faith effort involving Catholics, Protestants, Jews, and Muslims. Working out of places of worship, the program offered the destitute, who were treated as "welcomed guests, not difficult clients," a warm meal and shelter for the night. In 2005 there were twenty-five such sites in Greater Toronto providing an average of 125 beds on different nights once a week. Each place of worship raised its own funds and administered its own program. A small full-time staff, responsible for bedding, laundry, cleaning, security, and transporting the homeless to each site, was paid from city coffers. They were backed by an army of 3,000 volunteers. Bloor Street United, for example, dispensed two hundred meals and provided emergency shelter to sixty-five people once a week.[62]

Around the time of Out of the Cold's founding, Evangel Hall, the Presbyterian mission on Queen Street, identified Toronto's lack of affordable housing as a major social problem and one of its top priorities. In 1988 a subsidy from the Ontario Ministry of Housing allowed it to construct a forty-six-unit structure earmarked for the downtown's homeless at Portland Place just south of Queen Street. In 1991 the first seventy residents were welcomed. Long under the care of Knox Church and more recently the East Toronto Presbytery, Evangel Hall continued its long-established relief work among the needy, while extending its services to the mentally challenged and single mothers as well as refugees from Latin America and the Middle East. The mission created a summer garden program, offering plots of land in the suburbs to the socially disadvantaged "to provide some relief from the city core and develop a sense of accomplishment." This initiative recalled similar ones pursued by religious groups in late-nineteenth-century France and Germany. The Pentecostal Assemblies of Canada, for their part, opened the International Christian Centre in 1987 in a small mall on lower Spadina. Although intended for Chinese, the mission also targeted the destitute of neighbouring Alexandra Park. A café called Harvest Time and a fifty-bed shelter for the homeless operated seven days a week, staffed by members of Pentecostal congregations from across the city. The building was also the base for street evangelism in the area.[63]

A group attached to Western (Parkdale) Baptist Church before its closing in 1984 spearheaded a similar effort. By the 1980s the deterioration

of the social fabric was especially evident in Parkdale, where the proliferation of rooming houses attracted a disproportionately large number of socially marginalized people.[64] The Parkdale Neighbourhood
Church emerged in this context in a nearby community centre. A house
was purchased to provide shelter for disadvantaged church members
and as a base of operations. A pest-control business called "Good Rid-
dance" was started to provide work for a group described as "especially
poor ... yet incredibly devout." Later, a drop-in centre on Queen Street
offered short-term material and longer-term spiritual assistance to such
people as the unemployed, the mentally ill released from psychiatric
hospitals in the wake of deinstitutionalization, drug addicts, and others in trouble with the law.[65] A short time later, the Capuchin Fathers
opened a not-for-profit restaurant called St Francis Table in a Queen
Street storefront. With the help of donors and volunteers from different
parishes, two meals a day were offered on weekdays for a modest fee to
those in need.[66] A similar operation, styled psalm and soup, was operated by the United Church's Shalom House (now known as King–Dunn
community ministry) in a Victorian residence on King Street West; volunteers from nearby Holy Family Church shared the facility under the
name St Philip's Pantry. Shalom House distributed food, promoted
nutrition awareness, and sponsored immigrant outreach programs on
children's leisure.

Associational Life among Older Immigrant Groups

In many established parishes and congregations the ideal of a full-orbed
religion retreated as regular churchgoing steadily declined. This was
less the case, however, with immigrant parishes, at least in the early
years. The model remained strong, allowing that generational make-up
and the timing of arrival often determined the needs and priorities of
specific congregations.

The Chinese provide an interesting example of how the timing of
migration shaped the evolution of communal life. The oldest Chinese congregation and also the largest of its kind in Canada, First
Chinese Presbyterian, typified the full-orbed model: the church
included three floors of classrooms and a gymnasium so that "young
people become comfortable with a church in their lives."[67] At the
time, the congregation boasted a higher than average number of sec-
ond- and third-generation English speakers and professionals. So it
is not surprising that the same inter-generational tensions broke out
as at *Chevra Tehillim* in the 1930s (see chapter 5). An older group

of elders, characterized by an internal church report as ignorant of their responsibilities and as not respected by the congregation, jealously guarded its authority and dominance, leaving the English-speaking element feeling alienated. The discord was partly resolved in 1963 when a separate English-speaking congregation was instituted within the church.[68] Similar grievances surfaced twenty-five years later at Toronto Chinese Baptist. There, younger congregants complained of not being understood, of being the targets of church initiatives better suited to an older age cohort, and of having little scope for action. This conflict also followed linguistic lines, dividing the English from the Cantonese and Mandarin speakers.[69] At Chinese Gospel, a congregation founded roughly at the same time as Toronto Chinese Baptist, services were initially held in Cantonese with English translation for the Canadian-born. Later, English-language services were inaugurated for the second-generation members, as well as for those who did not understand Cantonese.[70]

Notwithstanding its internal divisions, First Chinese Presbyterian was the first Chinese church to develop a sophisticated structure. In 1964 its minister, Ronald Con, spearheaded the creation of the Mon Sheong Foundation. The organization's first major project was to raise funds to build a fifty-bed home for the elderly whose limited knowledge of English made it difficult to place them in existing facilities. The church's classrooms accommodated a pre-school program aimed at exposing Canadian-born Chinese children to their ancestral language and culture. These children were supervised by volunteers, both older and newer immigrants from different walks of life such as housewives, cooks, restaurant workers, and grandparents, some of whom had never studied English or even been in school before. A kindergarten was created that would grow into a large private elementary and secondary school.[71] While First Chinese Presbyterian confronted issues concerning the long-term care of the elderly, Our Lady of Mount Carmel was struggling to integrate newcomers in the wake of the immigration reforms of the late 1960s. The parish opened two hostels to provide food and shelter for new arrivals. It organized English-language classes funded in part by public school boards, as at First Chinese Presbyterian. It also dispensed information on housing, jobs, and schooling. After-school programs were organized for the children of working parents. The Franciscan Sisters opened a residence for high school girls from Hong Kong without family in Toronto. The Chinese Catholic Centre adjacent to the church, which housed a number of parish organizations, was renovated in 1985 to include a library, lecture rooms, and offices.[72]

Most West End churches frequented or founded by postwar immigrants peaked in the late 1960s and early 1970s. Weddings at St Patrick fell from 250 to 29 between 1958 and 1978. In the late 1970s, the parish sold its Richmond Hill farm. Now a seniors' club was instituted with a healthy membership of over two hundred. Clearly, St Patrick's population was aging and was not being replenished.[73] Be that as it may, the church persisted as a German-language downtown parish, unlike the neighbouring Hungarian ones. St Elizabeth and First Hungarian Presbyterian moved to the suburbs within a decade of each other. The visit in 1973 of József Cardinal Mindszenty (1945–75) to mark Hungary's millennium of Christianity undoubtedly was a high point in the life of the Catholic parish. The "Prince Primate" was returning to Canada for the first time since 1947, when he had attended the Marian Congress in Ottawa. He had spent many of his years between these two visits in detention because of his uncompromising opposition to the Communist regime in Budapest. Granted asylum by the US Embassy, where he resided for fifteen years, he had become a Cold War icon. Two years after this momentous visit, parishioners at St Elizabeth voted to remain downtown and renovate their church. But less than a decade later, the property was sold and the church demolished.

The more recently established Resurrection Lithuanian Catholic parish experienced a similar trajectory. Characterized by historian Milda Danys as "Lithuania-in-exile" for its range of activities, the church had a highly educated, articulate, and politicized cohort of DPs. They saw their church largely as a patriotic endeavour encompassing all elements of the community: immigrants, their children, and non-churchgoers alike. Besides the already mentioned credit union, sports club, and summer camp (chapter 5), the parish housed a library and offices for associations such as the Boy Scouts, university students, pensioners, and stamp collectors. A block away, the Sisters of the Immaculate Conception of the Blessed Virgin Mary, a community founded in Lithuania in 1918, ran a day care that reinforced Lithuanian language and culture among Canadian-born children and that gave mothers the opportunity to find paid employment outside the home. The parish also sponsored hundreds of exhibitions by Lithuanian artists, simultaneously amassing the largest collection of such art in Canada. While suburbanization had reduced the number of parishioners somewhat by the late 1970s, it was only at the end of the century that the parish moved to Etobicoke and the church was demolished.[74]

Highly politicized DPs were a significant presence at St Josaphat Ukrainian Catholic Cathedral. Believing themselves to be in temporary exile in Canada, many of them wanted their children to have a thorough education in Ukrainian in preparation for their eventual return to a free homeland. They refused to send their children to existing separate schools, considering them to be vehicles of Latinization – that is, cultural dispossession. So in 1961 the parish opened a nearby private Ukrainian-language day school with an initial enrolment of 150 children under the care of the Sisters Servants of Mary Immaculate. Two years later, the Toronto Separate School Board took it over, and within a few years, enrolment had doubled. Just as the church was for adults, the school was intended to be a centre of Ukrainian cultural and religious life. The parish created a chapter of *Plast*, the Ukrainian Boy Scout organization founded in Galicia in 1911, as well as a children's summer camp. Meanwhile, the credit union continued to prosper. In the late 1960s and early 1970s the parish welcomed Josyf Cardinal Slipyj, major archeparch of Lviv (1944–84), whom the Soviet authorities had detained in various jails and a Siberian gulag for eighteen years before finally allowing him to take up residence in Rome. His successor, Ivan Cardinal Lubachivsky (1984–2000), a DP who had spent more than forty years in the United States, was also a frequent guest of the cathedral.[75] The visits of these prelates-in-exile heightened parishioners' yearning for Ukrainian independence (as well as their anti-Soviet sentiments) in the 1970s era of détente and the subsequent one of Cold War confrontation inaugurated by US president Ronald Reagan (1981–1989).

Developments at St Wolodymyr Ukrainian Othodox paralleled those at St Josaphat. The parish experienced its most intense period of activity up to the mid-1970s, when the associations founded in the previous period reached their peak. Leadership courses were offered to counsellors aged fifteen and sixteen at Camp Kiev. The Ukrainian Democratic Youth Organization put together a folk dance troupe, a choir, and a band playing the bandura, a traditional Ukrainian stringed instrument similar to the lute. For a decade the parish ran a music school distinct from the elementary and secondary level classes offered to children of parishioners. These schools, together with the credit union, which had grown steadily since its inception, and a library of some 4,000 books, were all housed in the adjacent large brick building. In the 1970s, St Wolodymyr produced a radio program dedicated to Ukrainian Orthodoxy that aired weekly on CHIN radio, a multilingual broadcaster in Toronto. Despite this intense associational life, many Ukrainian families, whether Catholic or Orthodox, moved to Etobicoke, Mississauga, and Oakville in this period. Perhaps because both churches were the sites of metropolitan sees, they remained in their downtown locations.

The Ukrainian immigrants who came to Canada after the collapse of Communism disappointed St Wolodymyr's parishioners. The newcomers took advantage of the information and material assistance offered to them on arrival, but many ceased going to church once they became self-sufficient. Even the minority who continued to attend services, to send their children to Ukrainian school, and to involve themselves in associational life appeared to have a different mentality. Dismissed by the earlier DP wave as "economic migrants," they were resented for the aid they took so readily, in contrast to earlier immigrants, who claimed to have received none. Old-timers viewed the newcomers as lacking nationalist fervour, as shunning questions of language, politics, and culture, and as favouring the rapid assimilation of their children. The latter, for their part, regarded their accusers as living in the past, out of touch with the modern world. These divisions were deep enough that the parish tried to foster better understanding among the two groups, but to no avail. As the new millennium dawned, weekly attendance at Sunday worship remained at respectable levels of between three to five hundred parishioners. But parish life was largely in the hands of eighty-year-olds, while the younger generation was deprived of the administrative experience that might have been transmitted by the intermediate age group, whose interests evidently lay elsewhere.[76]

The trajectory of Holy Trinity Russian Orthodox was quite different. Founded by DPs, the parish benefited greatly from the influx of newcomers arriving after the fall of the Berlin Wall. One-quarter of these people came by way of Israel, where they had lived for a time. A Russian Orthodox Immigrant Aid Society with offices in the church was established. The Saturday school provided tangible evidence of the revitalization brought about by the newcomers' presence. Housed in a three-storey building complete with auditorium and classrooms, it actually increased enrolments from 120 students in 1966 to 180 by the end of the century. After the Sunday liturgy, a meal was prepared by the Sisterhood for about one hundred worshippers, reinforcing bonds of parish solidarity and financially assisting the women's organization. With parishioners coming from all over Greater Toronto, the church was able to resist the challenges of suburbanization. It attributed its success to its unadulterated dedication to Russian culture and Orthodoxy.[77]

In contrast to central and eastern European immigrants, southern European ones did not see themselves as a community-in-exile whose duty it was to keep alive a culture oppressed at home by Soviet military might. Their associational life was therefore not as intense or wide-ranging. This phenomenon was also related to the immigrant group's size. In 1975, thirty-three Catholic parishes in Metropolitan Toronto served Italians.[78] While not as numerous, Portuguese and Greeks also had a dense parish network. No single church came to represent the entire group or the postwar cohort, as did Resurrection for Lithuanians or Holy Trinity for Russians. The demographic weight of southern European immigrants meant that assistance in settlement and adaptation could be had from community agencies, such as the Italian Immigrant Aid Society, the International Institute of Metropolitan Toronto, or St Christopher House. These same organizations offered classes to adults trying to learn English, while school boards dispensed heritage language instruction to children of immigrants. As well, numerous regional or hometown societies, often associated with particular male-dominated café-bars, offered myriad opportunities for socializing, from card-playing to dances.

The overwhelmingly peasant origins of southern European immigrants also helps explain the disparity in parish life compared to that of eastern Europeans. The latter group had a higher proportion of better educated, more highly skilled, and more articulate professionals. Carmela Patrias contends that the peasant origins of interwar Hungarians made it more difficult for them to develop an associational life on their own. Being illiterate and uneducated, they simply lacked organizational skills and as a result had to rely on compatriots from other class backgrounds.[79] It is important to acknowledge, however, that while far from being autonomous historical actors, peasants were not mere putty in the hands of their social betters. Back home they had a degree of latitude in organizing their work in the fields. Europe even offers instances of organized peasant revolts. As Robert Harney has so well illustrated, in immigrating they navigated the complexities of state bureaucracies as well as cross-border and transatlantic travel.[80] In the religious sphere, they came together to coordinate festivals in honour of their hometown saints. An earlier chapter showed how the parishioners of St Stanislaus Polish Catholic stood up to their patrician pastor, who had dismissed them all as ignorant rustics. Clearly, then, peasants possessed their own class-based strategies and organizational skills, which were merely different from the ones of other social classes and cultures. In this regard, they would have been lost in formal meetings run in Toronto according to parliamentary procedures with motions moved, seconded, and carried by majority vote.

Southern European parishes typically resembled English-speaking ones with their devotional, charitable, and fundraising organizations. They provided catechism classes to children preparing to receive First

Communion or attending public schools, as well as marriage preparation courses for young couples. Scouts, Girl Guides, and seniors' clubs rounded out the picture. What distinguished these parishes was that they celebrated secular communal festivities marking the passage of the seasons. At St Sebastian, for instance, the winter carnival and autumn celebrations, such as the *matança do porco* (the killing of the pig) and the *festa da vindima* (the grape harvest), evoked happy memories of years past. But it is unlikely that Canadian-born children found much meaning in such observances. Young people who did get involved in parish-based initiatives seemed to prefer socially useful ones over purely leisure pastimes such as dances. In any event, at St Helen and St Sebastian, associational life was generally winding down by the end of the millennium as parishioners of the immigrant cohort were not replaced; whereas nearby, Our Lady of the Angels was apparently getting a new lease on life as young couples returned from the suburbs. The active youth of this parish were grouped into two age categories, with the younger ones focusing on fundraising for institutions such as the Hospital for Sick Children and the older ones on development work in countries such as Haiti and the Dominican Republic.[81]

St John Evangelical Lutheran, which had done so much to welcome and help integrate postwar DPs from the Baltic region, opened its doors to new refugee groups. By 1987, when Richard Drews took over as pastor, the church's prospects looked grim indeed: the Sunday school had closed a few years earlier, and the number of regular worshippers had perilously declined. It was at this point that Ernie Hahn, the missionary son of the long-serving pastor, instituted workshops and wrote tracts encouraging members of Christian congregations to recognize and interact with their Muslim and Hindu neighbours. As a result, the church once again became involved in refugee work. Two hundred asylum seekers were sponsored over a dozen or so years from such countries as Sri Lanka, Iran, Eritrea, and the Republic of Congo. Other groups, notably from Guyana, Ghana, and South Africa, were also welcomed. Small gatherings and picnics were organized so that parishioners could make contact with these new arrivals and help them integrate.

By 1990, worship at the church was being held in Tamil, Tigrinya, and Persian as well as English. The clergymen working in these idioms also took part in the English Sunday service. The church boasted five choirs singing common hymns in their native tongues. A special multicultural service was held five times a year where the Lord's prayer, the Apostles' Creed, and liturgical responses were recited in various languages. The pastor wanted to make this a regular feature of worship, which would have meant incorporating different musical traditions, but he encountered resistance from some older parishioners. In any event, the church was decorated with multilingual banners and images of Christ in different cultural settings. The Sunday school was revived, and the vacation Bible school became very much a multicultural affair. Meanwhile the church's weekly food bank served three hundred people divided fairly evenly between Portuguese and Spanish speakers. A religious service was held on the day the food bank operated. Congregants, however, showed little interest in bringing these people into their church. Newcomers came to comprise a majority at St John but were understandably reluctant to assume leadership positions, so the pastor instituted training classes for their benefit.[82]

Associational Life among More Recent Arrivals

Among the post-1967 immigrants, Koreans proved to be particularly fractious. The first congregation to be founded, Toronto Korean United, was in its early years the focus of community life. Besides organizing Korean language classes and an annual lecture series, the church was the spawning ground of Korean-language media, including the weekly *New Korea Times*; *Pioneer*, a monthly cultural and literary journal; *Voice of Hope*, a weekly radio broadcast of news, culture, and religion; and *Korean Celebration*, a regular television program. For more than thirty years, it hosted the Seoul pavilion during the Caravan Festival, an annual celebration of cultural diversity through food, music, and entertainment. In time, however, Toronto Korean United too experienced the problem of generational succession. Young people fell away from the church, using it only for rites of passage or preferring to attend a "Canadian" church. Some of them opted for the fervid and expressive atmosphere of evangelical-style worship. The introduction of an English-language service did little to change the situation. It attracted mostly recent immigrants, a number of whom had entered Canada under the investor category, and international students, both groups wanting to improve their English.[83]

For political as well as social reasons, Korean Presbyterian congregations had a much lower profile. Members tended to be shopkeepers, which imposed long hours of weekly labour on the entire family and severely constrained participation in church-sponsored programs. Although sporting activities were not a regular feature in these churches, an annual competition involving members of various Korean churches was arranged in badminton, bowling, volleyball, and table tennis. By contrast, some fundamentalist congregations, composed of more recent immigrants, had a younger profile and a more active social environment. Almost half the congregants at Toronto Korean Bethel Evangelical and two-thirds of those at Full Gospel Young Sung had been in Canada less than ten years. With three times more members, the first church offered a wide range of sports including gymnastics, soccer, and basketball.[84] Meanwhile, Pentecostal, Baptist, and the more evangelical Presbyterian congregations were either directly or indirectly involved in missionary work among First Nations peoples in the North or in countries in the developing world.

Non-Christian establishments also followed more closely the pattern set by English-speaking congregations, focusing on worship-related activities as well as charitable work and fundraising. At the core of Buddhist worship is meditation and chanting, in some cases performed daily, often under the guidance of monks and nuns. Formal services take place twice a month coinciding with the full and new moons, although most working congregants visit the temple on weekends when in addition to the service, a lecture (or Sangha talk) is delivered. The larger Chinese congregations, comprising 1,000 members, only manage to draw one hundred or so faithful to their weekend services, whereas temples serving mostly Westerners attract half that number or even less. In both cases, many times more congregants attend special festivities including *Wesak* (Buddha's birthday), *Ullambala* (remembrance of deceased ancestors), and the Lunar New Year.[85]

The Hong Fa Temple also sponsors retreats in which participants spend a long weekend within the temple itself. Each year a special children's retreat or summer camp is held on the Canada Day holiday. The library is stocked with books and numerous tapes relating to spiritual themes. In warm weather, Hong Fa and Ching Kwok organize fruit-picking and other excursions outside Toronto for core members. For the wider community, Fu Sien Temple runs a free weekly acupuncture clinic and a daily vegetarian food bank. Besides providing a weekly meal for the homeless, Fung Loy Kok Institute of Taoism offers English-language classes as well as assistance in filling out income tax and other government forms to Chinatown residents. Hong Fa financially supports a senior citizens' group through a bazaar held once a year. By contrast, the Chua Amida Temple, established by Vietnamese refugees in 1985, offers members no activities outside of worship and faces a severe crisis in generational succession. A youth club ceased operations when its members got older. Young congregants come to the site infrequently, do not understand its ceremonies and practices, and generally feel bored and unengaged.[86]

In Hindu, Daoist, and some Buddhist temples, as well as at the Sri Guru Singh Sabha *gurdwara*, worship is often accompanied by a vegetarian meal, reinforcing bonds of fellowship among congregants. Ming Sing Tao Tak, for example, had to be fitted with an industrial-standard kitchen for this purpose. Weekly attendance at Hindu temples ranges from a high of 150 at Prarthana Samaj, where services are held daily, to between 50 and 100 at Gayatri Mandir and Gandhi Bhawan, where the faithful gather only once a week. Special festivities such as *Diwali* (festival of lights), *Holî* (spring festival of colours), and *Navrati* (autumn festival of nine nights) bring in 200 to 400 worshippers. By contrast, at Sri Guru Singh Saba *gurdwara*, numbers apparently range between 700 and 1,000 weekly.[87] Besides preparing meals, the ISKCON (Hare Krishna) Temple holds classes on vegetarian cuisine and yoga. Prarthna Samaj and the Gayatri Mandir Hindu temples offer instruction in Hindi as well as sports activities for the children of congregants. The latter also imparts music classes, while the former dispenses yoga lessons to its seniors.[88]

Over the past half-century, the retreat of religion in Canada has had a powerful impact on parish and congregational life. The closing of numerous sacred spaces on the one hand and infrequent attendance at worship on the other have redefined the notion of fellowship. Some observers have wryly suggested that the shopping centre has replaced the church as a focal point of community life, a view that highlights the formidable impact of consumer capitalism on people's lives. In any event, few are the places of worship in West End Toronto that can claim today to have a similar level and range of activities as half a century ago. Of course, journalists and religious commentators can point to immigrant and evangelical congregations in the suburbs that are bursting at the seams. But statistics speak louder than such anecdotal evidence. Almost half of Canadians – and the percentage is higher among immigrants living in Toronto – can be termed lackadaisical churchgoers, attending services between once a month and once a year.[89] Although this temporal range is very broad and therefore imprecise (what percentage, for instance, does the once-a-month category represent?), it is evident that a vigorous community life cannot be sustained on such a basis. Historically, in the era of full-orbed religion, it was the larger congregations, most of them attached to mainstream denominations, that offered members the widest assortment of activities according to age, sex, social status, and ethnicity. Today these institutions are but a shadow of their former selves. At the same time, the West End has always had a plethora of smaller places of worship whose size necessarily restricts the scope of their activities. This continues to be the case today. Clearly there are limits to what a congregation of some fifty regular churchgoers can offer its members.

This chapter has provided vivid examples of robust community life under religious auspices. This was especially the case of parishes and congregations frequented by refugees from Iron Curtain countries, for whom attachment to religion became a badge both of national honour and of hostility to communism. A few short years after their arrival, these newcomers invested heavily in embellishing and equipping their churches, which became veritable community centres. These groups, however, later came to grips with two phenomena: generational succession and the fall of the Berlin Wall. The latter event did much to loosen the links that had been forged between religion, national identity, and opposition to communism. The Ukrainian immigrants who arrived after 1989 were deeply reluctant to take up the ideological struggles of the past or to commit themselves to perpetuating the ancestral culture in Canada, bitterly disappointing the earlier refugee wave. As a result, these parishes and congregations faced an uncertain future since neither the rising younger generation nor the new immigrant wave guaranteed continuity. A similar pattern can be observed at the other end of the ideological spectrum. Spurred by deep antagonism to the dictatorship in their country of origin, Toronto Korean United developed an intense community life, which, however, proved hard to sustain in times of generational succession and recurrent factionalism.

On the whole, newcomers arriving from South, East, and Southeast Asia have not significantly altered existing trends in religious fellowship. Patterns of attendance at worship are on the whole the same as in Christian congregations, if we take into account such considerations as time of arrival, generational position, and sustained immigration levels. Associational life outside of worship is certainly comparable to the Toronto norm. Rather than witnessing something startlingly new, we are in fact observing a more or less slow process of adaptation to Canadian religious standards.

Overall, parishes and congregations in the West End over the past half-century have displayed a wide array of responses to the challenges of consumer culture and society. Whether from the point of view of liturgy, religiosity, morality, theology, gender, or social and political involvement, these responses have ranged from the traditional to the modern, from the formal to the casual, from the accepting to the rejecting, from the engaged to the detached, from the proactive to the passive. Each position and its many variations, as well as the permutations and combinations among them, can be observed. Catholics, for example, may attend a Latin mass or one in the contemporary rite in a variety of languages, including English. The accompanying music includes the Gregorian, classical, and modern repertoire, with most parishes presenting a combination of each. A number of Eastern Rite churches provide liturgies in English, in addition to those in the vernacular or traditional tongues. Catholics and Anglicans can choose a barebones form of Sunday worship lasting half an hour or a more elaborate one over an hour long. Pentecostals, for their part, offer a highly expressive and emotional service with music embracing Latin rhythms, jazz, blues, reggae, and rock styles combined with Christian lyrics. Latin American and Caribbean Pentecostals, whose practices are more syncretic, incorporate holy water, holy oil, and other sacred objects in their services. Generally, synagogues in the West End are traditional in their form of worship, but Shir Lebeynu (Song of Our Hearts), a liberal congregation gathering monthly at the Jewish Community Centre, has a service that combines ancient and modern music as well as uncommon practices such as meditation.

West End places of worship have also assumed various stances on the issue of gender and sexual orientation. In Catholic parishes the role of women in the mass has been somewhat enhanced since the Second Vatican Council, but the key offices of priest and deacon are still denied them. This is also the case in Eastern Orthodox parishes. Other religious traditions, such as Judaism, Islam, Hinduism, and Buddhism, have assigned women subordinate roles. But, as we have seen, gender barriers were eliminated at First Narayever Synagogue in 1983, and a woman led the congregation at Tengye Ling Tibetan Buddhist Temple. In the past half-century, Protestant churches have intermittently had female pastors, priests, deacons, ministers, and elders, although in some parishes and congregations, this is still not a reality. A number of non-fundamentalist Protestant churches were in the forefront in welcoming homosexuals, but only after a gay Christian congregation was established in the area in the 1980s. By contrast, Catholic, Orthodox, fundamentalist Protestant, Jewish, and Muslim places of worship tend to regard homosexuality as a sin and practising homosexuals as recurrent and therefore unrepentant sinners. Be that as it may, two downtown synagogues, Shir Lebeynu and First Narayever, welcome gays. Also, two homosexual groups emerged within some of the above-mentioned denominations to try to conciliate sexual orientation and religious acceptance: Dignity Toronto (Catholic) has been in existence since the mid-1970s, and Salaam/Al Fatiha Toronto (Muslim) has been more or less active since 1991.[90]

Outside of regular worship, it is now possible for parishioners and congregants to express their religious sentiments and commitments in a number of different ways. Catholics and Anglicans can take part in street processions on liturgical feast days, observe other traditional rituals, or join a charismatic group. Some evangelical Christian and Muslim groups actively proselytize, an activity they view as a duty imposed by their faith, while mainstream Christian denominations, as well as most Muslims, Jews, Hindus, Buddhists, and Taoists, generally do not encourage missionary work or practise it discreetly. A number of parishes and congregations provide members with forms of direct social intervention, such as the Out of the Cold program and similar efforts to feed, clothe, and otherwise assist those in physical, emotional, or psychological need. Fundraising is a crucial activity to support such endeavours. Many worshippers, however, favour a less activist approach, quite content to make financial contributions to denominational organizations such as the United Jewish Appeal, ShareLife, Islamic Relief Canada, or non-denominational ones such as the United Way.

The West End, indeed Toronto as a whole, offers its inhabitants infinite varieties of worship, devotions, and pious practices. But this choice has not prevented religion's slow and steady decline. Some have attributed this drop to the fact that religion has become too liberal, indulgent, accommodating, or worldly. Others have argued instead that it is too dogmatic, outdated, hidebound, or otherworldly. Neither of these basic positions nor their many variations have succeeded in bringing back the disaffected or attracting the indifferent. This would seem to confirm that religion's eclipse is a Durkheimian social fact.

Conclusion: Blowing in the Wind

This is a story about religion, its rise and decline. It is set in a city that grew in wealth and power in just over a century. The decision-makers who anticipated Toronto's (and Ontario's) industrial rise saw religion as a key component in this process. They were well aware of its social utility, doubtless concurring with Voltaire's dictum: "si Dieu n'existait pas, il faudrait l'inventer." But it would be a mistake to conclude from this that religion was an elaborate plot hatched by rulers better to oppress the ruled: the opiate of the masses, to use Karl Marx's terms. For the masses, religion evidently satisfied some real needs. The preceding chapters have illustrated how it succeeded in bringing people together, giving them a sense of common purpose – how places of worship became building blocks of community, responding to myriad spiritual, intellectual, artistic, physical, and material needs. This is not to say that such responses were perfect or even adequate. However, they did contribute to the growing sense of community. Toronto's population at the beginning of the period under study was diverse in terms of ethnicity, religion, and nativity. At the turn of the twentieth century, it could be described as overwhelmingly British and evangelical Protestant, even though diversity had not vanished, as statistics on the foreign-born well show. While many factors contributed to the homogenization of the population, religion certainly played a key role. At the end of the Second World War, when Toronto had become the economic powerhouse of the country, attracting the most immigrants of any Canadian city, diversity came to express itself increasingly in non-British, non-Christian, and non-white terms. The population's growing differentiation coincided with the eclipse of religion in public life. But before drawing hasty conclusions based on factors of cause and effect, we would be well advised to remind ourselves that diversity was a hallmark of Toronto's early history and that religion had succeeded in bringing about social cohesion.

In the mid-nineteenth century, at the height of the Irish Famine, two-thirds of the city's population was born outside of Canada, and in 1871 that figure was still one in two, a level reached again only in the past few years. Of course it can be argued that, unlike today's foreign-born, the earlier ones all originated in the British Isles. But such a view ignores just how contested the term "British" was at the time. It is not clear that Irish Catholics, for example, identified themselves as such or were so identified by the Protestant majority. They were regarded as foreign and threatening because of language if they were Gaelic speakers, but mostly because of religion; at the time, Catholicism was seen by many as antithetical to British ideals in much the same way that today Islam raises suspicions or concerns in some quarters. The term "Black Irish," which equated them with a people associated in the hemisphere with slavery, starkly highlights their inferior status. But Scots too were wary of a designation that concealed their distinctive identity vis-à-vis the English. Since no group – whether English, Scots, or Irish – was clearly dominant at the time, we are indeed justified in referring to the city's ethnic diversity.

Religion was a key aspect of Toronto's variegated nature. Once again, while it can be claimed that the population was overwhelmingly Protestant, such a view discounts the distinct bodies to which mainstream Protestants – those of Methodist, Presbyterian, and Baptist lineage – belonged. Anglicans, for their part, navigated the polar extremes of High Church and Low Church with their separate parishes and institutions, including those for the training of clergy. Toronto Protestantism also encompassed fundamentalist and premillennial denominations that formed a number of small congregations across the city. Although not as numerous as their mainstream coreligionists, these groups certainly contributed to Protestantism's dynamism and diversity. As for Catholics, they were a solid minority, totalling one-quarter of the city's inhabitants at mid-century and forming the second-largest denomination after Anglicans. Irish immigrants, however, brought with them a peasant form of Catholicism that incorporated pre-Christian beliefs, folklore, and practices, a religion that fused dogmas with marvels. The institutional Church worked hard to expunge what it regarded as extraneous and adulterated elements so as to make Catholicism conform to the Ultramontane standards of the day. On the whole, this objective was achieved, but it took several years, perhaps one generation or more.

Prior to the First World War, centripetal forces were at work on the city's population. Canadian-born Torontonians increased their numbers substantially as large numbers of rural folk moved to the industrializing city in search of employment. At the same time, the Catholic proportion of the population declined steadily, bottoming out at half of what it had been in 1850. This was a consequence of the mostly Protestant migration from the countryside as well as Irish Catholics moving to other places of opportunity on the continent. During those years the disparate groups claiming Methodist and Presbyterian affiliation came together to form two Canada-wide denominations, putting aside the differences that marked their respective traditions. Together with evangelical Anglicans, these denominations promoted a number of common moral and social causes through the Social Gospel movement. The Boer War (1899–1902) revealed that the term "British" was now far less problematic than it had been a half-century earlier. Torontonians, including Irish Catholics, enthusiastically embraced an identity linking them to the foremost imperial power, whose determination to maintain and extend its dominion in the world they wholeheartedly endorsed. By the turn of the twentieth century, the census classified 90 per cent of Toronto's residents as British in origin and 85 per cent as Protestant, overwhelmingly affiliated with the Anglican, Methodist, and Presbyterian churches. The city could not have seemed less diverse.

But even within this homogenizing environment, difference found new forms of expression. With the arrival of large numbers of eastern European Jews in the early part of the new century, the idea of foreignness was redefined to designate non-Christian and non–English-speaking groups. This second category was reinforced with the coming of other continental Europeans, including Italians, Germans, Poles, and Ukrainians, who formed small clusters in the city. The newcomers had a different look and smell about them. They behaved differently. Like the Irish Catholics before them, they appeared to be wild, loud, impulsive, and unpredictable. Jews in particular seemed to be quarrelsome, requiring, it was thought, the inculcation of principles of British justice and fair play. As for the Italians, they were seen as hot-tempered, potentially violent, and therefore needing to be tamed. The religion practised by many of these newcomers was akin to the peasant one the Irish had brought with them, and this caused established religious leaders, be they Jewish or Irish Catholic, much embarrassment vis-à-vis the host society. Diversity was now also expressed in racial terms as small numbers of Chinese and African Americans made Toronto their home. Immigration from continental Europe during the 1920s strengthened the foreign element, which became ethnically and religiously more varied. The denominational landscape now included Eastern Orthodox, Lutherans, non-Scots Calvinists, non-British Baptists, and non–English-speaking Protestants generally. The percentage of Catholics and Jews increased somewhat in the interwar years, although by the Second World War the former only slightly surpassed levels achieved in 1891. The war brought Japanese Canadian internees from British Columbia to the city, adding Buddhism to the religious mix.

Fast becoming the economic capital of Canada, Toronto was the chief beneficiary of successive waves of postwar immigration, which significantly altered its ethnic, racial, and religious composition. Until 1970, Europe was the main source of newcomers as large numbers of Italians, Portuguese, and Greeks joined other populations fleeing the ravages of the war-torn continent. To this cohort can be added immigrants and their children who before the war had settled in other parts of Canada and who were now seeking employment in the metropolis's buoyant economy. Despite the high number of postwar newcomers from the United Kingdom, the British in 1961 were a bare majority of the inhabitants of Toronto (as opposed to the greater metropolitan area), a status lost by the time of the subsequent census. In fact, the overall increase in the population in that decade was largely due to the influx of southern European immigrants. Who could have foreseen that in a relatively short span of time, a city that had been so solidly British and that so proudly proclaimed its identity on the continent and in the Empire, would lose the ethnic base on which those claims rested? By 1961, Catholics, once vilified for their foreign character and allegiances, were a plurality of Toronto's inhabitants; by the time of the following census, their numbers exceeded the combined total of Anglicans, United Church members, and Presbyterians. Indeed, in 1971 the ratio of Catholics to the overall population was very close to levels for the country as a whole, including Quebec.

Toronto's British and Christian character had changed dramatically. The "colour-blind" criteria introduced in 1967 for the selection of immigrants would alter its racial and religious composition as well. Asia, followed by Latin America, now became the main source of new arrivals as Europe's postwar recovery stimulated overall economic growth and prosperity, thereby lessening people's drive to emigrate. With hundreds of thousands of Chinese, South Asians, and Southeast Asians settling in, the city became racially very diverse. Indeed, this has become for many observers the accepted, indeed the exclusive standard for defining diversity. In terms of religion as well, the newcomers were quite disparate. Some were Christian before migrating; some converted to Christianity after arriving; some had no religious affiliation back home and continued to eschew it here; others brought with them non-Christian religions that have since found public expression in the city.

For most of the period under study, worship was an important part of social and community life. Although it is perhaps difficult to appreciate this fact today, when so few people actually attend services at any given time, Toronto's many sacred structures (a number of which have been turned into condominiums) stand as mute reminders of how central worship once was. Churches were among the first community-based institutions to appear in the urban landscape. In the early years they were mainly plain wooden structures. Over time, brick or stone replaced clapboard and architects succeeded carpenters as the artisans who gave tangible and sometimes artistic expression to these communities of worship. Over half a century, the same church was often rebuilt twice over before achieving its final form. In this last stage, stained glass windows, wooden beams, oak furniture, wrought iron railings, and carpeting likely embellished interiors, heightening religious feelings and creating a sense of communal pride. This process illustrated the demographic growth and increasing wealth of parishes and congregations in the prosperous city. Some of them even offered high salaries to lure the best orators as ministers as well as the finest musicians. In so doing, they flaunted their status and prestige; but they also conveyed their commitment to meaningful worship. But this is not the whole story, for besides these larger churches were a multitude of others that mostly housed fundamentalist and premillennial groups. Everything about these latter churches suggested impermanence: their modest exteriors, often no larger than a private residence; their plain and unadorned interiors comprising at most a double room with the barest furnishings; their patterns of expansion consisting in the acquisition of additional small venues; and their instability as newer religious groups exerted a pull on members. Yet the congregation of Plymouth Brethren that gathered in a house on Gladstone Avenue above Queen remained there for more than seventy years, while the Grace and Truth Mission occupied a modest space on Westmoreland Avenue for close to a century.

The pattern of church building followed settlement quite closely. Towns on the outskirts of Toronto – Parkdale, Brockton, Swansea, Davenport, West Toronto Junction – each had their church, or more commonly their churches, which grew in size as congregations expanded. Speculators who spurred the development of these areas sought to give them an aura of respectability and stability by being among the first to subscribe to church-building projects. But they were not alone in doing so, for such projects responded to a genuine community need. Thus it is true that while promoter and mayor Daniel Webster Clendenan was prime mover in the erection of the Keele Street Church of Christ, his example spurred Methodists, Presbyterians, Baptists, and Catholics to erect their own places of worship. In Toronto proper, churches sprouted successively along College Street, Bloor Street, and St Clair Avenue as the city's older inhabitants abandoned the industrial core for the more bucolic suburbs. At the same time, some British immigrants were drawn to areas outside city limits in order to avoid taxes and by-laws that hamstrung their attempts to build a home. Westmoreland Methodist instituted a mission to these newcomers, which led to the founding of the Earlscourt congregation. Meanwhile, sacred spaces left behind by those leaving the downtown core were taken over by new groups.

By making places of worship among the first community-based institutions to be founded, immigrants repeated a pattern already well-established in the host society (see table 8.1). They were in this respect the prime beneficiaries of the flight to the suburbs. It might seem tedious to list here the transfer of sacred sites, but the information clearly illustrates the temporal and spatial scope of the phenomenon, as well as its dynamic quality. Table 8.1 does not include structures originally built as private residences, a number of which also changed hands.

Jews of course did not need to erect or occupy buildings specifically created for worship. They could and did take over private homes to gather and pray. A large number of these *stiblach* were found in the main area of interwar Jewish settlement. One of these, *Shaarei Tzedec* on Markham Street, survives, although it has been spruced up and embellished, notably with stained glass windows. The last authentic *stiblach*, Koil Yankov Anshei Emes, on Brunswick Avenue, was closed just a few

Table 8.1. Places of worship transferred to immigrant groups, 1886–1998

Immigrant Group	Original Occupant	Year of transfer
Jews	Wesleyan Methodist	1886‡
	New Richmond Methodist	1905‡
	Cecil Street Church of Christ	1925‡
	Gospel Mission Hall	1931‡
	Bathurst Street Disciples of Christ	1942‡
	Bethel Mennonite Brethren in Christ	1944
	West United	1947‡
Italians	St Patrick (first)	1908‡
	St Francis (first)	1914‡
	Christian Adventist	1922‡
	College Street Baptist (first)	1935‡
	St Columba United	1966
	Second Church of the Nazarene	1967
	Howard Park United	1970‡
	St Francis (second)	1970
Poles	Western Presbyterian	1911
	First Church of Nazarene	1954
	West Toronto Free Methodist	1962
Ukrainians	Christian Workers Missionary Tabernacle	1928
	Dale Presbyterian	1947
	Adath Israel Anshei Romania	1957
	Memorial Baptist	1959
Lithuanians	Grace Evangelical Association	1928‡
German speakers	St Patrick (second)	1929
	Achdus Israel Umerkaz Harav Synagogue	1955‡
	College Street Baptist (first)	1957
	Olivet Gospel Hall	1973‡
Russian speakers	St Paul Evangelical English Lutheran	1930‡
	St Cyprian Anglican	1966
	Beth Jacob Synagogue	1966
Hungarians	Robert Street Apostolic Church	1943
	St Philip Anglican	1944‡
	Brothers of Jacob Synagogue	1985
Japanese	Centennial United	1958‡
	St Alban the Martyr Anglican	1961‡
Belarusans	Central Church of Christ	1959
Slovaks	B'Nai Israel Synagogue	1959
Greeks	St Alban/North Parkdale United	1962
	St Paul Slovak Evangelical Lutheran	1971

Table 8.1. (concluded)

Immigrant Group	Original Occupant	Year of transfer
Serbs	Faith Apostolic	1966
Afro-Caribbean	Fischer Street Gospel Tabernacle	1968‡
	St Barnabas Anglican	1971‡
	Perth Avenue United	1973‡
	West End Revival Centre	1974
	West End Pentecostal	1980
	Salem Gospel Hall	1982
	Davenport Road Gospel Hall	1983
	Christian Mission Tabernacle	1986
	Torah Emeth Synagogue (second)	1990‡
	Dufferin Street Presbyterian	1995‡
	Glad Tidings Tabernacle	1997
	Bracondale Gospel Hall	1998
Portuguese	St Mary's Catholic	1969
	St Agnes	1970
	College Street Baptist (second)	1974‡
	St Helen's Catholic	1978
Muslims	High Park Presbyterian	1970
Chinese	Our Lady of Mount Carmel	1970
	Beverley Street Baptist	1975
	First Hungarian Presbyterian	1975
	Ukrainian Presbyterian	1986
	Anshei Szydłów Synagogue	1995
Koreans	Davenport Presbyterian	1974
	Humberside Baptist	1979‡
	Epworth United	1986‡
	Westmoreland United	1988‡
	Grace United	1990
Czechs	Annette Street Baptist	1977
Filipinos	Lippincott Street Salvation Army Hall	1979
	West Toronto Gospel Hall	1984
Maronites	Epiphany Anglican	1984
Hindus	Avenue Road Christian & Missionary Alliance	1975
	Fern Avenue Church of Christ	1979
	St Dunstan's Anglican	1982
	College Street Church of God	1998
Latinos	St John the Baptist Lithuanian Catholic	1985

‡ Either no longer occupied by the immigrant group indicated or demolished

years ago. Small fundamentalist congregations, which, as we saw, also met in private houses, began in the interwar period to move into storefronts on major thoroughfares in order to attract new members and conduct missionary work. This trend continued after the war, involving new immigrant groups, notably Afro-Caribbeans, Latin Americans, and Portuguese, as well as new religious ones, such as Hindus. Irrespective of the structure that was chosen, worship was important to all these groups.

But what mattered even more was the type of ritual practised. A defining feature of the evangelical consensus uniting mainstream Protestant denominations was anti-Catholicism. This sentiment was expressed explicitly and implicitly through such things as church interiors, clerical garb, and style of worship. The amphitheatrical structure was favoured in Protestant churches in the later nineteenth century because it was thought to express a sense of community, in contrast to the cruciform shape of Catholic and Anglican ones, which suggested hierarchy and authority. The Geneva gown worn by ministers represented learning and enlightenment, in contrast to the liturgical vestments of Catholic priests, which were considered to be relics of an obscurantist past. Protestant worship proudly featured the preacher's sermon and hearty congregational singing. By contrast, Catholic services took place in a language no one understood, the laity being mere passive witnesses of unseen rituals performed by a priest whose back was turned to them. This is why the impact of the Oxford Movement in nineteenth-century England raised so many hackles in Toronto and why its progress was the object of close attention in these pages. Questions such as candles in churches, surplices for clergy and choirs, and the veneration of the host became flashpoints of controversy. Ritual – or, as mainstream Protestants saw it, the absence of it – was central to their very identity as British Protestants. Their polarized world view would not admit traditions of worship existing in the past or expressed at the time in other cultures. Their Protestantism was inextricably linked to their ethnic identity and their sense of superiority as subjects of the British Empire.

Yet this form of worship was itself contested by fundamentalists and by advocates of premillennialism, who either felt disaffected within the larger Protestant denominations taking shape around them in the latter part of the nineteenth century or who believed that Christ's Second Coming was imminent. They dismissed mainstream worship as routinized, mechanical, and soulless. They yearned for worship that was warm, personal, spontaneous, even disruptive. Like the Apostles who expected Christ's pending return, they wanted to be born again in the Holy Spirit and to be ravished by him. Some hoped to display his gifts of divine healing and glossolalia for all to see. Their services featured the testimonies of plain men and women who were moved to speak by an inner force. Neither the Geneva gown nor the erudition it symbolized was a condition for speaking. Worshippers did not simply sit still in their pews passively absorbing a lifeless sermon; instead, they moved about expressing religion's vital force, or they rushed to the altar in response to the preacher's call. These Christians aimed to create a permanent state of spiritual excitement appropriate to their saviour's return to earth. Although they comprised a relatively small minority, Toronto was an important centre for them both as a spawning ground for their movements or as a hub of missionary work. John Salmon's Bethany Chapel, for example, was a forerunner of the Christian and Missionary Alliance, while James and Ellen Hebden's East End mission was part of a continent-wide network that in 1906 linked the city to Los Angeles and Chicago in the birth of Pentecostalism. Fundamentalists and premillennialists were very active, sponsoring well-attended rallies and revivals in large venues such as Massey Hall.

Protestants of various persuasions generally viewed European and other non-British immigrants as a potential menace to the Dominion's British character. Early on, Anglicans, Methodists, Presbyterians, and Baptists founded missions that targeted specific groups and offered them material assistance in settlement. Such missions had clear class and ethnic objectives in addition to religious ones. Immigrants would be brought to the light of Protestantism and would be taught English and encouraged to abandon their foreign and peasant ways for proper British or Canadian ones. That Finns, almost all of whom were baptized Lutherans, were also targeted shows that more than religion was at stake in such endeavours. Be that as it may, Bibles were printed in a number of languages, and bilingual ministers were hired to go into immigrant communities to fulfil the promise of an abundant harvest. Such contacts – often the first ones that newcomers had with the host society – were meant to ensure that their children would be socialized in a thoroughly Canadian environment.

Through missionary work, a few multilingual churches emerged in the downtown core, such as Beverley Street Baptist and the Church of All Nations, from which sprang small, language-based congregations that later occupied their own sites. In the interwar period, the Christian and Missionary Alliance and the Pentecostals also engaged in immigrant proselytism, but they pursued a different approach. Targeting Jews specifically, the former denomination inaugurated a "Christian synagogue" in the interwar years, following a path already well-trodden by Anglicans and Presbyterians, notably Morris Zeidman of the Scott Mission. Pentecostals, for their part, did not try to assemble disparate ethnic groups under one roof. Rather, whenever possible, distinct language-based congregations were encouraged, the only exception being the Slavic one, where Russian was the common language. Ukrainians arriving after the Second World War, however, rejected Russian as the idiom of worship. They left this congregation and formed their own, an example also followed by Ukrainian Baptists. Meanwhile, other fundamentalist denominations took advantage of the arrival in postwar Toronto of small numbers of coreligionists from various parts of Europe to pursue their own proselytizing projects among immigrant groups. However, as Enrico Cumbo has shown for Italians, conversion was not an option for most newcomers, who viewed Protestant worship as antithetical to their identity.

Indeed, immigrants had their own ideas about worship, and sought above all to create a familiar environment for themselves and their families. Eastern European Jews dismissed the liturgy at Holy Blossom as German, a reference to the Reformed Judaism that flourished in nineteenth-century Germany and whose worship was heavily influenced by the dominant Protestant culture. Determined instead to have liturgy reflect their particular traditions of Orthodoxy, eastern European Jews founded synagogues with unmistakable regional identities. Jews from Poland became so numerous that they formed, wherever possible, *shuls* based on their hometown of origin. The more local the identity, the more authentic was the worship. Such synagogues carried on for about half a century before being absorbed through a series of amalgamations that followed the movement of Jews out of the downtown. The hometown identity so cherished by founding members held little meaning for their grandchildren, who often had only the vaguest notions of their ancestors' geographical origins. Today these local identities persist largely in sections of Jewish cemeteries that bear hometown appellations.

In a similar way, Italians initially demanded priests who spoke their language. But when northern Italians were appointed, most parishioners were not pleased. For one thing, these clerics spoke a formal and educated Italian distinct from the speech of southerners. For another, their ideas of religious practice did not accord the same importance to the cult of the hometown saint that was central to peasants' conception of their faith. Questions of class and regional identities became entwined and – just as with Jews – found expression in conflicts over worship. In time, a *modus vivendi* was worked out, but not without turmoil. Similar clashes occurred in the early years between clergy and parishioners in Lithuanian and Polish churches. As for Ukrainian Catholics, they struggled to preserve the cherished Byzantine liturgy that set them apart from their coreligionists, even though their first churches were not particularly distinctive on the outside or the inside. Exasperated by what they saw as the growing Latinization of their religion and church, some members joined the Orthodox Church, where they felt they could remain faithful to their ancestral ways of worship.

The immigrant cohorts that settled in Toronto after the Second World War also called for their own religious spaces. As stated earlier, issues of class, education, professional training, and politicization separated them from earlier waves. They wanted clergy with backgrounds and political sensibilities similar to their own. Even if in some cases the two groups managed in the beginning to cohabit uneasily, later on they tended to opt for amicable separation. In the case of Afro-Caribbeans, while a number of them joined churches of mainstream or typically black denominations, such as the African Methodist Episcopal Church, many more formed their own places of worship affiliated to churches back home. Korean churches too proliferated throughout the city, either taking over sites or sharing them with existing congregations. The phenomenon was related to family and social networks that were decisive in determining where people went to church. This fact highlights once again the importance of the local character of worship for first-generation immigrants. Buddhist newcomers confirmed this pattern. On the whole, they did not frequent existing temples founded by whites; rather, they established ones reflecting their particular traditions, be they Chinese, Sino-Vietnamese, Vietnamese, or Tibetan.

Over the years, second-generation immigrants also demanded worship tailored to their own identity, not that of their parents. Mark McGowan has shown that the call for native-born clergy and bishops, as opposed to those coming from Ireland, became insistent in the latter part of the nineteenth century. This was a time when the children of Irish Famine immigrants were reaching maturity and doubtless growing weary of priests speaking in brogue and referring endlessly to events and situations "back home." In the same way, a twenty-seven-year-old, American-trained, English-speaking rabbi very much concerned with decorum in worship was hired a generation after *Goel Tzedec*'s founding, which had been instigated, we may recall, by staunch opposition to the assimilationist rituals of Holy Blossom. A few years later, women took their places on the ground floor of the sanctuary and participated in congregational singing. By 1939 the synagogue was considered British enough to merit the visit of King George VI and Queen Elizabeth on their cross-Canada tour. Similarly, the Nisei at the Toronto Buddhist Church needed to have their faith made meaningful to them by their Nisei minister, who stripped Buddhism of its Japanese peasant beliefs and ancestral practices. The result was a form of worship very closely resembling that of mainstream Protestants. Second- and third-generation Ukrainians left Slavic Pentecostal to create their own English-language congregation at the very time that newly arrived compatriots were forming their own Ukrainian-language one. Chinese Protestants likewise implemented English-language services in deference to second-generation members who chafed under the leadership and cultural hegemony of their Cantonese-speaking, Chinese-born elders.

Although worship was a focal point, indeed the raison d'être, of sacred sites, their associational life encompassed a wide range of activities connected to religion only to some degree. In the beginning, Sunday schools mobilized a great deal of (mostly women's) commitment. Women raised funds for their establishment and management. They also constituted the reserve army of labour of the teaching staff. Women's associations sprang up to promote fundraising for parish, congregational, or other ventures, as well as missionary work at home and abroad. Impressive sums of money were collected to rebuild, renovate, or embellish places of worship, as well as to financially support missionaries in the field and local projects to improve education and health. Over time, churches developed a social awareness that impelled lay men and women to work in the cause of temperance, sabbatarianism, and moral purity.

In late Victorian Canada, the emergence of the Social Gospel movement spoke to the church's ambition to exercise moral and social leadership. At the local level, it signalled a determination to be the focus of community life. Many Protestant churches became multipurpose sites housing bowling alleys, tennis courts, and gymnasiums for sporting events, as well as auditoriums for musical or theatrical performances and dances. Under church auspices, baseball, hockey, and boxing matches were held. Programs of social uplift were promoted through participation in denominational city missions or direct contact with "disadvantaged" congregations. A multitude of associations meeting within church precincts were formed according to gender, age, and class with the goal of inculcating strong religious and civic values in their members. This "full-orbed" model proved highly attractive to non-Protestants as well, especially to clerics born or trained in North America. Driven by the idea that youth-based leisure activities should occur under the aegis of religion, Julius Price of *Goel Tzedec* attempted in 1914 to amalgamate the city's Jewish athletic and social clubs. But it would take nearly a decade before the factionalism generated by the proposal was overcome and the YM/YWHA saw the light of day. In the interwar years, St Helen, St Agnes (then under the care of American Franciscans), and St Patrick (whose pastor was a Saskatchewan-raised Redemptorist) all emulated this model. Although waning in the post-war years, it still inspired associational life at Knox and First Chinese Presbyterian.

From the start, central and eastern European parishes exhibited a similar ambition to embody the life of their communities. This was largely because the culture of origin had been for so many years suppressed back home. Even when, as in the case of Poland and Lithuania, these countries achieved their independence after the First World War, there still existed an irrepressible need to express that culture in the land of adoption. In the event, drama, music, and dance groups, gymnastics clubs, reading societies, mutual aid associations, credit unions, language classes, and even child care services became integral to parish life. After eastern Europe fell under the Soviet sphere of influence following the Second World War, refugees arrived with a fresh determination to give full and free expression to their cultures in what they regarded as a land of temporary exile. Associational life took on new vigour, in some cases encompassing overtly political organizations as well. But this fervour later weakened, in part because the second generation could not maintain it and in part as a result of the fall of the Berlin Wall.

Only fundamentalist and premillennial groups seemed untouched by the ideal of a full-orbed religion, regarding social activities not strictly religious as distractions from the crucial goal of preparing for the Second Coming. Della Lageer's diary provides insights into the wholesome endeavours that Christians of her ilk engaged in. These included frequenting church for most of the day on Sunday and some other weeknights, participating in revivals at kindred places of worship, going to hear visiting evangelists, and attending conventions of mission workers. Many such groups expected members to take part in street evangelization, the distribution of tracts and Bibles, and door-to-door visits, and to coordinate and staff storefront missions.

In one way or another, worship and its related activities mobilized the energies of Torontonians for more than a century. To be sure, it was not their only or even their principal concern. But after work and family, it certainly enjoyed pride of place, especially in light of partly successful attempts to bring leisure under its purview. Except for the rare memoirs or correspondence of particular persons, it is difficult for the historian to determine how at an individual level the relationship to clerical leaders, religious institutions, denominations, and ultimately one's own place in the cosmos was understood and lived. But at the collective level, religion was often the way society articulated its ambitions, certitudes, preoccupations, fears, and hatreds. Places of worship touched many aspects of a community's life: its concern for its own material and physical well-being, as well as for that of others; its desire for the transcendent expressed in religious, educational, cultural, or artistic terms; its need for reassurance in times of crisis such as the Depression or the world wars; its sense of rootedness in tradition; its convictions about its own distinctiveness or superiority; and its impulse to embrace the new and modern.

All of that came to an end in the 1960s. People certainly continued to frequent places of worship, although some abandoned their long-standing affiliations, finding refuge in what seemed at the time more exotic forms of spirituality or in the moral certitude of fundamentalist congregations that rejected the situational ethics of the day. Still, the numbers of those who regularly attended a place of worship was dropping to the point that society could no longer be described as churchgoing. It was not merely a question of people leaving the downtown core to establish new congregations in the suburbs. The statistics on attendance and indeed on denominational self-identification tell another story: this was in fact a generalized social trend. As well, religion no longer was the medium through which society conveyed its state of being. The pronouncements of clerics and congregations were now one voice among many and no longer enjoyed primacy, or greater attention, or even respect.

The argument put forward in these pages is that the waning of religion had little to do with styles of liturgy or religiosity, issues of gender and sexuality, stances on contemporary moral questions, or indeed political and social relevance. The decline was a social fact caused by broader socio-economic forces at play in the Western world. This had an impact on the role of places of worship as building blocks of community. Successive church closings, as residents moved to the suburbs and as sacred sites succumbed to the wrecker's hammer or speculators transformed them into condominiums and lofts, has had devastating effects on parish and congregational life. But even in sacred sites frequented by immigrants, the range of activities and initial high rates of involvement were not sustained in subsequent generations. Today the associational life of parishes and congregations is centred essentially on devotional and charitable activities. The co-founder of the Out of the Cold project was the first to recognize the limitations of her program, describing it as a Band-Aid solution. This epithet can be applied to other initiatives promoted and staffed by places of worship, be they soup kitchens, clothes distribution depots, or community gardens: they do not go to the root of the social ills of our time, but merely bring temporary and partial relief that prevents them from reaching crisis proportions. While doubtless indispensable to both the needy individuals being served and to society's good operation, such efforts keep social problems out of the public eye and conscience.

Can the shopping centre replace the place of worship as a building bloc of community? Developers certainly think so, or at least they express that view for the public's edification. While it is true that these palaces of consumption attract masses of people of all ages, cultures, and social backgrounds, and are often *the* gathering place on the day of rest once set aside for worship, they do not and cannot mobilize the energies of men and women as sacred spaces once did. They encourage passive and individualized distractions rather than collective endeavours and ideals. They appeal to our baser instincts of acquisition, exhibition, and repudiation. The purpose here is not to call for a return of religion, which, given the broader socio-economic environment, is like shouting into the wind. It is rather to recall that what was once possible under its aegis might yet again find expression: an ethos beyond the self and the here and now, a concern for cultivating the spirit, the quest for a better world, and an awareness of the intangible and enduring aspects of existence. Religion was far from perfect in advancing such ideals, indeed it often shamefacedly betrayed them, but at least it stuck to them.

Places of Worship in the West End, 1840–2000

Year†, Name, Address, and Changes
† Indicates the year in which the site was occupied

1840   *Queen Street West, Methodist/United*   *423 Queen West*
(1857 third church; 1928 Church of All Nations; 1971
Hungarian Free Reformed; 1984 **demolished**)

1845   *St George the Martyr Anglican*   *197 John*

1857   *Davenport Road Methodist/United*   *1904 Davenport*
(1900 second church; 1973 Davenport–Perth after
merger with Perth Avenue United)

1858   *St John Garrison Anglican*   *31 Stewart*
(1892 second church; 1963 **demolished**)

        St Stephen-in-the-Fields   *103 Bellevue*
(1865 second church)

        St Mark's Carlton Anglican   *63 Connolly*
(1933 closed; joins Calvary Anglican; **demolished**)

1861   *West Presbyterian*   *12 Denison*
(1885 Church of Christ; 1892 Christian Workers; c. 1908
demolished)

1862   *St Anne's Anglican*   *270 Gladstone*
(1907 second church)

1869   *St Patrick Catholic*   *184 St Patrick*
(1908 Our Lady of Mount Carmel Italian; 1970 **Our Lady
of Mount Carmel Chinese**)

1871   *Wesleyan Methodist*   *153 University*
(1885 Goel Tzedec; 1913 African Methodist Episcopal; 1937
Church of God and Saints of Christ; 1948 **demolished**)

1872   *Church of the Redeemer Anglican*   *162 Bloor West*
(1879 second church)

1873   *St Matthias Anglican*   *45 Bellwoods*

1873   *College Street Baptist*   *410 College*
(1891 Christ Church Reformed Episcopal; 1923 Western
Congregational; 1931 First Holiness Pentecostal; 1935
St Paul's Italian United; 1943 Apostolic Church; 1957
St George's German Evangelical Lutheran)

1873   *College Street Presbyterian*   *452 College*
(1885 second church; 1986 **mostly demolished**)

1874   *Wesley Methodist/United/Westennial United*   *1146 Dundas*
(1957 **destroyed by fire**)

1875   *St Philip Anglican*   *515 Dundas West*
(1944 St Elizabeth of Hungary; 1983 **demolished**)

1875   *Anglican Church of the Ascension*   *137 Richmond*
(1919 closed; 1934 **demolished**)

1876   *Christ Church Reformed Episcopal*   *299 Simcoe*
(1891 First Church of Christ Scientist; 1925 **demolished**)

1876   *St Andrew's Presbyterian*   *73 Simcoe*

1878   *Erskine Presbyterian*   *18 Caer Howell*
(1915 **demolished**)

Spadina Methodist/Broadway Tabernacle   *Spadina/College*
(1879 second church; 1888 third church; 1929 **demolished**)

Zion/St Clair Avenue Methodist/St Matthew's   *729 St Clair*
  United
(1888 second church; 1924 third church)

1879 *West Presbyterian (second)*   *12 Denison*
(1911 **St Stanislaus Polish Catholic**)

1880 *St Mark's Parkdale Anglican*   *201 Cowan*
(1983 Epiphany Anglican merged with it)

Beverley Street Baptist   *78 Beverley*
(1886 second church; 1975 **Chinese Baptist**)

1882 *St Thomas Anglican (second)*   *383 Huron*

1883 *Chalmers Presbyterian*   *Dundas/Dovercourt*
(1889 second church; 1945 destroyed by fire; 1978 closed
and **demolished**)

Parkdale Congregational   *36 Brock*
(1911 closed and **demolished**)

1885 *St Alban the Martyr Anglican*   *112 Howland*
(1961 St Andrew Japanese Anglican; 1991 private **chapel
of Royal St George's school**)

St Mary's Catholic   *130 Bathurst*

Euclid Avenue Methodist/Queen Street United   *761 Queen*
(1904 second church; 1990 Worship centre Ruwach;
Open Bible Standard; **closed**)

1886 *New Richmond Methodist*   *McCaul/Grange*
(1905 Beth Hamidrash Hagodol Chevra Tehillim; 1955
closed and later **demolished**)

Cowan Avenue Methodist   *186 Cowan*
(1895 Cowan Avenue Presbyterian; 1928 Parkdale
Tabernacle; 1935 First Church of the Nazarene; 1954
St John's Polish National Catholic)

       Ossington Avenue Baptist   *720 Ossington*
(1906 second church)

       Lansdowne Baptist   *6 Lansdowne*
(1912 closed; 1914 church of the Social Revolution)

1887   *St Paul Methodist/United*   *112 Avenue Road*
(1985 closed; 1995 **demolished**)

       Bloor Street Presbyterian/United   *300 Bloor West*
 (1967 shares with Korean later Alpha United)

       Clinton Street Methodist/United   *90 Clinton*
(1930 closed; 1931 Mogen Abraham Synagogue; 1937
closed and later **demolished**)

       Dovercourt Road Baptist   *142 Argyle*
(1974 to Bloor and Dufferin; **Santa Cruz Portuguese
Catholic**)

       St Clarens Avenue Methodist   *Dundas/St Clarens*
(1907 **demolished**)

       St Barnabas Anglican   *43 Halton*
(1971 Toronto Church of God; 1998 **demolished**)

       Olivet New Jerusalem (Swedenborgians)   *Melbourne/Elm Grove*
(1958 to Etibicoke)

       St Olave's Anglican   *360 Windermere*
(1925 second church; 1936 third church)

1888   *Trinity Methodist/United*   *427 Bloor West*

       Bathurst Street Methodist/United   *736 Bathurst*
(1975 to Trinity United; 1981–85 MCC; Worship Centre
Ruwach; **Bathurst Theatre**)

       St Mark's Presbyterian   *King/Tecumseth*
(1912 **demolished**)

Western Congregational/United   *Spadina/D'Arcy*
(1921 Men of England synagogue; 1961 **demolished**)

Walmer Road Baptist   *188 Lowther*
(1892 second church)

College Street Baptist (second)   *506 College*
(1974 Portuguese Seventh Day Adventists;
 condominiums)

St Mary Magdalene Anglican   *477 Manning*

Epiphany Anglican   *Beatty/Queen*
(1910 new church; 1983 joins St Mark's; **Our Lady of
Lebanon Maronite**)

Epworth Methodist/United   *40 Yarmouth*
(1985 East Toronto Korean Presbyterian; 1998 **demolished**)

St Paul's Presbyterian   *Barton/Bathurst*
(1906 second church; 1969 merged with Dovercourt
Presbyterian; 1970 **demolished**)

Parkdale Presbyterian   *250 Dunn*
(1969 Bonar Presbyterian joined with it)

Sheridan Avenue Baptist   *Sheridan/Muir*
(1905 **demolished**)

Royce Avenue Baptist   *1622 Dupont*
(1915 Resurrection Russian Orthodox; 1919 Ukrainian
Presbyterian/United; 1953 St Andrew Ukrainian Orthodox;
1961 **demolished**)

Annette Street Baptist   *200 High Park*
(1906 second church; 1976 **Czechoslovak Baptist**)

Memorial Baptist   *148 Tecumseth*
(1897 second church; 1911 Memorial Institute; 1959
Ukrainian Baptist)

1889 St Mary the Virgin Anglican (first)   *212 Delaware*
(1919 Apostolic Faith; 1966 **St Michael the Archangel
Serbian Orthodox**)

St John's Anglican   *288 Humberside*
(1920 second church)

Parkdale Methodist/United   *171 Dunn*
(1984 **demolished**; congregation worships in apartment
tower)

St Alban's/North Parkdale Methodist/United   *136 Sorauren*
(1962 **Annunciation and Dormition Greek Orthodox
Cathedral**)

Perth Avenue Methodist/United   *243 Perth*
(1912 second church; 1973 joined to Davenport United;
Perth Avenue Seventh Day Adventist)

1890   *St Margaret Anglican*   *161 Spadina*
(1909 closed; 1931 Finnish Pentecostal; **factory**)

Fern Avenue Presbyterian   *62 Fern*
(1913 Church of Christ; 1979 **Hindu Prarthana Samaj**)

St Jude's Anglican   *437 Roncesvalles*
(1910 new church; 1983 parish closed; 1993 **demolished**)

Church of Christ   *97 Annette*

High Park Methodist/United   *260 High Park*
(1907 second church; 1970 Alhambra United merged
with it)

1891   *Church of the Messiah Anglican*   *240 Avenue*

Centennial Methodist/United   *701 Dovercourt*
(1908 second church; 1958 Japanese United;
condominiums)

Hope Congregational/Independent Bethel   *54 Clinton*
(1905 Christian Workers; 1915 Dewi Sant Welsh Presbyterian; 1928 Christian Standard tabernacle; 1933 Dewi Sant;
1960 St Paul's Slovak Evangelical Lutheran; 1971 **Holy
Trinity Greek Orthodox**)

Zion Congregatonal/Elim hall/Concord Pentecostal   *220 Concord*
(1920 closed and later **demolished**)

Brockton Gospel Mission   *48 Fisher*
(1922 Gospel tabernacle; 1969 Mount Zion Apostolic;
1979 First Seventh-Day Baptist; **demolished**)

Dovercourt/Westmoreland Avenue Methodist/   *246 Westmoreland*
    United
(1908 second church; 1988 Korean Cental Presbyterian;
2000 closed; **demolished**)

1892   *Crawford Street Methodist*   *74 Crawford*
       (1921 closed; 1986 **demolished**)

1892   *Church of Christ*   *58 Cecil*
       (1921 *Tiffereth Israel Bikur Cholim Anshei Ostrovtze*;
       1967 Chinese Catholic centre; 1970 **community
       centre**)

1893   *Bethany Chapel*   *University/*
                                                   Christopher

       (1910 **demolished**)

1894   *West Presbyterian Mission*   *160 Claremont*
       (1912 Italian Methodist mission; 1935 closed; **private
       residence**)

1895   *Church of Christ Scientist*   *189 Brunswick*
       (1900 Disciples of Christ; 1906 Bethel Mennonite; 1945
       First Narayever Synagogue)

Salvation Army   *124 Lisgar*
       (1968 **closed**)

1896   *Plymouth Brethren*   *67Gladstone*
        (1968 **closed**)

        Plymouth Brethren/Brock Avenue Gospel hall   *261 Brock*
        (1932 to 311 Brock)

1897   *Advent Christians*   *41 Argyle*
        (1913 Holiness Mission Hall; 1918 unnamed synagogue;
        1923 Sunflower Spiritualist Community Church; 1924
        closed)

        Grace and Truth Mission Hall (Brethren)   *189 Westmoreland*
        (1983 Mount Halibeth Christian church; 1985 Toronto
        Korean Prayer House; Cathedral church of Christ the
        King; **Bloor Community church**)

1898   *Queen Street Mission*   *1182 Queen*
        (1924–52 Door of Hope mission (second); to
        95 Gladstone)

        Gospel Hall   *3001 Dundas*
        (1938 closed; **demolished**)

1899   *Harmony Mission*   *799 Bathurst*
        (1910 **closed**)

        Covenant Presbyterian   *243 Avenue Road*
        (1906 church completed; 1935 Avenue Road Tabernacle;
        1941 Church of the Nazarene; 1948 Christian and
        Missionary Alliance; **1975 International Society for
        Krishna Consciousness**)

        Dovercourt Congregational   *100 Salem*
        (1903 Free Methodist; 1906 Gospel hall; 1913 **closed**)

1901   *Olivet Baptist*   *36 Margueretta*

        Brock Avenue People's Mission   *666 Brock*
        (1918 Salvation Army barrack; 1937 **closed**)

1902   *St Francis Catholic (first)*   *938 Dundas*
       (1914 St Agnes Italian; 1970 **St Agnes Portuguese**)

       Christie Street Baptist   *177 Christie*

       Holy Family Catholic   *1372 King*

1903   *Church of Christ*   *557 Bathurst*
       (1942 Adath Israel Anshei Romania; 1957 **First Ukrainian
       Pentecostal**)

       Advent Christian   *193 Montrose*
       (1922 Chiesa apostolica italiana; 1970 **demolished**)

       Grace Church Evangelical Association   *Gore Vale/Dundas*
       (1928 St John the Baptist Lithuanian Catholic; 1975
       Korean Catholic congregation; 1985 **San Juan Bautista
       Latino Catholic**)

       Victoria Presbyterian   *190 Medland*
       (1969 Royce Presbyterian merged with it)

1905   *Dovercourt Road Presbyterian*   *700 Dovercourt*

       Dufferin Street Baptist   *1219 Dufferin*
       (1918 second church)

1906   *Reorganized Church of Latter Day Saints*   *23 Soho*
       (1930 African Methodist Episcopal; 1994 Assemblea
       de Deus de Toronto; **demolished**)

       Christian Workers Missionary Tabernacle   *276 Bathurst*
       (1928 **Dormition of the Theotokos Ukrainian Catholic**)

       St Cyprian's Anglican   *102 Follis*
       (1966 joined St Mary the Virgin; **Christ the Saviour Rus-
       sian Orthodox cathedral**)

       St Peter's Catholic   *840 Bathurst*
       (1925 second church)

1907   *Goel Tzedec (second)*   *93 University*
        (1955 **demolished**)

        First Baptist   *Edward/University*
        (1954 **demolished**)

        Knox Presbyterian   *630 Spadina*

        Bonar Presbyterian   *186 St Clarens*
        (1969 merged with Parkdale; 1973 **demolished**)

        Runnymede Presbyterian   *680 Annette*
        (1950 second church)

        St Edmund's Anglican   *1223 Dovercourt*
        (1977 **St Nektarios Greek Orthodox**)

1908   *St. Patrick Catholic (second)*   *131 McCaul*

        St Helen's Catholic (second)   *1680 Dundas*

        St Paul's English Evangelical Lutheran   *College/Markham*
        (1915 demolished; to 4 Glen Morris)

        College Street Methodist/Grace United   *1155 College*
        (1967 merged with Carman to form Grace–Carman; 1983
        Christ Universal church for Better Living; 1990 **Toronto
        Korean Bethel Evangelical**)

        Davenport Road Presbyterian   *1183 Davenport*
        (1973 merged with Wychwood; Toronto Korean
        Presbyterian; 1997 **Galilee Presbyterian**)

        Markham Street Tabernacle   *Markham/Bloor*
        (1921 Christian Workers; 1938 Society of Truth (Brethren);
        1963 **demolished**)

        High Park Baptist   *9 Hewitt*
        (1910 second church)

1909   *Finnish Presbyterian/United*   *44 Mitchell*
        (1928 **closed**)

        Harbour Light Salvation Army   *Tecumseth/Queen*

        St Michael and All Angels Anglican   *611 St Clair*
        (1956 second church)

        Parkdale Tabernacle   *1239 Queen*
        (1928 to Cowan Avenue Presbyterian; 1935 **closed**)

        St Cecilia Catholic   *161 Annette*

1910   *Gospel Mission Hall*   *225 Brunswick*
        (1931 Shomrai Shabot Anshei Oistreich Minhag Sfard /
        Chevra Bais David; 1968 Petah Tikva Anshe Castille;
        1972 **closed**)

        Church of the New Jerusalem (Swedenborgians)   *532 College*
        (1951 Ukrainian Seventh Day Adventists; 1988
        demolished)

        Wychwood/St Columba Presbyterian/United   *540 St Clair*
        (1966 **St Alphonsus Catholic**)

        Dovercourt Road Salvation Army Citadel   *789 Dovercourt*

        Howard Park Methodist/United   *384 Sunnyside*
        (1970 Howard Park Church of God / Centro evangelico
        italiano; **condominiums**)

        Humberside Baptist   *754 Indian Road*
        (1980 Newgate Korean Presbyterian; **demolished**)

1911   *High Park Presbyterian/Erskine United*   *214 Wright*
        (1927 destroyed by fire and rebuilt; 1964 Emmanuel
        United after merger with North Parkdale; 1970
        Emmanuel–Howard Park after merger with Howard
        Park United)

Royce Avenue Presbyterian   *Dupont/Perth*
(1969 closed, joined Victoria Presbyterian, and
demolished)

Knesseth Israel Synagogue   *1 Shipman*

1912   *Shearith Israel Anshei Lida (first)*   *Grange*
        (1921 **closed**)

        Dale Presbyterian/Turner Memorial   *770 Queen*
        (1951 **St Nicholas Ukrainian Catholic**)

        West Presbyterian/United   *College/Montrose*
        (1947 Torah Chaim Synagogue; 1967 **demolished**)

        Dufferin Street Presbyterian   *1183 Dufferin*
        (1995 **Hope Centre Full Gospel**)

        St John's Evangelical Lutheran (first)   *762 Shaw*
        (1961–2 **demolished**)

        Western/Queen Street/Parkdale Baptist   *1620 Queen*
        (closed 1985; 1986 **demolished**)

1913   *Evangel Hall*   *573 Queen West*

        T. Eaton Memorial Methodist/United   *230 St Clair West*

        Pauline Avenue/Carman Methodist/United   *20 Pauline*
        (1967 **St Sebastian Catholic**)

        Seventh-day Adventist   *1 Awde*
        (1961 **Our Lady Queen of Croatia Catholic**)

        St Mary the Virgin (second)   *40 Westmoreland*
        (1966 St Cyprian Anglican joined it)

        St Clare Catholic   *1118 St Clair*

        St Josaphat Ukrainian Catholic   *110 Franklin*
        (1965 destroyed by fire; second church)

Royce Avenue Gospel Hall   *292 Royce*
(1920 Polish Baptist; 1944 Poles of Memorial Baptist
merged with it; 1952 closed; worship at Ossington
Avenue Baptist)

1914   *Anshei Szydłów*   *134 D'Arcy*
(1964 closed; 1995 **Fung Loy Kok Daoist temple**)

Tzemach Tzedec Anshei Libavitch Nusach Ari   *91 Denison*
(1969 **closed**)

Chevra Shaarei Anshei Lida   *239 Augusta*
(1954 closed)

Men of England (first)   *222 Simcoe*
(1920 **closed**)

Tiffereth Israel Bikur Cholim Anshei Ostrovtze   *72 William*
   (first)
(1919 **closed**)

Christian Workers   *8 Robert*
(1923 First Pentecostal Holiness; 1943 **Hungarian
Reformed Evangelical**)

St Paul's English Evangelical Lutheran   *4 Glen Morris*
(1930 Christ the Saviour Russian Orthodox;
1966 **closed**)

St Francis Catholic (second)   *101 Grace*

Methodist Italian Mission /Dufferin Street United   *1467 Dufferin*
(1961 **demolished**)

Door of Hope Mission   *152 Lappin*
(1924 Adriel chapel; 1932 closed)

Salvation Army Barrack   *Keele/Dundas West*

Windermere Methodist/United   *356 Windermere*

1915   *B'nai Abraham*   *44 Huron*
       (1961 **closed**)

       First Christian   *693 Bathurst*
       (1932 Grace Spiritualist; 1939 Springdale; 1956 **closed**)

       First Church of Christ Scientist (second)   *196 St George*

       St Clement/Our Lady of the Angels   *1481 Dufferin*

       St Vincent de Paul Catholic   *263 Roncesvalles*

       Our Lady of Czestochowa Polish Catholic   *1996 Davenport*

1916   *Anshei Minsk 1*   *10/12 St Andrew*
       (1930 second synagogue)

       Nathaniel Institute   *91 Bellevue*
       (1962 closed)

       Bible Truth Mission   *120 Brandon*
       (1950 **closed**)

       Morningside Presbyterian   *4 Morningside*
       (1968 absorbed High Park Presbyterian)

       St Martin-in-the-Fields Anglican   *151 Glenlake*

1917   *Zion Institute*   *16 Cecil*
       (**closed**)

       Chinese Presbyterian   *124/6 University*
       (1960 closed; **demolished**)

       Torah Emeth/Yeshivah Maril Graubart   *68 D'Arcy*
       (1965 **closed**)

       Maranatha hall for the Deaf (Brethren)   *783 College*
       (1945 **closed**)

Britten Memorial Spiritualist   *847 Dovercourt*
(1951 to 104 Clinton; 1965 to 657 Lansdowne)

Lansdowne Avenue Gospel Hall   *704 Lansdowne*
(1930 **closed**)

1918   *Rodfei Sholom-Anshe Kiev*   *28 Denison Square*

1919   *Anglican Church of the Ascension (second)*   *180 Simcoe*
(1933 closed; 1936 Trinity German Lutheran/
1940 Slovak Lutheran/1943 Finnish Lutheran;
demolished)

1920   *Rosh Pinah*   *27 Denison*
(1943 **closed**)

First Narayever (first)   *70 Huron*
(1943 Anshei Chmelnik; 1959 **closed**)

Kehillath Jacob Synagogue   *128 Markham*
(1959 **closed**)

Brothers of Jacob Synagogue   *75 Mackay*
(1955 Beth Israel; 1985 **Hungarian United**)

Église Ste-Jeanne-d'Arc/St Joan of Arc   *Dundas/Edna*
(1963 **demolished**)

1921   *First Moldovia Congregation of Romania Tifferes*   *53 Vanauley*
        Israel
(1928 **closed**)

Bikes Cholim Anshei Kielce   *450 Dundas West*
(1963 Chinese Gospel; 1972 **demolished**)

St Anthony's Catholic   *1041 Bloor*

St James Catholic   *728 Annette*
(1960 second church)

1922   *Stashever Synagogue*   *410 Dundas West*
        (1963 closed; **demolished**)

        Ezras Israel Anshei Apt   *216 Beverley*
        (1967 **closed**)

        Beth Jacob   *23 Henry*
        (1966 **Holy Trinity Russian Orthodox**)

        Chevra B'nai Israel   *257 Shaw*
        (1959 **Nativity of the Mother of God Slovak Catholic**)

        House of the Seekers After Truth Christian   *145 Major*
            Synagogue
        (1942 **closed**)

        Hillcrest Christian   *2 Vaughan Road*

        Alliance Tabernacle   *85 Christie*
        (1948 closed; United Jewish People's Order)

        Inasmuch Mission   *70 Ossington*
        (1944 **closed**)

        Central Church of Christ   *526 St Clarens*
        (1950 West End Gospel; 1961 **St Cyril of Turov Belarusan**
        Autocephalous Orthodox)

        Alhambra Presbyterian/United   *1573 Bloor*
        (1969 joins High Park United; **Lithuanian Hall**)

1923   *Christ the Saviour Russian Orthodox (first)*   *55 Spadina*
        (1930 **destroyed by fire**)

        Advent Christians (second)   *639 Crawford*
        (1936 **Crawford Street Congregational**)

        Christ Church Reformed Episcopal/Afro   *460 Shaw*
            Community
        (1945 merged with Afro Community church; 1998
        destroyed by fire)

St Dunstan's Anglican   *722 Lansdowne*
(1982 **Gandhi Bhawan Hindu Temple**)

Bible Faith Mission   *1355 St Clair*
(1935 Toronto Spiritual church; **closed**)

1923   *St Paul's Runnymede Anglican*   *404 Willard*

1924   *Toronto Jewish Mission*   *209 Borden*
(1930 closed; 1942 to 611 Dundas West; 1963 to
North York)

Chevra Mishnayes   *42 Cecil*
(1954 **closed**)

Chevra Tiferes Israel Anshei New York   *43 Huron*
(1967 **closed**)

Chevra B'nai Moshe   *37 D'Arcy*
(1973 **closed**)

Agudas Israel Anshei Sforad   *151 Palmerston*
(1979 **closed**)

Bracondale Gospel Hall   *58B Arlington*
(1998 **Faith Believers Gospel Apostolic**)

Olivet Gospel Hall   *778 Ossington*
(1973 **Evangelische Gemeinde**)

1925   *Bais Yahuda Synagogue*   *703 Ossington*
(1944 to 805 Dovercourt; 1968 Pentecostal Apostolic;
1973 **demolished**)

Reveille Mission   *383 Queen*
(1938 to 2184 Dundas; 1946 **closed**)

1926   *Holy Rosary Catholic*   *354 St Clair West*

1927   *Strettiner Synagogue*   *125 Huron*
(1937 **closed**)

First Moldovia Congregation of Tifferes Israel   *265 Augusta*
(1962 **closed**)

St Thomas Aquinas Chapel   *50 Hoskin*

Central/Avenue Road Presbyterian   *53 Avenue Road*
(1948 merged with Olivet Congregational)

Salem Gospel Hall   *228 Rosemount*
(1982 **Bibleway Church of God Apostolic**)

Runnymede Road United   *432 Runnmede*

1928   *B'Nai Israel Husyatiner Kloiz (first)*   *49 Ulster*
(1939 closed; to 96 Brunswick)

Grace Baptist (Fellowship)   *771 Dovercourt*
(1936 St Mark's Independent Anglican; 1949 **closed**)

Third Church of Christian Science   *70 High Park*

1929   *Church of God and Saints of Christ*   *117 Denison*
(1937 **closed**)

Italian Christian church (Pentecostal)   *335 Euclid*
(1945 Apostolic church; 1948 Holy Fellowship of the
Company of the Community of Israel of the Men of
Lagov Synagogue; c. 1956 **closed**)

St John Evangelical Lutheran (second)   *274 Concord*

1930   *Chevra B'nai Yankov Anshei Beizetchin*   *99 D'Arcy*
(1936 **closed**)

Knesses Israel Anshei Slipia   *43 Oxford*
(1967 **closed**)

Salvation Army Barrack   *382 Lippincott*
(1979 **First Filipino Baptist**)

West Toronto Independent Baptist   *3049 Dundas*
(1949 first church)

Runnymede Baptist   *60 Colbeck*

High Park Presbyterian   *58 Boustead*
(1969 **Jami Mosque**)

1931   *Reorganized Church of Jesus Christ of Latter*   *1443 Bathurst*
         Day Saints
(2000 changes name to Community of Christ)

Machzikei Torah Synagogue   *383 Markham*
(1974 **closed**)

St Paul the Apostle Maltese Catholic   *3226 Dundas*
(1955 second church)

1932   *Bathurst Street Hall*   *854 Bathurst*
(1950 **closed**)

1933   *Chevra Shas*   *32 McCaul*
(1965 **closed**)

St John's Polish National Catholic (first)   *1032 Queen*
(1953 to 186 Cowan Avenue)

1934   *Koil Yankov Anshei Emes*   *20 Brunswick*
(**closed**)

Agudas Israel Merkaz Harav   *257 Euclid*
(1955 German Baptists; 1970 Bethel Church of Jesus
Christ; 1979 Church of God Pillar and Ground of Truth;
1985 Assemblies of the First Born; **closed**)

1934   *Mach Zikei B'nai Israel Synagogue*   *270 Dovercourt*
(1982 **closed**)

1935   *Young Israel*   *15 Brunswick*
(1965 **closed**)

Second Church of the Nazarene   *1277 St Clair*
(1967 **San Nicola di Bari Catholic**)

1936   *First church of the Illuminate*   *531 Markham*
       (1950 **closed**)

       Temple (assembly, shrine, church) of Edith Cavell   *973 College*
       (1968 to 448 Shaw; 1970 **closed**)

1937   *Finnish Pentecostal (second)*   *21/3 Beverley*
       (1959 **closed**)

       Shaarei Tzedek Synagogue   *397 Markham*

       Wychwood–Davenport Presbyterian   *155 Wychwood*

       Marks Spiritual Church   *1247 Dundas*
       (1945 **closed**)

       Shaarei Shomayim Synagogue   *836 St Clair*
       (1967 closed; Hungarian Community Centre; **demolished**)

       Glad Tidings Tabernacle (Pentecostal)   *833 St. Clair*
       (1963 closed; 1998 Cornerstone Baptist Tabernacle;
       demolished)

       Christian Standard Tabernacle   *2017 Dundas*
       (1961 **closed**)

1938   *First Hungarian Presbyterian*   *206 McCaul*
       (1979 **Holy Word Chinese Evangelical**)

       Church of God   *1200 Lansdowne*
       (1950 **closed**)

       West Toronto Gospel Hall/Holiness mission   *425 Pacific*
       (1984 **Hallelujah Filipino Baptist**)

       Ukrainian Pentecostal   *322 Dupont*
       (1947 **closed**)

1939   *Plymouth Brethren*   *1176A St Clair*
       (1947 **closed**)

1940   *Husiatyner Kloiz (second)*   *96 Brunswick*
       (1964 **closed**)

       Church of the Crusaders (Associated Gospel)   *1307 Bloor*

       Church of Latter Day Saints   *851 Ossington*

       Central Baptist (second)   *965 Ossington*
       (1964 **Christadelphians**)

1941   *Sts Cyril and Methodius Slovak Catholic*   *38 Claremont*
       (1993 closed; **condominiums**)

       Ukrainian Presbyterian   *40 Claremont*
       (1981 Portuguese Pentecostals; 1987 **Grace Chinese
       Baptist**)

       Gospel Hall   *56 Tecumseth*
       (1980 **closed**)

       West End Pentecostal   *65 Ford*
       (1962 Congregazione pentecostale italiana; 1980
       Zion Apostolic Church of Jesus Christ)

1942   *New Apostolic*   *409 Dupont*

       Temple of Spiritual Guidance   *256 Lansdowne*
       (at various sites after 1934; 1956 **closed**)

       Beth Mordche Synagogue   *571 College*
       (1953 **closed**)

       Torah V'avodah Synagogue   *396 Markham*
       (1964 **closed**)

1943   *Yavneh Zion*   *651 Spadina*
       (1963 **closed**)

Russian-Ukrainian Pentecostal   *1090 Queen*

1946 *Toronto Buddhist Church (first)*   *134 Huron*
      (1954 closed; to 918 Bathurst)

1947 *St Wolodymyr Ukrainian Orthodox*   *400 Bathurst*

      Redeemer Lithuanian Lutheran   *1691 Bloor*

1948 *Scott Mission*   *502 Spadina*

1949 *Drildger Synagogue*   *414 Markham*
      (1971 **closed**)

      West Toronto Free Methodist   *2611 Dundas*
      (1962 **Pierwszy Kosciol Baptystow (Polish Baptist)**))

1950 *Farmer Memorial Baptist*   *293 South Kingsway*

1951 *Pride of Israel*   *578 Spadina*
      (1963 **closed)**

      Russian Ukrainian Church of Evangelical   *24 Carr*
        Christians

1952 *First Unitarian*   *175 St Clair*

      St Casimir Polish Catholic   *156 Roncesvalles*

1953 *Shlomei Amunei Yisroel*   *153 Huron*
      (1967 **closed**)

      Torah Emeth (second)   *1344 Bathurst*
      (1972 St Nikon Greek Orthodox; 1978 **Church of God/
      Church of God Sabbath Keeping**)

      West Toronto Salvation Army Citadel   *343 Keele*

      Door of Hope Mission (third)   *95 Gladstone*
      (1969 **Slavic Evangelical Baptist**)

1954   *St Mary Help of Christians Slovene Catholic*   *611 Manning*

Grace Lutheran   *1424 Davenport*
(1973 **St Paul Slovak Evangelical Lutheran**)

St Pius X Catholic   *2305 Bloor*

1955   *First Baptist (second)*   *101 Huron*

Toronto Buddhist Church (second)   *918 Bathurst*

Resurrection Lithuanian Catholic   *1000 College*
(2000 **demolished**)

Davenport Road Gospel Hall   *2037 Davenport*
(1982 Apostolic Church of God; 1985 **Newborn Church of God**)

1956   *Trinity College Chapel (second)*   *6 Hoskin*

Society of Friends (Quakers)   *60 Lowther*

Assemblea cristiana pentecostale italiana   *686 Ossington*

Grace Church of the Nazarene   *624 Annette*

1957   *Kingdom Hall of the Jehovah's Witnesses*   *285 Christie*

St Paul Italian United   *1120 Ossington*
(1980 joined by Pietro Valdo United)

St Euphrosinia of Polatsk Belarusan Orthodox   *1008 Dovercourt*

1958   *Agudath Israel Council of Toronto Synagogue*   *608 Bathurst*
(1966 **closed**)

Ukrainian Evangelical   *869 Dovercourt*
(1982 **closed**)

1959   *Chinese Evangelical Baptist*   *155 Spadina Road*
(1975 **closed**)

Christian Mission Tabernacle   *2733 Dundas*
(1965 to 3200 Dundas)

1960   *Chinese Presbyterian (second)*   *177 Beverley*

       Westennial United   *256 Ossington*
       (1999 **closed**)

1961   *Kingdom Hall (Jehovah's Witnesses)*   *959 College*

1962   *St Andrew Ukrainian Orthodox (second)*   *1622 Dupont*

       West End Revival Centre   *1780 St Clair*
       (from 65 Ford; 1974–86 Church of God of Prophecy;
       1987 **Faith Impact ministry**)

       Muslim Society of Toronto Islamic Centre   *3047 Dundas*
       (1957 renamed Albanian Muslim Society of Toronto and
       moved to 564 Annette)

1963   *St John Latvian Evangelical Lutheran*   *200 Balmoral*

       St Wenceslaus Czech Catholic   *496 Gladstone*

1964   *Holy Protection Ukrainian Catholic*   *18 Leeds*

1965   *Full Gospel Tabernacle*   *159 Claremont*
       (1989 **Living Water Chinese assembly**)

       Calvary Assembly   *3200 Dundas*
       (from 2733 Dundas; 1986 **Church of God of Prophecy/
       Iglesia de Dios de la Profecia universal**)

1967   *St Joan of Arc Catholic (second)*   *1701 Bloor*

1970   *Assemblea Cristiana/chiesa apostolica (second)*   *703 College*
       (1978 **Toronto Spiritualist temple**)

1971   *Toronto Zen Centre*   *569 Christie*
       (1983 closed; to 33 High Park Gardens)

1972   *Church of Scientology*   *124 Avenue Road*
(1980 **closed**)

1973   *Lighthouse Community Ministry (Dutch*   *1008 Bathurst*
      Christian Reformed)

1975   *Our Lady of Good Counsel Caribbean Catholic*   *867 College*

      Sri Guru Singh Saba Sikh Gurdwara   *331 Weston*

      Kingdom Hall of the Jehovah's Witnesses   *3003 Dundas*
(1998 Shiloh Pentecostal Church of Jesus Christ from
977 College)

1977   *Emmanuel Pentecostal*   *3079 Dundas*
(1991 **closed**)

1978   *Church of God*   *369 Harbord*
(1981 Hungarian Pentecostal; 1987 True Jesus church;
1997 **closed**)

      College Street Church of God   *54 Moutray*
(1981 First Born Apostolic; 1998 **Assemblea de Deus**)

      Pentecostal Church of God   *3339 Dundas*
(1995 **Celestial Church of Christ** (Ayo parish))

1979   *Unification Church*   *87 Bellevue*
(1992 **closed**)

1980   *St Ann's Spiritual Bathurst*   *645 Dupont*

      Church of God of Prophecy   *1071 Bloor*
(1986 to 3200 Dundas)

      College Street Church of God   *1871 Davenport*
(1998 **Shri Satya Narayan mandir**)

1981   *Taoist Tai Chi Society*   *1376 Bathurst*

1981	*Gaden Choling Buddhist Centre*	*637 Christie*
1982	*Oakwood Wesleyan*	*33 Brandon*
1984	*First Portuguese Evangelical*	*132 Nassau*
	Tai Bai Buddhist Temple (1991 becomes Ching Kwok temple at 300 Bathurst)	*960 Dundas*
	Toronto Zen Centre (second)	*33 High Park Gardens*
1985	*Fu Sien Tong Buddhist Temple*	*185 Niagara*
	Chua Adiba Buddhist	*1118 College*
	Buddhist Association of Canada/Hong Fa Temple	*1330 Bloor*
	Shiloh Pentecostal Church of Jesus Christ (1998 to 3003 Dundas)	*977 College*
	Parkdale Neighbourhood Church	*197 MacDonell*
	Kingdom Hall of Jehovah's Witnesses	*2393 Dundas*
1986	*Chuen Te Buddhist Society*	*294 Beverley*
1987	*International Christian Centre*	*184 Spadina*
1988	*Toronto Shambala Meditation Centre*	*670 Bloor*
	Fung Leun Tong Sit and Seto Society	*20 Cecil*
1989	*Brahma Kumaris Raja Yoga*	*897 College*
	St Francis Table	*1485 Queen*
1990	*Good News Pentecostal/Living Water Church*	*695 St Clair*
	Nine Mountains Zen Society (Korean Buddhist)	*1000 Queen*

	First Spanish United Pentecostal (1995 **closed**)	*3346 Dundas*

Missionary Church of Christ (1993 **Nazarene Church of God/Iglesia de Dios Evangelica Pentecostal**)   *1909 Davenport*

Riwoche Pemavajra Tibetan Buddhist Temple   *566 Annette*

1991   *Canadian Chinese Ming Yuet Buddhist Society*   *22 Cecil*

Mount Maria   *3291 Dundas*

1992   *Covenant Christian*   *455 Huron*

Igreja universal do reino de Deus (to 1653 Dundas under name Novas de Alegria)   *1305B Dundas*

Restitution Bethesta Tabernacle   *134 Hallam*

1993   *The Church in Toronto*   *24 Cecil*

Toronto Bahá'í Centre   *288 Huron*

1994   *The Quays Community Church (Baptist)*   *1087 Queen*

International Pentecostal City Mission Prayer Centre   *1764a St Clair*

Brotherhood of Christ Healing Temple of the Full Gospel Tabernacle   *Bathurst/Alcina*

1995   *Ming Sing Tao Tak Temple*   *38 St Patrick*

Karma Sonam Dargye Ling Tibetan Buddhist Temple   *39 Triller*

1996   *Gayatri Mandir Hindu Temple*   *983 Dupont*

Islamic Information and Da'Wah Centre International   *1168 Bloor*

	Tengye Ling Tibetan Buddhist	*11 Madison*
1997	*Igreja central do evangelho pleno*	*1170 Dupont*
	Chua Linh Son Sacred Mountain Vietnamese Buddhist	*1 Howard Park*
1998	*Kingdom Hall of Jehovah's Witnesses*	*2101 Dundas*
c1998	*Deus e Amor Igreja Pentecostal*	*1535 Dundas*

Notes

1. Consolidating Protestantism

1 Wilson, *The Orange Order in Canada*.

2 Canada, *Census of Canada 1851–2*, 67; Canada, *Census of Canada 1880–1*, 174–5. In 1851, 418 people declined to state their denominational affiliation, while the faith of 269 others was "not known." In 1871, 57 Torontonians indicated that they had no religion, while 108 others did not give their religious attachment. See Canada, *Census of Canada 1870–1*, 117.

3 See Gibson, *The Church of England,*.

4 Donaldson, *The Scottish Reformation*.

5 Hempton, *Methodism*; Heitzenrater, *Wesley and the People Called Methodists*.

6 deMattei, *Pius IX*; Delville and Jacov, eds., *La Papauté contemporaine*. 64.

7 Clarke, *Piety and Nationalism*, ch. 3. For Irish Catholicism, see Larkin, *The Historical Dimensions*.

8 Only two churches were constructed in the 1840s, five in the 1850s, and another five in the 1860s.

9 Champion, *The Methodist Churches of Toronto*, 272.

10 Carlton Village was annexed to West Toronto Junction in 1889. Samuel Thompson bought land and had a house built on Davenport Road in 1853. See his *Reminiscences*.

11 Robertson, *Landmarks*, vol. 4, 113–14; St Mark and Calvary Anglican Church, *St Mark's West Toronto 125th Anniversary*. Unless other wise indicated all references to Robertson's work are taken from volume 4.

12 Robertson, *Landmarks*, 420; [N.A.], *A Meeting Place Forever*.

13 *DCB*, vol. 13, "Kivas Tully." Tully was the architect of Trinity College.

14 Robertson, *Landmarks*, 88–90.

15 Ibid., 94–6, 268–72, 377–9; PCCA, Cherry, *Sixty Years of Growing*, 1–4.

16 This description appears verbatim in both Robertson, *Landmarks*, 409, and Champion, *Methodist Churches of Toronto*, 266, as if each author had written it.

17 Robertson, *Landmarks*, 408–11; Champion, *Methodist Churches of Toronto*, 266–7.

18 Gagan, *The Denison Family of Toronto*.

19 Robertson, *Landmarks*, 24–9; Cochrane, *Kensington*.

20 Arthur, *Toronto: No Mean City*, 268. The building contractor was William Henry Pim, a native of Middlesex in England.

21 Angus was Allan Macdonell's brother, discussed in Knight and Chute, "A Visionary on the Edge."

22 Robertson, Landmarks, 384–5.

23 UCA, Gray, *Diamond Jubilee*; Champion, *Methodist Churches of Toronto*, 177–87; DCB, vol. 10, "Robert Wilkes."

24 The jurists were John Godfrey Spragge and David Breakenridge Read and the businessmen were Lewis Moffatt and Frederick Chase Capreol. See *DCB*, vol. 11, for Spragge and Capreol; vol. 12 for Moffatt; and vol. 13 for Breakenridge.

25 Butler, "St. Andrew's Presbyterian Church." The prolific Lionel Yorke, a Cambridgeshire immigrant, received the building contract. See Arthur, *Toronto*, 271.

26 Mulvany, *Toronto Past and Present*, 166.

27 *DCB*, vol. 11, "John Macdonald"; *DCB*, vol. 11, "William Cayley."

28 Robertson, *Landmarks*, , 253.

29 Ibid., 395–7; Champion, *Methodist Churches of Toronto*, 272–3; Mulvany, *History of Toronto* vol. 2.

30 Elliott, "The English," in Magocsi, ed., *Encyclopedia of Canada's Peoples*, 482.

31 Arthur, *Toronto*, 147.

32 Ibid., 248. Gordon had trained with Henry Langley, striking out on his own in 1877, shortly before this commission.

33 *DCB*, vol. 8, "John Henry Dunn."

34 Champion, *Methodist Churches of Toronto*, 292.

35 Simmins, *Fred Cumberland*, claims that Wilcock was the church's contractor, although the latter's name does not appear in the list of builders and contractors in Arthur, *Toronto*.

36 The 1871 expansion also gave the church three hundred draw seats so that its total seating capacity was 1,800 to Metropolitan's 1,900. Robertson, *Landmarks*, 370–3; Champion, *Methodist Churches of Toronto*, 293; Simmins, *Fred Cumberland*. Robertson (371) claims that the organ cost $4,000, whereas Champion puts the price at $1,000.

37 A sketch of the Methodist chapel that became the Primitive Methodists' Elm Street mission and later became Goel Tzedec Synagogue is found in Robertson, *Landmarks*, 562.

38 Champion, *The Methodist Churches of Toronto*, 366–7.

39 Clarke, *Piety and Nationalism*, 54. In contrast, Robertson asserts that the debt was paid off by 1881. See Robertson, *Landmarks*, 337. See also Toronto Public Library's website *Toronto's Sanctuaries*.

40 UCA, "The Amplifier," June 1925; UCA, Gray, ed., *Diamond Jubilee*.

41 CBA, College Street Baptist, *A Short History of the Church*.

42 Galvin, "The Jubilee Riots in Toronto."

43 Greig, *In the Fullness of Time*, 4.

44 Robertson, *Landmarks*, 63.

45 Ibid., 66.

46 Ibid., 62–9; Ruggle, "The Saints in the Land," 202–8. For an evangelical Anglican perspective, see Blake, "The Protestant Episcopal Divinity School," 172–5.

47 Bartlett, *Genealogy*.

48 Robertson, *Landmarks*, 69–75; Reeves, *Over 100 Years*.

49 Tully contested the election on the grounds that women pew-holders did not have the right to vote. See Ruggle, "Saints in the Land," 190.

50 Smith left over $200,000 to beneficiaries, including Wycliffe College, the seminary for Low Church clergymen, founded in 1877 as the Protestant Episcopal Divinity School and located on College Street west of Queen's Park near Christ Church First Reformed Episcopal church. See the *Globe* article "A Grasping Church," 7 June 1883.

51 Robertson, *Landmarks*, 61; Jones, "Reaching Out," 150.

52 Sir Adam Wilson was mayor of Toronto from 1859 to 1861. Charles Henry Ritchie was one of three arbitrators in the dispute between the City of Toronto and the Toronto Street Railways Company settled in 1891. Middleton, *The Municipality of Toronto*, vol. 3, 179.

53 *DCB*, vol. 12, "William George Storm."

54 Robertson, *Landmarks*, 40.

55 *DCB*, vol. 12, "Daniel James Macdonnell"; McCurdy, ed., *Life and Work of D.J. Macdonnell*.

56 Robertson, *Landmarks*, 124.

2. An Era of Exuberance

1 Robertson, *Landmarks*, 223–8; PCCA, Erskine Annual Report, 1892.

2 "Downtown Life Will Engulf Erskine Church," *Toronto Daily Star*, 29 May 1915, 4.

3 See Careless, *Toronto to 1918*, ch. 4.

4 Canada, *Census of Canada 1880–1*, I, 174–5. In 1881, only 59 people said they had no religion and 474 others declined to state what their religion was. Forty years later, the census indicated 50 atheists, 56 free thinkers, 518 without religion, and 1,213 people who chose not to give their religious affiliation. See Canada, *Sixth Census*, 756.

5 Other churches in this category were New Richmond, Broadway Tabernacle, St Paul's, and Euclid.. All but the latter have disappeared from the landscape.

6 Other larger Baptist churches included Memorial, Humberside, and Western, all put up between 1897 and 1912.

7 Sawatsky, "Looking for the Blessed Hope."

8 Barker, *The Story of Memorial Institute, Toronto*; CBA, "History of Olivet Baptist Church, 1889–1937," *Canadian Baptist*, 16 September 1937.

9 Mercer, *Toronto, Old and New*, 86.

10 *Biographical Dictionary of Architects in Canada*, http:// dictionaryofarchitectsincanada.org/architects; Architectural Index for Ontario, www.archindont.torontopubliclibrary.ca; Thomas, "A Thoroughly Traditional Architect"; Carr, *Toronto Architect Edmund Burke*.

11 The censuses of 1911 and 1921 listed around six hundred Mormons in the entire city of Toronto. Canada, *Fifth Census*, vol. 2; Canada, *Sixth Census*, vol. 1, 756. The first church was located on Camden Street and was built in 1900. The second was on Soho Street just north of Queen Street.

12 See the entry on Wilm Knox in *Biographical Dictionary of Architects in Canada*.

13 Fraser, *A History of Ontario*, 756–7. Architect Charles Frederick Wagner attended Upper Canada College and married the daughter of Major James Bennett, Grand Master of the Orange Lodge at the time of the wedding. T.C. Robinette, the best man, would become a prominent Liberal lawyer. The first church, which stood at the corner of College and Markham Streets, was sold within a short time, the congregation moving to a larger site on Glen Morris Street near Huron Street. See *Toronto Globe*, "Lutherans to Build Two More Churches, 8 December 1913, 9. Heritage Toronto gives M. Klein as the architect of this second St Paul's Church. According to *Biographical Dictionary of Architects in Canada*, however, Maurice Dalvin Klein, aged eighteen in 1914, was still a student when the church was built. From 1880 to 1920, the total number of Lutherans in Toronto went from 500 to 1,600. The peak was reached in 1911 at 2,700. See Canada, *Census of Canada 1880–1*, vol. 1, 174; Canada, *Sixth Census of Canada 1921*, vol. 1, 707.

14 [N.A.], *The Reverend Ernest Hahn*. The chapel was located at Shaw and
    Irene Streets.

15 See Frager, *Sweatshop Strife*; Zucchi, *Italians in Toronto*; Petroff, *Sojourners
    and Settlers*; Harney ed., *Gathering Place*.

16 Robertson, *Landmarks*, 495–7; Dendy, *Lost Toronto*; Reynolds, *Footprints*.

17 "Church Services To-Morrow," *Toronto Daily Star*, 18 September 1909, 17;
    Reid, "Toward a Fourfold Gospel.

18 Hayes, "Repairing the Walls," in Hayes, *By Grace Co-Workers*, 88–9.

19 Robertson, *Landmarks,*, 30–1.

20 Butler, "St Andrew's Presbyterian Church"; Robertson, *Landmarks*, 126–31.
    The minister who resigned was W.J. McCaughan.

21 "Methodist Church to Become a Synagogue?," *Toronto Daily Star*,
    8 March 1905, 1–2; "To Sell the Old Church: Hebrews McCaul Street
    Place of Worship," *Globe*, 3 June 1905, 24; "McCaul Street Church Sale,"
    Globe, 14 June 1905, 8.

22 CBA, "Beverley's Battle for a Building," *Canadian Baptist*, 15 April 192?;
    meeting of the executive committee, Home Missions Board, 14 December
    1914.

23 Robertson, *Landmarks*, 449.

24 Carr, *Toronto Architect Edmund Burke*, 28; *DCB*, vol. 15, "William Davies."

25 *Globe*, 3 May 1897; *Mail and Empire*, 3 May and 13 September 1897. See
    also Barker, *The Story of Memorial Institute*.

26 According to the Canadians census, Christian Scientists numbered fewer
    than 1,000 in 1911 and 2,200 in 1920.

27 For example, James Beaty, James Lesslie, and Thomas Chalmers Scott
    were early members. See *DCB*, vol. 12, "James Beaty"; and *DCB*, vol. 11,
    "James Lesslie". For Scott, see Middleton, *The Municipality of Toronto*,
    vol. 3.

28 In 1919, individual congregations were given leave to introduce the
    organ in worship, but only after a unanimous vote of members. The
    same issue divided Mennonite Brethren in Christ, and a similar policy
    was adopted.

29 Robertson, *Landmarks*, 500–3; UCA, Butchart, "Fragments of Church
    History"; UCA, Butchart, "A Jubilee Year"; Cox, ed., *The Campbell–Stone
    Movement in Ontario*.

30 See the excellent article by Draper, "A People's Religion."

31 Robertson, *Landmarks*, 505–7.

32 The census reported that Congregationals numbered 2,000 in 1881, rising
    to 3,700 in 1901. Their numbers dropped in the 1910s to 2,700 in 1921.

33 See *DCB*, vol. 13, "Joseph Wild."

34 Robertson, *Landmarks*, 494–5.

35 "Church Services Tomorrow," *Toronto Evening Telegram*, 2 December 1905.

36 TRL, Banfield Memorial Church, Diaries of Della Lehman Lageer, 1910.

37 Ibid., 30 August 1910. In the same entry, she described as "grand" the sermons of Pastor William Roffe of the Missionary Tabernacle. On 19 March 1918 she commented positively on a Prophetic conference she had attended at Knox Presbyterian at which Philpott spoke, adding that US Methodist preacher C.F. Wimberley denounced the lack of spirituality in contemporary churches, which had to resort to bazaars and ice cream socials to raise money. On 16 January 1921, she attended Annette Street Baptist, observing: "Great revival ... Prayer meeting until five in the morning."

38 TRL, Banfield Memorial Church, Good, "Here Are Some Happenings."

39 Ukrainians originated largely from the counties of Ternopil and Stanislaviv in eastern Galicia. Interview with John Barczek, 29 September 2000. Poles came from the counties of Sanok, Skole, and Drohobych in eastern Galicia. Some Jews came from Berezhany county, which is adjacent to Ternopil.

40 Zucchi, *Italians in Toronto*, ch. 5; Robertson, *Landmarks*, 594; see also www.stfrancis.ca.

41 *DCB*, vol. 15, "Eugene O'Keefe"; Shahrodi, "The Experience of Polish Catholics."

42 *Almanach Torontoiskoi Eparchii / Yearbook of the Eparchy of Toronto* (Toronto: 1964), 328–9.

43 Yaworsky-Sokolsky, "The Beginnings of Ukrainian Settlement in Toronto."

44 See Cook, *The Regenerators*, ch. 5.

45 Hebrew Men of England moved to 222 Simcoe Street next door to the Associated Hebrew Charities and down the street from the Talmud Torah. Tiffereth Israel Bikur Cholim Anshei Ostrovtze (Men of Ostrowiec) settled into 72 William (now St Patrick). Anshei Minsk and Anshei Kiev took over houses on streets where their synagogues currently stand. Finally, Chevra B'Nai Israel probably began on the second floor of a garage on Argyle Street.

46 Speisman, *The Jews of Toronto*, 174–5.

47 Righteous Scion is a reference to Menachem Mendel Schneersohn, grandson of Zalman Shneur and third spiritual leader of the Lubavitch movement. Nusach Ari refers to the prayer book used by the Lubavtich and compiled by Shneur.

48 "Toronto Jewish News," *Toronto Star*, 6 November 1917, 13; Kayfitz, "How Synagogues Named." Montreal Rabbi Zibbe Cohen presided over the proceedings.

49 "Jews Carried Out Many Ancient Rites," *Toronto Daily Star*, 19 September 1917, 9.

50 Interview with Sam Huizinga, 22 May 2005; Robertson, *Landmarks*, 523–6. The *Might's Directory* for 1901 lists Donald Munro as an evangelist.

51 The censuses of 1911 and 1921 listed a little over 1,000 Brethren in all of Toronto.

52 Lindström-Best, *Defiant Sisters*, 132–3.

53 PCCA, David Smith, "A Short History of Chinese Work in Toronto" (c. 1960).

54 Di Stasi, *Fifty Years of Italian Evangelism*; Pizzolante, "The Growth of Italian Protestant Churches."

55 Robertson, *Landmarks*, 84–6; *Eye Weekly*, 1 September 2003.

56 Robertson, *Landmarks*, 290–1.

57 McCurdy, ed., *Life and Work of D.J. Macdonnell*; Robertson, *Landmarks*, 280–3.

58 PCCA, *Diamond Jubilee 1890–1950*.

59 PCCA, Wychwood–Davenport, file 1976–4058, "A Short History of Wychwood Presbyterian Mission" (Toronto, 1902); "New Church in Wychwood," *Toronto Globe*, 4 July 1910, 9.

60 I am indebted to Dr Frank Peddy for providing me with the material on this congregation in his possession.

61 PCCA, "The Story of Dale Presbyterian Church"; CBA, C. Kent Duff, *Walmer Road Baptist: Seventy-Fifth Anniversary* (Toronto: 1963); Grant, *George Pidgeon*; Hayes, "Repairing the Walls," in Hayes, *By Grace Co-Workers*, 88; CBA, Program for the Fiftieth Jubilee; Di Stasi, *Fifty Years of Italian Evangelism*; CBA, "A Sixty Year Crusade."

62 Table 8.3 in McGowan, *The Waning of the Green*, 259. The table does not single out ethnic parishes.

63 "Church Services Sunday," *Toronto Daily Star*, 18 December 1915.

64 Ayer, *A Great Church in Action*, 49.

65 "Church Services Sunday," *Toronto Daily Star*, 10 April 1915.

66 "Church Services To-morrow," *Toronto Telegram*, 10 April 1915.

67 "Jews Pray for Allies' Triumph," *Toronto Daily Star*, 4 January 1916, 7.

68 "Great Jewish Host Prays for the Allies," *Globe*, 8 March 1915, 6.

69 "Pulpit Speaks Out in Righteous Wrath," *Globe*, 10 May 1915, 6.

70 Banfield Memorial Church, conference resolutions. Banfield is the current name of the original Bethel Mennonite chapel.

71 Shahrodi, "The Experience of Polish Catholics."

72 Anglican Archives (AA), Diocese of Toronto, Church of the Epiphany; www.theredeemer.ca/space; Ferres, *The First Fifty Years*; Jackson,

"Toronto's St Anne's Anglican Church"; [N.A.], *Open Doors and Open Windows*; TRL, Sands Collection, Baldwin Room, "The History of St Martin-in-the-Fields; BA, Parkdale Baptist, "The Memorial Window," n.d.; PCCA, *Fiftieth Anniversary: Dufferin Street Presbyterian Church*, 1958; Reeves, *Over 100 Years*; AA, R.B. Salter, *Church of the Messiah, 1891–1962*; Keeble, "St Mary Magdalene and the ROM."

73 Handera, "The Russian Orthodox Church in Toronto"; Kazymyra, "The Defiant Pavlo Krat."

74 CBA, Baptist Year Book 1923.

75 Yaworsky-Sokolsky, "The Beginnings of Ukrainian Settlement in Toronto."

76 "Toronto's Jewry Laments for Slaughters in Ukraine," *Globe*, 12 December 1919, 9.

77 Shahrodi, "The Experience of Polish Catholics."

3. Fulsome Fellowship

1 This is the full-orbed Christianity analyzed in Christie and Gauvreau, *A Full-Orbed Chrisitianity*.

2 In the late nineteenth century, for example, Redeemer Anglican had 400 students (average attendance was 270) and 34 teachers. See Robertson, *Landmarks*, 42. Erskine Presbyterian's Sunday school engaged 30 teachers for 300 children, with an average attendance of 200. The library had 600 books. See PCCA, Erskine Presbyterian, Annual Report, 1892. Olivet Baptist's 100 scholars were taught by 14 adults. See Robertson, *Landmarks*, 461. Parkdale Congregational had similar numbers.

3 Champion, *Methodist Churches of Toronto*, 243.

4 PCCA, *Diamond Jubilee 1890–1950*.

5 The expression is from Robertson, *Landmarks*, 10. Similarly, Evangel Hall, Knox Presbyterian's outreach program on Queen Street, ran a Sunday school with three hundred children. See PCCA, Helen Telford, *Evangel Hall Golden Anniversary*. Erskine, Parkdale, and West Presbyterian each had mission schools.

6 Fitch, *Knox Church of Toronto*, 112–13. Parkdale Presbyterian hired a full-time instructor for its spacious gymnasium. See PCCA, Cherry, *Sixty Years of Growing*.

7 Ayer, *A Great Church in Action*, 17, writes that the church had a bowling alley in the basement.

8 Kent, *Household of God*, 25; Fitch, *Knox Church of Toronto*, 113.

9 This was the case for College Street Presbyterian; see UCA, "The Amplifier," June 1925. Dufferin Street Baptist ran a youth camp at Kleinburg; see TRL, *Dufferin Street Baptist Church.*

10 See Noel, *Canada Dry*; Clarke, *Piety and Nationalism*, ch. 6.

11 TRL, *St Paul's Avenue Road Methodist/United Church*, 1.1.

12 Champion, *Methodist Churches of Toronto*, 254. The author identifies Farley as the president of the West End Christian Temperance Society. Robertson, *Landmarks*, 390–2, makes no mention of Farley.

13 Grant, *George Pidgeon*, 37; Cox, *The Campbell–Stone Movement*, 231; Robertson, *Landmarks*, 467.

14 See Tuesday Literary Club, Web.

15 Middleton, *The Municipality of Toronto*, vol. 3, 172.

16 "Church Services To-morrow," *Toronto Telegram*, 4 December 1915.

17 Clarke, *Piety and Nationalism*, 92.

18 Zucchi, *Italians in Toronto*, 169.

19 Shahrodi, "The Experience of Polish Catholics."

20 Robertson, *Landmarks*, 694.

21 TRL, local history files, Westmoreland Methodist church; Di Stasi, *Fifty Years of Italian Evangelism.*

22 Kent, *Household of God*, 25.

23 Clarke, *Piety and Nationalism*, ch. 4; McGowan, *The Waning of the Green*, 158–65.

24 Greig, *In the Fullness of Time*, 143; UCA, Gray, *Diamond Jubilee*, 9; Shirley Ayer, *A Great Church in Action*, 17.

25 At Erskine Presbyterian, the Society of Christian Endeavor had a flower committee responsible for beautifying the church. See PPCA, Erskine Annual Report, 1892.

26 See Smyth, "Christian Perfection"; and Cooper, "A Re-Examination."

27 Zucchi, *Italians in Toronto*, 123–4; Capurri, "Italian Catholic Immigrants in Toronto."

28 Coome, *A Memoir*; Cochrane, *Kensington*; Ruggle, "The Saints in the Land"; Hayes, ed., *By Grace Co-Workers*, 211.

29 Robertson, *Landmarks*, 100; Ferres, *The First Fifty Years.*

30 Sherk, *Keeping Faith.*

31 Grant, *The Church in the Canadian Era*, 58.

32 McCurdy, *Life and Work of D.J. Macdonnell*, 303, ch. 31. See also Fraser, *The Social Uplifters*; Allen, *The Social Passion.*

33 UCA, Gray, *Diamond Jubilee*, 17; UCA, "The Amplifier," June 1925, 6.

34 PCCA, Bryson, "Brief Historical Sketch."

35 Kent *Household of God*, 35 and 309–11.

36 Fitch, *Knox Church of Toronto*, 113.

37 PCCA, Cherry, *Sixty Years of Growing*, 16.

38 Hayes, "Repairing the Walls," in Hayes, ed., *By Grace Co-Workers*, 78–9.

39 Grant, *George Pidgeon*, 58; Gauvreau, "Baptist Religion."

40 Grant, *The Church in the Canadian Era*, 55–7.

41 "Church Services To-morrow," *Toronto Telegram*, 10 December 1910; "Church Services Sunday," *Toronto Daily Star*, 3 December 1910; Ayer, *A Great Church in Action*, 19.

42 "Church Directory," *Toronto Daily Star*, 6 April 1895; *DCB*, vol. 15, "Charles Samuel Eby."

43 "Church Services To-morrow," *Evening Telegram*, 2 April 1910; and see Brouwer, *New Women for God*.

44 "Church Services To-morrow," *Toronto Daily Star*, 16 December 1905.

45 "Church Services To-morrow," *Evening Telegram*, 24 December 1895.

46 "Church Services To-morrow," *Evening Telegram*, 2 April 1910.

47 "Church Services To-morrow," *Evening Telegram*, 18 December 1915.

48 PCCA, Erskine, Annual Report, 1892.

49 Robertson, *Landmarks,*, 488–90; CBA, Minute Book, West Toronto Baptist Church, 1886–91.

50 Fitch, *Knox Church of Toronto*, 113.

51 See www.bloorstreetunited.org; Grypma, *Healing Henan*, 1. According to the author, the church subscribed $1,200 per month for this work.

52 UCA, Gray, *Diamond Jubilee*, 9, 16.

53 TRL, *Jubilate Deo*.

54 UCA, Butchart, *The Disciples of Christ in Canada*, 258.

55 UCA, Toronto Chinese Mission, *Strangers Within Our Gates*; Plante, "Answering the Call for Reform."

56 Thompson and Blackstone, *A Century of Jewish Missons [sic]*, 278.

57 Some of the pastors who held two-year charges here served in the Guelph area: W.E. Beese and J.G. Domm were ministers in Morriston, while J.L. Merner later was pastor in Hespeler. See Marjorie Clark, "The Morriston Church," 1980, www.clarksoftomfad.ca/MorristonChurch.htm, as well as Puslinch Historical Society, Web.

58 Speisman, *The Jews of Toronto*, 133–4; Greig, *In the Fullness of Time*, 166, 174.

59 Di Stasi, *Fifty Years of Italian Evangelism*; Zucchi, *Italians in Toronto*, 123.

60 Yaworsky-Sokolsky, "The Beginnings of Ukrainian Settlement."

61 "Church Services Sunday," *Toronto Daily Star*, 10 December 1910.

62 Speisman, *The Jews of Toronto*, 199; TRL, *St Paul's Avenue Road*, 10–11; Arthur, *Toronto*, 198.

63 Champion, *Methodist Churches of Toronto*, 219–22.

64 [N.A.], *Open Doors and Open Windows*; *DCB*, vol. 13, "Joseph McClausland"; www.stfrancis.ca/ENG/history.htm.

65 See the Registry of Stained Glass Windows in Canada, www.yorku.ca/rsgc, produced by its director, Shirley Ann Brown of York University; Robertson, *Landmarks*, 323.

66 Jackson, "Toronto's St Anne's Anglican Church."

67 Arthur, *Toronto*, 189, 198; www.saintcecilia.ca/history.

68 Roberson, *Landmarks*,, 65; Kent, *Household of God*, 22.

69 TRL, local history files, Westmoreland Avenue Methodist; AA, *A Brief Historical Sketch of the Church of the Epiphany*.

70 PCCA, Erskine, Annual Report, 1892; "Seventh Day of Passover," *Toronto Daily Star*, 16 April 1906, 4. The cantor's name was Schorr.

71 "Sir Ernest Alexander Campbell MacMillan," *Canadian Encyclopedia*.

72 "William Reed," *Encyclopedia of Music in Canada* [hereafter *EMC*].

73 "Ada Kent," *EMC*. Kirby was also the owner of one of the largest building and contracting companies in Toronto. See Middleton, *The Municipality of Toronto*, vol. 3, 1923, 223.

74 "Dalton Baker," *EMC.*

75 "Jews Carried Out Many Ancient Rites," *Toronto Daily Star*, 19 September 1917. The cantor's name was Manovitch.

76 Robertson, *Landmarks*, 101–2.

77 "Church Services To-rorrow," *Evening Telegram*, 7 December 1895.

78 PCCA, session minutes, Dale Presbyterian, 27 December 1916.

79 "Gospel Music," *EMC*.

80 "Would Not Allow Choir to Sing," *Toronto Daily Star*," 7 December 1910, 3.

81 Speisman, *The Jews of Toronto*, 223. Disruptions occurred in synagogues, such as at Chevra Tehillim, when, just before prayers, a baker named Temperman publicly accused the owner of a boarding house, Abraham Charwinsky, of serving unkosher meat to his tenants, who then left in disgust. The matter was referred to the courts. See "Says That Baker Sought Revenge," *Toronto Daily Star*, 17 March 1908, 2.

82 Butler, "St Andrew's Presbyterian church"; Ruggle, "The Saints in the Land," 207; Ayer, *A Great Church in Action*, 119; Grant, *George Pidgeon*, 136.

83 See Robertson, *Landmarks*, 65–7, for a detailed description of the Sunday liturgy at St Matthias written in the mid-1880s and later brought up to date for publication in 1904; Kent, *Household of God*, 20–1. Reeves, "Over 100 Years," attributes the introduction of bells at St Thomas to John Charles Roper, future bishop of Ottawa.

84 Kent, *Household of God*, 36–8.

85 *Toronto Daily Star*, 18 March 1901.

86 Coome, *A Memoir*, 86.

87 Kent, *Household of God*, 25, 28.

88 See Miller, *Equal Rights*; Crunican, *Priests and Politicians*; Perin, *Rome in Canada*.

89 See PCCA, Bryson, "Brief Historical Sketch of Chalmers"; Butchart, *Disciples of Christ in Canada*, 518.

90 *Evening Telegram*, 1 and 22 April 1905 and 3, 10, and 17 December 1910. J.L. McCombe employed similar techniques in Victoria, British Columbia. See "Evangelistic Campaign," *Victoria Colonist*, 19 January 1907.

91 *Evening Telegram*, 7, 14, and 21 April 1900. On Crossley and Hunter, see Kee, *Revivalists*, ch. 1.

92 *Evening Telegram*, 7 December 1895 and 1 April 1900.

93 See Armstrong and Nelles, *The Revenge of the Methodist Bicycle Company*, ch. 5. Macdonnell's quote appeared in the *Mail*, 21 December 1891.

94 "Coronation Day in Toronto," *The Globe*, 11 August 1902; Kent, *Household of God*, 27; "Laid Stone in the Rain," *The Globe*, 14 May 1906, 12; "Jews Are Thankful," *Toronto Daily Star*, 14 May 1906, 7; "New Synagogue Opened," *The Globe*, 4 February 1907, 14. The guest rabbi was Herman Abramowitz.

95 *Toronto Daily Star*, 22 October 1894.

96 Church Advertisements, *The Globe*, 18 October 1899; "Pastors Talk of War," Church Advertisements, *The Globe*, 16 October 1899, 5; Church Advertisements, *Toronto Evening Telegram*, 3 December 1910.

97 *The Globe*, 5 August 1904, 10.

98 "Massacre of Russian Jews," *The Globe*, 10 November, 1904, 12; "The Oppressed Russian Jews" and "Russian Horrors Were Recounted," *The Globe*, 13 November 1905, 6, 12; "Jews Hold Memorial Service," *The Globe*, 6 December 1905, 4; "Men Sobbed, Women Wailed," *Toronto Daily Star*, 13 November 1905.

99 *The Globe*, "Besieged in Synagogue," 24 April 1908, 12.

100 "Hebrew Citizens for Robinette," *Toronto Daily Star*, 31 October 1904, 3; "The Jews for Robinette," *The Globe*, 31 October 1904, 8; "Shall Hebrews Have Man in the Council?," *Toronto Daily Star*, 22 October 1906. A prominent member of Trinity Methodist, Robinette attended the meetings called to protest the Kiev pogrom and persecutions in Romania. See "To Help Roumanian Jews," *The Globe*, 8 April 1907, 12.

101 Canadian Baptist Archives (CBA), Duff, *Walmer Road Baptist*; "Pastor Resigns Heresy Charged," *Toronto Daily Star*, 15 January 1906, 8. Might's Directories, *The Toronto City Directory, 1909*, dropped the term "Baptist,"

and Horsman was no longer its pastor in 1910. A church continued to exist at this site, on Markham Street just north of Bloor, until the 1960s.

102 "Over the Border," *The Globe,* 26 June 1899, 10; Bryson, "Brief Historical Sketch of Chalmers."

103 "Distinguished Rabbi May Come to Toronto," *The Globe,* 13 April 1914, 9; Speisman, *The Jews of Toronto,* 183–4.

104 "News of the City Seen at a Glance," *Toronto Daily Star,* 4 June 1914, 13. The following year, Joseph Gurowsky was named interim president of a new Jewish federation that would look after the educational and domestic affairs of Jews. "Three Million Jews Starving in Europe," *The Globe,* 9 August 1915, 7.

105 The literature on modernity is vast. See Taylor, "Two Theories of Modernity"; and Giddens, *Modernity and Self-Identity.* For discussions of it in the Canadian context, see among others Francis, "Modernity and Canadian Civilization"; Christie and Gauvreau, *A Full-Orbed Christianity;* Mackay, *The Quest for the Folk;* and Walden, *Becoming Modern in Toronto.*

106 Kee, *Revivalists,* 36.

107 Cumbo, "'Impediments to the Harvest.'"

4. Ecclesiastical Musical Chairs

1 Dominion Bureau of Statistics (DBS), *1961 Census of Canada,* vol. 1.1: *Population, Incorporated Cities, Towns and Villages* (Ottawa; Roger Duhamel, Queen's Printer, 1962), A-11; *Ninth Census of Canada 1951,* vol. 1: *Population* (Ottawa: Queen's Printer, 1953), 6–54.

2 Harris, *Unplanned Suburbs,* 23, 32–34.

3 DBS, *Ninth Census of Canada,* vol. 1, 35–9, 36–3.

4 Ibid., 42–9, 43–3.

5 DBS, *1961 Census of Canada,* vol. 1.1, 52–17, 53–1.

6 Ibid., 38–17, 39–5.

7 Ibid., 38–18, 39–5 by ethnicity; 45–18, 46–5 by religion.

8 Ibid., 38–18.

9 Ibid., 45–17.

10 DBS, *Ninth Census of Canada 1951,* vol. 1: *Population,* 42–9, 42–10, 43–3, 43–4.

11 DBS, *Census of Canada 1931,* vol. 4: *Population Cross-Classification* (Ottawa; J.O. Patenaude,1934), 912–13.

12 PCCA, "Historical Notes," Morningside-High Park Presbyterian Church; PCCA, *Wychwood Presbyterian Church;* PCCA, Nicol, "History of Wychwood Presbyterian Church."

13 "Church May be Sold for Use as a Synagogue," *The Globe*, 14 July 1920, 6, 8.

14 Robertson, *Landmarks*, 488–9 ; UCA, Western Congregational, interview with J.W. Pedley, 16 December 16, 1930. The building had been occupied by Christ Church Reformed Episcopal.

15 "Benjamin Brown," *Biographical Dictionary of Architects in Canada 1800–1950* [hereafter *BDAC*].

16 Ontario Vital Statistics Project, Ontario Marriage Registrations, 1925, City of Toronto, 6624–25.

17 Ibid., 1923, City of Toronto, pt 10, 007205/23. Sprachman served as best man at Kaplan's wedding.

18 Dubylko, ed., *Fiftieth Anniversary*, 338. .

19 UCA, *The Amplifier*, June 1925.

20 "Old Congregational Church is Threatened by Flames," *The Globe*, 2 April 1926, 18.

21 OJA, *Daily Hebrew Journal*, 24 February 1956.

22 These are *Rodfei Shalom Anshei Kiev* (Seekers of Peace Men of Kiev); First Narayever after the town of Naraiv, Berezhany County, Galicia, now in Ukraine, situated at 70 Huron and later at 189 Brunswick Avenue; the already mentioned First Moldovia on Augusta Avenue; *Shearith Israel Anshei Lida* (Remnant of Israel Men of Lida) after the town in Belarus, also on Augusta Avenue; *B'nai Israel Husyatiner Kloiz* after Husiatyn, a border town in Galicia; Anshei Minsk after the capital of Belarus; and *Adath Israel Anshei Romania. Shaarei Tzedec* (Gates of Righteousness) was also known as the Russian synagogue; *Shomrai Shabot* was also referred to as the Galician synagogue; and of course Beth Jacob was the Polish synagogue.

23 Zimmerman, "The Ladies of the Henry Street Shul," 12.

24 OJA, *Daily Hebrew Journal*, 10 April 1959.

25 "Kelmans Set to Celebrate Rav Zvi's 50th Yahrzeit," *Canadian Jewish News*, 27 November 1986, 31. Kelman was born in Vyshnivchyk in neighbouring Ternopil County.

26 Although this congregation used a Sephardic prayer book, it was not Sephardic.

27 "World Agudath Israel," and "Hapoel HaMizrachi," in Wikipedia; "Varieties of Orthodox Judaism," http://people.ucalgary.ca/~elsegal/index.html#.

28 OJA, Rabbi Nachman Shemen Papers, Finding Aid, MG6 CS1.

29 OJA, Publications 1930–91, *50th B'nai Israel/B'nai David 10th Congregation Jubilee* (Toronto: 1966).

30 "The New, United Shaarei Tefillah and Bais Yehuda Congregation," *Canadian Jewish News*, 21 September 1960, 5.

31 Buzzelli, "From Little Britain to Little Italy," 576, 580.

32 "Ask M.O.H. to Report on New Synagogue," *Toronto Daily Star*, 5 October 1920, 3; "Horse Stables Are Unpopular," *The Globe*, 2 November 1920, 17.

33 OJA, Speisman, "Shaarei Shomayim's First Fifty Years"; Warschauer, *The Story of Holy Blossom Temple* (Toronto; Holy Blossom, 1959); Olitzky, *The American Synagogue*, who claims (378) somewhat erroneously that Brothers of Jacob was founded in 1928 and that congregants built it.

34 "Wears Rabbi's Cap When he Preaches," *Globe*, 13 August 1923, 12.

35 BA, Home Mission Board, Minutes of the annual meeting, 1914.

36 Zeidman, *Good and Faithful Servant*; Davies and Nefsky, *How Silent Were the Churches*, 67–9.

37 Danys, "Lithuanian Parishes in Toronto"; Stankus-Saulitis, "Toronto Lithuanian," 26–28.

38 PCCA, *Acts and Proceedings of the General Assembly, Report for 1929* (1930).

39 Patrias, *Patriots and Proletarians*, 118–20; *50 Ev/Years*.

40 PCCA, *Acts and Proceedings of the General Assembly, Report for 1932* (1933); *Report for 1934* (1935).

41 PCCA., *Report for 1938* (1939).

42 PCCA., *Report for 1939* (1940); *Report for 1941* (1942); Dreisziger, *Struggle and Hope*, 152–4.

43 CBA, G. Balla, *A Brief History of the First Hungarian Baptist Church, 1929–1939*; "The First Hungarian Baptist Church: Toronto Baptist Church Extension Board Objective for 1943," 15 January 1943; Patrias, *Patriots and Proletarians*, 116.

44 Shuba, "I'm just Reminiscing"; Kirschbaum, *Slovaks in Canada*, 232–3.

45 *Might's Toronto Directory*, 1940–51. During the 1950s, Lutherans worshipped in the East End, but returned to the West End at the beginning of the next decade.

46 Schindler, *Aussaat und Ernte*, 3, 7, 22.

47 "George Ryerson," *DCB*, vol. 13.

48 Duquin, *They Called Her the Baroness*, ch. 11. The author does not explain how de Hueck, whose son was baptized at St Clair Catholic Church, could also be involved with a Russian Orthodox church.

49 Handera, "The Russian Orthodox Church in Toronto"; MHSO, interview with Stephen Cocherva-Curtis. The wife of Derwyn Owen, Anglican bishop of Toronto, opened the bazaar at Christ the Saviour Church in 1934; see *Toronto Telegram*, 31 October 1934. My thanks to Dr Benjamin Bryce for the information concerning the merger of the two Lutheran parishes.

50 According to *Might's Toronto Directory*, the Ukrainians worshipped at 335 Euclid and 322 Royce Avenue (now Dupont Street). Interview with

Ludmilla Kolesnichenko, First Ukrainian Pentecostal church, 24 August 2001.

51 Cumbo, "A Brief History"; Portelli, "Father Fortunato Mizzi's Contributions."

52 Zucchi, *Italians in Toronto*, ch. 5.

53 Pizzolante, "The Growth of Italian Protestant Churches"; Cumbo, "'Your Old Men Will Dream Dreams.'"

54 Ibid.; www.polishheritage.ca/news_detail.aspx?news_page_id=4&news _id=320.

55 Shahrodi, "The Experience of Polish Catholics," 151–2.

56 Yaworsky-Sokolsky, "The Beginnings of Ukrainian Settlement," 293.

57 Dubylko, *Fiftieth Anniversary*, 337; Gregorovich, "The Ukrainian Community in Toronto."

58 UCA, 83.050C, box 13, file 57, J.I. Mackay to Colin Young, 28 May 1928.

59 Interview with Michael Fesenko, two sessions, May 1998.

60 UCA, J.I. MacKay, "Report on Non-Anglo-Saxon Work," 1 October 1929.

61 UCA, MacKay and Smith, *One Lord One Door One People*.

62 UCA, 83–050C 26–404, file 21, George Dorey, "Memorandum re Visit to Church of All Nations, Toronto," 10 March 1944.

63 CBA, Baptist Yearbook, Home Mission Reports, 1927 and 1929.

64 Ibid., 1934.

65 Ibid., 1929.

66 Pentecostal Assemblies of Canada Archives (PACA), *Pentecostal Testimony*, May 1937, March 1938; see also Makela-Varvas, "Finnish Pentecostal Church of Toronto and the Impact It Had on the Finnish Immigrants," undergraduate paper in the author's possession.

67 CBA .Baptist Yearbook, Home Mission Reports, 1943; interview with Terry and Diane Borisenko, Slavic Evangelical Baptist church, 29 April 2001.

68 CBA .Baptist Yearbook, Home Mission Reports, letter to Archie (surname not indicated) from pastor Joseph Novak of the Czechoslovakian Baptist church, 8 January 1969; Manitoba Historical Society, memorable Manitobans, Frank Dojacek, www.mhs.mb.ca/docs/people/dojacek_f.shtml.

69 CBA, *Baptist Yearbook*, Home Mission Board Annual Report, 1936.

70 Ibid., Home Mission Board Annual Report, 1931.

71 PCCA, *Acts and Proceedings of the General Assembly*, 1934, report for 1933.

72 Ibid., report for 1942 (1943).

73 Patrias, *Patriots and Proletarians*, 181.

74 Martens, "The German Community of St Patrick's Parish," 99; Schindler, *Ausaat und ernte*, 3, 16–17, 20; Duquin, *They Called Her the Baroness*, ch. 17.

75 Ibid., chap. 17; Beck, "Contrasting Approaches." Beck illustrates the close and at times somewhat overbearing relationship between the Redemptorists and Sisters of Service, especially between key figures such as George Daly, director of the female order, and Catherine Donnelly, its foundress.

76 Zucchi, *Italians in Toronto*, 174–5; Pennacchio, "The Torrid Trinity"; Pennacchio, "Exporting Fascism to Canada," 56–7; Principe, *The Darkest Side of the Fascist Years*, 55.

77 Interview with Sam Huizinga, Brock Avenue Gospel Assembly, 22 May 2005.

78 CBA, Home Missions Board Minutes, 30 August 1939.

79 Smale, "For Whose Kingdom?," 148.

80 Cumbo, "A Brief History." At the Ukrainian Orthodox parish of St Wolodymyr, the youth organization SUMK formed a relief committee that sent four hundred parcels to Canadian troops stationed in England. See Dubylko, *Fiftieth Anniversary*, 355–7. Meanwhile, Ukrainian Presbyterians sent donations in kind and money to Ukrainians in war camps in Europe. See Fesenko interview.

81 CBA, Baptist Year Book, Home Mission Board Annual Reports, 1942 and 1944; see Keshen, *Saints, Sinners, and Soldiers*, Chapter 5.

82 Schindler, *Aussaat und Ernte*, 37–8, 43.

83 Sauro, "The Work of the Rev. Libero Sauro"; Di Stasi, *Fifty Years of Italian Evangelism*. Di Stasi makes no mention of Sauro's internment.

84 Schindler, *Aussaat und Ernte*, 38, 46.

85 UCA, MacKay and Smith, *One Lord*, 22–3; Dowe, "The Protestant Churches."

86 Watada, *Bukkyo Tozen*, 284.

87 McLellan, *Many Petals of the Lotus*, 51–4.

88 Reform Rabbi Ferdinand Isserman of Holy Blossom had already addressed the congregants of Carlton Street United, situated to the east of our area., in 1925. Davies and Nefsky, *How Silent Were the Churches*, 34; Slonim, *To Kill a Rabbi*, 145–9.

89 Ferres, "The First Fifty Years"; TRL, Runnymede United Church, W.T. Vance, "Resumé of the Early History of Runnymede United Church," 1960; CBA, "A Sixty Year Crusade for Christ in the Parkdale District of Toronto," *Canadian Baptist*, 1 September 1947; Anglican Archives, Diocese of Toronto, "A Brief Historical Sketch of Church of the Epiphany"; PCCA, Nicol, "A History of Wychwood Presbyterian Church."

90 Salter, *Church of the Messiah*; BA, "Seventy-Five Years of History."

91 OJA, *Golden Jubilee Book, 1902–1952, Adath Israel Congregation*; "A Brief Historical Sketch."

92 Wukasch, "Baltic Immigrants in Canada."

93 Dubylko, *Fiftieth Anniversary.*

94 Iacovetta, *Gatekeepers.*

95 Interview with Wiktor Holowacz 23 March 2001; interview with Myron Stasiyw, 29 September 2000.

96 Interview with William Dawidiuk, 11 October 2000.

97 Interview with Ludmilla Kolesnichenko 24 August 2001.

98 PACA, Brown, *Fifty Years of Pentecostal History*, 139–40.

99 "The Ultra-Orthodox Congregation Machzikei Torah," *Canadian Jewish News*, 21 September 1960, 5.

100 Handera, "The Russian Orthodox Church"; interview with Vladimir Malchenko, 21 April 2001.

101 www.polishheritage.ca.

102 CBA, "Church in Action: Ossington Avenue Baptist Church" 15 April 1961.

103 Kirschbaum, *Slovaks in Canada*, 256–7; "Bishop Michael Rusnak," www.byzcath.org.

104 Kaye, "Canadians of Byelorussian Origin"; Madelyn Ziniak, "Belarusans," in Magocsi, ed., *Encyclopedia of Canada's Peoples*. The first parish was affiliated with the Belarusian Autocephalous Orthodox Church; the second, to the Ukrainian Greek Orthodox Church in exile; both were headquartered in the United States.

105 Ausra, "Lithuanian Lutherans"; Wukasch, "Baltic Immigrants in Canada."

106 *50 Ev/Years*; Papp, "The Hungarian Community of Toronto."

107 UCA, 83.05C, box 26, file 411, George Dory, Memorandum re visit to Church of All Nations, 10 March 1944.

108 Ibid., report "Church of All Nations," 1967–8.

109 OJA, *Daily Hebrew Journal*, 7 January 1958; "Flying Rabbi Is February Good Citizen," *Toronto Star*, 25 March 1973, 5.

110 AO, Our Lady Help of Christians, Tone Zrnec Papers, MFN 109–1 and 2, microfilm, Report to the archdiocese of Toronto, 1961–62.

111 AO, H.A. Gleason Papers, MU 9771, MSR 7817, F 1405–75; Stermole and Gleason, "Residential Patterns of Ethnic Subgroups in Toronto"; "Priest Pioneered Heritage Language," *Toronto Star*, 24 May 2005, A12.

112 The congregation now calls itself Humbervale Park Baptist and is located in Etobicoke. See www.humbervalepark.org. The synagogue was at this site since 1934.

113 Schindler, *Aussaat und Ernte*, 53, 72; wedding and baptism statistics are found at the front of the book; Martens, "The German Community of St Patrick's Parish."

114 Iacovetta, *Such Hardworking People*, 130–41; "Priest Pioneered Heritage
    Language," *Toronto Star*, 26 July 2005; Paróquia de Santa Inês/Saint-
    Agnes Church, *O Seu Centenário 1903–2003 Our Centenary* (Toronto:
    2003), 8. Giuseppe Sbrocchi, a priest from Puglia, was visiting relatives
    in Toronto in 1959 when he was asked to serve the Italians of St Clare
    parish.
115 Sauro, "The Work of the Rev. Libero Sauro"; Di Stasi, *Fifty Years of Italian
    Evangelism.*
116 Pizzolante, "The Growth of Italian Protestant Churches."
117 See Maurutto, *Governing Charities.*

5. The Empire of Full-Orbed Religion

 1 Martens, "The German Community of St. Patrick's"; von Vulte, "The
   German Canadian Identity"; Schindler, *Aussaat und Ernte*, 90.
 2 "For Spies and Critics Father Asks Prayers," *Toronto Daily Star*, 6 March
   1922, 11. The reporter not only questioned the legality of reciting the Hail
   Marys, but pointed out that it was done at the end of mass at the foot
   of the altar, as if these circumstances proved its shadiness. The fact is,
   however, that in Catholic churches this is precisely when and where these
   prayers are said. The reporter was obviously more intent on displaying
   his prejudices than his knowledge of the liturgy.
 3 After the Second World War, incense still provoked negative reactions
   among Protestants. Members of the church of All Nations complained
   about the smell that lingered after the liturgy was performed by the
   newly established Russian Orthodox Parish of the Holy Trinity, which
   briefly rented the facilities. See Handera, "The Russian Orthodox Church
   in Toronto,"
 4 Kent, *Household of God*, 49–51, 60.
 5 Ibid., 49, 56, 55.
 6 Ayer, *A Great Church in Action*, 117–20.
 7 See, in *Encyclopedia of Music in Canada*, "Healey Willan," "Walter
   MacNutt," "Weldon Kilburn," "David Ouchterlony," and "Gerald Bales."
 8 Ayer, *A Great Church in Action*, 57–9, 80–83.
 9 See, in *Encyclopedia of Music in Canada*, "Sir Ernest MacMillan," "Albert
   Jordan," "Thomas Crawford," "Eileen Law," "Jeanne Pengelly," "Dorothy
   Allan Park," "Mario Bernardi," "Evelyn Gould," and "Esther Gahn."
10 PCCA, Morningside-High Park Presbyterian Church, file 1973–4145.
11 Greig, *In the Fullness of Time*, 134.
12 Speisman, *The Jews of Toronto*, 217–34.

13 Slonim, *To Kill a Rabbi*, 30.

14 "Does Not Believe Moses Mere Pen in God's Hands," *Toronto Daily Star*, 23 August 1937.

15 Slonim, *To Kill a Rabbi*, ch. 3. In this chapter the author presents the synagogue executive as closed-minded, mean-spirited, legalistic, and devious; in doing so he displays all of the impatience and intolerance a second-generation immigrant feels towards the previous generation. On Breslin, see Traub, ed., *History of the McCaul Street Synagogue.*

16 Slonim, *To Kill a Rabbi*, 169–71.

17 Ibid., 92.

18 Slonim gave the example of the *shamas* or sexton who, in order to ward off the evil eye, would count the members of the *minyan* as "not one," "not two," and so on. The author also mentioned that following *Yahrzeit* or the anniversary of the death of a loved one, family and *beth midrash* members would symbolically drink to life. What was left over was placed in a bottle containing a mixture of all leftovers, whether whisky, gin, or vodka. On days when there was no *Yahrzeit*, members freely partook from this bottle. Slonim, *To Kill a Rabbi*, 86–7.

19 Ibid., 130–2.

20 See Vecoli, "Cult and Occult"; Cumbo, "Salvation in Indifference."

21 OJA, Stephen Speisman, "Shaarei Shomayim's First Fifty Years."

22 Kent, *Household of God*, 50–51, 131–6; Greig, *In the Fullness of Time*, 52–3.

23 Salter, *Church of the Messiah.*

24 [N.A.], *Open Doors and Open Windows.*

25 http://homes.chass.utoronto.ca/~floyd/ACW125an.pdf, 21.

26 These figures were James MacGregor (1759–1830), Presbyterian scholar, composer, and preacher; William Case (1780–1855), Methodist circuit rider and superintendent of the Methodist Episcopal Church in Canada; James Evans (1801–1846), Methodist missionary to the First Nations; Henry Wilkes (1805–86), pastor of Zion Congregational in Montreal; Egerton Ryerson (1803–1882), Methodist circuit rider and superintendent of education, Canada West/Ontario; James Robertson (1839–1902), superintendent of missions in the West and Northwest; and the three leaders of the churches that joined the United Church in 1925, the Congregationalist William Gunn (1867–1930), the Presbyterian George Pidgeon (1872–1971), and the Methodist Samuel Chown (1853–1933).

27 The first of these windows depicted Presbyterian pastor James MacGregor delivering his first sermon in Pictou, Nova Scotia, in 1786. The next three, dedicated to home missions, featured Congregationalist Henry Wilkes actively engaged in the conversion of French Canadians;

George McDougall (1821–76), Methodist missionary in the Northwest; and Thomas Crosby (1840–1914), Methodist missionary on the Pacific Coast. The fifth window represented different aspects of world missions, while the sixth, focused on city missions, highlighted the Fred Victor mission. TRL, Baldwin Room, W.T. Vance, "Resumé of the Early History of Runnymede United Church" (1960); UCA, Foley, "The Stained Glass Windows."

28 Marchetto, *A Vision Shared*.

29 *Toronto Daily Star*, photograph and caption, 7 May 1927, 3; Archves of the Archdiocese of Toronto (AAT), Holy Rosary file. The article from *The Parishioner* (May 1965) incorrectly identifies the composer as Rheinberg.

30 See St Cecilia, Parish history, on the Web.

31 *Svoboda Ukrainian Daily*, 28 April 1962, reprinted from the *Toronto Telegram*, 9 April 1962.

32 Suhačev lived with his parents in a displaced persons camp near Hamburg, Germany, and studied at the city's Academy of Arts. In 1949, the family immigrated to Ethiopia, where Igor and his father Petr spent seven years decorating churches. They then moved to Canada. See www.russianhouse.ca.

33 MHSO, interview with Cocherva-Curtis; Dubylko, *Fiftieth Anniversary*, 340; Barida and Syrotynsky, *Ikonohrafiya Svyato-Mikolaivskoi Tserkvy*, 20–32, 57–8; Urbanc and Tourtel, *Slovenians in Canada*, 78–9, 160; ARCAT, Our Lady Help of Christians, Architectural Finding Aid (1982), Slovenian Album (1954); Maver, "Contemporary Diasporic Literature in Canada," 389–93; 50 *Ev/Years: Szent Erzsebet Egyharzkozseg*.

34 Levitt, Milstone and Tenenbaum, *Shuls*; Online Exhibitions, Ontario Jewish Archives; "Opening of New Synagogue Climax of Ten Years' Effort," *Toronto Daily Star*, 1 October 1948, 27.

35 Johan Tangelder, "Dr Oswald J. Smith: A Unique Church" (February 1969), in http://www.reformedreflections.ca/biography/dr-oswald -smith.pdf.

36 Church Advertisements *Toronto Daily Star* 11, 18, and 25 September 1926 and 1 December 1928.

37 Reid, "Toward a Fourfold Gospel." See also "At Alliance Tabernacle," *The Globe*, 19 September 1925, 12; and "24 Hours in Toronto," *Toronto Daily Star*, 21 June 1926, 3.

38 Templeton, *An Anecdotal Memoir*, 34.

39 Church Advertisements, *Toronto Daily Star*, 15 November 1924, 10; Pentecostal Assemblies of Canada Archives (PACA), David Kennedy and Jaye Torley, "Evangel Temple: its Past, Present and Future."

40 "Offers Explanation of Faith Healing," *Toronto Daily Star*, 4 October 1924, 3. Two days later the newspaper reported that 6,000 people had turned up at the arena to hear the testimonials of those who had been cured by Price.

41 Church Advertisements, *Toronto Daily Star*, 9 May 1925, 10.

42 PACA, *Pentecostal Testimony*, November 1925.

43 Ibid., October 1923, March and September 1925. It is unclear whether this congregation was the original Christian Workers one that had become "pentecostalised."

44 Ibid., February 1939.

45 Might, *City of Toronto Directories*, 1941. The congregation remained at 65 Ford until 1964, changing its name to West End Full Gospel Tabernacle.

46 See *DCB*, "Ralph C. Horner"; Whiteley, "Sailing for the Shore"; Might, *City of Toronto Directories*, 1922–61. Between 1929 and 1933 the Standard Church briefly took over the church situated at 54 Clinton from the Welsh Presbyterians.

47 E-mail from Heather Heibein, 28 February 2007. Heibein's parents and siblings had been actively involved at Bonar since childhood.

48 Ayer, *A Great Church in Action*, 76.

49 Dirks, "Reinventing Christian Masculinity."

50 Prang, "'The Girl God Would Have Had Me Be.'"

51 Grant, *George Pidgeon*, 58; Ayer, *A Great Church in Action*, 74–5.

52 [N.A.], *A Meeting Place Forever; 1875–2000 St. Helen's Parish*, 20; UCA, 83.050C, box 26, file 406, Home Missions Institution Survey 1943–44: Queen Street United Church, Visit of Member of the Commission, 9 February 1944.

53 Ayer, *A Great Church in Action*, 85; Grant, *George Pidgeon*, 139.

54 [N.A.], *The Reverend Ernest Hahn*, 8.

55 *Encyclopedia of Music in Canada*, "Gospel Music."

56 Schmidt, *Shabbes Goy*, 157–63; *Catholic Register*, 9 May 2008.

57 PCCA, Central/Avenue Road Presbyterian, session minutes, 24 March 1937 and 12 June 1940; CBA, C. Kent Duff, *Walmer Road Baptist: 75th Anniversary*.

58 For somewhat contrasting views of the Oxford Group, see Christie and Gauvreau, *A Full-Orbed Christianity*, 227–34; and Grant, *George Pidgeon*, 129–32. Pidgeon refuted criticisms made by W.B. Creighton, editor of the denomination's newspaper, *New Outlook*. He also wrote an open letter to the *Times* (London) in defence of the movement.

59 Ayer, *A Great Church in Action*, 97n44.

60 Jackson, "Toronto's St. Anne's Anglican Church," 28.

61 UCA, 83.050C, box 26, file 406, Home Missions Institution Survey, 1943–44: Queen Street United Church, Visit of Members of the Commission to Queen St Church, Toronto, 9 February 1944; Barker, *The Story of Memorial Institute*.

62 See Comacchio, *The Dominion of Youth*.

63 Ayer, *A Great Church in Action*, 76–7; UCA, 83.050C, box 26, file 406, Home Missions Institution Survey, 1943–44: Queen Street United Church.

64 Ibid., file 405, Home Mission Institution Survey, 1943–44: St Christopher House, Memo re St Christopher House, 17 March 1944.

65 Fitch, *Knox Church Toronto*, 71, 79, 108–9.

66 OJA, MG6 CS1-i, publications 1930–1991, *Dinner to Honour Rabbi Gedalia Felder*, September 26, 1989. Joseph Kelman was the author of Gedalia Felder's biographical sketch.

67 Ibid., MG3 A15, Bais Yahuda Congregation, Toronto, *Bulletin*, 3, 1 (January 1953); OJA, Speisman, "Shaarei Shomayim's First Fifty Years," 20–21.

68 Schmidt, *Shabbes Goy*, ch. 9; "Toronto Youth Gangs to Spring Up Again Pastor Fears, Asks Aid," *Toronto Star*, 26 April 1951, 25. The reporter emphasized how gang members affirmed their difference. Rejecting convention, the Beanery Boys refused to take off their hats at a dance organized in the church basement and insisted as well that the girls choose their dance partners. The article noted with a sense of relief that "before long" the boys willingly took off their hats. Ernest Howse, minister at Bloor Street United, made the assembly hall of his church available to the Christie Pitts gang for Saturday night dances. See "Our History," on the Bloor Street United website.

69 TRL, "St. Paul's Avenue Road Methodist/United Church"; Stott and Fallis, "25th Anniversary Reflections;," Douville, "The Uncomfortable Pew"; Henderson, *Making the Scene*, 65–72. Henderson's attempt to make a connection in these pages between greasers and ethnicity remains, however, unconvincing. The young men belonging to the Ramsden Park Gang appear to have been Protestant, for they initially turned to Crysdale for assistance and a number of them eventually joined his congregation.

70 The nomination was also supported by the Toronto Methodist Ministers Association. See Christie and Gauvreau, *A Full-Orbed Christianity*, 143–9.

71 "Father Minehan Hits Back," *Toronto Daily Star*, 23 June 1923, 8.

72 Smale, "For Whose Kingdom?," 170–1.

73 "He Got $40 and Horse for Six Months' Work," *Toronto Daily Star*, 7 March 1925, 3. The organizational meeting of the Federated Jewish Farmers took

place at Anshei Ostrovtze synagogue in the spring. See "Jewish Mass Meeting," *The Globe*, 23 May 1925.

74 Davies and Nefsky, *How Silent Were the Churches?*, 40.

75 "Striker is Arrested on Assault Charge," *Toronto Daily Star*, 28 June 1924, 3.

76 Greig, *In the Fullness of Time*, 157–60. See also Lettre pastorale collective de leurs excellences Nosseigneurs les archevêques et évêques de la province civile de Québec, *Le problème ouvrier en regard de la doctrine sociale de l'Église*.

77 "Toronto Youth Gangs," *Toronto Daily Star*, 26 April 1951, 25. See Patrias and Frager, "'This Is Our Country'"; Patrias, "Race, Discrimination."

78 In the *Toronto Daily Star*, see the following: "'Never a Communist' Rev. G. Domm Urges Fellowship for All," 16 February 1953, 5; "Pastor Says 'Good' Will Come of Split Over Church Rental," 10 February 1953, 21, 39; "Ban Four Groups Domm to Call Congregation," 17 March 1953, 1; "Bathurst Street Members Vote Confidence in Domm by 197 to 4," 31 March 1953, 1. See also Endicott, *James G. Endicott*, chs. 23 and 24. The petition against arms sales to Chiang Kai-shek was also signed by Lavell Smith, minister of the Church of All Nations. See Endicott, 246. The minister of Trinity United, Ernest Crossley Hunter, son of evangelist John D. Hunter, invited Endicott to his church after the latter's controversial statement of support for the Chinese Revolution. See www.trinitystpauls.ca/content/about-tsp.

79 Slonim, *To Kill a Rabbi*, 215, 208–16.

80 Schindler, *Aussaat und Ernte* 18–45; Shahrodi, "The Experience of Polish Catholics," 152; Gebhard, "Credit Unions in Ontario"; Kirschbaum, *Slovaks in Canada*, 234.

81 See Gerus, "Consolidating the Community."

82 MHSO, Russian–Canadian Papers, MFN 108, Mary Diachina Papers, Notice of the White Russian Red Cross Group, 24 July 1940; Dubylko, ed., *Fiftieth Anniversary of St. Vladimir's*, 355.

83 *Canadian Jewish News*, 24 October 1985. Price worked with the Canadian Jewish Congress, Senator Arthur Roebuck, and government officials on this question. On the internment of Jews, see Draper, "The 'Camp Boys.'"

84 Genizi, *The Holocaust*, 68.

85 UCA, Mackay and Smith, *One Lord*, 28. At the request of the World Council of Churches, the Church of All Nations sponsored thirty refugees, who were temporarily sheltered in a house purchased for that purpose in Parkdale. Christ the Saviour Russian Orthodox sponsored

thirty-two Russian-speaking families. MHSO, interview with Mary Diachina, May 1979.

86 Schindler, *Aussaat und Ernte*, 51–3.

87 For an excellent discussion of these policies, see Danys, *DP*, pt 2.

88 Wukasch, "Baltic Immigrants in Canada," 7–8.

89 MHSO, Rus-0337-DJA, interview with Mary Diachina; and Rus-0739-COQ, interview with Stephen Cocherva-Curtis, September 1977.

90 These included St Elizabeth of Hungary, Sts Cyril and Methodius Slovak Catholic, Nativity of the Mother of God Eastern-Rite Slovak Catholic, St Paul's Slovak Evangelical Lutheran, Holy Trinity Russian Orthodox, Redeemer Lithuanian Lutheran, and Grace Lutheran, as well as the Latvian and Estonian congregations nurtured at St John's Evangelical Lutheran.

91 "Charges Reds Burned Church, Dissuaded from Buying a Gun, Priest Says," *Globe and Mail*, 3 January 1963, 5.

92 See Wukasch, "Baltic Immigrants in Canada," 14–18; Obituary: Michael Rusnák, *Toronto Star*, 21 January 2003; Kirschbaum, *Slovaks in Canada*, 271; "The Ultra-Orthodox Congregation Mach Zikei Torah," *Canadian Jewish News*, 21 September 1960; "Toronto's Youngest Rabbi to be Installed Dec. 13," *Toronto Star*, 2 December 1953.

93 PCCA, Presbytery of East Toronto, First Hungarian, box 15, file A-20 XX, 26 November 1959.

94 Interview with Bishop Yurij Kalistchuk, 10 October 2000.

95 Stanger-Ross, *Staying Italian*, 62.

96 Urbanc and Tourtel, *Slovenians in Canada*, 147; Danys, *DP*, 297–8.

97 Martens, "The German Community," 100; Dubylko, *Fiftieth Anniversary of St. Vladimir's*, 363.

98 Martens, "The German Community," 99; *50 Ev/Years Szent Erzsebet*; MHSO, interview with Vladimir Malchenko, Rus 0734-MAL, October 1977; Dubylko, *Fiftieth Anniversary of St. Vladimir's*, 340–1, 349; Urbanc and Tourtel, *Slovenians in Canada*, 203; Wukasch, "Baltic Immigrants in Canada," 15–17; Danys, *DP*, 108.

99 The Afro Community church, founded in 1937 by Cecil Stewart, which later occupied Christ Church Protestant Episcopal on Shaw Street, had a credit union that later merged with the United Negro Credit Union. See Moore, *Don Moore*. The following are the chartered institutions and their dates of foundation: St Stanislaus Polish in 1945; So-Use (St Wolodymyr Ukrainian Orthodox), 1950; St Josaphat Ukrainian Catholic, 1950; Czechoslovak, 1953; Resurrection Lithuanian Catholic, 1953; St Elizabeth of Hungary, 1956; St Nicholas Ukrainian Catholic, 1957; Our Lady Help of

Christians Slovenian Catholic, 1957; St Casimir Polish Catholic, 1958; Our Lady Queen of Croatia, 1958. See Cujes, "The Involvement of Canadian Slavs."

100 Plawiuk, "Ukrainian Credit Unions in Canada." Plawiuk (147) overestimated the number of Ukrainians living in Toronto (he gave a figure of 65,000 as opposed to the 46,650 listed in the 1961 census for the metropolitan area) and therefore came up with a lower percentage. His membership figures were drawn from the reports of seven Ukrainian credit unions in Toronto. By contrast, Stanger-Ross shows that postwar Italian immigrants adopted a more personal, less institutional approach for acquiring a home, relying on the seller to provide them with a first mortgage. See his Stanger-Ross, *Staying Italian*, 52–3.

101 Plawiuk, "Ukrainian Credit Unions in Canada," 147; Cujes, Cujes, "The Involvement of Canadian Slavs,"159–60, cited figures from a survey he conducted in 1969 of twenty-two Slavic credit unions in Toronto.

102 Ibid., 161. See also Milos Greif, Czechoslovak (Toronto) Credit Union Ltd., "Kampelička History," in author's possession. Greif was the chair of the board of directors of the credit union.

103 The expression is from an advertisement for Parkdale Tabernacle on the religious page in the *Toronto Star*, 2 April 1910.

6. To Every Thing Turn! Turn! Turn!

1 Michael Ondaatje's *In the Skin of a Lion* strikingly portrays a play organized for and by left-wing Finns at Toronto's Harris Filtration Plant, whereas Steven Haywards' *The Secret Mitzvah of Lucio Burke* brings to life the baseball culture of interwar Toronto's Jewish and Italian youth with its local games and stars.

2 A case in point is the statement on social justice issued in 1983 by the Social Affairs Committee of the Canadian Catholic Conference of Bishops, which was publicly repudiated by Emmett Cardinal Carter, Archbishop of Toronto. See Higgins and Letson, *My Father's Business*, ch. 13.

3 See Gidney and Millar, "The Christian Recessional in Ontario's Public Schools"; Miedema, *For Canada's Sake*.

4 UCA, Centennial-Japanese United Church, n.d. (c. 1995).

5 See among others Bibby, *Restless Gods*; and Fay, *New Faces of Canadian Catholics*.

6 Émile Durkheim, *Les règles de la méthode sociologique*, 18, http://classiques .uqac.ca/classiques/Durkheim_emile/durkheim.html.

7 Stanger-Ross, *Staying Italian*, 13.

8 Ibid., 14–15. See Miranda, "Not Ashamed or Afraid," 265.

9 Statistics Canada, "Toronto City and CMA, Population, 1971–2006."

10 Bibby, *Unknown Gods*, 26.

11 City of Toronto, *Toronto Social Atlas*, Religious Affiliation by Census Tract, 2001, No Religious Affiliation, www1.toronto.ca.

12 Ibid., Judaism, Islam, Greek Orthodox, Eastern Orthodox, Orthodox Not Included Elsewhere, Buddhism, Hinduism.

13 See Kelley and Trebilcock, *The Marking of the Mosaic*, ch. 10; Dirks, *Controversy and Complexity*, chs. 6 and 7.

14 Berton, *The Comfortable Pew*, 1965.

15 For the Second Vatican Council, see Alberigo, *A Brief History of Vatican II*; and O'Malley, *What Happened at Vatican II?*.

16 Ramirez, *Italians in Canada*, 7; Carlos Teixeira, "Portuguese," in Magocsi, ed., *Encyclopedia of Canada's Peoples*, 1076; Chimbos, *The Canadian Odyssey*, 29–30; Nagata, "Adaption and Integration."

17 Li, "The Rise and Fall," 12–13.

18 Tran, Kaddatz, and Allard, "South Asians in Canada," 20–2.

19 Toronto Church of God (formerly St Barnabas Anglican) on Givens Street in 1998, and Assemblea de Deus Pentecostal (formerly African Methodist Episcopal) on Soho Street in 2000.

20 City of Toronto, *Toronto Social Atlas*, Toronto Neighbourhood Profiles, www1.toronto.ca.

21 Interview with John Barczek St. Josaphat Ukrainian Catholic Cathedral, 29 September 2000.

22 PCCA, David Smith, "A Short History of Chinese Work in Toronto," n.d. (c. 1960).

23 Interview with W.S. Tai, church elder, Chinese Gospel Church, 26 September 2000; Chinese Gospel Church, Calendar: 1963–1988.

24 Interview with George and Veronica, parishioners of St Andrew's Ukrainian Orthodox, 7 November 2011.

25 Interview with Poyu Fa Shih, head monk at Fu Sien Tong Temple, 30 July 2000, and with Gian Wong, a nun at Ching Kwok Temple, 31 July 2000.

26 Marchetto, "The Catholic Church and Italian Immigration," 109.

27 City of Toronto, *Toronto Social Atlas*, Toronto Neighbourhood Profiles.

28 Pizzolante, "The Growth of Italian Protestant Churches," 73.

29 "Breve Biografia di Michele Sauro, un uomo di Dio," in the author's possession; see Weston Road Church on the Web. "Our History: Weston Road Pentecostal Church."

30 Mónico, *Bodas de Prata*, 16; Marchetto, *A Vision Shared*, 18–19. Also, interviews with John Mendonça, pastor of St Sebastian, 5 February 2008; John Cabral, pastor of St Mary of the Angels, 29 January 2008; and Fernando Couto, pastor of St Helen, 12 July 2007.

31 St Agnes had 15,000 parishioners in 1983; ten years later that figure was cut in half. See Mónico, *Bodas de Prata*, 22. Baptismal, marriage, and first communion statistics show that the parish had reached its peak by 1980. The Mendonça and Cabral interviews confirm the decline of the Portuguese population.

32 City of Toronto, *Toronto Social Atlas*, Toronto Neighbourhood Profiles

33 Portuguese speakers shared facilities at Olivet Baptist and Dovercourt–Paul's Presbyterian (*igreja evangélica presbiteriana*), as well as the Kingdom Halls of the Jehovah's Witnesses at Christie Street and Yarmouth, and College Street at Dovercourt.

34 UCA 77.075L, box 18, file 2, "A Report of the Portuguese Mission for the year 1964," Vernon Kimball, 5 February 1965. *Deus é Amor* (God Is Love) is located at 1535 Dundas West; *Igreja Universal do Reino de Deus* (Universal Church of the Kingdom of God) used to be at 1305B Dundas West before moving to larger facilities on Dufferin Street just north of Eglinton; *Assembleias de Deus* (Assemblies of God) was for a time at 54 Moutray; and *Igreja evangélica Vida Nova* (New Life Evangelical Church) is at 2365 St Clair West. Another Pentecostal congregation shares space at High Park–Alhambra United.

35 Grafos, "The Greeks in Toronto," ch. 1.

36 See, in *Toronto Star*, "Cathedral Gutted in Early Morning Fire," 4 April 2000, B1; "Congregation Will Stay Put," 5 April 2000, 2; and "Cathedral Reborn from Ashes," 27 June 2002, B4.

37 This was confirmed in interviews conducted with Chinese, Korean, and Filipino informants.

38 CBA, Russian Ukrainian Evangelical Baptist Church, Rev. Bondarenko to D.A. Burns, 13 April 1964; D.A. Burns to Bondarenko, 14 August 1964. Meanwhile, Polish Baptists, most of whom were postwar immigrants, left the old Royce Gospel Hall they had occupied since 1920 and moved into the former West Toronto Free Methodist, a couple of blocks away. Meanwhile, Full Gospel Polish Evangelical, a Pentecostal congregation comprised of an older immigrant cohort who worshipped in English with the occasional Polish hymn, shared Howard Park Pentecostal with the Italians. See CBA, First Polish Baptist Church, Program for the Opening of the Church at Dundas, 18 October 1962; and Radecki with Heydenkorn, *A Member of a Distinguished Family*, 156–7.

39 AAT, Our Lady Queen of Croatia Parish, Branko Mihic, president of Canadian-Yugoslav Cultural Association Bratstvo I Jedinstvo, to James Cardinal McGuigan, 7 April 1961.

40 AAT, Kamber to Thomas Fulton, 2 January 1963. See also "Charges Reds Burned Church, Dissuaded from Buying a Gun, Priest Says," *Globe and Mail*, 3 January 1963, 5. To the chancellor of the archdiocese, he confided: "They, very probably, or directly (or indirectly by provoking revenge) caused the fire in this church." Regarding their mental condition, he added: "Some few need psychiatrist, and some were (and some still are) in Mental Institutions. If your parish priest yielded a bit, he could every day be surrounded with mentally and emotionally disturbed people and transform the Rectory in Mental hospital, with the time left for nothing else." Ibid., Kamber to Chancery Office, 28 June 1963.

41 Hockenos, *Homeland Calling*, 38–41.

42 He was accused, among other things, of having had a liaison with Radmila Milentijević, then in her twenties, the daughter of a prominent Chetnik exile, on whom the bishop apparently showered extravagant gifts. After completing her doctorate at Columbia University, she became a history professor and dean at the City College of the City University of New York and, later, Minister of Information in the government of Slobodan Milošević. See Hockenos, *Homeland Calling*, 109–24.

43 The schism resulted in a court case launched in Illinois by Bishop Dionisije that went all the way to the US Supreme Court, which in 1976 dismissed the bishop's claims, invoking the constitutional principle of separation of church and state. See "Serbian Eastern Orthodox Diocese vs Milivoijevich." A reconciliation between the two branches of Serbian Orthodoxy was achieved in 1992. Škorić and Tomashevich, *Serbs in Ontario*.

44 The building was situated on Mackay Street near St Clair and Dufferin. A Pentecostal group briefly rented a commercial space on Harbord Street and Shaw in the early 1980s before moving to North York.

45 Interview with Pastor Meyer, 28 November 2000.

46 "The Sephardim Are Now Here," *Canadian Jewish News*, 15 March 1968, 3; http://www.petahtikva.ca/history. In 1958, Gedalia Felder, rabbi of Shomrai Shabot, offered the synagogue's banquet hall to Michael Nesry, whose father had been chief rabbi of the Tangier Bet Din (Religious Tribunal) for community worship.

47 "Leader of Sephardim," 19 June 1970, 2 and 1 January 1971. Edery had created the Torah Fund for Sephardic children to permit these youngsters to attend Jewish day schools. The initiative prompted various responses

from other Sephardic leaders ranging "from praise to unprintable criticism."

48 "Lack of Communication Among Sephardim," *Canadian Jewish News*, 7 April 1971, 1, 7.

49 "Toronto Synagogues," *Canadian Jewish News*, 19 February 1971, 2.

50 www.churchintoronto.org/history.htm

51 www.tjc.org

52 AAT, C.K. Cheung, "History of the Chinese Catholic Centre"; CBA, "Toronto Chinese Baptist Church, Thirtieth Anniversary Booklet, 1967–1997."

53 CBA, Grace Chinese Baptist church. Church officials declined to be interviewed for this project.

54 Interview with David Ko, 20 October 1998. The garage had earlier served a Pentecostal congregation called Full Gospel Tabernacle.

55 Interview with Steven Lee, 22 February 2001, and with Brad, 26 July 2000; "New Taoist Temple Rare and Unique in North America," *Toronto Star*, 1 September 2007, A15.

56 Interview with Jane Lai, 12 May 2001.

57 Interview with May Lui, 2 June 2001, and Tai Sau Sofu, 24 July 2000, of Hong Fa temple; interview with Mr Lam of Chuen Te Buddhist Society; "Statement of Activities," 31 January 1995, for registration as a charity under the Income Tax Act.

58 They are Fung Leun Tong Sit and Seto Society and the Canadian Chinese Buddhist Ming Yuet Society, the latter combining Pure Land and Tiantai traditions.

59 City of Toronto, *Toronto Social Atlas*, 2001 Census, Visible Minorities, Chinese.

60 Rosemary Sadlier, "The BME: Memories of My Church," *Toronto Star*, 24 April 1998, A26; interview with Desmond Ottley of St Matthew United, 3 June 2003. St Mark and the Epiphany is the result of the merger of two Parkdale parishes that now worship together at St Mark's. St Matthew's was created when two United Church congregations, St Clair and St Columba, were merged at the St Clair church site.

61 St Barnabas Anglican became the Toronto Church of God. A white congregation of the same denomination existed from 1938 to 1950 at Lansdowne Avenue and Davenport. Perth Avenue United became an Adventist church; Dufferin Street Presbyterian turned into Hope Centre Full Gospel. Finally, Glad Tidings Tabernacle changed into Cornerstone Baptist tabernacle.

62 Mount Zion Apostolic church of Jesus Christ, comprised largely of Jamaicans, bought the historic one on Fisher Street; see Mount Zion

Apostolic website for its history. When this congregation moved to Mississauga, the Fisher Street hall was passed on to a First Seventh-Day Baptist group, also of Caribbean origin. Two other Gospel Halls, Salem on Rosemount Avenue and Bracondale on Arlington Avenue, became respectively Bibleway Pentecostal Church of God Apostolic and Faith Believers Gospel Apostolic. Jamaicans, mostly from Clarendon Parish, established the Church of God of Prophecy, which, after meeting in various halls and commercial buildings, finally found permanent quarters at Calvary Assembly. By that time the congregation included Trinidadians, Guyanese, and Bermudans.

63 Three congregations with equally elaborate names belong to the Canadian Apostolic Ministries. They are First Born Apostolic (known today as Praise Sanctuary Church of the First Born [Apostolic]), Zion Apostolic Church of Jesus Christ, and Shiloh Apostolic Church of Jesus Christ.

64 See Iacovetta, *Such Hardworking People*, chapter 7.

65 St Germain of Melchisedec briefly occupied a synagogue on Euclid Avenue.

66 Henry, *The Caribbean Diaspora in Toronto*; "Mother Del Tends 'Wild' Flock," *Toronto Star*, 19 July 1997, L14.

67 "Church's Joyful Noise a Headache Next Door," *Toronto Star*, 17 July 2001, A1, B2.

68 City of Toronto, *Toronto Social Atlas*, 2001 Census, Visible Minorities: Black.

69 Interview with Richard Drews, pastor of St John's Evangelical Lutheran, 28 September 2000.

70 Anglican Archives, Diocese of Toronto "Ethiopian Gain Leaves Anglicans at a Loss," 20 February 1997.

71 City of Toronto, *Toronto Social Atlas*, 2001 Census, Visible Minority – South Asian.

72 "Bogus Charity Receipts Issued," *Sunday Star*, 24 February 2002, A-1, A-10.

73 Since 1998 the Shri Satya Narayan *mandir* has been in the building previously occupied by the College Street Church of God at 1871 Davenport Road at Symington.

74 Interview with Richard Drews, 28 September 2000.

75 See Jami Mosque on the Web.

76 Anita Beltran Chen, "Filipinos," in Magocsi, ed., *Encyclopedia of Canada's Peoples*.

77 City of Toronto, *Toronto Social Atlas*, 2001 Census, Visible Minority – Filipino.

78 Nagata, "The Role of Christian Churches," 41–60.

79 www.hallelujahfellowshipbaptistchurch.org/history.html; CBA, Filipino Baptist Church at Parkdale, Minister's Annual Report, January 1981; and Deacon's Report, October–December 1984. Nagata maintains that Toronto's Filipino Baptist congregations were controlled by rival groups of extended kin and that ministers who were themselves members of these clans competed with one another for influence and control. A Filipino Christian and Missionary Alliance congregation met at Wychwood–Davenport Presbyterian.

80 Nagata, "The Role of Christian Churches." Vietnamese congregations share facilities at Olivet Baptist and the Jehovah's Witnesses Kingdom Hall on Dundas West north of Bloor.

81 McLellan, *Many Petals of the Lotus*, 109–11.

82 CBA, Department of Canadian Missions, *Baptist Yearbook*, 1980, 1981.

83 Hispanics were present at the Kingdom Halls of the Jehovah's Witnesses at College and Dovercourt and at Dundas West just east of Roncesvalles. With Afro-Caribbeans they shared the Church of God of Prophecy on Dundas West and Restitution Bethesta Tabernacle Pentecostal on Hallam near Dovercourt. Spanish services were available at these two Portuguese-language places of worship: Deus è Amor, and World Mission Centre on Dufferin at Dupont.

84 City of Toronto, *Toronto Social Atlas*, 2001 Census, Visible Minority – Latin American.

85 Kim, "How Koreans Came to Call Toronto Home"; interview with Hyungshik Lee, Nagwan Presbyterian, 18 March 2006.

86 Apart from Bloor Street United, these were Victoria-Royce United, High Park United, Runnymede Road United, Christie Street Baptist, High Park Baptist, Farmer Memorial Baptist, West Toronto Baptist, and Ossington Avenue Pentecostal. The congregation at Ossington Avenue Baptist (Convention) later joined High Park Baptist (Fellowship).

87 Kim, "How Koreans Came to Call Toronto Home."

88 Ibid.; Lee and Weingartner, *The Wanderer*.

89 Interview with D.J. Kim, 26 May 2006. The church at first gathered at College Street United. Today it is located at 23 Fasken Drive in Etobicoke.

90 Interview with Pastor Kim of Newgate Presbyterian, 16 May 2006. Since 2003 the church has been located at 240 The Westway in Etobicoke; the one on Indian Road has since been demolished.

91 See interviews by Inkee Kim, Livingstone Presbyterian, 23 November 2006; Hyungshik Lee, Nagwon Presbyterian, 18 March 2007; and Pastor Kim, Toronto Newgate Presbyterian, 16 May 2006/

92 Interview with D.J. Kim, Central Toronto Presbyterian, 28 May 2006;
   interview with Young Lee and Sam Ho, Galilee Presbyterian, 27 January
   2007.
93 Interview with Young-ha Cho and Sarah Yoon, Alpha Korean United,
   17 June 2006.
94 City of Toronto, *Toronto Social Atlas*, 2001 Census, Visible Minority – Korean.
95 Franco Famularo, *A History of the Unification Church in Canada, 1965–1991*,
   http://www.tparents.org/Library/Unification/Books/UcCan/UcCan-2
   -5c.htm
96 "Seeking Meaning Within," *Toronto Star*, 12 May 2002, F6–7.
97 Interview with Ian Henderson, 13 September 2000.
98 Interview with Donald Eckler, 20 July 2000.
99 Interview with Choje Namse, 30 July 2000.
100 Interview with Sandra Monteath, 5 August 2000.
101 Interview with Tenzin Kalsang, 26 July 2000.
102 CBA, Dufferin Street Baptist; Hazeh Parent, "The Establishment of Baptist
    Work among Spanish Immigrants in Toronto," n.d..
103 Grieg, *In the Fullness of Time*, 174,
104 Brown, "The History of the Keele St. Church of Christ," 244, 248.
105 CBA, Home Mission Board Annual Report 1962, *Baptist Yearbook*.
106 CBA, Dufferin Street Baptist, Report of the Spanish Ministry at Dufferin
    Street Baptist Church, n.d.; Report to the Department of Canadian Missions
    on the Spanish Ministry at Dufferin Street Baptist Church, 21 September
    1981; letter from D. Quinton, Dufferin Street Baptist, to A.E. Coe, secretary,
    Department of Canadian missions, 22 October 1981.
107 CBA, Quays Community Church, Department of Canadian Missions/
    Division of Shared Missions, *Baptist Yearbook*, 1986, 1987, 1991, 1994.
108 The storefront had two congregations, the first called Good News
    Pentecostal and the second Ethiopian Living Water. The latter became the
    Eritrean Full Gospel Church with Mussie Teklay as pastor.
109 See the Lighthouse on the Web.
110 See in this regard Fay, *New Faces of Canadian Catholics*, Introduction.

7. Fellowship in the Time of the Shopping Centre

1 Stott and Fallis, "25th Anniversary Reflections"; UCA, Smith, *I Wish I
  Were a Fish*; "Lives Lived: Murray MacInnes," *Globe and Mail*, 22 March
  1999.
2 Lindsay, "Canadians Attend." By 2005, only one in five Canadians
  claimed to go weekly, and one in three declared that they never attended.

3 A Spiritan missionary to Africa, Lefebvre became bishop and then archbishop of Dakar (1947–62). From 1962 to 1968 he was the head of his order.

4 Interview with John Cabral, 29 January 2008.

5 In the late 1990s the fresco above the apse in St Anthony's Church was lovingly restored to its former splendour by artists Calos Nunes and Gordon MacDonald. See Marchetto, *A Vision Shared*. At St Cecilia, paintings on the back wall of the apse and the western and eastern walls, as well as the ceiling, were painted over. See St Cecilia Parish on the Web.

6 Greig, *In the Fullness of Time*, 181–2.

7 http://www.ocp.org/artists/61546

8 Douville, "The Uncomfortable Pew," 349–52.

9 Schindler, *Aussaat und Ernte*, 150, 153.

10 Iacovetta, *Such Hardworking People*, 135–6.

11 Douville, "The Uncomfortable Pew," 347.

12 Greig, *In the Fullness of Time*, 184–90.

13 www.trinitystpauls.ca/content/our-history, Trinity United Church and St. Paul's Avenue Road United Church, 1887–1997, "TSP at 100 – Our Preoccupations in 1987," section on Inclusive Language.

14 Kent, *Household of God*, 214, 85.

15 K. Schindler, *Im Dienst des Volkes*, 83–4.

16 Templeton, *An Anecdotal Memoir*, 55, http://www.templetons.com/charles/memoir/evang-graham.html.

17 Interview with Pastor Meyer, 28 November 2000.

18 Interview with L. Kolesnichenko, 24 August 2001. Enrico Cumbo noted similar behaviour among Italians in the first part of the twentieth century. They were religiously experimental, sometimes attending Pentecostal places of worship, sometimes Catholic ones. See Cumbo, "As the Twig Is Bent," chs. 5 and 6.

19 Interview with John Cabral, 29 January 2008.

20 "Tongues Catholic Style," *Toronto Daily Star*, 6 May 1967, 15.

21 Church Advertisements, *Toronto Daily Star*, 2 April 1966, 16.

22 "Jury Wants All Cults Probed," *Toronto Daily Star*, 4 October 1967, 1–2. See also Hayes, *By Grace Co-Workers*, 120.

23 "Devil Cult Priest Needs Psychiatrist, Church Says," *Toronto Daily Star*, 30 May 1968, 1, 4.

24 "'Devil Cult' Canon Goes Back to Work," *Toronto Daily Star*, 30 January 1969, 1.

25 James Hanrahan, "The Nature and History," 317.

26 See Fay, *New Faces of Canadian Catholics*. Ch. 4 highlights the importance of the charismatic movement to the individual Filipinos featured.

27 Hanrahan, "The Nature and History," 319.

28 McLellan, *Many Petals of the Lotus*, 46, 54–8.

29 "Imaginative Hard-Driving Churchmen Aid Immigrants," *Toronto Star*, 11 December 1971, 89; BA, "Changes in Immigration Procedures," Department of Canadian Missions Minute Book, 1967.

30 Schindler, *Aussaat und Ernte*.

31 Interviews with Wiktor Holowacz, 23 March 2001, and Bishop Yuri Kalistchuk, 10 October 2000.

32 "Doris Way, 88: 20 Years at the Pulpit," *Toronto Star*, 7 April 2006. After being served by the Ways for sixty-five years, the congregation survived only a few years longer, becoming a Buddhist temple in 2006.

33 Kent, *Household of God*, 92–4, 348–9.

34 Korinek, "No Women Need Apply."

35 PCCA, Wychwood-Davenport, file 1976–4058, James Nicol, "History of Wychwood Presbyterian Church."

36 Interview with Pastor Meyer, 28 November 2000.

37 Interview with Sam Huizinga, 22 May 2005.

38 In *Canadian Jewish News*, see interview with Stuart Schoenfeld, March 2000; "Downtown Community Expands Services," 18 January 1979, 7, and 29 July 1982, 6; "Congregants Return to Downtown Shul," 7 October 1982, 16; and "Expanding Role for Women Sparks Controversy," 5 January 1984, 5.

39 "Bishop Served Ukrainian Catholics," *Globe and Mail*, 9 August 2003, F10.

40 "Gay Pastor Called 'to Lead People to Freedom,'" *Toronto Star*, 17 December 2000, 1.

41 "Give Us This Gay," *Now Magazine*, 7–14 September 2000.

42 Greig, *In the Fullness of Time*, 193.

43 Stanger-Ross, *Staying Italian*, 77–81; Borges, "United and Not Without Agency," 50–3.

44 The circumstances surrounding this decision remain obscure and can only be clarified through access to the archives of the eparchy, the archdiocese, and the Vatican.

45 It followed Benedict XVI's *motu proprio* of 2007 titled *Summorum Pontificum*, which relaxed the rules governing its celebration.

46 Dubylko, *Fiftieth Anniversary of St. Vladimir's*, 341.

47 MHSO, interview with Vladimir Malchenko, Rus0734-MAL, October 1977; interview with V. Malchenko, 10 April 2001.

48 Interview with Vladimir Malchenko, 10 April 2001; see the website Synod in Resistance to which Holy Michael the Archangel is affiliated and www.orthodoxyinfo.org for St Nektarios.

49 www.theredeemer.ca/Page/History.html. The chapel was restored to its former purpose as a transept in 2010.

50 "Lives Lived: William McElcheran," *Globe and Mail*, 26 February 1999.

51 See Sarah Hall Studio on the Web.

52 "Yougoslav-Born Brothers Keep Alive Art of Carving Wood," *Globe and Mail*, 1 January 1971, 10.

53 He was identified as N. [*sic*] Suchachev in Kirschbaum, *Slovaks in Canada*, 256.

54 On Vanin, see Pugliese, "Beautifying the City." In *Toronto – a City in Between* (Toronto; Anik Press, 2009), a pretentious work. Anna Manolkin claims that it was Sukhacheva who installed the mosaic. See her *Toronto – a City in Between*, 109.

55 "Artist Used Wife, Self as Models," *Globe and Mail*, 12 December 1968, W5; see also http://www.holyprotection.ca/index.php/en/about-us/church-history.

56 Dubylko, *Fiftieth Anniversary of St Vladimir's*, 343.

57 "Designed to Nudge People 'Close to God,'" *Toronto Star*, 23 March 1985, L12. See as well St Francis of Assisi Parish on the Web.

58 My thanks to Professor Olga Pugliese of the Italian Studies Department at the University of Toronto for sharing this information with me.

59 Gyatso, *Understanding the Chinese Buddhist Temple*.

60 http://www.riwoche.com/tara.html

61 No author indicated, *A Century of Praise: Dovercourt Baptist Church: 100th Anniversary, 1879–1979* (Toronto: 1979).

62 "Church Shelters Scrutinized," *Toronto Star*, 4 January 2005, C3; *Catholic Register*, 23 April 2012.

63 Interview with John Simeon, 12 February 2001, and with Yvette Duhamel-Moore, 9 March 2001.

64 The deterioration of Parkdale is attributed to the construction beginning in 1955 of the Gardiner Expressway, which killed local businesses and severed the community from its waterfront, which had provided myriad leisure activities in the past. Large Victorian homes were transformed into rooming houses, and high-rise apartments proliferated in the 1960s.

65 BA, Parkdale Baptist Church, Department of Canadian Missions, *Baptist Yearbook*, 1985, 1986; "Gerri's World," www.christianity.ca/church/outreach/2004/02.001.html.

66 www.capuchinoutreach.org; "One Million Served, but No Reason to Celebrate," *Toronto Star*, 19 November 2010.

67 "Community Leader Also Man of Faith," *Toronto Star*, 14 June 2004, B5. The words are from Edward Ling, a church elder, who led the fundraising drive to build the new church.

68 PCCA, Chinese Presbyterian, R.J. Con, "A Critical Report on the Various Centres of Chinese Work from March to November 1963."

69 BA, Toronto Chinese Baptist Church, "The Twenty-First Anniversary of the Toronto Baptist Church: The English Ministry," included pieces by Ken Wong, "Reflections 1987–88"; Danny Yu, "Youth Work or Youthful Work"; and Timothy Cheung, "Thoughts on Christian Serving."

70 Interview with W.S. Tai, church elder, 26 September 2000.

71 PCCA, Chinese Presbyterian, David Chan to A.L. Milloy, secondary school superintendent, Toronto Board of Education, 18 October 1968; See Mon Sheong Foundation on the Web.

72 AAT, Our Lady of Mount Carmel, Louis Tchang, "Social Service Report 1970 to mid-1971"; anonymous, "A History of Canada's Chinese Catholic Church." Tchang was pastor of the parish in the early 1970s.

73 Schindler, *Im Dienst des Volkes*, 83–4; and *Aussaat und Ernte*, 163–73.

74 Danys, "Lithuanian Parishes in Toronto."

75 "Immigrant Faith and Culture," *Globe and Mail*, 23 November 1968, 28; www.saintjosaphat.com, Історія парохії Катедри Св. Свщм. Йосафата; interview with John Barczek, 29 September 2000. Cardinal Slipyj died in exile in Rome in 1984; his remains were transferred to St George Cathedral in Lviv only in 1992. Cardinal Lubachivsky returned to Lviv in 1991, where he died nine years later.

76 Interview with Bishop Yurij (Kalistchuk), 10 October 2000.

77 MHSO, interview with Vladimir Malchenko, Rus0734-MAL, October 1977; interview with V. Malchenko, 10 April 2001; Handera, "The Russian Orthodox Church in Toronto." Full communion was restored in 2007 between the Russian Orthodox Church and the Russian Orthodox Church Outside Russia after the schism caused by the October Revolution.

78 Marchetto, "The Catholic Church and Italian Immigration," 110.

79 Patrias, *Patriots and Proletarians*, introduction.

80 Harney, "The Commerce of Migration."

81 Interview with John Mendonça, 5 February 2008; interview with John Cabral, 29 January 2008.

82 Interview with Richard Drews, 28 September 2000.

83 Kim, "How Koreans Came"; interview with Young-ha Cho and Sarah Yoon, 17 June 2006.

84 Interview with Seok Jae Kim, Full Gospel Young Sung Church,
17 November 2006.

85 Interviews with Mr Lam, Chue Te Buddhist Society; May Lui, Hong Fa
temple, 2 June 2001; Gian Wong, Ching Kwok temple, 31 July 2000;

86 Interviews with May Lui and Tai Sau Sofu, Hong Fa Temple, 2 June 2001
and 24 July 2000; Gian Wong, Ching Kwok Temple, 31 July 2000; Poyu Fa
Shih, Fu Sien Temple, 30 July 2000; Jane Lai, Ming Sing Tao Tak Temple,
12 May 2001; Brad, Fung Loy Kok Institute of Taoism, 26 July 2000; and
Chan Bon, Amida Temple, 20 July 2000.

87 An article in the *Toronto Star* put the number of worshippers at 500. See
"Radical Sikh Temples Continue to Issue Phony Charitable Receipts,"
24 February 2002, A10.

88 Interviews with Ganesh Persaud, Gayatri Mandir, 19 October 2008; and
Ksiracova Cooper, ISCKON Temple, 9 October 2008.

89 "City of Cultures, City of Faith," *Toronto Star*, 24 January 2004, B4–5.

90 See "Toronto Priest Backs Same-Sex Marriage," *Toronto Star*, 5 February
2004, A1; and El Farouk Khaki, "For the Love of Allah: Gay Muslims'
Pride Prayer," posted on Muslimunion.ca. See also "Progressive Muslims
Launch Gay-Friendly, Women-Led Mosques in an Attempt to Reform
American Islam," *Huffington Post*, 29 March 2012. The article mentions two
such mosques in Canada, the first in Toronto and the second in Ottawa.

Bibliography

Primary Sources

Archival Sources

Anglican Archives, Diocese of Toronto, Anglican Church of Canada (AA)

"A Brief Historical Sketch of the Church of the Epiphany."
"Ethiopian Gain Leaves Anglicans at a Loss," 20 February 1997.
R.B. Salter, "Church of the Messiah, 1891–1962."

Archives of the Archdiocese of Toronto (AAT)

C.K. Cheug, "History of the Chinese Catholic Centre."
Robert Chow, "An Oriental Twilight," *Globe Magazine*, 4 April 1970.
"A History of Canada's Chinese Catholic Church."
Louis Tchang, "Social Service Report 1970 to mid 1971."

Archives of Ontario (AO)

Peter Markes papers, MU 9772, MSR 4868, F 1405-75.
Otmar Mauser papers, MU 9771, MSR 6299 and 6548, F 1405–25.
H.A. Gleason papers, MU 9771, MSR 7817, F 1405-75.
Tone Zrnec papers, MFN 109–1 and 2.

Baldwin Room, Toronto Reference Library (TRL)

"Addresses Presented on the Thirty-Fifth Anniversary Runnymede United
  Church, 1960."
"Brief History of Earlscourt United Church, 1905–1950."
"Carman Memorial United Church, 50th Anniversary, 1912–1962."

C. Kent Duff, *Seventy-Five Years in Walmer Road, 1884–1964*.
Dufferin Street Baptist Church, Toronto, "Sixty Years of Witness, 1906–1966."
F.J. Telford, *High Park–Alhambra United Church* (1970).
History of the First Baptist Church (1959).
"*Jubilate Deo*: A Record of the Good Hand of God Upon High Park Baptist
   Church during Fifty years of Sunshine and Shadow, 1908–1958."
"Ossington Avenue Baptist Church: Serving the Community for 75 Years,
   1886–1961."
St Paul's Avenue Road Methodist/United Church. Toronto: the Project, 1993.
Sands Collection, "The History of St Martin-in-the-Fields."
W.T. Vance, "Resumé of the Early History of Runnymede United Church" (1960).
Westmoreland United Church.

Banfield Memorial Church, 89 Centre Avenue, Willowdale,

Diaries of Della Lehman Lageer, 1910–11, 1918–24.
C.H. Good, "Here Are Some Happenings during My 50 Years of Ministry."

Canadian Baptist Archives (CBA)

"Beverley's Battle for a Building," *Canadian Baptist*, 15 April 192?.
College Street Baptist, *A Short History of the Church*.
"History of Olivet Baptist Church, 1889–1937," *Canadian Baptist*, 16 September
   1937.
Program for the Fiftieth Jubilee Celebrations of College Street Baptist.
"Seventy-Five Years of History of the Ossington Avenue Baptist Church,
   1886–1961."
"A Sixty Year Crusade for Christ in the Parkdale District of Toronto," *Canadian
   Baptist*, 1 September 1947.

Community of Christ, 1443 Bathurst Avenue

Meeting of the executive committee, Home Missions Board, 14 December 1914.
Norma Oliver, "History of the Toronto Branch," 2 pp.
"History of the Reorganized Church of Jesus Christ of Latter day Saints in
   Toronto," September 1984, 2 pp.

Multicultural History Society of Ontario (MHSO)

Interview with Stephen Cocherva-Curtis, Rus 0739-COQ, September 1977.
Interview with Mary Diachina, Rus 0337-DJA, May 1977.
Interview with Vladimir Malchenko, Rus 0734-MAL, October 1977.

***Ontario Jewish Archives* (OJA)**

Howard Markus, "A History of Beth Jacob V'Anshe Drildz."
Stephen Speisman, "Shaarei Shomayim's First Fifty Years."

***Pentecostal Assemblies of Canada Archives* (PACA)**

Victor G. Brown, *Fifty Years of Pentecostal History, 1933–1983*.
David Kennedy and Jaye Torley, "Evangel Temple: its Past, Present, and Future."
Pentecostal Testimony, 1920–39.

***Presbyterian Church in Canada Archives* (PCCA)**

G.G. Bryson, "Brief Historical Sketch of Chalmers Presbyterian Church"
     (1927).
Leeta McCully Cherry, *Sixty Years of Growing: Parkdale Presbyterian Church:
     Diamond Jubilee 1879–1939* (Toronto, 1939).
"A Critical Report of the Various Centres of Chinese Work from March 1963
     to November 1963."
Diamond Jubilee 1890–1950: Dovercourt Road Presbyterian Church, Toronto.
     Toronto, 1950.
Erskine Annual Report 1892.
Evangel Hall Non-Profit Housing Corporation, "Official Opening and Service
     of Dedication" (1991).
Fiftieth Anniversary: Dufferin Street Presbyterian Church (1958).
*Historical Notes on the Founding and Development of Davenport Road Presbyterian
     Church* (1964).
"Historical Notes," Morningside–High Park Presbyterian Church, session
     minutes, file 1988–4004.
Historical Sketch of St Paul's Presbyterian Church, prepared for the Twenty-Fifth
     Anniversary (1914).
L.P. Kan, "Glimpses of Our Chinese Mission."
[N.A.], "What the YMCI Can Do for the Chinese."
Fay McTavish, "Report of the Chinese Presbyterian Mission, 1946."
James Nicol, "History of Wychwood Presbyterian Church," n.d.
David Smith, "A Short History of the Chinese Work in Toronto" (c. 1960).
"A Short History of Wychwood Presbyterian Mission" (Toronto, 1902)
"The Story of Dale Presbyterian Church," in *Dale Anniversary Cook Book*, Dale
     Presbyterian Church, Toronto, c. 1926, file 1989-4064.
Helen Telford, *Evangel Hall Golden Anniversary 1913–1963*, n.d.
Wychwood Presbyterian Church, Twenty-Fifth Anniversary, 1925–1950.

United Church Archives (UCA)

"The Amplifier," monthly of the Men's Association of College St Presbyterian, ed. J.C. Torrance, June 1925.

Reuben Butchart, "Fragments of Church History," *Christian Messenger*, February 1918.

– "Jubilee Year for Toronto Churches," *Canadian Disciple*, February 1932.

George Dorey, "Memorandum re Visit to Church of All Nations, Toronto," 10 March 1944.

Roy S. Foley, "The Stained Glass Windows in Runnymede United Church: Story and Interpretation," Toronto, 1969.

R.A. Gray, ed., *Diamond Jubilee: College Street United*, 1934.

J.I. MacKay and Lavell Smith, *One Lord One Door One People: The Church of All Nations, Toronto*, 1963.

Outreach: Eye Witness Accounts of the Wider Work of the Church, Board of Information, United Church of Canada, 1962.

Toronto Chinese Mission, *Strangers within Our Gates*. Toronto: Armac Press, 1906.

Western Congregational, interview with J.W. Pedley, 16 December 16, 1930.

Oral Interviews

John Barczek, St Josaphat's Ukrainian Catholic Cathedral, 29 September 2000.

Chan Bon, resident monk, Amida Buddhist temple, 20 July 2000.

Terry and Diane Borisenko, Slavic Evangelical Baptist Church, 29 April 2001.

Brad, Fung Loy Kok Institute of Taoism, 1376 Bathurst Street, 26 July 2000.

John Cabral, pastor, Our Lady of the Angels Portuguese Catholic Church, 29 January 2008.

Young-ha Cho and Sarah Yoon, Alpha Korean United Church, 17 June 2006.

Choje Namse, Karma Sonam Dargye Ling Buddhist Temple, 30 July 2000.

C. Ksiracora Cooper, Iskcon Temple, 8 October 2008.

Fernando Couto, pastor, St Helen's Portuguese Catholic Church, 12 July 2007.

William Dawidiuk, Ukrainian Baptist Church, 11 October 2000.

Richard Drews, pastor, St John's Evangelical Lutheran Church, 28 September 2000.

Yvette Duhamel-Moore, International Christian Centre, 9 March 2001.

Donald Eckler, Toronto Shambala Centre, 20 July 2000.

Michael Fesenko, Ukrainian Presbyterian minister, two interviews, May 1998.

Ian Henderson, Toronto Zen Centre, 13 September 2000.

Wiktor Holowacz, St Nicholas Ukrainian Catholic Church, 23 March 2001.

Sam Huizinga, Brock Avenue Gospel Assembly, 22 May 2005.

Bishop Yurij Kalistchuk, St Vladimir Ukrainian Orthodox Cathedral, 10 October 2000.

Tenzin Kalsang, Tengye Tibetan Buddhist Temple, 26 July 2000.

Kim, Toronto Newgate Korean Presbyterian Church, 16 May 2006.

D.J. Kim, Toronto Central Presbyterian Church, 28 May 2006.

Inkee Kim, Livingstone Presbyterian Church, 23 November 2006.

Seok Jae King, Full Gospel Young Sung Korean Church, 17 November 2006.

David Ko, pastor, Living Water Assembly, 20 October 1998.

Ludmilla Kolesnichenko, First Ukrainian Pentecostal Church, 24 August 2001.

Jane Lai, Ming Sing Tao-Tak Taoist Temple, 29 July 2000 and 12 May 2001.

Lam, director and vice-president, Chuen Te Buddhist Society.

Hyungshik Lee, Nagwon Korean Presbyterian Church, 18 March 2007.

Nolan Lee, pastor, Toronto Chinese Baptist church, 16 May 2001.

Steven Lee, Fung Loy Kok Institute of Taoism, 22 February 2001.

Young Lee and Sam Ho, Galilee Korean Presbyterian Church, 27 January 2007.

Evan Lowig, priest, Christ the Saviour Russian Orthodox Cathedral, 23 October 2000.

May Lui, Hong Fa Buddhist Temple, 2 June 2001.

Igor Makuchev, Slavic Evangelical Pentecostal Church, 12 July 2001.

Vladimir Malchenko, priest, Holy Trinity Russian Orthodox Church, 10 April 2001.

John Mendonça, St Sebastian's Portuguese Catholic church, 5 February 2008.

Reverend Meyer, pastor, Deutsche Evangelische Gemeinde, 28 November 2000.

Kee Mim, Livingstone Korean Presbyterian Church, 23 November 2006.

Sandra Monteath, Gaden Choling Buddhist Temple, 5 August 2000.

Desmond Ottley, St Matthew's United Church, 3 June 2003.

Ganesh Persaud, Gayatri Mandir Hindu Temple, 19 October 2008.

Mrs Ram, Gandhi Bhawan Hindu Temple, 18 October 2008.

Poyu Fa Shih, head monk, Fu Sien Tong Buddhist Temple, 30 July 2000.

Stuart Schoenfeld, president, First Narayever Synagogue, March 2000.

John Simeon, International Christian Centre, 12 February 2001.

Tai Sau Sofu, Hong Fa Buddhist Temple, 24 July 2000.

Myron Stasiyw, Holy Protection Ukrainian Catholic Church, 29 September 2000.

W.S. Tai, church elder, Chinese Gospel Church, 26 September 2000.

Gian Wong/Jian Hong See, Ching Kwok Taoist Temple, 31 July 2000.

Po Yu, monk, Fu Sien Tong Buddhist Temple, 12 May 2001.

Internet Sources

Bloor Street United Church – History.

The Church in Toronto.

Church of the Messiah.
Church of the Redeemer, www.theredeemer.ca
Ontario Heritage Trust, www.heritagetrust.on.ca/PlacesOfWorship/Public/
  Inventory
Arthur Zimmerman, "The Ladies of the Henry Street shul," *Ivansk Project
  e-Newsletter*, 17 (March–April 2006). The Ivansk Project.

Reference Works

Architectural Index for Ontario. www.archindont.torontopubliclibrary.ca
Biographical Dictionary of Architects in Canada. http://dictionaryofarchitectsincanada
  .org/architects
City of Niagara Falls, New York. *Architectural Overview.* http://www.buffaloah
  .com/surveys/nf/4.pdf
Jewish Community Directory Update, 1 November 1995.
Gilles Potvin and Helmutt Kallmann, eds., *Encyclopedia of Music in Canada.*

Secondary Sources

1875–2000 St Helen's Parish 12th Anniversary. Toronto; Basilian Press, 2000. 36 p.
*50 Ev/Years: Szent Erzsebet Egyharzkozseg / St Elizabeth of Hungary Church,
  Toronto.* Toronto: 1978.
Alberigo, Giuseppe. *A Brief History of Vatican II.* Maryknoll: Orbis Books, 2006.
Allen, Richard. *The Social Passion: Religion and Social Reform in Canada, 1914–1928.*
  Toronto: University of Toronto Press, 1990.
Almanach Torontoiskoi Eparchii / Yearbook of the Eparchy of Toronto (Toronto:
  1964)
*A Meeting Place Forever: A Brief History of the Davenport–Perth United Church and
  its Surrounding Neighbourhood.*
Archevêques et Évêques de la province civile de Québec, *Le problème ouvrier en
  regard de la doctrine sociale de l'Église.* Montréal: Éditions Bellarmin, 1950.
Armstrong, Christopher, and Vivien Nelles. *The Revenge of the Methodist Bicycle
  Company: Sunday Streetcars and Municipal Reform in Toronto, 1888–1897.*
  Toronto: Peter Martin, 1977.
Arthur, Eric Ross. *Toronto: No Mean City*, 3rd ed. Toronto: University of
  Toronto Press, 1986.
Ausra, Valdas. "Lithuanian Lutherans in North America." *Lituanus: Lithuanian
  Quarterly Journal of Arts and Sciences* 41, no. 2 (Summer 1995).
Ayer, Shirley. *A Great Church in Action: A History of Timothy Eaton Memorial
  Church, Toronto, Canada, 1909–1977.* Toronto: Plum Hollow Books, 1978.

Barida, Michael, and Ivan Syrotynsky. *Ikonohrafiya Svyato-Mykolaivskoi Tserkvy / The Iconography of St Nicholas Church*. Toronto: St Nicholas Ukrainian Catholic Parish, 1977.

Barker, Alfred J. *The Story of Memorial Institute, Toronto*. Toronto: c. 1980.

Bartlett, John Russell. *Genealogy of that Branch of the Russell Family which comprised the Descendants of John Russell of Woburn, Massachusetts, 1640–1878*. Providence: 1879.

Beck, Jeanne. "Contrasting Approaches to Catholic Social Action during the Depression: Henry Somerville the Educator and Catherine de Hueck the Social Activist." In *Catholics at the "Gathering Place*," ed. Mark McGowan and Brian Clarke, 213–31. Toronto: Canadian Catholic Historical Association, 1993.

Berton, Pierre. *The Comfortable Pew: A Critical Look at Christianity and the Religious Establishment in the New Age*. Toronto: McClelland and Stewart, 1965.

Bibby, Reginald. *Restless Gods: The Renaissance of Religion in Canada*. Toronto: Novalis, 2004.

– *Unknown Gods: The Ongoing Story of Religion in Canada*. Toronto: Stoddart, 1993.

Blake, S.H. "The Protestant Episcopal Divinity School, Wycliffe College, Toronto." In John George Hodgins, *Establishment of Schools and Colleges in Ontario, 1792–1910*, vol. 3. Toronto: L.K. Cameron, 1910.

Bland, Salem. *James Henderson D.D.* Toronto: McClelland and Stewart, 1926.

Block, Tina. "'Boy Meets Girl': Constructing Heterosexuality in Two Victoria Churches, 1945–60." *Journal of the Canadian Historical Association*, 1999.

Blumhofer, Edith. "'Canada's Gift to the Sawdust Trail': The Canadian Face of Aimee Semple McPherson." In *Aspects of the Canadian Evangelical Experience*, ed. George Rawlyk 387–402 Montreal and Kingston: McGill–Queen's University Press, 1997.

Borges, Christian. "United and Not without Agency: Misinterpretations and Misrepresentations of the Azorean Community in Toronto, 1953–1967," Major Research Paper in History, York University, 2002.

Brouwer, Ruth Compton. *New Women for God: Canadian Presbyterian Women and India Missions, 1876–1914*. Toronto; University of Toronto Press, 1990.

Brown, Mary Ann. "The History of the Keele St. Church of Christ, Toronto." in *The Campbell-Stone Movement in Ontario: Christian Church (Disciples of Christ), Churches of Christ, Independent Christian Churches/Churches of Christ*, ed. Claude Cox. Lewiston: Edwin Mellen Press, 1995.

Butchart, Reuben. *The Disciples of Christ in Canada Since 1830:Ttheir Origins, Faith, and Practice, Their Striving for Christian Unity through a Single Christian*

Fellowship, and Their Integration with American and Other Churches in a World Brotherhood. Toronto: Canadian Headquarters Publication, 1949.

Butler, Janine. "St Andrew's Presbyterian Church, Toronto's Cathedral of Presbyterianism." *Ontario History* 83, no. 3 (September 1991): 169–92

Buzzelli, Michael. "From Little Britain to Little Italy: An Urban Ethnic Landscape Study of Toronto." *Journal of Historical Georgraphy*, 27, no. 4 (2001): 573–87.

Canada. *Census of Canada 1851–2: Personal Census*, vol. 1. Québec; John Lovell, 1853.

– *Census of Canada 1870–1*. Ottawa: I.B. Taylor, 1873.

– *Census of Canada 1880–1*, I. Ottawa: Maclean, Roger & Co., 1882.

– *Fifth Census of Canada 1911*, vol. 2. Ottawa; C.H. Parmalee, 1912.

– *Sixth Census of Canada 1921*, vol. 1: *Population*. Ottawa; F.A. Arcand, 1924.

Canadian Council of Christians and Jews, Ontario Region. *Multireligious Expressions: A Directory of Christian Religious Organizations in Toronto with an Ethnic Expression*. Toronto: n.d., [1977].

Capurri, Valentina. "Italian Catholic Immigrants in Toronto at the Beginning of the Twentieth Century: A Case of Religious Citizenship." MA thesis (Geography), York University, 2003.

Careless, J.M.S. *Toronto to 1918: An Illustrated History*. Toronto; James Lorimer, 1983.

Carlson, Enrico. "'Impediments to the Harvest': The Limitations of Methodist Proselytization of Toronto's Italian Immigrants, 1905–1925." In *Catholics at the "Gathering Place*," ed. Mark McGowan and Brian Clarke, 155–76 . Toronto: Canadian Catholic Historical Association, 1993.

Carr, Angela. *Toronto Architect Edmund Burke*. Montreal and Kingston: McGill–Queen's University Press, 1995.

Champion, Thomas E. *The Methodist Churches of Toronto: A History of the Methodist Denomination and Its Churches in York and Toronto*. Toronto: G.M. Rose & Sons, 1899.

Chimbos, Peter *The Canadian Odyssey: The Greek Experience in Canada*. Toronto; McClelland and Stewart, 1980.

Christie, Nancy, and Michael Gauvreau. *A Full-Orbed Chrisitianity: The Protestant Churches and Social Welfare in Canada, 1900–1940*. Montreal-Kingston; McGill-Queens Press, 1996.

Clarke, Brian. *Piety and Nationalism: Lay Voluntary Associations and the Creation of an Irish Catholic Community in Toronto, 1850–1895*. Montreal and Kingston: McGill–Queen's University Press, 1993.

Cochrane, Jean. *Kensington*. Erin: Boston Mills Press, 2000).

Comacchio, Cynthia. *The Dominion of Youth: Adolescence and the Making of a Modern Canada, 1920–1950*. Waterloo: Wilfrid Laurier University Press, 2006.

Cook, Ramsay. *The Regenerators: Social Criticism in Late Victorian English Canada*. Toronto: University of Toronto Press, 1985.

Coome, Hannah Grier. *A Memoir of the Life and Work of Hannah Grier Coome*. London: Oxford University Press, 1933.

Cooper, Barbara. "A Re-Examination of the Early Years of the Institute of the Blessed Virgin Mary (Loretto Sisters), in Toronto." In *Catholics at the "Gathering Place,"* ed. Mark McGowan and Brian Clarke, 89–104. Toronto: Canadian Catholic Historical Association, 1993.

Cox, Claude, ed. *The Campbell–Stone Movement in Ontario* . Lewiston: Edwin Mellen Press, 1995.

Crunican, Paul. *Priests and Politicians: Manitoba Schools and the Elections of 1896*. Toronto: University of Toronto Press, 1968.

Cujes, Rudolf. "The Involvement of Canadian Slavs in the Co-operative Movement in Canada." In *Slavs in Canada*, vol. 3, ed. Cornelius Jaenen. Toronto: Inter-University Committee on Canadian Slavs 1970.

Cumbo, Richard S. "As the Twig Is Bent, the Tree's Inclined: Growing Up Italian in Toronto, 1905–1940," PhD diss. (History), University of Toronto, 1996.

– "A Brief History of the Maltese Community of Toronto." *Polyphony* 6, no. 1, special issue: "Toronto's People" (Spring-Summer 1984): 101–3.

– "Salvation in Indifference: Gendered Expressions of Italian-Canadian Catholicism, 1900–1940." In *Households of Faith: Family, Gender, and Community in Canada 1760–1969*, ed. Nancy Christie. Montreal and Kingston: McGill-Queen's University Press, 2002.

– "'Your Old Men Will Dream Dreams': The Italian Pentecostal Experience in Canada, 1912–1945." *Journal of American Ethnic Studies* 19, no. 3 (Spring 2000): 35–81

Curtis, Heather. *Faith in the Great Physician: Suffering and Divine Healing in America Culture*. Montreal and Kingston: McGill–Queen's University Press, 2007.

Danys, Milda. *DP: Lithuanian Immigration to Canada after the Second World War*, pt. 2. Toronto: MHSO, 1986.

– "Lithuanian Parishes in Toronto." *Polyphony* (Spring–Summer 1984): 104–9

Davies, Alan, and Marilyn Nefsky. *How Silent Were the Churches: Canadian Protestantism and the Jewish Plight during the Nazi Era*. Waterloo: Wilfrid Laurier University Press, 1997.

DCB (Dictionary of Canadian Biography). 16 vols. Toronto: University of Toronto Press, 1959–.

Delville, J.-P., and Marko Jacov, eds. *La Papauté contemporaine. Hommage au chanoine Roger Aubert*, Louvain-la-Neuve – Rome, 2009. Bibliothèque de la Revue d'histoire ecclésiastique, 90 – Collectanea Archivi Vaticani, 64.

de Mattei, Roberto. *Pius IX*. Translated by John Laughland. Gloucester;
    Gracewing, 2004.

Dendy, William. *Lost Toronto: Images of the City's Past*. Toronto: McClelland and
    Stewart, 1993.

Dirks, Gerald. *Controversy and Complexity: Canadian Immigration Policy during
    the 1980s*. Montreal and Kingston: McGill–Queen's University Press, 1995.

Dirks, Patricia. "Reinventing Christian Masculinity and Fatherhood: The
    Canadian Protestant Experience, 1900–1920." In *Households of Faith: Family,
    Gender, and Community in Canada, 1760–1969*, ed. Nancy Christie. Montreal
    and Kingston: McGill–Queen's University Press, 2001.

Di Stasi, Michael. *50 Years of Italian Evangelism: The Story of St Paul's Italian
    United Church Toronto*. Toronto: 1955.

Donaldson, Gordon. *The Scottish Reformation*, rev. ed. London; Cambridge
    University Press, 1972.

Dowe, David. "The Protestant Churches and the Resettlement of Japanese
    Canadians in Urban Ontario, 1942–1955." *Canadian Ethnic Studies* 39, nos.
    1–2 (2007): 51–77.

Draper, Kenneth. "A People's Religion: P.W. Philpott and the Hamilton Christian
    Workers Church." *Histoire sociale / Social History* 36, no. 71 (2003): 99–1201

Draper, Paula. "The 'Camp Boys': Interned Refugees from Nazism." In
    Enemies Within: Italian and Other Internees in Canada and Abroad, ed. Franca
    Iacovetta, Roberto Perin and Angelo Principe. Toronto: University of
    Toronto Press, 2000.

Douville, Bruce. "The Uncomfortable Pew: Christianity, the New Left and
    the Hip Counterculture in Toronto, 1965–1975," PhD diss. (History), York
    University, 2011.

Dreisziger, N.F., et al. *Struggle and Hope: The Hungarian-Canadian Experience*.
    Ottawa: Department of Supplies and Services Canada, 1982.

Dubylko, Ivan, ed. *Fiftieth Anniversary of St Vladimir's Ukrainian Greek Orthodox
    Cathedral in Toronto, 1926–1976*. Toronto: Harmony Printing, 1979.

Duquin, Lorene Hanley. *They Called Her the Baroness: The Life of Catherine de
    Hueck Doherty*. New York: Alba House, 1995.

Endicott, Stephen. *James G. Endicott: Rebel Out of China*. Toronto: University of
    Toronto Press, 1980.

Famularo, Franco. *A History of the Unification Church in Canada, 1965–1991*.
    http://www.tparents.org/Library/Unification/Books/UcCan/UcCan
    -2–5c.htm.

Fay, Terrence. *New Faces of Canadian Catholics: The Asians*. Toronto: Novalis, 2009.

Ferres, James. *The First Fifty Years, 1907–1957: The Anglican Church of St Michael
    and All Angels*. Toronto: 1957.

Ferretti, Lucia. *Entre voisins: la société pariossiale en milieu urbain. Saint-Pierre Apôtre de Montréal, 1848–1930*. Montréal: Boréal, 1992.

Fitch, William. *Knox Church Toronto: Avant-Garde, Evangelical, Advancing*. Toronto: np 1971.

Forsyth, Barbara, and Barbara Myrvold. *Most Attractive Resort in Town: Public Library Service in West Toronto Junction, 1888–1989*. Toronto: Toronto Public Library Board, 1989.

Frager, Ruth. *Sweatshop Strife: Class, Ethnicity and Gender in the Jewish Labour Movement of Toronto 1900–1939*. Toronto: University of Toronto Press, 1992.

Francis, Douglas. "Modernity and Canadian Civilization: The Ideas of Harold A. Innis." In *Globality and Multiple Modernities: North American and Latin American Perspectives*, ed. Louis Roniger and Carlos Waisman. Eastbourne: Sussex Academic Press, 2002.

Fraser, Alexander. *A History of Ontario: Its Resources and Development*, vol. 2. Toronto: Canada History Company, 1907.

Fraser, Brian J. *The Social Uplifters: Presbyterian Progressives and the Social Gospel in Canada, 1875–1915*. Waterloo: Wilfrid Laurier University Press, 1988.

Gagan, Paul. *The Denison Family of Toronto, 1792–1925*. Toronto; University of Toronto Press, 1973.

Galvin, Martin. "The Jubilee Riots in Toronto, 1875." Canadian Catholic Historical Association, *Report*, 26 (1959).

Gauvreau, Michael. "Baptist Religion and the Social Science of Harold Innis." *Canadian Historical Review* 76. No. 2 (June 1995): 161–204.

Gebhard, Krzysztof. "Credit Unions in Ontario: St-Stanislaus–St Casimir's Parish Credit Union." *Polyphony* 2, 1 (Winter 1979): 43–4.

Genizi, Haim. *The Holocaust, Israel, and Canadian Protestant Churches*. Montreal and Kingston: McGill–Queen's University Press, 2002.

Gerus, Oleh. "Consolidating the Community: The Ukrainian Self-Reliance League." In *Canada's Ukrainians: Negotiating an Identity*, ed. Lubomyr Luciuk and Stella Hryniuk. Toronto: University of Toronto Press, 1991.

Gibson, William. *The Church of England, 1688–1832*. London and New York; Routledge, 2001.

Giddens, Anthony. *Modernity and Self-Identity: Self and Society in the Late Modern Age*. Cambridge: Polity Press, 1991.

Gidney, R.D., and W.P.J. Millar. "The Christian Recessional in Ontario's Public School." In *Religion and Public Life in Canada: Historical and Comparative Perspectives*, ed. Marguerite van Die, 275–93. Toronto: University of Toronto Press, 2001).

Goheen, Peter. *Victorian Toronto, 1850–1900: Pattern and Process of Growth*. Chicago: University of Chicago Press, 1970.

Gottesman, Eli. *Canadian Jewish Reference Book and Directory* (Montreal, 1965).
– *Who's Who in Canadian Jewry*. Montreal: 1965.
Grafos, Dimitrios James. "The Greeks in Toronto: Constructing a Greek Identity." MA thesis (Geography), York University, 2001).
Grant, John Webster. *The Church in the Canadian Era*. Toronto; McGraw-Hill Ryerson, 1972.
– *George Pidgeon: A Biography*. Toronto: Ryerson Press, 1962.
Gregorovich, Andrew. "The Ukrainian Community in Toronto from World War I to 1971." *Polyphony* (Spring–Summer 1984): 123–6.
Greig, David. *In the Fullness of Time: A History of the Church of Saint Mary Magdalene, Toronto*. Toronto: 1990.
Grypma, Sonya. *Healing Henan: Canadian Nurses at the North China Mission, 1888–1947*. Vancouver; UBC Press, 2008.
Gualtieri, Antonio. "Domenico Roberto Gualtieri and the United Church of Canada." *Italian Canadiana* 13 (1997): 38–46.
Gyatso, Karma Yönten. *Understanding the Chinese Buddhist Temple*.Richmond Hill: The Sumeru Press, 2010.
Handera, Vladimir. "The Russian Orthodox Church in Toronto." *Polyphony* (Spring–Summer 1984): 83–5.
Hanrahan, James. Canadian Catholic Historical Association. "The Nature and History of the Catholic Charismatic Renewal in Canada." *Study Sessions* 50 (1983).
Harney, Richard. "The Commerce of Migration." *Canadian Ethnic Studies*, 9, no. 1 (1977): 42–53.
Harney, Robert, ed. *Gathering Place: Peoples and Neighbourhoods of Toronto 1834–1945*. Toronto: Multicultural History Society of Ontario, 1985.
Harris, Richard. *Unplanned Suburbs: Toronto's American Tragedy, 1900–1950*. Baltimore: Johns Hopkins University Press, 1996.
Hayes, Alan L., ed. *By Grace Co-Workers: Building the Anglican Diocese of Toronto, 1780–1989*. Toronto: Anglican Book Centre, 1989.
Heitzenrater, Ralph. *Wesley and the People Called Methodists*, 2nd ed. Nashville: Abingdon Press, 2013.
Hempton, David. *Methodism: Empire of the Spirit*. New Haven: Yale University Press, 2005.
Henderson, Stuart. *Making the Scene: Yorkville and Hip Toronto in the 1960s*. Toronto: University of Toronto Press, 2011.
Henry, Frances. *The Caribbean Diaspora in Toronto: Learning to Live with Racism*. Toronto: University of Toronto Press, 1994.
Higgins, Michael, and Douglas Letson. *My Father's Business: A Biography of His Eminence G. Emmett Cardinal Carter*. Toronto: Macmillan, 1990.
Hockenos, Paul. *Homeland Calling: Exile Patriotism and the Balkan Wars*. Ithaca: Cornell University Press, 2003.

Hudson, Edna. *Bellevue Avenue: An Architectural and Social Study*.Toronto: Toronto Region Architectural Conservancy, 1993.

Iacovetta, Franca. *Gatekeepers: Reshaping Immigrant Lives in Cold War Canada*. Toronto: Between the Lines, 2006.

– *Such Hardworking People: Italian Immigrants in Postwar Toronto*. Montreal and Kingston: McGill–Queen's University Press, 1992.

Jackson, W.A. Douglas. "Toronto's St Anne's Anglican Church: A Unique Canadian Heritage." *New Scholars – New Visions in Canadian Studies* 11, no. 3 (Winter 1998).

James, Kathy. "Reforming Reform: Toronto's Settlement House Movement, 1900–1920." *Canadian Historical Review* 82, no. 1 (March 2001): 55–90.

Jones, Elwood. "Reaching Out for Two Hundred Years: Church Growth and Church Extension, 1780–1989." In *By Grace Co-Workers: Building the Anglican Diocese of Toronto, 1780–1989*, ed. Alan L. Hayes. Toronto: Anglican Book Centre, 1989,

Jones, Humphreys. "A Short History of Dewi Sant Welsh United Church." *Polyphony* (Spring–Summer 1984): 75–8.

Kaye, V.J. "Canadians of Byelorussian Origin." *Revue de l'Université d'Ottawa* 30, no. 3 (juil.–sept. 1960): 300–14.

Kayfitz, Ben. "A History of Toronto Jewry." *Canadian Jewish Reference Book and Directory*. Montreal: 1965.

– "How Synagogues Named." *Globe and Mail*, 17 September 1955,

Kazymyra, Nadia. "The Defiant Pavlo Krat and the Early Socialist Movement in Canada." *Canadian Ethnic Studies* 10, no. 2 (1978): 38–54

Kee, Kevin Bradley. *Revivalists: Marketing the Gospel in English Canada 1884–1957*. Montreal and Kingston: McGill-Queen's University Press, 2006.

Keeble, K. Corey. "St Mary Magdalene and the ROM." *Rotunda* 28, no. 3 (Winter 1995–6): 41–2.

Kelley, Ninette, and Michael Trebilcock. *The Marking of the Mosaic: A History of Canadian Immigration Policy*.Toronto: University of Toronto Press, 1998.

Kent, David. A., general editor *Household of God: A Parish History of St. Thomas's Church, Toronto*. Toronto: St Thomas Church, 1993.

Keshen, Jeffrey. *Saints, Sinners, and Soldiers: Canada's Second World War*. Vancouver; UBC Press, 2004.

Kim, Jung-Gun. "How Koreans Came to Call Toronto Home." *Polyphony* 6 (Spring–Summer 1984): 176–80.

Kirschbaum, Joseph. *Slovaks in Canada*. Toronto: Canadian Ethnic Press Association of Ontario, 1967.

Knight, Allan, and Jane E. Chute. "A Visionary on the Edge: Allan Madonell and the Championing of Native Resource Rights." In *With Good Intentions: Euro-Canadian and Aboriginal Relations in Colonial Canada*, ed. Celia Haig-Brown and David Nock. Toronto: University of Toronto Press, 2006.

Korinek, Valerie. "No Women Need Apply: The Ordination of Women in the United Church, 1918–1965." *Canadian Historical Review* 24, no. 4 (December 1993). 473–509.

Kydd, Ronald. "Canadian Pentecostalism and the Evangelical Impulse." In George Rawlyk, ed., *Aspects of the Canadian Evangelical Experience. 289–300* Montreal and Kingston: McGill–Queen's University Press, 1997.

Larkin, Emmet J. *The Historical Dimensions of Irish Catholicism*. New York; Arno Press, 1976.

Laycock, Margaret, and Barbara Myrvold. *Parkdale in Pictures: Its Development to 1889*. Local History Handbook no. 7 (Toronto: 1991).

Lee, Sang-Chul, and Erich Weingartner. *The Wanderer: The Autobiography of a United Church Moderator*. Winfield: Wood Lake Books, 1989.

Levitt, Sheldon, Lynn Milstone, and Sid Tenenbaum. *Shuls: A Study of Canadian Synagogue Architecture, Ontario 1979–80*. Toronto: Canadian Jewish Congress, 1980.

– *Treasures of a People: The Synagogues of Canada*. Toronto; Lester & Orpen Dennys, 1985.

Li, Peter. "The Rise and Fall of Chinese Immigration to Canada: Newcomers from Hong Kong Special Administrative Region of China and Mainland China, 1980–2000." *International Migration* 43, 3 (2005): 12–13.

Lindsay, Colin. "Canadians Attend Weekly Religious Services Less than Twenty Years Ago." Statistics Canada, June 2008.

Lindstrom-Best, Varpu. *Defiant Sisters: A Social History of Finnish Immigrant Women in Canada*. Toronto: Multicultural History of Ontario, 1988.

Litvak, Marilyn. *Edward James Lennox: Builder of Toronto*. Toronto: Dundurn Press, 1995.

Mackay, Ian. *The Quest for the Folk: Anti-Modernism and Cultural Selection in Twentieth-Century Nova Scotia*. Montreal and Kingston: McGill-Queen's University Press, 1994.

Magocsi, Paul Robert, ed. *Encyclopedia of Canada's Peoples*. Toronto: University of Toronto Press, 1999.

Manolkin, Anna. *Toronto – a City in Between*. Toronto; Anik Press, 2009.

Marathon Realty. *A Street Called Front*. Toronto: 1983).

Marchetto, Ezio. *A Vision Shared: The Fresco at St. Anthony's Church*. Toronto: Basilian Press, 1998.

Marshall, David. *Secularizing the Faith: Canadian Protestant Clergy and the Crisis of Belief, 1850–1940*. Toronto: University of Toronto Press, 1992.

Martens, Hildegard. "The German Community of St Patrick's Parish, 1929 to the Present." *Polyphony* 6 (Spring–Summer 1984): 98–100.

Marchetto, Ezio. "The Catholic Church and Italian Immigration to Toronto: An Overview," *Polyphony* 7 (1985): 106–10.

Maurutto, Paula. *Governing Charities: Church and State in Toronto's Catholic Archdiocese, 1850s–1950s*. Montreal and Kingston: McGill–Queen's University Press, 2003.

Maver, Igor. "Contemporary Diasporic Literature in Canada: Introduction." In *Migrating Memories: Central Europe in Canada*, vol. 1: *Literary Anthology*, ed. Vesna Lopičić. Brno/Niš: Central European Association for Canadian Studies, 2010.

McCurdy, J.F., ed. *Life and Work of D.J. Macdonnell*. Toronto: William Briggs, 1897.

McGowan, Mark. *The Waning of the Green: Catholics, the Irish, and Identity in Toronto, 1887–1922* (Montreal and Kingston: McGill–Queen's University Press, 1999.

McLellan, Janet. *Many Petals of the Lotus: Five Asian Buddhist Communities in Toronto*. Toronto: University of Toronto Press, 1999.

Mercer, Adam. *Toronto, Old and New: A Memorial Volume, Historical, Descriptive and Pictorial to Mark the Hundredth Anniversary of the Passing of the Constitutional Act of 1791*. Toronto; The Mail Printing Company, 1891.

Middleton, Jesse. *The Municipality of Toronto: A History*, vol. 3. Toronto: Dominion Publishing Company, 1923.

Miedema, Gary. *For Canada's Sake: Public Religion, Centennial Celebrations, and the Remaking of Canada in the 1960s*.Montreal and Kingston: McGill–Queen's University Press, 2005.

Miller, J.R. *Equal Rights: The Jesuits' Estates Act Controversy*. Montreal and Kingston: McGill-Queen's University Press, 1979.

Miller, Lorne, and Neil Ross. *One Hundred Years at the Junction Shul*. Toronto: ECW Press, 2011

Miller, Thomas William. "The Canadian 'Azuza': The Hebden Mission in Toronto." *PNEUMA: The Journal of the Society for Pentecostal Studies* 8, no. 1 (Spring 1986): 5–29

Miranda, Susana. "Not Ashamed or Afraid: Portuguese Immigrant Women in Toronto's Cleaning Industry, 1950s–1995," PhD diss., York University, 2010.

Monico, Joao. "Bodas de Prata: Paroquia Portuguesa de Santa Inês, 1970–1995." Toronto: 1995.

Moore, Donald. *Don Moore: An Autobiography*.Toronto: Williams-Wallace, c. 1985.

Mulvany, Charles Pelham. *History of Toronto and county of York, Ontario, containing an outline of the history of the Dominion of Canada, a history of the city of Toronto and the county of York, with the townships, towns, villages, churches, schools, general and local statistics, biographical sketches, etc., etc.*, vol. 2. Toronto; C. Blackett Robinson, 1885.

– *Toronto Past and Present: A Handbook of the City*. Toronto: W.E. Caiger, 1884.

Nagata, Judith. "Adaption and Integration of Greek Working Class Immigrants in Toronto: A Situational Approach." *International Migration Review* 4 (Fall 1969): 44–69.

– "The Role of Christian Churches in the Integration of Southeast Asian Immigrants in Toronto." *Contributions to Southeast Asian Ethnography* 6 (1988): 41–60.

Noel, Jan. *Canada Dry: Temperance Crusades before Confederation.* Toronto: University of Toronto Press, 1995.

Olitzky, Kerry M. *The American Synagogue: A Historical Dictionary and Sourcebook.* Westport: Greenwood Press, 1996.

O'Malley, John. *What Happened at Vatican II?* Cambridge, MA: Belknap Press of Harvard University Press, 2008.

O'Neill, Joseph H. "Archbishop McGuigan of Toronto and the Holy Name Society: Its Role as a Force against Canadian Communism." Canadian Catholic Historical Association, *Historical Studies* 55 (1988): 61–77.

[N.A.], *Open Doors and Open Windows: A Contemplative Guide to the Windows of St John's Church, West Toronto.* Toronto: 2003.

Papp, Susan. "The Hungarian Community of Toronto: Over Fifty Years of Change," *Polyphony* 6, no. 1 (Spring–Summer 1984): 131–34.

Paroquia de Santa Inês / Saint Agnes Church: o seu Centenario / Our Centenary. Toronto; Toledo Graphics, 2003.

Patrias, Carmela. *Patriots and Proletarians: Politicizing Hungarian Immigrants in Interwar Canada.* Montreal and Kingston: McGill–Queen's University Press, 1994.

– "Race, Discrimination, and State Complicity in Wartime Canada, 1939–1945." *Labour/Le Travail,* 59 (Spring 2007): 10–42.

Patrias, Carmela, and Ruth Frager. "'This Is Our Country, These Are Our Rights': Minorities and the Origins of Ontario's Human Rights Campaigns." *Canadian Historical Review* 82, no. 1 (March 2001): 1–35.

Patterson, Cynthia, Carol McDougall, and George Levin. *Bloor–Dufferin in Pictures.* Local History Handbook No. #5. Toronto: Toronto Public Library Board, 1986.

Pennacchio, Luigi. "Exporting Fascism to Canada: Toronto's Little Italy." In *Enemies Within: Italian and Other Internees in Canada and Abroad,* ed. Franca Iacovetta, R. Perin, and A. Principe. Toronto: University of Toronto Press, 1999.

– "The Torrid Trinity: Toronto's Fascists, Italian Priests, and Archbishops during the Fascist Era, 1929–1940." In *Catholics at the "Gathering Place,"* ed. Mark McGowan and Brian Clarke, 233–54. Toronto: Canadian Catholic Historical Association, 1993.

Perin, Roberto. *Rome in Canada: The Vatican and Canadian Affairs in the Late Victorian Age.* Toronto: University of Toronto Press, 1990.

Petroff, Lillian. *Sojourners and Settlers: The Macedonian Community in Toronto to 1940.* Toronto: Multicultural History Society of Ontario, 1995.

Pizzolante, Joseph. "The Growth of Italian Protestant Churches in Ontario and Quebec." *Italian Canadiana* 13 (1997): 56–79.

Plante, Jeff. "Answering the Call for Reform: The Toronto and Montreal Chinese Missions, 1894–1925." MA thesis (History), University of Guelph, 1997.

Plawiuk, Mykola. "Ukrainian Credit Unions in Canada." In *Slavs in Canada*, vol. 2. Toronto: Inter-University Committee on Canadian Slavs , 1968.

Portelli, John. "Father Fortunato Mizzi's Contributions to Maltese Catholics in Toronto." Canadian Catholic Historical Association, *Historical Studies* 67 (2001), 57–80.

Prang, Margaret. "'The Girl God Would Have Had Me Be': The Canadian Girls in Training, 1915–1939." *Canadian Historical Review* 66 (June 1985): 154–84.

Principe, Angelo. *The Darkest Side of the Fascist Years: The Italian Canadian Press 1920–1942*. Toronto: Guernica Editions, 1999.

Pugliese, Olga Zorzi. "Beautifying the City: 1960s Artistic Mosaics by Italian Canadians in Toronto." *Quaderni d'Italianistica* 28, no. 1 (2007): 93–113.

Radecki, Henry, with Benedykt Heydenkorn. *A Member of a Distinguished Family: The Polish Group in Canada*. Toronto: McClelland and Stewart, 1976.

Ramirez, Bruno. *Italians in Canada*. Ottawa: Canadian Historical Association, 1989.

Reeves, Evanne. *Over 100 Years: A Personal History of St Thomas*. Toronto: 1979?

Reid, Darrel. "Towards a Fourfold Gospel: A.B. Simpson, John Salmon, and the Christian and Missionary Alliance of Canada." In George Rawlyk, ed., *Aspects of the Canadian Evangelical Experience*. 271–88. Montreal and Kingston: McGill–Queen's University Press, 1997.

The Reverend Ernest Hahn: His Life, Work, and Place among Us. Toronto: St John's Evangelical Lutheran Church, n.d.

Reynolds, Lindsay. *Footprints: The Beginnings of the Christian and Missionary Alliance in Canada*. Beaverlodge: Buena Books Services, 1982.

Rice, Allan B. *West Toronto Junction Revisited: Excerpts from the Writings of A.B. Rice*, ed. Joan Miles. Erin: Boston Mills Press, 1989.

Robertson, John Ross. *Robertson's Landmarks of Toronto* vols. 4 and 6. Toronto: 1904, 1914.

Rosenberg, Stuart. *The Jewish Community in Canada: A History*, vol. 1. Toronto: McClelland and Stewart, 1970.

Rudd, Douglas *When the Spirit Came upon Them: Highlights from the Early Years of the Pentecostal Movement in Canada*. Burlington: Antioch Books, 2002.

Ruggle, Richard. "The Saints in the Land, 1867–1939." In *By Grace Co-Workers: Building the Anglican Diocese of Toronto, 1780–1989*, ed. Alan L. Hayes. Toronto: Anglican Book Centre, 1989.

St Mark and Calvary Anglican Church. *St Mark's West Toronto 125th Anniversary 1854–1979: From Village to Inner City.* Toronto: 1979.

"Sankey Partnership Architects," *Canadian Interiors* 17, no. 5 (May–June 1980): 43–7.

Sauro, Albertindo, "The Work of the Rev. Libero Sauro in the Italian Community." *Italian Canadiana* 13 (1997): 47–55.

Sawatsky, Ronald George. "Looking for the Blessed Hope: The Roots of Fundamentalism in Canada, 1878–1914." PhD diss. (History), University of Toronto, 1985.

Schindler, Karl. *Aussaat und Ernte: Jahrbuch zum fünfzigjährigen Jubiläum der deutschsprachigen katholischen Gemeinde von Toronto, 1929–1979.* Toronto: 1979.

– *Im Dienst des Volkes, 1929–1969. Jahrbuch zum 40-Jahrigen Jubiläum der deutschsprachigen katholischen Gemeinde in Toronto.* Toronto: St Joseph Press, 1969.

Schmidt, Ted. *Shabbes Goy: A Catholic Boyhood on a Jewish Street in a Protestant City.* Toronto: 2001.

"Serbian Eastern Orthodox Diocese vs Milivoijevich: The Continuing Crusade for the Separation of Church and State." *William and Mary Law Review* 18, 3 (1977): 655–76.

Shahrodi, Zofia. "The Experience of Polish Catholics in the Archdiocese of Toronto, 1905–1935." In *Catholics at the "Gathering Place,"* ed. Mark McGowan and Brian Clarke, 141–54 . Toronto: Canadian Catholic Historical Association, 1993.

Shantz, Mary-Ann. "Centring the Suburb, Focusing on the Family in Calgary's Anglican and Alliance Churches, 1945–1969." *Histoire sociale/Social History* 42, no. 84 (November 2009): 423–46.

Sherk, F. Arthur. *Keeping Faith: A Centennial History of Banfield Memorial Church.* Toronto: 1997.

Shuba, Michael. "I'm Just Reminiscing." *Polyphony* 6, no. 1 (Spring–Summer 1984): 219–20.

Simmins, Geoffrey. *Fred Cumberland: Building the Victorian Dream.* Toronto: University of Toronto Press, 1997.

Škorić, Sofija, and George Vid Tomashevich. *Serbs in Ontario: A Socio-Cultural Description.* Toronto: Serbian Heritage Academy, 1987.

Slonim, Reuben. *To Kill a Rabbi.* Toronto: ECW Press, 1987.

Smale, Richard. "For Whose Kingdom? Canadian Baptists and the Evangelization of Immigrants and Refugees, 1880–1950," PhD diss. (Education), Ontario Institute for Studies in Education, 2000.

Smith, James E. *I Wish I Were a Fish: A Search for Live Options in Yorkville.* Toronto: Yorkville Area Community Services Organization, 1972.

Smyth, Elizabeth. "Christian Perfection and Service to Neighbours: The Congregation of the Sisters of St. Joseph, Toronto, 1851–1920." In *Changing Roles of Women within the Christian Church in Canada*, ed. Elizabeth Gillan Muir and Marilyn Färdig Whiteley. Toronto: University of Toronto Press, 1995.

Speisman, Stephen. *The Jews of Toronto: A History to 1937*. Toronto: McClelland and Stewart, 1979.

Stackhouse, John. *Canadian Evangelicalism in the Twentieth Century*. Toronto: University of Toronto Press, 1993.

Stanger-Ross, Jordan. *Staying Italian: Urban Change and Ethnic Life in Postwar Toronto and Philadelphia*. Chicago: University of Chicago Press, 2009.

Stankus-Saulitis, Algirdas. "Toronto Lithuanian Roman Catholic St John the Baptist Benefit Society." *Polyphony* 2, no. 1 (Winter 1979): 26–8.

Stermole, David, and H.A. Gleason. "Residential Patterns of Ethnic Subgroups in Toronto." *Proceedings of the East Lakes Division of American Geographers, Selected Papers* (1979).

Taylor, Charles. "Two Theories of Modernity." In *Alternative Modernities*, ed. Dilip Parameshvar Gaonkar. Durham: Duke University Press, 2001.

Templeton, Charles. *An Anecdotal Memoir*. Toronto: McClelland and Stewart, 1983.

Thomas, Christopher A. "A Thoroughly Traditional Architect: A.W. Holmes and the Catholic Archdiocese of Toronto, 1890–1940." *Bulletin of the Society for the Study of Architecture in Canada* 10, no. 1 (March 1985): 3–9.

Thompson, A.E., and W.E. Blackstone. *A Century of Jewish Missons [sic]*. Chicago: Fleming H. Revell Co., 1902.

Thompson, Samuel. *Reminiscences of a Canadian Pioneer: The Last Fifty Years, 1833–1883: An Autobiography*. Toronto: Hunter Rose, 1884.

Toronto Chinese Mission. *Strangers Within Our Gates*. Toronto; Armac Press, 1906.

Tran, Kelly, Jennifer Kaddatz, and Paul Allard. "South Asians in Canada: Unity through Diversity." In Statistics Canada, *Canadian Social Trends*, Autumn 2005, 20–2.

Traub, S. ed. *History of the McCaul Street Synagogue. Golden Anniversary (1887–1937)*. Toronto: n.d.

Trudelle, Clermont, and Pierre Fortier, *Toronto se raconte: la paroisse du Sacré-Coeur*. Toronto: Société d'histoire de Toronto, 1987.

Urbanc, Peter, and Eleanor Tourtel. *Slovenians in Canada*. Hamilton: Slovenian Heritage Festival Committee, 1985.

Vagners, Martin. "Latvian Settlement in the City." *Polyphony* 6, no. 1 (Spring–Summer 1984): 113.

Vecoli, Rudolph. "Cult and Occult in Italian-American Culture: The Persistence of Religious Heritage." In *Immigrants and Religion in Urban America*, ed. R.M. Miller and T.D. Marzik. Philadelphia; Temple University Press, 1977.

von Vulte, Manfred. "The German-Canadian Identity: A Shared History Unites and Defines a People in Toronto." MRP (History), York University, 1998.

Walden, Keith. *Becoming Modern in Toronto: The Industrial Exhibition and the Shaping of Late Victorian Culture*. Toronto: University of Toronto Press, 1997.

Warschauer, Heinz. *The Story of Holy Blossom Temple*. Toronto: Holy Blossom, 1959.

Watada, Terry. *Bukkyo Tozen: A History of Jodo Shinshu Buddhism in Canada 1905–1995*. Toronto: 1996.

Westfall, William. *Two Worlds: The Protestant Culture of Nineteenth-Century Ontario*. Montreal and Kingston: McGill–Queen's University Press, 1989.

Whiteley, Marilyn Fardig. "Sailing for the Shore: The Canadian Holiness Tradition." In George Rawlyk, ed., *Aspects of the Canadian Evangelical Experience*. 257–270 Montreal and Kingston: McGill–Queen's University Press, 1997.

Wilson, David. *The Orange Order in Canada*. Dublin: Four Courts Press, 2007.

Wukasch, Peter. "Baltic Immigrants in Canada, 1947–1955," *Concordia Historical Institute* 50 (Spring 1977): 4–22.

Yaworsky-Sokolsky, Zoriana. "The Beginnings of Ukrainian Settlement in Toronto, 1891–1939." In *Gathering Place: Peoples and Neighbourhoods of Toronto*, ed. Robert Harney, 279–302 . Toronto: Multicultural History Society of Ontario, 1985.

Yu, Bradley Chin. "'New' Immigration, Sacred Spaces, and Identity Transformations: Catholic National Parishes in West Toronto Junction, 1900–1925," MA thesis (Geography), York University, 2007.

Zeidman, Alex. *Good and Faithful Servant: The Biography of Morris Zeidman*. New York: Crown, 1990.

Zucchi, John. *Italians in Toronto: Development of a National Identity*. Montreal and Kingston McGill–Queen's University Press, 1988.

Index